Islands of Discontent

ASIA/PACIFIC/PERSPECTIVES

Series Editor: Mark Selden

Identity and Resistance in Okinawa
by Matthew Allen
Woman, Man, Bangkok: Love, Sex, and Popular Culture in Thailand
by Scot Barmé
The Mongols at China's Edge: History and the Politics of National Unity
by Uradyn Bulag
Transforming Asian Socialism: China and Vietnam Compared
edited by Anita Chan, Benedict J. Tria Kerkvliet, and Jonathan Unger
China's Great Proletarian Cultural Revolution: Master Narratives and Post-Mao Counternarratives
edited by Woei Lien Chong
North China at War: The Social Ecology of Revolution, 1937-1945
edited by Feng Chongyi and David S. G. Goodman
Islands of Discontent: Okinawan Responses to Japanese and American Power
edited by Laura Hein and Mark Selden
Women in Early Imperial China
by Bret Hinsch
Local Democracy and Development: The Kerala People's Campaign for Decentralized Planning
by T. M. Thomas Isaac with Richard W. Franke
Postwar Vietnam: Dynamics of a Transforming Society
edited by Hy V. Luong
Wife or Worker? Asian Women and Migration
edited by Nicola Piper and Mina Roces
Contentious Kwangju: The May 18th Uprising in Korea's Past and Present
edited by Gi-Wook Shin and Kyung Moon Hwang

Islands of Discontent

Okinawan Responses to Japanese and American Power

Edited by
Laura Hein and Mark Selden

ROWMAN & LITTLEFIELD PUBLISHERS, INC.
Lanham • Boulder • New York • Oxford

The musical instrument used as a design element on the title page and the chapter opening pages in this book is the sanshin, a three-stringed, plucked lute. It is the quintessential Okinawan musical instrument. A black-lacquered ebony neck extends from a snakeskin-covered body. The strings, originally of silk, are plucked with a water-buffalo horn. Its sounds can be heard reverberating wherever Okinawan communities thrive.

ROWMAN & LITTLEFIELD PUBLISHERS, INC.

Published in the United States of America
by Rowman & Littlefield Publishers, Inc.
A Member of the Rowman & Littlefield Publishing Group
4501 Forbes Boulevard, Suite 200, Lanham, Maryland 20706
www.rowmanlittlefield.com

PO Box 317
Oxford
OX2 9RU, UK

British Library Cataloguing in Publication Information Available

Library of Congress Cataloging-in-Publication Data

Islands of discontent : Okinawan reponses to Japanese and American
power / edited by Laura Hein and Mark Selden.
p. cm. — (Asian Voices)
Includes bibliographical references and index.
ISBN 0-7425-1865-5 (cloth) — ISBN 0-7425-1866-3 (paper)
1. Okinawa-ken (Japan)—Civilization. 2. Okinawa-ken
(Japan)—Relations—United States. 3. United
States—Relations—Okinawa-ken. I. Hein, Laura II.
Selden, Mark. III. Asian voices (Rowman and Littlefield, Inc.)
DS894.99.O374 I85 2003
952'.29033—dc21

2002014944

Printed in the United States of America

∞™ The paper used in this publication meets the minimum requirements of American National Standard for Information Sciences—Permanence of Paper for Printed Library Materials, ANSI/NISO Z39.48-1992.

Contents

1

Culture, Power, and Identity in Contemporary Okinawa

Laura Hein and Mark Selden

Okinawa has been the site of intense cultural creativity and cultural conflict in recent years. By debating and transforming Okinawan politics and values, and by creating a vibrant Okinawan musical and literary scene, Okinawans are embroidering an intricate tapestry of Okinawanness. What it means to be Okinawan is being contested, redefined, and inscribed in the consciousness and praxis of Okinawans today. Much of that creativity is linked to new understandings of Okinawa's past, particularly of the Ryūkyū Kingdom of the fourteenth to the nineteenth centuries; incorporation into the Japanese imperium in the nineteenth and early twentieth centuries through World War II; subjugation to U.S. military designs after the Battle of Okinawa; and Okinawa's postreversion experience since 1972. Reframing that history is central to redefinition of the Okinawan-Japanese relationship. That interpretive act affects Okinawan attitudes toward the U.S. military as well. The burst of creativity involved in rethinking Okinawa's historical experience, the diverse meanings ascribed to it, and its implications for Okinawa, Japan, and the United States comprise the subject of this volume.

The chapters explore contemporary Okinawan claims to citizenship and cultural identity through war remembrance, peace education, community organizing, antibase protest, feminist analysis, movements to protect the environment and revive spiritual traditions, literature, new musical trends, and cinema. We start from the premise that these explorations in the realm of culture and identity are not only inherently political acts, but also metaphorical calls to arms. As Linda Angst puts it, "identity politics is implicitly one of resistance—in this case against the Japanese state and the powerful myth of Japanese cultural homogeneity, and against U.S. military power." Much Okinawan creativity today directly wrestles with the problem of expressing Okinawan identity within the context of Japanese culture and society and, to a lesser extent, American power.[1] As the essays here show, differing visions of their collective past and imagined future reveal major internal tensions among Okinawans in addition to those that divide them from others. The spirited exchange of these different visions, rather than any unanimity over what it means to be Okinawan, fuels the efforts to reimagine Okinawan identity today.

Contemporary Okinawan cultural and aesthetic expressions reveal important ways in which both Okinawan and mainland Japanese social attitudes about Okinawans are being transformed. Greater acceptance of Okinawans as both distinctively Okinawan and indubitably Japanese is one important development. However, more is at stake. That conceptual shift also carries within it the redefinition of Japanese national identity toward one that is more accepting of heterogeneity, diversity, and hybridity. By challenging Japanese nationalist premises, Okinawans are not adding their voices to the national anthem, but are changing its song.

Modern Japan is famously committed to the ideal of purity and homogeneity, presented especially sharply in the postwar era, following the dissolution of Japan's colonial empire, in terms of ethnic homogeneity.[2] That contemporary Japanese ideology of racial homogeneity and cultural assimilation has made it difficult for Okinawans to both honor their own distinctive heritage and gain acceptance within Japan. As Michael Molasky observes here, "Japanese national subjectivity does not yet admit the possibility of hyphenated identities such as 'Okinawan-Japanese.'" Nor is Japanese society organized in some other way that simultaneously honors cultural difference and full citizenship. Nevertheless, as these chapters suggest, there are ample signs of change.

Okinawan encounters with Japan, and explanations of Okinawa's "proper" place within the Japanese order, have always been couched in terms of the special characteristics of Okinawan culture. Okinawans suffered severe discrimination at the hands of Japanese, before, during, and after World War II. Presurrender assimilation policy was particularly brutal: It was designed to strip Okinawans of all distinctive cultural attributes, above all language, and remake them as Japanese.[3] Much recent scholarship, notably the work of Tomiyama Ichirō, has documented how hard it is for Okinawans to be simultaneously Japanese and Okinawan. The answer to the question posed by Tomiyama, "Are Okinawans Japanese?" clearly is both yes and no—in ways that define Okinawans as imperfect Japanese—and this is the exact source of Okinawans' uneasy place within the Japanese imaginary.[4]

The structures of discrimination that confront Okinawans are not just the product of social prejudice but have been shaped and enforced by state power. Attempts to change discriminatory social attitudes are thus a bid for full political citizenship as well as respect for cultural-ethnic differences. As Tessa Morris-Suzuki observes, even though the precise explanation of what constitutes "Japanese culture" has varied wildly depending on who was formulating it and at what time and place, "the implicit equation of Japanese citizenship with ethnic markers (appearance, names, language), and of these ethnic markers with cultural characteristics (group consciousness, social order), has had profound consequences for the negotiation of citizenship in postwar Japan."[5] If being Japanese requires an amalgam of ethnic and national purity, then admitting the possibility of "Okinawan-Japaneseness" (or Korean-Japaneseness, Ainu-Japaneseness, or American-Japaneseness) forces a reappraisal not only of the meaning of Okinawan culture and identity but of Japaneseness as well. For these reasons, the most emotionally fraught dimension of Okinawan identity is the Okinawan-Japanese relationship, as it has been for more than a century.

Renegotiating a better place for Okinawans within Japan—one that is more autonomous and more respectful of Okinawan values and daily lives—is clearly the overriding priority for nearly all the people discussed in these pages. Okinawans disagree over how to best accomplish this goal: Some are convinced that only complete political independence will be effective, while others seek to blend into mainland society. Yet, at present, those both seem to be minority positions. Most Okinawans are searching for ways to affirm Okinawan distinctiveness while still enjoying full Japanese citizenship, something that was impossible in the past under conditions of extremely discriminatory policies and attitudes on the part of mainland Japanese. Despite their unusually strong emphasis on an ideology of homogeneity, Japanese attitudes toward Okinawans—as well as toward Ainu, Burakumin, Koreans, and other marginalized peoples—share much in common with the attitudes of powerful groups elsewhere toward those they deem inferior. Indeed, modern scientific racial prejudice developed in Japan at roughly the same time as it did in Europe and North America, and it was clearly influenced by international racial "science" and Western colonial practices.[6]

Despite a very different national imaginary as a cultural "melting pot," American treatment of minorities exhibits many features in common with Japan. Native Americans faced comparable policies suppressing their languages, as did Okinawans, ones similarly enforced through compulsory education in the dominant language. As late as 1987, for example, the state of Hawai'i forbade education in the Hawai'ian language in public schools.[7] Likewise, the rationales Osaka landlords gave for refusing to rent to Okinawans as described in Steve Rabson's chapter are reminiscent of those deployed by landlords in Chicago or Los Angeles over the last century when they excluded minorities. Similarly, World War II created an atmosphere of heightened anxiety about the loyalty of Japanese Americans who were treated as spies by the U.S. government on purely racial and linguistic grounds as were Okinawans by the Japanese military. Japanese and American racial attitudes also converged in their treatment of Okinawans. During the twenty-seven years of direct military rule (1945–1972), Americans living on the islands (not to mention official military policy) displayed over and over again their strong sense of superiority toward Okinawans.[8]

The specific terms in which the ethnic nation is imagined in Japan are distinctive, but the logic of inclusion and exclusion mirrors stances elsewhere, as do battles to challenge that logic. Those battles are likewise simultaneously about both respect for cultural distinctiveness and aspirations to achieve full citizenship rights. The stakes are always about the nation as a whole, not just the members of the minority. Just as state repression of Okinawan aspirations in the postwar years has undercut the Japanese government's claims to full-fledged democracy, American denial in practice of the privileges of full citizenship to African Americans through segregation and discrimination has forced, and continues to force, reappraisal of what it means to be an American, the nature of American society, and the legitimacy of the American government. Indeed, Okinawan critiques of mainstream Japanese ideology and politics both inspire and are richly informed by struggles by minorities in other parts of the world.

Equally important, the national context is new. Japanese society, too, is changing, and one important element of that evolution follows from the fact that Okinawans are better integrated into national society than at any time in the past. That integration provides a larger and more secure space from which Okinawans can forge new understandings of their own place as simultaneously Okinawan and Japanese. As a result, Okinawans appear to be moving from the periphery toward the center of Japanese consciousness in ways that are sure to affect the lives of Okinawans and mainland Japanese in the years ahead.

BETWEEN JAPAN AND THE UNITED STATES: OKINAWA'S ECONOMIC AND STRATEGIC IMPASSE

Two closely linked problems have long shaped and lent urgency to Okinawan cultural life: political subordination and economic malaise. Political subordination has primarily meant two things over the long twentieth century: Okinawan subordination to the Japanese state and, beginning in 1945, to American Cold War military designs in the Pacific region. The overriding Okinawan grievance against both the Japanese and the U.S. governments is the disruptive presence of thirty-two U.S. military bases on the main island of Okinawa and six more on smaller islands within the prefecture. Although Japan has forty-seven prefectures, Okinawa, with just 1 percent of the Japanese landmass, is home to 75 percent of U.S. bases and the majority of U.S. forces stationed in Japan. The bases occupy 20 percent of the main island, concentrated in the most densely populated southern areas. Okinawans have persistently fought to diminish the number and scale of these installations, but policymakers in Tokyo and Washington insist on maintaining the bases at current levels. Many local inhabitants view the U.S. military as an occupying power, both because their own police are powerless to control the lawless behavior of U.S. troops and their dependents, and because the bases officially exist to protect them from enemies that few fear. The salient fact for many Okinawans is that both Japanese and American officials insist that they accept incorporation into national and international military systems on terms they find not only repugnant but discriminatory against Okinawans. After the USSR dissolved, marking the end of the Cold War, it seemed possible that the U.S. military might at least partially withdraw from the bases, and Okinawans stepped up pressure for base reduction. But the United States has rejected even preliminary discussion on reducing its military presence, and following September 11, 2001, the U.S. began radically re-expanding its military bases throughout Asia.

Okinawa has chronic economic problems. It was Japan's poorest prefecture from its incorporation in 1879 and it has remained so since. Okinawa's early poverty was reinforced by government policies, particularly exceptionally heavy taxes. Another major blow dealt the Okinawan economy by Tokyo was the decision in the 1920s, just when world sugar prices collapsed, to encourage sugar cultivation in the colony of Formosa at the expense of Okinawan producers.[9] Throughout the first half of the twentieth century, impoverished Okinawans went abroad in droves, while many others sought employment in the Osaka textile mills, as detailed in the chapter by Rabson. Between 1899 and 1935, about 15 percent of the Okinawan population emigrated either to the mainland or overseas. The largest number of emigrants went to Hawai'i, Brazil, the Philippines, and Peru, mainly as agricultural laborers. By 1945, about 332,000 Okinawans (some born overseas) were living abroad.[10]

The Battle of Okinawa ravaged the main island. In many communities, nothing was left but scattered bones, as eloquently described here by Asato Eiko. In May 1945, even as the battle raged, U.S. military authorities bulldozed abandoned villages and scraped precious topsoil for landfill to build ten B-29 air strips, as well as military roads and storage depots in preparation for the planned invasion of mainland Japan. By 1947, more than one-third of the arable land had been paved over or was behind barbed wire, and many more farmers were forced to leave by a regulation that declared off-limits all land within one mile of larger American housing sites.[11] During the nearly three decades of U.S. occupation, the Okinawan economy was effectively reduced to the provision of support services for the U.S. military bases, including many bars and brothels. Following reversion to Japan in 1972, the economy grew in size and diversity with the infusion of government investment and some private capital, and Okinawan standards of living improved substantially, as did those on the mainland. But the subsidized economy neither achieved self-sustaining growth nor approached mainland levels. Moreover, as Asato points out, Japanese development devastated the environment, particularly when measured against the meager economic benefits to Okinawans.[12]

Nor is this inequity abating. The economic recession that has continued in Japan since 1990 began earlier in Okinawa and its impact has been harsher there. Per capita income has hovered around 70 percent of the national average for the last decade. Unemployment rates in Okinawa Prefecture have been substantially higher than the national average every year since 1973, often more than twice the national rate. In 2000, prefectural unemployment was 7.9 percent, while nationally 4.7 percent of the population was unemployed.[13]

The issue that most intimately links Okinawa's economic problems to the military bases is payments for use of land by the United States. After appropriating huge tracts of land, the U.S. military offered Okinawan landowners small lump-sum payments for their property. This proposal sparked islandwide protest among landowners, who insisted on retaining ownership rights and the legal framework for eventual return of their land. In 1952, the United States issued twenty-year leases on confiscated land, with payment at 6 percent of its assessed value, to fifty-seven thousand landowners, including some who had been forcibly evicted by American military forces in tanks and then arrested for resisting the expropriation.[14] At reversion in 1972, the Japanese government assumed responsibility for rental payments to landowners. The conflict over land rights, a flashpoint in the antibase movement throughout the 1950s and 1960s, ebbed only after the Japanese government inserted itself financially between the U.S. military and the local landowners and substantially increased payments. However, in 1982, a landowner began selling one-tsubo plots of land (3.3 square meters), initiating a movement that eventually produced three thousand landowning antibase activists. That tactic expanded the ranks of property owners protesting the expropriation of land for bases and also shifted protest toward a moral argument over symbolic property rights and collective quality of life rather than one over direct compensation for lost rights to farm or build on the land.[15] (See figure 1.1)

The central government's response to Okinawan discontent with the military bases in recent years has been to silence opposition by dramatically increasing payments to local Okinawan governments. In December 1999, for example, it pledged an astonishing annual one hundred billion

Figure 1.1. U.S. Military bases on Okinawa.
Source: Critical Asian Studies 33, no. 1 (March 2001). Used with permission.

yen supplementary stimulus package, mainly earmarked for large construction projects. The money was promised just after Inamine Keiichi, who supported the Tokyo government's position on keeping the bases in Okinawa, wrested the governorship of Okinawa from longtime opponent to the bases, Governor Ōta Masahide, and was universally seen as a quid pro quo for muting opposition to the bases.[16]

Tokyo's money reinforces subordination to American and Japanese priorities, even as it creates temporary construction jobs for unemployed Okinawans. Since many Okinawans want both greater autonomy from the central government and closure of the bases, this economic strategy of accepting money for keeping the bases, however lucrative, is profoundly frustrating.

Alternative economic strategies, however, have been unsuccessful to date. One much-discussed concept is to develop Okinawa as "the southern exchange hub of Japan"—that is, a free-trade zone for regional Asian trade, a concept rooted in part in memories of the historical Ryūkyū Kingdom as a regional crossroads. In preparation, they have designated Okinawa as a free-trade zone with low investment taxes for new businesses, relaxed import quotas, streamlined visa requirements, and special incentives for high-technology ventures, including a new "high-tech" School of Graduate Studies with an international focus. However, few Japanese or international enterprises have relocated to the development zones. The decade-long recession throughout Japan makes this a singularly unpromising moment to begin ambitious new ventures that rely heavily on foreign investment.[17]

Some Okinawans have turned to a vision of an Okinawan economy based on the rhythms of nature and the sea. In this volume, Asato celebrates that idea of resurrecting the ancient subsistence economy. Her story of community initiatives on Kudaka Island illustrates both the hopes of its proponents and the problem in miniature: Community action on this tiny island has protected the land from rapacious and ugly economic development, but it has been unable to keep young people from leaving in search of opportunities elsewhere. As in many other nations, full-time farmers in Japan, including Okinawa, have almost disappeared in the last forty years. The Okinawan experience of rapid urbanization is part of a global trend away from small-scale agriculture, and there is little likelihood that the outcome will be different there.

Okinawans have no obvious alternative to economic reliance on central government subsidies, which carries the heavy price tag of continuing their role as hosts to the American bases. It is no accident that the cinematic fantasy of secession from Japan described by Aaron Gerow in this volume includes the fortuitous (and geologically improbable) discovery of petroleum on the territory of the breakaway island. Without such a windfall, it is hard to see how Okinawans can transform their economy in ways that give them substantial autonomy from Tokyo. The intractability of that problem makes all the more striking the current burst of cultural creativity in Okinawa.

OKINAWA, MAINLAND JAPAN, AND THE LESSONS OF THE PAST

Although Okinawans have been unable to overcome those daunting political and economic realities, they have made important gains in carving out space for themselves as accepted members of Japanese society, not least through the effective deployment of cultural symbols and narratives of Okinawan identity. The symbols themselves are not new, but the intensity and creativity with which they are being positioned, the sheer scale of Okinawan cultural inventiveness, and the positive reception to Okinawan culture throughout Japan and internationally are significant and new. Many of the narratives of Okinawan identity examined in this volume center on remembrance of the past, particularly of three moments: the Ryūkyū Kingdom, the Battle of Okinawa, and the contemporary Okinawan-Japanese relationship. People everywhere construct and reconstruct narratives of national history in order to create a sense of collective identity.[18] Our focus is on the specific ways in which bygone eras are now being remembered, the lessons drawn from them, and the significance of those lessons for redefining Okinawan relations with Japan and the United States.

The Ryūkyū Kingdom

The history of the Ryūkyū Kingdom from the fourteenth to the seventeenth century is among the most widely invoked elements of the past. The Ryūkyū Kingdom, like Japan, was long part of the Chinese political world order, while its trading relationships extended throughout maritime Asia. In the early seventeenth century, shortly after Japan was unified under Tokugawa rule, the Japanese domain of Satsuma brought the Ryūkyū Kingdom under its control. The Ryūkyūs maintained tribute relations with China, however, and a modicum of independence for the next 250 years, before being subsumed into the new Meiji state in 1879.[19] Throughout the eighteenth and nineteenth centuries, Satsuma insisted that the Ryūkyū Kingdom was a foreign (and "barbarian") land, forbade Okinawans from wearing Japanese clothing or adopting Japanese names, and required tribute payments to Satsuma. Satsuma inscribed difference on the Okinawans, but then the Meiji state redefined those very differences as marks of inferiority. That two-step process shares much with the historical construction of racial hierarchies throughout the world.[20]

For Okinawans, the key point of the Ryūkyū Kingdom narrative is that they were not always Japanese. Rather, they carefully positioned themselves between China and Japan, welcomed ideas and travelers from many lands, and for centuries conducted peaceful diplomatic relations throughout East and Southeast Asia and the Pacific region. The economic success of the Ryūkyū Kingdom and its far-flung trading networks is another important theme of remembrance, leading a recent chronicler to state that "the former commercial importance of the sixty-odd islands of the Ryūkyūan Archipelago stirs the imagination of modern Okinawans."[21]

This vision of a proud past is deployed against the suggestion that Okinawan inferiority explains its present position as the economically least successful prefecture on Japan's periphery. It also directly counters the idea that Okinawa today is trapped in the *Japanese* past. In prewar Japan, the key figure who reframed Okinawa as not just backward but as the primitive and unchanging repository of *Japanese* tradition was the ethnographer Yanagita Kunio. Harootunian has called that assumption "the sign of a colonial unconscious that stalked the cultural sciences in Japan during the interwar period." Okinawan remembrance of the Ryūkyū Kingdom is incompatible with the long-dominant idea that the mainland advanced to modernity, leaving Okinawa behind, still mired in the primitive traditions it once shared with mainland Japan.[22]

The Ryūkyū Kingdom is invoked in James Roberson's analysis here of the images that Okinawan pop musicians celebrate and disseminate in their songs. He shows that they envision Okinawa as historically located "betwixt and between" powerful external forces but also as embodying social and moral virtues that set them apart from others, including mainland Japanese and Americans. Two such virtues stand out in this presentation. The first is peacefulness, or "gentle kindness," as the Rinken band phrased it. The other is "mixed," meaning both cosmopolitan and internally diverse, in a deliberate criticism of the purportedly homogeneous mainland. The musicians trace the sources of cultural tolerance and local diversity to Okinawa's historic location astride the great maritime trading routes of Asia, its many visitors and overlords, and the extensive diasporic experience of Okinawans themselves.

Roberson's musicians are part of a larger group of Okinawan intellectuals and artists who are exploring the association of Okinawa with peacefulness, tolerance, and hybrid identity. They are also rejecting the assumption that Okinawa is following in the footsteps of Japanese history, or escaping from the fate, as Kushi Fusako put it, of "always seem[ing] to be at the tail end of history, dragged along roads already ruined by others."[23] Their collective project seeks to promote the image of Okinawans as peaceful, tolerant, and "mixed," and they have achieved some success in exporting this image throughout Japan and around the globe by packaging it in accessible musical form.

The most important physical symbol of an autonomous Okinawan past is Shuri Castle, whose fortunes over the last 150 years mirror (and reinforce) other forms of remembrance of the Ryūkyū Kingdom. Shuri Castle was constructed as the royal residence, home of government, and religious center in approximately 1427. It served as the seat of government until 1879, when Okinawa was incorporated as a Japanese prefecture and the monarchy abolished. Subsequently, a Japanese army detachment was quartered in the castle complex, parts of which became barracks. Other buildings were used as school classrooms. In 1929, the Japanese government designated the Seiden or Main Hall as a national treasure and restored it. Prior to the invasion of Okinawa, Japan's Thirty-second Army located its wartime headquarters in a tunnel complex beneath the castle.[24] The castle was destroyed during the Battle of Okinawa when, as Ronald Nakasone informs us, it was also looted by American officers.[25] Under U.S. military rule, the site housed the postwar University of the Ryukyus, from 1951 until it was moved to a new location in 1982. In 1992, on the twentieth anniversary of Okinawa's reversion, the partially reconstructed castle reopened. It soon became the central site of Okinawa's tourist industry, as well as the iconic center of Okinawan remembrance of the Ryūkyū Kingdom. Additional construction was completed in 1999 when the castle was designated a UNESCO World Heritage Site. The Japanese government also celebrated the reconstruction of the castle and highlighted its historical significance by hosting the international G-8 summit there in 2000.

The Shuri Palace gate is featured on the reverse side of a new two-thousand-yen note, first issued in 2000. It is hard to think of a more powerful symbolic claim by the Japanese state that the Ryūkyū Kingdom was an integral part of Japanese as well as Okinawan history. The national celebration of Shuri Palace and the Ryūkyū Kingdom as simultaneously distinctively Okinawan and central to the Japanese national heritage undercuts Yanagita's claim that twentieth-century Okinawa is the lingering trace of Japan's past. By formally acknowledging Okinawa's history—and its modern trajectory since the days of the Ryūkyū Kingdom—the Japanese state is distancing itself from the idea that the mainland is modern while Okinawa is still stuck in premodernity. It likewise implicitly recognizes the historical linkages between the Ryūkyū Kingdom and China. The gate was originally built to welcome Chinese emissaries, and its commemoration on the two-thousand-yen note also validates the image of Okinawa as a gateway to Asia within the Japanese imagination (see figure 1.2).

Figure 1.2. The Shureimon gate from the palace of the Ryūkyū kings was originally built to commemorate peaceful relations with China. It has since become a symbol of pride in the Okinawa heritage. The Japanese government recently displayed it on the new 2,000-yen note, incorporating Ryūkyūan history into the national narrative.
Source: Photograph by Gerald Figal.

One could interpret the decision to picture the gate on the new note as an imperialist gesture: By appropriating Shuri Castle as a symbol of Japanese nationhood suitable to grace the currency, Tokyo is again asserting control over Okinawans and subordinating them to the nation. Yet symbolic exchange works by a different logic than does financial exchange. Even if the new bill is such an attempt, recognition of the Ryūkyū Kingdom as a distinct, important part of the national political and cultural heritage strengthens the concept of a hybrid Okinawan-Japanese identity. It also institutionalizes the assertion that Ryūkyū history can make valuable contributions to the present, particularly its tradition of amicable relations with Asia. To the extent that this symbolism gains acceptance, it will also further legitimate a multicultural Japan.

The Battle of Okinawa

The Battle of Okinawa is the most traumatic event in Okinawan history and the most controversial site of remembrance in contemporary Okinawa. Not surprisingly, alignment of Okinawan and Japanese official remembrance of World War II in general and of the Battle of Okinawa in particular is far more difficult than is that of the Ryūkyū Kingdom. The Battle of Okinawa, the only major land battle fought on Japanese soil, was the largest and most deadly conflict in the Pacific theater. The United States marshaled over half a million troops and massive air and naval power against 110,000 well-entrenched Japanese defenders. The battle stands out for the intensity of the fighting, the heavy casualties, and, especially, the number of civilians who perished. For twelve weeks, beginning on April 1, 1945, there was no food, no medicine, and nowhere safe for people to hide. Unable to escape the deadly crossfire, an estimated 130,000 to 140,000 civilians died during the combat, more than one-fourth of the population. Few Okinawan families were untouched.[26]

The chapters by Matt Allen and Gerald Figal explore the controversies inherent in remembrance of the war for Okinawans. Elementary schools in Okinawa now regularly invite survivors to tell their stories to the pupils, while memorials, museums, exhibitions, and tours commemorating the battle have proliferated. Okinawan educators have designed a circuit of museums and memorials commemorating the battle for school groups (from both Okinawa and the mainland) and tourists. Tens of thousands of people visit these sites each month. The most important of the new monuments, the Okinawan Cornerstone of Peace, opened in 1995. Building on an approach pioneered in Maya Lin's Vietnam War memorial in Washington, the cornerstone avoids any stance on the goals or prosecution of the war and merely honors all who fell in battle by listing their names. The Cornerstone of Peace extends Lin's logic in two ways. First, it presents the names of the military dead on each side, Allied forces as well as Japanese, Okinawans, Koreans, and Taiwanese. Second, it names civilian as well as military victims. Lin's memorial honored only American forces, eliding not only the vastly larger numbers of Vietnamese dead but also the soldiers who fought and died alongside the Americans, such as South Koreans and Australians. Expanding the commemoration to all those who died in the battle made the monument an internationalist commemorative site.[27] In contrast to most war memorials, which celebrate nationalist memories, the dominant message of the cornerstone is a peace statement that commemorates the victims of war and endorses no national agenda.

Such internationalism in commemorative sites is rare. War memorials virtually everywhere not only explicitly pay homage to the state's wartime goals but also suggest that the sacrifice of the lives of its nationals, mainly those in uniform, was a worthy exchange for defending those goals. In listing the names of all the dead, the Cornerstone of Peace encourages the viewer to ponder the fact that commemoration of their deaths does not conform to a single logic of assailant and victim, certainly not one that can be fully captured by nationality.

The Cornerstone of Peace is effective precisely because it honors the dead without endorsing the wartime Japanese government's priorities. Okinawans have never accepted the view that the battle was either unavoidable or ennobling. A set of 1993 public opinion polls cited by Ishihara Masaie reveals that 87.5 percent of Okinawans thought that the battle was "a reckless battle which sacrificed countless Okinawan lives." Just 6.2 percent thought it was "an unavoidable battle necessary for the defense of the fatherland."[28] The historical evidence supports the opinion of most Okinawans on this—crucial—issue. By spring 1945, on the eve of the battle, Japan had lost the war. But the emperor and the military insisted on pressing on fruitlessly despite the gloomy assessment of the inner circle. At least 130,000 Okinawans died simply to put off the inevitable surrender just a little longer and to warn the Americans of the high cost of invading the main Japanese islands.[29]

There are other critical reasons why many Okinawans reject orthodox Japanese interpretations of the battle. As both Allen and Figal show in this volume, the most controversial issue centers on the fact that soldiers of the Imperial Japanese Army turned on the civilians they were sworn to protect, sometimes ordering them to commit "compulsory group suicide" rather than surrender to the enemy and sometimes callously killing Okinawans—men, women, and children—in order to claim safe shelter for themselves. On March 26, 1945, when U.S. troops first landed in the Kerama Islands just off Okinawa, the Japanese commander confiscated all food and ordered the people to prepare to commit suicide. On March 28, on Tokashiki, the largest of the Keramas, 329 civilians died. Sixteen-year-old Kinjō Shigeaki recalled the events years later: Kinjō watched as a middle-aged village leader snapped a limb off a nearby tree, and "Once he had that stick in his hand, he turned into a madman. Striking his wife and children over and over again, bludgeoning them to death." That act triggered a murderous frenzy in which families and relatives set upon each other with knives, sickles, cudgels, and rocks. Kinjō recalls attacking his own mother. "'When we raised our hands against the mother who bore us, we wailed in our grief. . . . In the end we must have used stones. To the head. Then my brother and I turned against our younger brother and younger sister. Hell engulfed us there.'" After many villagers obeyed orders to kill themselves and family members, military units on the island avoided combat, and many soldiers survived.[30]

Many of the new commemorative sites in Okinawa emphasize the Japanese military's brutal treatment of the Okinawan people. Allen's storytellers on Kumejima soften the message by placing the blame for the murder of local civilians on one particularly vicious local commanding officer, while Figal's tour guides emphasize decisions made in Tokyo. Both nevertheless make clear that the wartime state was oppressor far more than it was protector of Okinawans. They seek to counter the official position that the state valued all Japanese highly and equally. That official story, reiterated by the veterans who erect monuments to the bravery and loyalty of Japanese soldiers during the war, emphasizes the willing self-sacrifice of national subjects to the state and the nation's postwar gratitude. Close examination of the history of the Battle of Okinawa troubles that narrative deeply.

Many Okinawans believe that Japanese soldiers sacrificed local civilians because they were despised as Okinawans and so were considered undeserving of the protection the soldiers would have offered "real" Japanese. That suspicion explains why recent museum depictions of the battle have been the focus of such heated popular and official controversy, as discussed by Figal. There is abundant evidence that the wartime Japanese officers stationed in Okinawa suspected local residents of being traitors. During the war, as Allen explains, Japanese officers treated utterances in an Okinawan language as evidence of disloyalty and sometimes as cause for summary execution. The officers were particularly suspicious of Okinawans who had traveled overseas to find work, presuming their ability to speak English or other evidence of cosmopolitanism was an indication of treachery. In this respect, Japanese wartime anxieties about Okinawans resemble World War II–era European suspicions of Jews, who were also seen as dangerously "cosmopolitan" aliens. And, just as in the case of European Jews, Okinawans were considered particularly insidious because their difference from "true" Japanese was often difficult to detect.[31]

Remembrance of Japanese military cruelty toward Okinawans during the battle also has directed attention to Okinawa's position in Japan's colonial empire.[32] Okinawan remembrance of the Japanese Empire today is frequently framed as solidarity and sympathy for other victims of Japanese imperialism, such as Koreans, Chinese, and Taiwanese. As recent scholarship has demonstrated, Japanese government policies toward Okinawa were part of a larger imperial project, just as English overlordship of Ireland and Scotland is inextricably connected to the development of the British Empire. Okinawans, like North Irish and Scots, now have full legal rights in the metropolitan society, but in the past their position had much in common with colonized people, such as Koreans and Taiwanese, who have since broken free of the empire. The similarity should not be surprising, since the Japanese closely studied European imperialist practices and often borrowed ideas and justifications for their own imperial policies.

Okinawans now are calling attention to the ethnic/racial hierarchy of the presurrender Japanese Empire, particularly the similarities between Japanese treatment of Okinawans and of colonial subjects. Okinawans did share special hardships with Koreans and Taiwanese during the war, when they were not only drafted as soldiers but also conscripted as (forced) civilian laborers and deployed to the most dangerous outposts of the empire. While many Okinawans at the time sought to differentiate themselves from the even-lower-status colonial subjects, contemporary remembrance focuses more on their common experience of oppression.

For example, although the textbooks approved for use in schools throughout Japan barely mention former colonial subjects, a supplementary high school text *Ryūkyū・Okinawa shi* (A History of the Ryukyus-Okinawa) used in Okinawa discusses at length the fate of Koreans, Taiwanese, Chinese, and Filipinos during the war.[33] One detailed map shows the locations of 130 comfort stations in Okinawa where women were forced to provide sex to the Japanese military, and it identifies the women as nearly all Korean.[34] The text emphasizes the theme that "lesser" national subjects were treated as expendable by the Imperial armed forces. The issue became a point of contention in Okinawan war memory when Governor Inamine ordered a similar map removed from the prefectural museum in 1999.

The Peace Memorial Park also includes a stele dedicated to the memory of the Koreans who died in the Battle of Okinawa. An inscription states that over ten thousand Koreans were dispatched to Okinawa during the war and, despite facing the same dangers as did Japanese recruits, were treated badly by their Japanese officers. The stele explains in Korean, Japanese, and English that Korean soldiers and conscripts "suffered innumerable hardships, and some of them were killed in battle and even slaughtered here in Okinawa." Survivors also dwell on the fate of Korean civilians who lived in Okinawa and were singled out for summary execution, as in the massacre of the Tanegawa family on Kumejima described by Allen.[35] The memory of that family, the cruelty of the soldiers toward them, and the horrified sympathy of the Okinawan bystanders are all themes stressed by the elderly narrators. That stance of solidarity with former colonial subjects is one of the most important ways that Okinawans are calling for reevaluation of the modern Japanese past as a whole, not just of the place of Okinawans within it.

In reflecting on motivations for Japanese violence against Okinawans, it is not entirely clear whether the government and military took such a cavalier attitude toward Okinawan lives out of racial prejudice or out of a more general lack of concern for civilian suffering. Simply put, the difference turns on the following question: Did wartime brutality toward Okinawans mainly reveal racist discrimination, or did it primarily spring from a profound official disregard for all but the most elite Japanese?

Prewar policies in Okinawa were not, after all, so different in their callousness from those applied, for example, to poor farmers throughout Japan's mountain villages who likewise confronted aggressive programs of linguistic and cultural assimilation. Nor did the plight of Okinawans during the war differ so greatly from that of the impoverished Japanese settlers left behind on the northern Manchurian border when the retreating Kwantung Army commandeered all trains, leaving settlers to an uncertain fate. Japanese military personnel were also treated as cannon fodder by their superior officers. Like Okinawan soldiers and civilians, tens of thousands of Japanese soldiers throughout Southeast Asia were ordered to fight to the death or die by their own hands rather than surrender. The Battle of Okinawa in this scenario was the penultimate step in a murderous logic that had begun with the prohibition on surrender by officers, then expanded to include enlisted men, and finally, grotesquely, was extended to all civilians. The Okinawans may have had the worst experience, but, from this perspective, they were essentially the canaries in the coal mine inhabited by all but the most elite national subjects.

Some Okinawan as well as some Japanese remembrance of the war emphasizes this interpretation, for example, the collaborative peace education curriculum developed jointly by people from Hiroshima, Nagasaki, and Okinawa. In fact, there is a long tradition in this vein of Japanese scholarship and activism rooted in pacifism and defense of the constitution's prohibition against war. Either way, remembrance of official Japanese cruelty and—at the very least—utter callousness toward civilian suffering shines a very harsh light on the wartime government's ideas about the duties of its national subjects and the reciprocal responsibilities of the state. Nor are these two scenarios mutually exclusive: Not only was the murderous logic of Japan's wartime leaders almost certainly racist, it also undervalued *all* human life.[36]

Although many Okinawans have criticized the Japanese racial hierarchy, far fewer have addressed Okinawan complicity with it. Okinawan author Medoruma Shun is a notable exception. In his short story "Taiwan Woman," discussed here by Molasky, Medoruma depicts Okinawan efforts to claw their way up that hierarchy at the expense of Taiwanese. Medoruma is unusual for the extent to which he insists that Okinawans judge their own past actions by the same standards they apply to mainland Japanese. The same theme also appeared in his prize-winning story "Droplets," in which an elderly Okinawan man is haunted by his wartime companions who remind him of how he had left them to die, thirsty and alone. The old man had often spoken about the war to schoolchildren, each time omitting those shameful details. Medoruma reminds us that even once-suppressed memory may contain its own biases, no less than do the national textbooks.

Remembrance of Okinawans who traveled overseas in the presurrender years is generally framed as a diaspora spurred by Japanese oppression of Okinawans at home. Yet that wave of emigration likewise occurred within the enabling context of Japanese imperialism. Okinawans who went to the Philippines and Saipan, for example, benefited from Japanese military domination of others. Here, too, remembrance of the extent to which Okinawans embraced the power they enjoyed as "nearly Japanese" lags behind remembrance of their suffering.[37] That history of emigration, and the resultant diasporic Okinawan community, is often cited by Okinawans as evidence of a distinctive level of Okinawan cosmopolitanism in contrast to an allegedly homogeneous Japan, explaining why the close involvement of Okinawan emigrants with the empire is so easily forgotten.

Surprisingly to us, Okinawan remembrance of the war and the Battle of Okinawa has not focused nearly as much on the American role, even though American bullets, grenades, rockets, and artillery barrages were the overwhelming immediate cause of civilian deaths. As Takemae Eiji observes, "In the heat of battle, GIs, too, showed no quarter, incinerating with flame-throwers combatants and non-combatants alike who had taken refuge in caves and vault-like ancestral 'turtleback' tombs."[38] Not only are these facts largely elided from Okinawan memorials and museum exhibits, there is even little attention to actions generally thought of as war crimes, such as the use of poison gas by U.S. troops during the invasion of Okinawa.[39] Rather, many Okinawans recall the Americans as the dreadful and impersonal culmination of the logic of Japanese militarism more than as people who could have chosen less deadly tactics against Okinawan civilians in the waning months of the war.

One reason why the American onslaught in Okinawa is remembered as relatively benign is that the Americans in victory proved to be far less cruel an enemy than the Okinawans had been led to believe. The Americans killed many civilians, sometimes deliberately, in the heat of battle, but they did not pursue a policy of torture, rape, and murder of civilians as Japanese military officials had warned. Some GIs did attack civilians, but the U.S. military also provided food and medical care to survivors—something that the Japanese military had not done in the last desperate month of the battle. In fact, American policy was to treat Okinawans as a subjugated people who were being liberated, rather than as the Japanese enemy in the immediate aftermath of the battle. In subsequent years, as discussed earlier, Okinawans discovered how little their welfare mattered to the Americans, but in the spring and summer of 1945, the enemy troops were less vicious than expected. Fears of American brutality had led many Okinawans to kill themselves or take the lives of loved ones as an act of mercy. When the survivors discovered that those precautions had been unnecessary, their sense of betrayal by their Japanese leaders exceeded their anger at the destruction wrought by the Americans.

Postwar Okinawa and Mainland Japan

Okinawan feelings of betrayal by Japan extend to the postwar years, too. The most obvious instance was the use of Okinawa by Japanese officials as a bargaining chip to achieve their own independence in 1952, leaving Okinawa as an American military colony. The diplomatic exchanges between American and Japanese officials show surprising levels of agreement on Okinawa's proper place in international affairs. General Douglas MacArthur expressed the views of the U.S. military on September 1, 1947, when he protested a State Department proposal to return Okinawa to Japan at the end of the occupation. That same month, Emperor Hirohito sent a secret message to MacArthur, requesting that the United States maintain control of Okinawa after the occupation of the mainland ended as protection against the Soviet Union.[40]

Okinawa became the strategic centerpiece of a string of American military bases extending from Micronesia to Japan. The 1952 peace treaty simultaneously ended the U.S. occupation of Japan, brought Japan into the Cold War treaty system, and transferred Okinawa to the exclusive control of the United States, rather than to the United Nations or any other civilian or international body. The treaty also granted Japan "residual sovereignty"—over Okinawa, that is, "the fiction of a long-term lease" of the islands to the United States, as Emperor Hirohito had proposed in 1947. Although the Americans talked of bringing democracy to Okinawa, military logic trumped all else. In both 1952 and 1957, when the laws were rewritten, the highest-ranking American officer in Okinawa retained the right to "promulgate laws, ordinances or regulations," "veto any bill," "annul any law," "remove any public official from office," and "assume, in whole or in part, the exercise of full authority in the islands."[41] The chain of command was so absolute that at least two ranking American government officials considered Okinawa an outright colony of the United States and a liability for international relations on those grounds. George Ball and Edwin O. Reischauer both complained in 1961 that, in Ball's words, it was "preposterous" that the United States "should still be treating [Okinawa] as our colony," especially since the United States had taken a strong stand against European colonialism.[42]

There were plenty of reasons for Okinawans to resent harsh American military rule. Not only were the Americans responsible for the destruction of their land and homes both during the battle and later, but the United

States Civil Administration of the Ryukyu Islands (USCAR) paid Okinawan workers extremely low wages, compensated them for their land at pitifully low levels, and denied workers at military bases the right to organize or strike. (A 1959 USCAR memorandum conceded that Americans earned twelve times, Japanese eight times, and Filipinos five times as much as Okinawans in jobs on the military bases while categorically rejecting the possibility that anyone was underpaid.) Like colonial rulers elsewhere, Americans lived in sumptuous houses with electricity, manicured lawns, and servants to do the work, while Okinawans lived in tiny dirt-floored shacks without running water or electricity.[43]

The military installations made dangerous neighbors: Sometimes ordnance exploded in nearby towns, planes crashed into buildings, and artillery fired in the wrong direction. The troops were and are frequently a menace, too. As Angst notes, most were bored young men who saw the crowded streets of Okinawan towns as their personal playground. Local civilians have had to put up with a steady stream of traffic accidents, brawls, drunken attacks, and petty theft by American soldiers and sailors. During the period of American rule, U.S. military courts blatantly and routinely favored American over Japanese parties in legal disputes over those issues, just as they did for the more serious crimes of rape, felonious assault, and murder. And, as Asato reminds us, the ongoing land seizures were a major source of Okinawan frustration. USCAR's control over travel between Japan and Okinawa allowed officials to punish Okinawans it considered subversive, providing another abiding spur to anger for Okinawans during the occupation years.

Between 1945 and 1972, USCAR officials also put considerable energy into manipulating the cultural symbols of Okinawan identity in an effort to create a permanent divide between Okinawans and Japanese, including celebrating the history of the Ryūkyū Kingdom and renaming the territory the Ryukyu Islands. The highest-ranking USCAR official, General Donald P. Booth, sponsored radio broadcasts on Ryukyu history, urged adoption of a flag based on the official regalia of the Ryūkyū court, and ordered an American Army Band leader under his jurisdiction to find a local folk song that could be made into an anthem. The American goal was to generate as many symbols as possible that would "represent the true spirit of the Ryukyus" and thereby diminish Okinawan desire to rejoin Japan, as Booth put it in 1960.

U.S. efforts to define Okinawa culturally were frequently heavy-handed and indicative of an unwillingness to allow Okinawans to define themselves. One example will suffice to illustrate the point. Baseball is an important element of national sports culture in Japan, as it is in the United States. In 1958, Shuri High School became the first Okinawan team to reach the national championship tournament. High school baseball was and is enormously popular throughout Japan, and the games were avidly followed by millions of Japanese. The Shuri team did not win, but the players marked their presence in Kōshien Stadium by digging up a little of the earth to bring back as a memento of their moment at the epicenter of Japanese popular culture. USCAR, on learning of their action, was so disturbed by the implication of that act that, when the team's ship arrived in Okinawa, military officials forced them to dump the dirt in the ocean. As David Obermiller has observed, "USCAR obviously feared that this symbolic soil from the 'homeland' challenged its authority."[44] Reversion to Japan, most Okinawans came to believe, would end such petty tyranny.

Chafing under U.S. military rule, most Okinawans favored reversion to Japan. As Obermiller and Yoshida both show, the reversion movement in the 1950s and 1960s was extremely popular, attracting 76 percent of the Okinawan electorate on a 1951 petition calling for reunification with Japan, for example. In the 1960s, many Okinawan political and intellectual leaders pushed hard for reunification, anticipating that the bases would close, the American military would leave, and Okinawans could fully enjoy the new social and economic opportunities available on the mainland.

Those expectations were not met. The bases and the American military occupiers remain in Okinawa. The land is still unavailable for local use. Military exercises are still dangerous and disruptive. American troops still regularly escape punishment for crimes against Okinawans.

Nevertheless, since 1972, some of the most egregious problems faced by Okinawans have been addressed. Japanese government health, pension, workers' compensation, and unemployment programs now cover Okinawans, for example. During the occupation years, they had no such safety net. Although incomes are still significantly lower than in other parts of Japan, they have risen substantially and the income disparity is far smaller than when Okinawa was ruled directly by the Americans. The number of people living in absolute poverty has diminished as well. Okinawans regained Japanese citizenship following reversion, and from 1972 they could obtain passports from Tokyo rather than having to apply for temporary travel documents from USCAR.

Okinawan anger since reversion has been directed at the Japanese government and society at least as much as at the Americans. The Okinawan sense of betrayal by Japan is obvious in the comments of many who reversed their stance in 1972 after realizing that reversion would not bring the benefits they most desired. One of the most prominent to change his mind was the highest local official in 1972, Yara Chōbyō, then chief executive of the government of the Ryūkyū Islands who had fought fiercely to achieve reversion.[45] While the U.S. military presence in Okinawa has remained huge since 1945, the number of American troops stationed on mainland Japan steadily diminished: from two hundred thousand in 1952 to forty-six thousand in 1964. Even at the height of the Vietnam War, U.S. forces in mainland Japan continued to decrease. In contrast, the American presence on Okinawa grew with the transfer of units from the mainland. In 2001, there were eighty thousand Americans in Okinawa, including thirty thousand active duty personnel. Most of the rest were either civilian employees of the military or family members. By contrast, there were fewer than twenty thousand active duty personnel at all the U.S. bases in mainland Japan combined. The United States also used Okinawa as a nuclear arsenal throughout the postwar era, both before and after reversion, with secret Japanese government approval.[46]

The reaction to the 1995 gang rape of the elementary school girl highlighted the issue of victimization of Okinawans by both the American and the Japanese governments. A mass rally of ninety thousand people on October 21, 1995, was the largest rally in Okinawa since reversion.[47]

As Angst shows here, Okinawan anger over the repeated brutality of American GIs against Okinawan civilians, and especially women and girls, is directed at least as much at Japan as at the United States. Okinawans are certainly angry at American soldiers who attack civilians and at the failure of the American military command to prevent such violence or prosecute offenders. Many are even angrier at Japanese officials whose indifference and inaction seems like yet another betrayal. The 1995 rape was treated by nearly all the Okinawans who discussed it publicly as a metaphor for a violent attack on Okinawa as a whole. For many Okinawans, the most intimate violence was the failure of the patriarchal Japanese "father" to protect his Okinawan "daughter" rather than the actual violence directly perpetrated by the three American men. The widespread use of the metaphor of a family—in which Okinawa is the daughter sacrificed by the father who defines the good of the family in ways that exclude her—helps explain why this is the most searing aspect of the experience for many Okinawans. As in the Battle of Okinawa forty years earlier, Okinawans felt betrayed by a Japanese state that demands great sacrifice but values them little.

As Angst demonstrates, the tropes of sacrificed young women, sexual violence, and patriarchal families suffuse contemporary debates on both the U.S. military presence in Okinawa and Okinawan-Japanese relations. Most of the protests underscored the idea that Okinawans were peaceful, pure, and innocent and therefore had powerful moral authority for their claims for better treatment from both Americans and Japanese. Yet, framing Okinawan peacefulness, purity, and innocence in gendered terms poses problems for Okinawan identity. Angst explores from a feminist perspective the pitfalls of an analysis suggesting that women require patriarchal protection when the invocation of one young girl raped by U.S. servicemen is extended to the metaphorical image of all Okinawa as Japan's young daughter sacrificed to the American lust for domination. That trope may actually impede feminist efforts to institutionalize public policies that benefit women, because it focuses attention so completely on the violation of the collective Okinawan body politic. The shared indignation about the rape—and compassion for the victim—by all Okinawans obscures the instances in which the specific concerns of women differ from those of the Okinawan male political elite. Angst argues further that the feminist agenda probably will be passed over, since male leaders successfully reframed the rape as the metaphorical violation of *Okinawan* property rights.

The author of "Taiwan Woman" mentioned earlier, Medoruma Shun, explores from a different perspective the problem of working within a gendered discourse about authority in Okinawa. When imagined in gendered terms, powerlessness connotes feminization or, worse, emasculation, especially since the specific issue raised by the 1995 rape was sexualized violence. For Medoruma, as Molasky shows here, celebrating "peacefulness" or claiming the moral high ground of victimization carries with it the danger of accepting old stereotypes of Okinawans as meek and dependent. The sheer passivity of that stance did nothing to appease his rage about the 1995 rape, imaginatively and chillingly rendered as homicidal in a 1999 short story made even more disturbing by its title, "Hope."[48] Medoruma and others are searching for ways to reframe Okinawan identity so that it includes more energy, assertiveness, and power. While "peacefulness" may be a favored weapon of the weak in many parts of the world, Medoruma is frustrated by its ineffectiveness at pressuring either the U.S. or Japanese governments to close the bases.

NEW INTERNATIONAL AND LOCAL CONTEXTS

Okinawan identity and its relationship to Japanese national identity has been a matter of public debate at least since an affronted Okinawan newspaper editor objected to Japanese display of Okinawans as exotic specimens at the 1903 Osaka Exhibition. Why, then, has the renegotiation of Okinawa's place within Japan gained such momentum and been the basis for so much creative energy in recent years? We see four major contributing factors.

First, and crucially, the international context has changed profoundly. In many ways, the Okinawan story is like that of many others, in which minorities all over the world have challenged their subordination within nations on racial-ethnic grounds and successfully forced reconsideration of discriminatory attitudes long unquestioned in the halls of power everywhere. Those efforts have impelled change both in societies that think of themselves as ethnically homogeneous, such as Germany, and ones that think of themselves as ethnically diverse, such as the United States. Japanese nationalists argue that Japan should become a "normal state," by which they mean a militarized one, but more and more in the minds of many people a "normal state" means a self-consciously multiethnic and multicultural one that strives to serve all its citizens well. In the 1980s, the corrosive effects of ethnic contempt became excruciatingly clear in Yugoslavia and Rwanda when ruling groups sought to create ethnically pure states by ruthlessly expelling and massacring all their minority residents. The viciousness with which they carried out those projects did much to discredit conceptions of national racial homogeneity and further legitimized ethnic and religious minorities around the globe who were demanding full rights as citizens on equal terms with the majority.

Okinawa's dilemma, fundamentally, is that of a small place forced to pick its way carefully through a world full of more powerful groups. Okinawans have had to accept incorporation into projects framed by powers far greater than their own whose concern for their well-being has been at best minimal. This is a dilemma familiar to many others. For example, Puerto Ricans face many of the same issues within the United States that Okinawans do within Japan. Their island, too, is home to a large and unpopular military base, their economy is highly dependent on special tax arrangements and other forms of government subsidy, and linguistic and cultural differences distinguish them from mainland society. Puerto Rican history has been one of conquest and partial assimilation on unequal terms, first by Spain and subsequently by the United States.

Yet, these cases are not completely parallel. Perhaps the greatest contrast is a result of the differing international positions of the Spanish and Okinawan languages. Puerto Ricans are linguistically and culturally part of the richly diverse Hispanic world, opening up a large cultural sphere separate from English-centered mainland life. Nor are Okinawans on the Japanese mainland part of a major diaspora community comparable in size and economic and political clout to the Hispanic populations in the United States. Thus, Hispanics not only have wide access to Spanish-language broadcast media but also have secured institutional measures such as bilingual education in American public schools for their children that allow them to live primarily in a Spanish cultural milieu. Okinawan languages are disappearing, while in San Juan, New York, Chicago, and Los Angeles, among other cities, Spanish thrives.

The international context is not just a reminder that the dilemmas Okinawans face are similar to those confronting many others around the world. It is also a source of models. Contemporary Okinawans are drawing on a global language of minority and human rights that is reinforced by international organizations such as the United Nations, as well as on concepts of ethnic identity, political pluralism, and multiculturalism that presently animate social, cultural, and political movements worldwide. Those international currents are one important reason why Okinawans are reconceptualizing themselves right now in ways that stimulate significant new cultural expression and redefine parameters of citizenship and historical memory in Japan.

One example, provided by Roberson, is the Uchinā pop musicians, who participate in a global network of music producers and consumers. In that global circuit, Latin, African, and African American musicians working in jazz, folk, salsa, blues, and many other idioms have provided Okinawans not only with new musical ideas, but also with compelling examples of minority groups asserting pride in their distinctive cultures and criticizing oppression through musical expression. Okinawan feminists have drawn on yet another global model of oppressed peoples (although not a minority) when they reframed attacks on women as human rights abuses.[49] Similarly, as Molasky argues, some of Okinawa's finest writers have found inspiration in the magical realism of Latin American authors, who pioneered that literary genre in order to express more directly the complexity of their lives within a highly politicized and hierarchical world.

Many of the other practices discussed in this volume that are contributing to a strong sense of Okinawan identity are influenced by global trends, such as those in history education, environmental activism, cinematic technique, and museum exhibit and public monument design. Moreover, many of those trends emerged explicitly as strategies to empower the disenfranchised. Oral history, for example, developed in the 1970s as a way to democratize history education and tell the stories of people formerly excluded from the official narratives of the nation. This impulse is evident in the invitation to elderly Kume Islanders to relate their experiences to local young people. *Tsuru-Henry,* the film Gerow identifies as cinematically most successful in expressing Okinawan aspirations, draws heavily on video production, both in the plot and on the screen. Far cheaper and more technically accessible than traditional film technology, video has been the preferred medium of expression for minorities in many parts of the world. Of all the films set in Okinawa, *Tsuru-Henry* most self-consciously experiments with imaginative ways of representing multiculturalism and hybridity.

Okinawans have been able to draw effectively on international cultural models in part because of their vision of themselves as open to the world beyond Okinawa's shores. One way that Okinawans became aware of the world music scene was through Peruvian-Okinawan musical groups, who combined Okinawan folk motifs with Latin music. This development suggests that the contrast drawn earlier with Puerto Rico is one of degree rather than kind. Okinawa, too, is tied into the global circuits of people and culture that are currently transforming our world. Moreover, it has become easier to connect to those circuits as greater access to the Internet and opportunities for international travel accelerate the pace of change.[50] So, for example, a group of Okinawan activists traveled to Puerto Rico in late 2001 to join a protest against live ammunition testing at Vieques. Puerto Ricans and Okinawans alike saw opportunities to support each other as participants in an international movement where inspiration, ideas, and strategies flow in multiple directions. Such cross-fertilization across national lines is customary behavior in all modern societies, including mainland Japan, but in Okinawa, these ideas are being framed as evidence that Okinawans are "global citizens" in a world-wide imagined polity.

Second, the end of the Cold War focused attention specifically on the assumptions behind the global deployment of U.S. military power. Far more than at any time in the previous fifty years, people in both Japan and the United States questioned the need for any U.S. bases in Okinawa at all. The end of the Cold War also created a political climate that opened new opportunities for former Japanese colonial subjects and Asians who had suffered under Japan during World War II to air their long-neglected grievances internationally. The former military comfort women and victims of the Nanjing massacre, for example, began to mount effective international demands for redress. Those developments also provided Okinawans with a new context and set of arguments to protest their treatment by both Japanese and Americans.[51] The new themes of remembrance of World War II in the textbook and memorials described earlier are one prominent result.

Japan also is changing, and this is the third factor contributing to new levels of attention to Okinawa's place within it. Even though many Japanese and international observers cling to essentialized notions of what it means to be Japanese, Japan is a very fast-changing society. Several different minority groups have launched sophisticated and highly visible challenges to Japanese ideas of homogeneity in the last decade.[52] Among the most vocal are the resident Koreans in Japan. By now, most of them are the children, grandchildren, and great-grandchildren of the colonial subjects who were brought to Japan as laborers before 1945 and were stripped of Japanese citizenship in the same peace treaty that relegated Okinawans to life under U.S. military command. All but the oldest Korean residents have lived in Japan their entire lives and, like Okinawans, speak native Japanese and are thoroughly acculturated to Japanese society. They have been protesting their exclusion from Japanese civic life since the early 1980s, beginning with the requirements that they register as aliens by being fingerprinted and carry their alien registration books with them at all times. The Japanese government only granted Koreans permanent residency and allowed them to travel abroad freely after it was pressured to do so on the basis of the Human Rights Convention, ratified by Japan in 1979, and the United Nations Refugee Convention of 1981.[53] In 1990, Korean residents were still barred from all government jobs, including teaching in public schools, working in municipal governments, and delivering the mail. By 2002, however, as a result of steady pressure for change from Korean residents, many local governments had eased those restrictions, even though the central government continues to resist changing the laws barring noncitizens from most jobs in the public sector.

Japan's other major ethnic minority, the Ainu, have also demanded and won significant recognition in the last decade. Both Ainu and Okinawans have forged political links, not only with each other but also with indigenous peoples in other parts of the world, including Native Americans and Australian Aborigines. The Ainu have been particularly active in embracing the concept of an indigenous people, but some Okinawans have also sought to establish Fourth World solidarity bonds.[54] The concert schedule of Okinawan musician Kina Shoukichi's White Ship tour in 1998, which included stops at the Ute and Pine Ridge Reservations and ended at the Onondaga Iroquois Nation, is one such example of Okinawan cultural outreach. That imagined community of indigenous peoples is partly a rebuke to the environmentally destructive and intolerant majority societies in Japan, Australia, the United States, and elsewhere, but it is also a celebration and elaboration of minority culture. The invocation of indigenous rights also provides an internationally sanctioned context for claims to specific tracts of land as a powerful spiritual source of community identity, as argued here by Asato for Okinawa.

The antibase "one-tsubo landowner" movement described earlier is another important example of a modern claim to power framed in terms of Okinawan identity. In addition to being an astute political and legal tactic to expand the number of Okinawan landowners who publicly demand return of base land, it is a powerful cultural invention as well. By buying just enough land to lie down on (or be buried in), propertyless Okinawans become symbolically connected to the land, invested in the natural habitat, and part of a larger egalitarian community of fellow Okinawans who are acting in concert toward the elimination of the alien military bases.

Fourth and finally, a major reason why Okinawans have been so productively engaged in recent years in debating the nature of Okinawan-Japaneseness and Okinawan identity is that Okinawans are significantly more integrated into Japan than at any time in their history. In the presurrender years, as Rabson shows, discrimination and impoverishment made it extremely difficult for Okinawans to assimilate into Japanese society, even for those determined to do so. At that time, linguistic and cultural barriers were enormous for many Okinawans. Between 1945 and 1972, travel and cultural exchange between Okinawa and the mainland was difficult, and in the early postwar years most Okinawans were still struggling to repair their war-shattered lives. But since 1972, Okinawans have studied the same school curriculum; watched the same movies; read the same books, magazines, and *manga* (graphic fiction); and traveled freely back and forth to the mainland. (Within Okinawa, life has also become more uniform as the smaller islands have become more integrated with the main one and distinctive local dialects and cultural forms have disappeared.) The life experience of Okinawans now in their midadult years and younger has been far closer to that of mainland Japanese than was true of their parents' and grandparents' generations. It may well be that precisely because full assimilation into mainland norms is for the first time truly achievable, so many Okinawans now feel free to reject that goal. Instead, they are exploring an identity that simultaneously expresses their ability to maneuver smoothly in Japanese culture and their Okinawan cultural heritage. Stated differently, Okinawans are making significant headway in carving out space for "hyphenated identity" by reimagining their cultural and political heritage: as Okinawans, as Japanese, and as Asians.

In the 1980s, for the first time since 1945, a significant number of foreigners came to Japan from Asia and Latin America in search of work. Although most of the Latin Americans were ethnically Japanese or Okinawan—the descendents of emigrant laborers—they were Latin in language, sensibility, and life experience. The presence of these newcomers demonstrated for many in Japan how similar resident Koreans, Ainu, and Okinawans are to mainland ethnic Japanese by comparison.

The essays gathered here suggest that Okinawans are having some success in changing mainland attitudes as well—both at the level of government and of society. Many of the contributors here are pessimistic about the degree to which both government officials and mainland Japanese will accept Okinawan demands for change, but Okinawans certainly are engaging Japanese attention to an unprecedented degree. Julia Yonetani shows that the Japanese government is now explicitly treating Okinawan protest against hosting 75 percent of the U.S. bases as an ideological challenge, in addition to using familiar tactics of compensatory payment and political pressure on elected officials. In the "Okinawa Initiative" debate of 2000, the national government mobilized pro–Liberal Democratic Party Okinawans to reframe its political relationship to Okinawa. The proponents of the Okinawa Initiative began by acknowledging that wartime policies were deeply prejudicial toward Okinawans. They also conceded that the Japanese government's postwar willingness to cede Okinawa to the United States in 1952 and to leave all U.S. bases intact at reversion was deeply unfair. Such concessions clearly were made in the hope that rhetorical apology—together with higher cash payments—would suffice to mollify Okinawan ire over being forced to continue hosting the bases in the future. As critics of the initiative pointed out, words of contrition would be very welcome if accompanied by policies of redress, but they are unacceptable as a ploy to perpetuate the highly unequal distribution of the bases and the sacrifice of Okinawan to mainland Japanese interests. The Okinawa Initiative is clearly intimately connected to the Japanese government's attempts to respond to the challenge posed by the wave of Okinawan protests following the September 1995 rape. This tacit recognition of the legitimacy of Okinawan grievances has appeared in recent pronouncements by Japanese officials. Tellingly, in early 2002, the Japanese consul general in Chicago, Yabunaka Mitoji, told a local audience that the single greatest challenge to the Japanese government's *international* agenda was "the sensitivities of the Okinawan people" regarding the bases.[55] Tokyo officials can no longer ignore Okinawan remembrance and its associated political demands.

Gerow focuses on the diffuse but powerful ways that the ideology of Japanese homogeneity is reinforced through popular culture rooted in the relentless cultural logic of contemporary capitalism. In many of the films he discusses, Okinawan distinctiveness is both attractive and offers an implicit critique of Japanese homogeneity, but, in subtle and not so subtle ways, most of the films guide the viewer back toward the message that there is no alternative to the Japanese mainstream. Some of the movies present that message as reassuring, others as bleak, but only one, *Tsuru-Henry*, views it as surmountable. Similarly, Roberson and Rabson report that many Okinawan musicians are wary of their popularity on the mainland, anxious that they are merely the fashion of the moment and their deepest statements of difference will be reduced to a trivial "tidbit" to be consumed and forgotten by mainland Japanese. As Rabson notes, some Okinawan performers see their primary audience as other Okinawans, at times even barring mainlanders from performances on the grounds that they are religious observances. Yet, many Okinawan musicians also welcome their popularity among mainland Japanese. That wider audience not only allows them to earn a living from their music, it also signals that they are a distinctive part of a shared musical culture that embraces both Japanese and world music.

Collectively, these demands to rethink Okinawan-Japaneseness necessarily imply interrogating the idea of Japaneseness as well. Demands for full civic and social inclusion also require rethinking fundamental questions about the war, the alliance with the United States, economic development priorities, and the routes to social mobility in contemporary Japan. Japan's economic stagnation over the last decade has meant significant erosion of the preeminent postwar social compact in Japan: that conformity and hard work will lead to success on a narrowly defined (and highly gendered) social ladder of achievement. For most of the postwar era, all boys who did well on school exams could expect to move directly from school to decades of secure employment and steady advancement in a single firm. There were significant barriers to Okinawans, Ainu, resident Koreans, and Burakumin, but still the rewards to conformity were considerable. After more than a decade of economy-wide retrenchment, few Japanese believe that social compact is still in effect for young people today. Long-term recession has loosened once-tight links between "proper" behavior and opportunity to participate in economic prosperity.

For some Japanese, those changes are deeply alarming, precisely because they validate heterogeneity and democracy and challenge ethnic and gender hierarchies. One such group is the Japanese Institute for Orthodox History Education, analyzed at length in our earlier study.[56] Ishihara Shintarō, a noted writer and conservative politician who became governor of Tokyo in 1997, has belittled Koreans and Chinese residents in Japan by referring to them as "third-country nationals," the highly derogatory phrase used in the immediate postwar years, to emphasize their foreign and dangerous nature. Other officials have engaged in petty harassment of Okinawans for expressions of pride in local identity. In 1999, for example, an Okinawan high school baseball team returned to Kōshien Stadium to compete in the national championship for the first time since 1958. Officials forbade Okinawan fans from wearing colorful Okinawan robes at the stadium, even though fans from other parts of Japan were allowed regionally distinctive clothing. Just as the Americans had feared the symbolic power of Okinawan identification with Japanese baseball in 1958, Japanese officials forty-one years later clearly feared the symbolic power of Okinawan difference within the highly ritualized sphere of sports rivalries.

Other mainland Japanese, however, find the efforts by Okinawans and other minority groups to expand the meaning of contemporary Japaneseness deeply satisfying. These include activists in the peace movement, Japanese women's and human rights organizations, and environmental and "small is beautiful" movements, but they are not alone. In recent years, critical and popular interest in literature by Okinawan writers on Okinawan themes has skyrocketed in Japan as has academic research on Japan's minorities. Some mainland Japanese have joined the ranks of "one-tsubo" landowners by buying symbolic amounts of Okinawan land in solidarity with the Okinawan antibase movement. More and more mainland Japanese agree with those Okinawans who believe that conforming to the rigid cultural and social requirements of middle-class life in Japan is not worth the considerably reduced chances of joining the "elite course." They, too, deploy the theme that Okinawans are better able to communicate with foreigners, especially other Asians, appreciating it as a skill that all Japanese need for the new century. This view of Okinawans as cosmopolitan is sometimes naïve and highly romantic, but the romantic fantasy is of redemption and renewal rather than tropical escape. It expresses the hope that Okinawan challenges to the status quo and cultural resourcefulness will help transform all Japan into a more lively, vibrant, cosmopolitan, and humane place to live.

NOTES

1. This is a major theme in Michael Molasky and Steve Rabson, eds., *Southern Exposure: Modern Japanese Literature from Okinawa* (Honolulu: University of Hawai'i Press, 2000).

2. Tessa Morris-Suzuki, *Reinventing Japan: Time, Space, Nation* (Armonk, N.Y.: Sharpe, 1998); Donald Denoon, Mark Hudson, Gavan McCormack, and Tessa Morris-Suzuki, eds., *Multicultural Japan: Palaeolithic to Postmodern* (Cambridge: Cambridge University Press, 1996); Harumi Befu, *Hegemony of Homogeneity: An Anthropological Analysis of "Nihonjinron"* (Melbourne: Trans Pacific, 2001).

3. See Steve Rabson, chapter 4 in this volume; also Hugh Clarke, "The Great Dialect Debate: The State and Language Policy in Okinawa," in *Society and the State in Interwar Japan*, ed. Elise K. Tipton (London: Routledge, 1997), 193–217.

4. Tomiyama Ichirō, "Colonialism and the Sciences of the Tropical Zone: The Academic Analysis of Difference in 'the Island Peoples,'" *positions: east asia cultures critique* 3, no. 2 (September 1995): 367–91; Tomiyama Ichirō, *Senjō no Kioku* (Battlefield Commemorations) (Tokyo: Nihon Keizai Hyōronsha, 1995); Tomiyama Ichirō, "The Critical Limits of the National Community: The Ryukyuan Subject," *Social Science Japan Journal* 1, no. 2 (1998): 165–79, especially 175; Tomiyama Ichirō, "'Spy': Mobilization and Identity in Wartime Okinawa," in *Japanese Civilization in the Modern World: Vol. XVI. Nation State and Empire*, ed. T. Umesao, T. Fujitani, and E. Kurimoto, *Senri Ethnological Studies*, no. 52 (Osaka: National Museum of Ethnology, 2000). For one individual who was driven mad by this dilemma, see Gregory Smits, "Jahana Noboru: Okinawan Activist and Scholar," in *The Human Tradition in Modern Japan*, ed. Anne Walthall (Wilmington, Del.: SR Books, 2002), 99–114.

5. Morris-Suzuki, *Reinventing Japan*, 204–05. The statement is at least equally true for presurrender Japan.

6. Morris-Suzuki, *Reinventing Japan*; John Higham, *Strangers in the Land: Patterns of American Nativism, 1860–1925*, 2d ed. (New Brunswick, N.J.: Rutgers University Press, 1988; Ian Neary, "Burakumin in Contemporary Japan," in *Japan's Minorities*, ed. Weiner (London: Routledge, 1997), 50–78, especially 64–69; Frank Upham, *Law and Social Change in Postwar Japan* (Cambridge, Mass.: Harvard University Press, 1987).

7. Schools could offer Hawai'ian only as a foreign language. "Master's Degree in Hawaiian," National Public Radio, *Morning Edition*, May 30, 2002.

8. Kensei Yoshida, "Democracy Betrayed: Okinawa under U.S. Occupation," *Studies on East Asia*, vol. 23 (Bellingham: Center for East Asian Studies, Western Washington University, n.d.).

9. Chih-ming Ka, *Japanese Colonialism in Taiwan: Land Tenure, Development, and Dependency, 1895–1945* (Boulder, Colo.: Westview, 1995).

10. Ronald Y. Nakasone, ed., *Okinawan Diaspora* (Honolulu: University of Hawai'i Press, 2002), 17.

11. Takemae Eiji, *Inside GHQ: The Allied Occupation of Japan and Its Legacy* (London: Continuum, 2002), 122, 441.

12. For a comprehensive critique of Japanese-style developmentalism in Okinawa, see Gavan McCormack, "Okinawan Dilemmas: Coral Islands or Concrete Islands?" in *Okinawa: Cold War Island*, ed. Chalmers Johnson (Cardiff, Calif.: Japan Policy Research Institute, 1999), 261–82.

13. Okinawan per capita income was 72.8 percent of the national average in 1998, the most recent year given. Ministry of Economic Trade and Industry—Okinawa website: llogb.go.jp/move/English/index.e_html, accessed April 20, 2002.

14. Takemae, *Inside GHQ*, 514.

15. Miyume Tanji, "The Dynamic Trajectory of the 'Okinawa Struggle,' since 1972," in *Japan and Okinawa: Structure and Subjectivity*, ed. Glenn Hook and Richard Siddle (London: Routledge, 2002). See also Angst, chapter 5 in this volume.

16. Julia Yonetani, "Playing Base Politics in a Global Strategic Theater: Futenma Relocation, the G-8 Summit, and Okinawa," *Critical Asian Studies* 33, no. 1 (March 2001): 70–95.

17. Report by the Committee of Industrial and Economic Promotion and Deregulation Study, posted on the Okinawa Prefectural Government website: www.pref.okinawa.jp/97/kokusaitoshikeisei/, accessed April 25, 2002.

18. A good comparative treatment is John R. Gillis, ed. *Commemorations: The Politics of National Identity* (Princeton, N.J.: Princeton University Press, 1994); the classic text is Benedict Anderson, *Imagined Communities: Reflections on the Origin and Spread of Nationalism*, 2d ed. (London: Verso, 1991); see also Laura Hein and Mark Selden, eds., *Censoring History: Citizenship and Memory in Japan, Germany and the United States* (Armonk, N.Y.: M. E. Sharpe, 2000).

19. Hamashita Takeshi, *Okinawa Nyūmon: Ajia o Tsunagu Kaiiki Kōza* (Introduction to Okinawa: Blueprint for Understanding the Asia Connected by the Sea) (Tokyo: Chikuma Shobō, 2000). See also his "Tribute and Treaties: Maritime Asia and Treaty Port Networks in the Era of Negotiation, 1800–1900," in *The Resurgence of East Asia: 500, 150 and 50 Year Perspectives*, ed. Giovanni Arrighi, Takeshi Hamashita, and Mark Selden (London: Routledge, 2003).

20. See Stephen Steinberg, *The Ethnic Myth: Race, Ethnicity, and Class in America*, 2d ed. (Boston: Beacon, 1989).

21. Ronald Y. Nakasone, "An Impossible Possibility," in *Okinawan Diaspora*, ed. Nakasone, 9. On prehistoric Okinawa, see Mark J. Hudson, *Ruins of Identity: Ethnogenesis in the Japanese Islands* (Honolulu: University of Hawai'i Press, 1999).

22. See H. D. Harootunian, "Figuring the Folk: History, Poetics, and Representation," and Hashimoto Mitsuru "Chihō: Yanagita Kunio's 'Japan,'" both in *Mirror of Modernity: Invented Traditions of Modern Japan*, ed. Stephen Vlastos (Berkeley: University of California Press, 1998). Quote from 155.

23. Kushi Fusako, "Memoirs of a Declining Ryukyuan Woman," in *Southern Exposure,* ed. Molasky and Rabson, 73–80.

24. Okinawa Commemorative National Government Park Office, ed., *The Tale of Shurijo Castle: Enjoy Learning about Shurijo Castle* (Naha: Shurijo Castle Park Management Center, n.d.). See also Gerald Figal, "The Battle of Tropical Ryukyu Kingdom Tourist Okinawa," unpublished manuscript.

25. Ronald Y. Nakasone, "An Impossible Possibility," in *Okinawan Diaspora,* ed. Nakasone, 3, 22–23.

26. Former governor Ōta Masahide is the foremost historian of the battle. See Yonetani chapter here and Ōta, "Re-examining the History of the Battle of Okinawa," in *Okinawa: Cold War Island,* ed. Johnson, 13–38.

27. For a perceptive discussion of internationalism, see Perry Anderson, "Internationalism: A Breviary," *New Left Review* 14 (March–April 2002): 5–25. For related discussions, see Lisa Yoneyama, "Memory Matters: Hiroshima's Korean Atom Bomb Memorial and the Politics of Ethnicity," in *Living with the Bomb: American and Japanese Cultural Conflicts in the Nuclear Age,* ed. Laura Hein and Mark Selden (Armonk, N.Y.: Sharpe, 1997), 155–72; and Hein and Selden, eds., *Censoring History,* particularly Hein and Selden, "The Lessons of War, Global Power, and Social Change," and Gregory Wegner, "The Power of Selective Tradition: Buchenwald Concentration Camp and Holocaust Education for Youth in the New Germany," 226–57.

28. Ishihara Masaie, "Memories of War and Okinawa," in *Perilous Memories: The Asia–Pacific War(s),* ed. T. Fujitani, Geoffrey M. White, and Lisa Yoneyama (Durham, N.C.: Duke University Press, 2001), 87–106, especially 88.

29. Herbert P. Bix, "Japan's Delayed Surrender: A Reinterpretation," in *Hiroshima in History and Memory,* ed. Michael J. Hogan (Cambridge: Cambridge University Press, 1996), 80–115.

30. Haruko Taya Cook and Ted Cook, *Japan at War: An Oral History* (New York: New Press, 1992), 354–72; Norma Field, *In the Realm of a Dying Emperor: Japan at Century's End* (New York: Vintage, 1991).

31. See Omer Bartov, "Defining Enemies, Making Victims: Germans, Jews, and the Holocaust," *American Historical Review* 103, no. 3 (June 1998): 771–816.

32. Michael Weiner, "The Invention of Identity, 'Self' and 'Other' in Pre-war Japan," and Koji Taira, "Troubled National Identity: The Ryukyuans/Okinawans," both in *Japan's Minorities,* ed. Weiner, 1–16 and 140–77, especially 154.

33. The text was written by high school teacher Arashiro Toshiaki and the Okinawa Rekishi Kyōiku Kenkyūkai (Okinawan History Education Research Association) (Naha: Tōyō Kiku, 2001). Since the Japanese Ministry of Education did not formally approve this book, it can only be used as a supplementary text in schools. See also Koji Taira, "The Battle of Okinawa in Japanese History Books," in *Cold War Island,* ed. Johnson, 39–49.

34. See also Yoshimi Yoshiaki, *Comfort Women: Sexual Slavery in the Japanese Military during World War II* (New York: Columbia University Press, 2000), chapter 5; Yuki Tanaka, *Japan's Comfort Women: Sexual Slavery and Prostitution during World War II and the US Occupation* (London: Routledge, 2002), 26–28.

35. *A History of the Ryukyus-Okinawa* (Naha, 2001), 226–27. For further discussion of the Korean memorial in Okinawa, and comparisons with the Korean memorial located near Hiroshima Peace Park, see Gerald Figal, "Historical Sense and

Commemoration Sensibility of Okinawa's Cornerstone of Peace," *Positions: East Asia Cultures Critique* 5, no. 3 (Winter 1997): 748–49, and Lisa Yoneyama, *Hiroshima Traces: Time, Space, and the Dialectics of Memory* (Berkeley: University of California Press, 1999).

36. Comparative study of the issues is critical. John Dower's *War without Mercy: Race and Power in the Pacific War* (New York: Pantheon, 1986) is the classic study of Japanese and American racism in the Pacific War. The willingness to inflict mass civilian casualties on enemy populations was one of the distinctive features of all the major combatants in World War II, not just Japan. Japan stands out only for extending that attitude to its own subjects and perhaps for the cruelty with which it treated civilians. On questions of technology and the bombing of civilians, see Mark Selden, "The Logic of Mass Destruction," in *Hiroshima's Shadow: Writings on the Denial of History and the Smithsonian Controversy,* ed. Kai Bird and Lawrence Lifschultz (Stony Creek, Conn.: Pamphleteer's, 1998); on broader comparison of Japanese and American war atrocities in the twentieth century, see Selden, "State Terrorism and Human Rights: The United States, Japan and the Civilian in Twentieth Century Asian Wars," in *Asia and the U.S. at War: The Twentieth Century Experience,* ed. Mark Selden and Alvin So (Lanham, Md.: Rowman and Littlefield, 2003).

37. But for a recent exception, see Edith Kaneshiro, "'The Other Japanese': Okinawan Immigrants to the Philippines, 1903–1941," in *Okinawan Diaspora,* ed. Nakasone, 71–89.

38. Takemae is sharply critical of both the American and Japanese military for their indiscriminate destruction of civilians. *Inside GHQ,* 33.

39. Significantly, most of the Japanese commanding officers in Okinawa had participated in the Nanjing Massacre. Cook and Cook, *Japan at War,* 357, for poison gas. Kinjō Shigeaki, "Now They Call It 'Group Suicide,'' 363–66, and Miyagi Harumi, "I Learned about the War from Grandma," 472–77, inform the following paragraph.

40. Herbert P. Bix, *Hirohito and the Making of Modern Japan* (New York: HarperCollins, 2000), 626–27; see also Ōta Masahide, "War Memories Die Hard in Okinawa," *Japan Quarterly* 35, no. 1 (January–March 1988): 9–16; Takemae, *Inside GHQ,* 443–44.

41. Yoshida, "Democracy Betrayed," especially 54 and 78–79.

42. Michael Schaller, *Altered States: The United States and Japan since the Occupation* (New York: Oxford University Press, 1997), 171–72.

43. Yoshida, "Democracy Betrayed," 67–68, 94. This USCAR memorandum was prepared to ward off criticism of U.S. policy in Okinawa from the American Civil Liberties Union, which played an important role in publicizing infringements of civil liberties in Okinawa.

44. David Tobaru Obermiller, "The Okinawan Struggle over Identity, Historical Memory, and Cultural Representation," *Japan Foundation Newsletter* 27, nos. 3–4 (March 2000): 12–16; quote is from 14.

45. Obermiller, "The Okinawan Struggle," 12–16. Arakawa Akira, Kawamitsu Shin'ichi, and others anticipated many of the problems of reversion, notably continued Okinawan subjugation to Japanese goals and priorities, ongoing U.S. bases, and lack of Okinawan autonomy, in their antireversion writings in the early 1970s. Publishing in *Sekai* and other Japanese journals, they alerted Japanese in-

tellectuals to many problems that would become clear following reversion. See Michael Molasky, "Arakawa Akira: The Thought and Poetry of an Iconoclast," in *Japan and Okinawa*, ed. Hook and Siddle.

46. Figures from 2001 are from Yoshida, "Democracy Betrayed," 177. Nuclear weapons were first introduced to Okinawa in 1954. Yoshida, "Democracy Betrayed," 62, and Schaller, *Altered States*, 195–96. For recently classified details on the secret U.S.–Japan agreement to store nuclear weapons in Okinawa, see the National Security Archive website: www.gwu.edu/~nsarchiv/japan/okinawa/okinawa.htm, accessed May 11, 2002.

47. Yoshida reports that since reversion 4,800 U.S. servicemen and their dependents have committed nearly 5,000 crimes, including 520 "atrocious" and 970 "violent" crimes. "Democracy Betrayed," 179. See also Taira, "Troubled National Identity," in *Japan's Minorities*, ed. Weiner, 173.

48. Medoruma Shun, trans. Steve Rabson, *JPRI Critique* 6, no. 12 (December 1999).

49. For more analysis, see Laura Hein, "Claiming Humanity and Legal Standing: Contemporary Demands for Redress from Japan for its World War II Policies," in *Politics and the Past: On Repairing Historical Injustices*, ed. John Torpey (Lanham, Md.: Rowman & Littlefield, 2003). See also Linda Angst, "In a Dark Time: Community, Memory, and the Making of Ethnic Selves in Okinawan Women's Narratives," Ph.D. diss., Yale University, 2001.

50. Donald M. Nonini, "Introduction: Transnational Migrants, Globalization Processes, and Regimes of Power and Knowledge," *Critical Asian Studies* 34, no. 1 (March 2002): 3–18, is an excellent Asia-centered explication of this theme.

51. Johnson, ed., *Cold War Island*, is the best indicator of the changing intellectual and political climate in the United States, Japan, and Okinawa on base issues.

52. John Lie estimates a minority population of 4 to 6 million out of 125 million Japanese. Of that group, Ainu compose 25,000 to 30,000; Burakumin, 2 to 3 million; Okinawans, 1.6 million; Koreans, 700,000 to 1 million; and Chinese, 200,000. *Multiethnic Japan* (Cambridge, Mass.: Harvard University Press, 2001), 4.

53. "Introduction: Resident Koreans in Japan," in *Koreans in Japan: Critical Voices from the Margin*, ed. Sonia Ryang (London: Routledge, 2000), 6.

54. A March 2001 Okinawan appeal to the United Nations claimed, "The people of Okinawa possess their own history and culture. As such, their rights are those of an indigenous people, including the right to self-determination." "Information on OKINAWA Concerning the Initial and Second Periodic Report of the Japanese Government Submitted to CERD," submitted jointly by the Association of Indigenous Peoples in the Ryukyus (AIPR), the Okinawa Citizens' Information Centre (OCIC) and the Shimin Gaikō Centre (SGC; Citizens' Diplomatic Centre for the Rights of Indigenous Peoples), a nongovernmental organization in special consultative status with the Economic and Social Council (ECOSOC) of the United Nations.

55. Yabunaka Mitoji, speech on "Japan–U.S. Relations in the Aftermath of September 11," Chicago, January 30, 2002.

56. Hein and Selden, eds., *Censoring History*, particularly Hein and Selden, "The Lessons of War, Global Power, and Social Change," and Gavan McCormack, "The Japanese Movement to 'Correct' History," 53–73.

I

Making Sense of the Past

2

Wolves at the Back Door

Remembering the Kumejima Massacres

Matthew Allen

ILLEGITIMATE VIOLENCE?

Between 26 June and 20 August 1945, the Japanese army stationed on Kumejima, a small island sixty miles to the west of the main island of Okinawa, executed twenty civilians on charges that ranged from spying to profiteering. Among those executed were six children under eleven years of age and two women. What makes these incidents particularly shocking is that they all occurred after the Japanese army on Okinawa had surrendered (25 June). Sworn to protect civilians, the army's commander, Lieutenant Kayama, refused to acknowledge that the war was over and took actions to enforce discipline. This use of violence revolved around the idea of identity: Were Kume islanders the "enemy within"? Were those executed really spies? Were they Japanese? Were they Okinawan?

The executions, which have come to be known as "the Kumejima Massacres," have been used as evidence to demonstrate that Okinawans were victims of Japanese illegitimate violence.[1] One of the massacres—that of the Korean Tanegawa family—has also been cited as evidence of atrocities against Koreans by the Japanese army.[2] Other writers have cited the massacres as examples of Japanese war crimes.[3] Tomiyama[4] has suggested that the citizens' group that eventually forced Kayama to surrender was an example of popular uprisings against the Japanese army in Okinawa.

On Kumejima remembrance of the massacres is more complex than any of these accounts would suggest. Accommodating most of the themes described, oral accounts of the massacres are fragmented and disjointed personal recollections of events, which until 1999 had no forum in which to emerge publicly. The introduction of the "living history" program (discussed later) in the Nakazato district was an attempt by islanders to provide an accessible, popular form of education for children about the wartime experiences of islanders.

Although the stories presented to the audience portray the commander, Kayama, as an extreme, obsessive, and ultranationalist aberration of Japanese rule and are understood by listeners primarily as antiwar parables, they implicitly revolve around the issue of islanders' identity. Kayama's suspicions that islanders were spies was driven by official army policy of 1945, which banned the speaking of dialect (which was incomprehensible to Japanese army personnel) in public on penalty of death. The simple fact that Tokyo believed Okinawans were capable, indeed likely, to betray Japan to the Americans belies the rhetoric of Okinawans as Japanese citizens. It was this ambivalence about Okinawans' status, as much as any other factor, that led to the massacres of civilians on Kume Island.

"LIVING TREASURES" AND RESURRECTED PASTS

In 1999, the Nakazato Board of Education (*kyōiku iinkai*) on Kumejima introduced the new "living history" program (*nen warabi gakkyū*) for junior high school second-year students. In "living history" elderly people present to students stories of their experiences during the Pacific War and the Battle of Okinawa. It was the first time that such an enterprise had been attempted on the island, and it took place at a time of surging political activity in Okinawa. Members from the Nakazato Board of Education recognized that as the people who experienced this particular history die, the opportunity to articulate these events from firsthand experience diminishes.[5]

Although conducted in the summer holidays, the program has attracted large numbers of local children; in 1999, about seventy junior high school children attended the two-day workshop. This program is notable in that these stories represent deeply held, *local* memories of a period in history that had not been part of the formal education curriculum since the war. This is not to suggest that the act of remembering and the act of speaking of one's memories are the same thing. In this case, until the workshop no public forum for the memories existed. However, the act of remembering the war and the events described later had been eclectically performed at many sites, some textual and, by implication, official (as in the Gushikawa and Nakazato official district histories[6]), some informal and anecdotal (as in people's homes, age association meetings, etc.), and some in U.S. investigations into war crimes.

The narratives that are produced run counter to the discourse of war and memory that dominates Japan's official record of activities during World War II. They provide counternarratives to those sponsored by the Ministry of Education (Monbusho). Although historians have written about the Kumejima massacres[7] and other political commentators have referred to those events in arguing for historical revision within Okinawa, for the most part the massacres, and indeed the Battle of Okinawa, have been omitted from the historical record available to schoolchildren. The workshop is the first official attempt to publicly engage people in discussions about what happened on the island more than half a century ago. It is also an attempt to come to terms with the past and reexamine relationships between Japan and Okinawa or, more specifically in this case, the relationship between Japan's war and Kume Islanders.[8]

This attempt to engage the public in new ways about the war is done through the medium of storytelling.[9] As I will demonstrate, the stories chosen emphasize themes including the victimization of islanders by Japanese soldiers, the massacres themselves, and the hardiness of the islanders in looking after each other as circumstances deteriorated. In short, they are narratives of plucky survival in the face of ruthless attack. Some storytellers demonstrate how islanders' fear of the Americans was displaced by fear of their Japanese military "protectors" and portray the Japanese commander, Lieutenant Kayama, as the devil incarnate. In fact, he is presented as the evil of war personified, thus enabling many elderly islanders to displace anger toward Japan by pointing at Kayama as both an aberration and a personal symbol of war and its consequences.

In providing a forum for the elderly to communicate their own experiences of the war to the younger generations, the Nakazato Board of Education is actively teaching young people about their identity. That is, a consciousness about the "lack" of islanders' knowledge about themselves drove the process. Using the existing community *rōjinkai* (old people's associations), representatives of the board of education convinced some elderly raconteurs to participate in the program for the sake of the island's future.[10] Although most of the storytellers are not teachers or former teachers, they have the authority of age and personal experience, and once the program got under way, many seemed to embrace their new role enthusiastically.[11]

Some excerpts from the program will provide insights into how people remember their wartime experiences and how these memories are being transmitted to the children. In particular, the illegitimate and cruel actions of the Japanese (represented by the Japanese army, and Lieutenant Kayama in particular) are contrasted with the (mostly) dutiful behavior of Kume Islanders, who struggled to survive in the wartime conditions. The informality of the setting, the educational method and the content reinforce the idea that this is "popular history," as opposed to "official history" sponsored by the Japanese state.[12] I think that it could also be interpreted as an attempt by the community to empower itself through control of the narrative of history at the local level. This application of local knowledges challenges the ubiquitous national history learned at school, and it foregrounds people's memories and experiences in understanding the impact of war, on the one hand, and the ambivalent relations that existed between Kume Islanders and Japanese, on the other.

Titled "A Class for Young and Old," the program lists dates and events relevant to Kumejima and the Battle of Okinawa. These include the formal beginning of hostilities (the U.S. invasion of the Kerama Islands on 28 March 1945), dates for the conclusion of hostilities, and dates for events that transpired on the island both during the battle and after the formal cessation of hostilities. It is these latter stories that dominate the discourses of the elderly storytellers, most in their seventies and eighties, and it is the violence and immediacy of these accounts that shock the students, as I shall demonstrate. At the center of war memories lie the infamous Kumejima massacres. A strong sense of identity/identification and belonging/alienation underscores the memory of these events.

Program: "A Class for Young and Old"

25 June 1945: Public announcement of the surrender of Japan's armed forces in Okinawa to the United States military.

26 June: 1,000 United States marines arrive on Kumejima.

27 June: The slaughter of Asato Shojiro.

Asato-san who had sought refuge in the mountains, was carrying home some floorboards and other materials for his hut when he was spotted by some American soldiers and captured. Sent to the Japanese army base with a letter from the Americans demanding their surrender, he was executed by the Japanese. (His wife later committed suicide.)

29 June: The Japanese army's defense garrison.

Two people from Kitahara who had been picked up by the Americans were apprehended by Japanese soldiers on their way home from the American base; on suspicion of being spies they were killed on the spot. Furthermore, the village head and the head of the volunteer unit, along with a further five people were executed for failing to report the "spies" to the Japanese garrison on the island. They were gathered together at Miyashiro's house, beheaded and the house with their bodies inside burned to the ground. This is how they were made to pay for their disloyalty to Japan.

5 July: Corporal Hanaoka's execution.

> Corporal Hanaoka and Corporal Uchida, commanding five other men, conducted a raid on Kokoban (the United States headquarters). Uchida and one other man died in the attack. Corporal Hanaoka was executed by Lieutenant Kayama for failure to carry out orders.
>
> 26 July: Potsdam Agreement announced.
>
> 6 August: Atomic bomb dropped on Hiroshima.
>
> 9 August: Atomic bomb dropped on Nagasaki.
>
> 15 August: End of the Pacific War. Emperor makes surrender announcement over the radio.
>
> 18 August: Japanese garrison massacres locals.
>
> Nakandakari Meiyu, his wife, and his one-year-old son were executed after being suspected of spying.
>
> Nakandakari-san had been captured by Americans in fighting on the main island. Told that there was no Japanese resistance left on Kumejima, he returned home on an American ship. When the Japanese garrison became aware of this fact they accused him of being a spy, killed him and his family, and set fire to their house with their bodies inside.
>
> 20 August: Japanese garrison massacres the Tanegawa family—all seven are killed.
>
> The entire Tanegawa family (two adults and five children aged ten, eight, six, five, and an infant not yet one), a Korean family who had lived on the island since before the war, were accused of profiteering by selling American military goods in defiance of Kayama's orders, and executed. Their bodies were burned in the house.[13]

The program then presents in graphic detail an eyewitness account of the execution of the Tanegawa family: how the children clung to their mother's dead body after she was decapitated; how the infant was skewered with a sword, her body thrown on top of the mother's; how the oldest child was hunted down and killed.[14]

The stories present the Japanese military as refusing to acknowledge the humanity of islanders. Believing they were being "protected" by Kayama's group, islanders were shocked by the actions of the army, which turned loyal citizens into "traitors," killed many, and effectively dehumanized all. Implicit in their dehumanization was their transformation in status from those to be protected to those who allegedly betray their "protectors."

The presentation of facts in the program is critical; the use of language is direct but relatively mild, and there is some attempt at evenhandedness in the representation of reasons for what are extreme and violent actions committed against islanders by their erstwhile protectors. However, the order of dates and the words chosen to represent the victims of Japanese violence emphasize the *illegitimacy* of the acts recorded—that is, that those acts occurred after the war was officially over, and that they were the acts not of a "friendly" army but of an oppressor.

Although the U.S. military was perceived to be an aggressive enemy during the war, there was a concomitant perception that aggression was appropriate in an enemy.[15] In this workshop, islanders do not debate the accounts of the American involvement in the battle—it is accepted that violence was endemic during the conflict—but rather focus on the transformation of the "friendly" Japanese army's attitude toward them. From Japanese citizens to be protected in war, they were transformed into impediments on the battlefield and people whose loyalty would be mortally interrogated.

Michel Foucault[16] has said that historical memories are constantly restructured to suit the circumstances of the time. At this juncture in Okinawan history, when interest in the construction of Okinawan identity is strong, memories of the war have been mobilized as a collection of voices that together produce a vivid set of overlapping, ambivalent, and still horrified images. In the act of remembering and passing on to others their memories of the violence and illegitimacy of the acts perpetrated against them by the Japanese army, the storytellers cast their characters as innocent (or certainly guileless) victims in a battle between incomprehensible forces. These are seminal memories. They are memories of Japanese becoming the enemy, of betrayal, of distrust, of violence directed against entire families. These are not the memories of a homogeneous Japanese "self." In passing on these stories to the students, the storytellers have empowered their listeners with the knowledge of who they are and have set in place troubling questions about their "Japanese-ness." Putatively, Okinawans were and are Japanese; in practice, though, the memories of such actions in the Battle of Okinawa must call into question the legitimacy of such claims.

In this workshop, memory paints vivid pictures of the past. Those who lived through the Kumejima massacres are now critically reassessing their significance. The result has been a reconsideration of the basis of the relationship between Japan and Okinawa, a circumstance that is linked to the timing of wider political movements and an increasing consciousness about what it means to be Okinawan. It has also led to a synthesis of local and more official understandings of the war on Kumejima.

It is clear, too, that the memories transmitted to the children are not those of some Arcadian past but rather antiwar parables par excellence. While the characters in the stories are important, the message "This must never happen again" is the recurrent and dominant theme. The storytellers emphasize the personal nature of their anecdotes, which lends them credibility. They tell students not only of the massacres but also of how they were forced to shelter from the American bombings, the scarcity of food, the jingoistic Japanese education system, and how they lived in fear of the American invasion. In other words, they discuss how the war rudely interrupted the rhythm of their lives.

How did the children react to the workshop? They were asked to write essays of their impressions, and these are revealing:

> The thing that made the biggest impression on me was that after the Emperor had surrendered and the war was over, the Japanese army killed those people they suspected of being spies. They killed one family of three people (the Nakamura family) and a Korean family of seven. That's ten people they killed *after* the war was over.
>
> There were others killed on suspicion of being spies too. I think it sucks (*chimui*) that when the father was accused of spying, the whole family was killed. . . . There was also this old lady (*obaasan*) who told us that when she was at primary school they were taught the following rule: "If each of you kills one American soldier, we will win." It seems that they were taught things we wouldn't even think of these days. It's so great to have been born when I was. (Yutaka, twelve years old)

> I got a huge shock when I heard about the war from people who had lived through it. The things that happened were terrible. Also, I learnt a lot about how people actually survived during the war, something I'd never heard before. I think that the people who lived through that time were so brave. I think that the thing called war is an evil thing.
>
> And I never want to see another war. So I think that people of my generation, those who have never experienced war, should think about war and peace very carefully. (Yumi, thirteen years old)

> First we went on a bus to a number of places. When we looked inside the air raid shelters, they were dark and I couldn't believe people lived in those places. Inside it was dark, and there were heaps of insects. Even though it was dark, at least it was a safe place.
>
> Anyway, for our sakes, we were told sad stories of 54 years ago. Every time I hear stories about the war, I think that it is a cruel thing. From now on, I really, really want to keep our country at peace. (Shoki, twelve years old)

These brief excerpts illustrate a strong sense of "otherness" in the representation of the Japanese army's involvement on the island. The children's primary impressions are of the horrors of war, the sacrifices made by their relatives, and the victimization of islanders by the Japanese army. Their ignorance of the war and the shock at the level of sacrifice made by the old people on the island were also important elements of the essays.[17] For many students, however, the most enduring impression they have of the workshop is how lucky they are to be living in a time of peace. These students identified strongly with the stories and demonstrations of living and schooling conditions and with the small children who were executed as spies after the war. Those children's social nationality as Koreans, rather than situating them as "others" within the narrative, instead acted as a rhetorical device to tie Okinawans with Koreans as "liminal subjects" in the Japanese Empire.[18] To most it was incomprehensible that the Japanese army should kill the people they were sworn to protect, no matter who they were, particularly with little or no evidence and after the war was over.

These themes are pertinent to our understanding of the massacres, but they require the context of the Battle of Okinawa in order for their importance as signifiers of identity to emerge. Underscoring the narrative of the battle that follows, like the narratives of the Kumejima storytellers, is the thread of identity: Who was trustworthy? How could people demonstrate their trustworthiness and, by extension, their "Japanese-ness"? Underlying such distrust was the issue of identity—in identifying Okinawans as potentially disloyal to Japan, the Japanese army applied the label of "otherness" to Okinawans.

SPYING ON THE JAPANESE ARMY

The Battle of Okinawa, which took place between March and September 1945, was among the bloodiest and most savage battles of World War II. Both the American and Japanese forces were intensely motivated and engaged each other in an all-out confrontation. The American forces were massively equipped, numbered more than 540,000, and had powerful naval and air support, while the Japanese forces were poorly equipped, numbered about 110,000, had neither naval nor air support, but had established strong defensive positions throughout Okinawa. Caught between these two homicidal forces was the population of Okinawa, which, at the time, totaled just under 500,000 people. By the end of hostilities, between one-quarter and one-third of the civilian population of Okinawa, 400,000 of whom had been mobilized in the defense of the islands, was dead; by one estimate, civilian deaths (130,000 to 140,000) outnumbered Japanese military deaths (73,000) by almost two to one.[19] For the United States the victory came at the cost of an estimated 14,000 dead, with many more wounded.

Okinawa's strategic importance as the last obstacle standing between the Japanese mainland and the U.S. forces ensured that resistance to the Americans would be intense. The Japanese army deployed more suicide bombers and boats (*kamikaze*) than in any other battle in the Pacific War in an attempt to stall the advance of the Americans and to make them pay so heavily that they would reconsider their invasion plans and surrender terms. As the tide of battle turned against Japan (it was plain to all who were informed of the military situation that the war had really already been lost by Japan a year or so earlier), this desperation was also manifested in increasingly paranoid and restrictive measures designed to control civilians.[20] The Japanese military perceived Okinawan civilians both as a resource that could be employed to slow the American advance and also as a nuisance and even a potential threat. In short, the "spy" ordinances were introduced so that the military could control the Okinawan people. At the same time, while the military saw Okinawans as a potential impediment to its war plans, it also recognized the importance of civilians as labor to support the efforts of the Thirty-second Army. Able-bodied adult males and high school students—both boys and girls—were conscripted into the military or nursing services, and the military mobilized tens of thousands of villagers to build air strips, military housing, and other facilities. Others were forcibly evacuated from their villages to the mountains and caves along the coast with their possessions restricted to the clothes they wore,[21] and personal property, in particular food and animals, was commandeered for military use.

The Pacific War ultimately exacerbated the ambivalence in relations between Okinawa and Tokyo. While the rhetoric of empire placed Okinawa within the purview of Japanese territory, in practice the war demonstrated that by 1945 the Japanese military was far from regarding Okinawans as Japanese. Okinawans, on the other hand, had experienced almost seventy years of direct Japanese rule and had been educated and socialized to become Japanese. Although on the geographic and cultural periphery of Japan, Okinawans had largely accommodated Japanese demands that they become loyal Japanese citizens; indeed, they were mobilized during the war, they were conscripted along with other Japanese and were sent to battle zones throughout the Pacific.[22] In short, they served as did others on the periphery of the empire, such as Taiwanese and Koreans. However, as documentation recovered from the Thirty-second Army's records indicates, in the context of the Battle of Okinawa, many in the military perceived Okinawans as unreliable, gullible, and capable of betraying the Japanese state.[23] Implicit in many directives was the notion that Okinawans were *not* Japanese, their formal status as Japanese citizens notwithstanding. Ōta Masahide[24] asserts that the rhetoric of the Japanese military increasingly distanced Okinawa in order to justify concentrating resources to defend the home islands.

High Command in Tokyo had known from as early as 1943 that Okinawa would likely become a strategically important territory if the United States was able to successfully prosecute its "island-hopping" campaign in the Pacific. This influenced Tokyo's perception of the prefecture. While rhetorically it remained a prefecture of Japan, in practice, from late 1944 onward, as Japan bolstered its defense, Okinawa was perceived as a potential and expendable battle zone, and its inhabitants as both logistic and military labor, and increasingly as potential impediments in the defense of the home islands.

As the Americans advanced, the importance of Okinawa increased. However, consistent with many decisions taken by Japan's military leaders during World War II, practical solutions to problems were not forthcoming.[25] In particular, the issue of how to deal with the civilian population in Okinawa became an increasingly difficult problem for policymakers. In the end, as battle loomed, the military closed the schools and mobilized student support as aides and nurses, evacuated citizens from the major towns, and distributed hand grenades to groups of people.[26] Civilians in the line of fire were left to fend for themselves, while the military continued to conscript all able-bodied persons into military or nursing groups. In the heat of battle, as desperation mounted, Japanese forces drove some of the civilians from the caves in which they had been hiding onto the open battlefield and, in some instances, such as on Kerama, gave entire villages orders to commit "mass suicide" (*shūdan jiketsu*).[27]

Ōta Masahide says in response to the question of what lessons can be learned from the Battle of Okinawa that "military forces cannot protect people."[28] He raises a point of some significance. Perhaps more pertinent, though, is to ask whether Okinawans were considered people worth protecting by the military (were they "Japanese enough"?). With these questions in mind, Tomiyama Ichirō[29] has studied Japanese fears of spies in Okinawa during the war, especially during the Battle of Okinawa. The Japanese military imposed increasingly harsh restrictions on a population they suspected of being disloyal, while doing nothing to protect them. Included in these restrictions was a decree of April 1945 that prohibited the use of Okinawan dialects in public, a crime punishable by death.[30] Seeing the Okinawans as Other became both a central government policy and a local army priority.

Documents collected after the war demonstrate that over one thousand Okinawans were executed under this emergency provision.[31] As both Ōta and Tomiyama point out, people were executed as spies on the flimsiest of evidence.[32] These acts flew in the face of Japanese claims that Okinawa was an unsinkable aircraft carrier (e.g., *Ryūkyū Shinpō,* 14 April 1945) and government propaganda and other claims that encouraged Okinawans to expect that the army would defend them in return for their (un)dying support of Japan. As many Okinawans tragically discovered, these expectations would not be met. This was graphically foreshadowed in a chilling comment made by Major-General Chō Isamu, the chief of staff in Okinawa, in an interview in early 1945: "The military's important mission is to win the war. We are not allowed to lose the war in order to save civilians."[33]

Such attitudes were reinforced in the "Absolute Rules to be Observed in the Battle for the Mainland," as Ōta points out:

> Article 2 states, "The wounded and the sick should not be sent back from the front during the battle. Keep in mind that the greatest thing you can do for your wounded comrades is to annihilate the enemy as quickly as possible. . . ." Article 5 states, "It is expected that the enemy will use non-combatants, women, children and the elderly as their shields in order to destroy our fighting morale. In such a case, have faith that our compatriots share our hope for our country's victory rather than wanting to have their own lives saved, and do not hesitate to demolish the enemy." Such was the attitude of the military toward civilian safety.[34]

These regulations clearly illustrate the military's preparations in advance of the battle to sacrifice Okinawan civilians as necessary in the service of military strategy. Japan's leaders knew that they would be defeated and the prefecture lost, but it was clear that the wounded were to be consigned to a glorious death, rather than being treated. It was also made clear that soldiers should be suspicious of women, children, and the elderly, who could be compromised by the enemy, and that they should not hesitate to kill those civilians who may stand between themselves and the Americans. This view was consistent with the requirement that there should be no prisoners.[35]

While these rules were widely disseminated among the military, Okinawans labored under the impression that the Japanese military would protect them in the battle. As the Japanese military girded for all-out war with the United States, many Okinawans were less inclined to adopt the ideology that embraced death as glorious and surrender as ignominious, and these doubts deepened as the crisis unfolded, as many survivors' accounts demonstrate.[36]

It was at such moments of crisis that the ambivalence of Okinawan identity came to the fore. Distrusted by the military but treated as Japanese by the Americans,[37] Okinawans were in a desperate situation. The spy edicts had intimidated the people and reinforced the total control of the Thirty-second Army.[38] Moreover, the edicts had raised the issue of the "enemy within." In this case, the enemy was the "Okinawan" who was almost, but not quite, the same as the Japanese. Unable to become "perfect" Japanese,[39] Okinawans retained the Okinawan other within the Japanized self, but as Bhabha points out, this ambivalence can only be resolved through the elimination of the internalized other. The spy edict made the internalized Okinawan other the enemy. As Tomiyama says, summing up the Japanese military's perspective, "There is an Other within, which should be killed!"[40]

SPIES AND SUSPICION ON KUMEJIMA

People on Kumejima experienced the war differently in many ways from those on Okinawa itself. In June 1944, the first detachment of the signal corps of the Thirty-second Japanese Army, led by Lieutenant Kayama Tadashi, landed on Kumejima. The garrison was briefed to build a defendable fortress in the mountains in preparation for the coming battle. By January 1945, forty-three soldiers were stationed on Kumejima. At this time the island's population was a little over ten thousand.[41] Although subjected to limited American bombing, most of the population stayed in their homes until the very end of the battle. The American marines did not land on Kumejima until after the Battle of Okinawa was officially over; hence, there was none of the intense shelling and hand-to-hand fighting that took place across much of the main island, and fewer than 20 percent of homes were destroyed.

As the situation for Japanese forces on the main island worsened and morale amongst the civilian populations declined, the Japanese military issued increasingly restrictive decrees. All military personnel and civilians were required to follow these measures, including those on the outer islands, which included Kumejima. As mentioned earlier, one of the more important of these measures forbade the speaking of Okinawan dialects.[42] According to Tomiyama, this decree provided the basis for a campaign of selective violence by the Japanese army against the people of Okinawa in the last months of the battle and provoked resistance amongst Okinawan civilians on the battlefields and in the caves.[43] Moreover, it cemented the status of Okinawa as beyond the pale of Japan "proper." By conversing in a proscribed language that was incomprehensible to most members of the Japanese army, Okinawans were employing symbols of culture that could have been a secret code of resistance, something that eventually it became, arguably due in large part to the proscriptions against its use.[44]

On Kumejima, the island population had practiced air raid drills and fire drills and built air raid shelters from the beginning of hostilities in the Pacific. They had also developed a plan to evacuate all inhabited areas in the event of American landings on the island.[45] As in other Japanese prefectures, the villagers on Kumejima were bound by the National Mobilization Law (1938) and by the laws that promoted the Imperial Assistance Association (1940). Required to contribute special war taxes, food levies, property, wages, and even young people to corvée labor to support the war, local government on Kumejima had reorganized as required by the state. This included formation of a volunteer force (home guard), consisting mainly of older men and women who were prepared to serve as lookouts along the coast. They also strengthened the reporting structures within the hamlets and districts. Individuals were elected or appointed to positions within the emergency services and local government, all theoretically under the jurisdiction of the Japanese military.[46]

As the battle on the main island intensified, Kayama's actions had become increasingly paranoid. It was rumored that he kept a notebook with the names of people suspected of disloyalty or spying and that, if one's name was in it, one could expect an early morning visit from the army.[47] The Japanese army on Kumejima issued the following directive in mid-June 1945, in preparation for the enemy's arrival:

> Civilians who are captured by Americans while attempting to return to their homes (from their mountain hide-outs) are to be identified. Their presence must be reported immediately to the *ku-chō* (headman) and to the head of volunteer forces, who will report the actions and location of the perpetrator to the Japanese military. Failure to do so will result in the executions of the entire family of the perpetrator, the *ku-chō*, the head of the volunteer forces, and any other culpable persons.[48]

Capture by the Americans thus was taken as proof of treachery.

When the Americans landed on Kumejima on 26 June, three days after the Japanese army on Okinawa surrendered, there was no resistance, and there were few civilians visible. Most had made their way to the mountains, where they hid in caves and makeshift huts, a plan coordinated by the Japanese military. Over the next week or so, the Americans visited the villages and hamlets, distributed food to the few local people they encountered, and provided some medical assistance, as some islanders returned home.[49] However, the people from the hamlets near Lieutenant Kayama's mountain headquarters remained hidden in the hills, initially unwilling and eventually unable to come down. Many had lost their homes, their land, and their possessions in the air raids. Fear of the Americans had driven them to the hills, but above all fear of Lieutenant Kayama's forces kept them in the hills. In any event, they had little to return to.

Lieutenant Kayama with thirty men under his command refused to give up, despite the fact that the Japanese military on the main island had already surrendered. In fact, he was not prepared even to look at the surrender terms, as the Asato case so tragically informs us (discussed later in more detail). Unable to directly engage the superior American forces, the military hid in the mountains, from where they conducted largely ineffectual guerilla actions. Indeed, while the Japanese army killed no Americans during their "postwar" guerilla campaign, they executed twenty islanders, including six children.

The following story, published in 2000, was written by a Japanese sailor who was washed ashore on Kumejima in June 1945:

> The story of Asato Shojirō is a terrible one. He was executed in front of the village chairman and the voluntary guards' leader, for carrying the surrender documents from the Americans. With his hands tied behind his back, he was lashed to a tree, and two soldiers stabbed him from both sides with their bayonets, but they did not kill him. Lieutenant Kayama dispatched him with a shot to the head. Before he was executed, the Lieutenant stood in front of Shojirō and said "You, being a Japanese, on top of having brought us the surrender documents, will have made your preparations, I suppose?" Shojirō, hearing this, bowed his head and said, "Thank you." Why did he answer in this way? According to a soldier who witnessed the event, it was because he didn't understand what was happening. But the story doesn't end here. His wife Kane's body was found lying face down in a stream near their mountain hut not long after.[50]

Asato was the messenger who was literally shot for bearing bad news. An innocent man by all accounts, he was in the wrong place at the wrong time. His wife, shocked by what occurred, committed suicide almost immediately after his execution in despair. The tragic element in the deaths of such upright young people (Asato was an Okinawan karate champion) remains central in today's retelling of the stories. With the Americans already on the island, and a messenger dispatched to demand the surrender of the Japanese (the Americans by now differentiated between Japanese and Okinawan), the killing of a young, guileless Kume man was a futile act of immense cruelty.

The tale presents some subtle themes of identity. The question Asato was asked by Kayama just before he died has significant implications for the construction of "self" and "other" on Kumejima. By prefacing his rhetorical question with the phrase "You, being Japanese," Kayama invoked the sameness or commonality of both parties' origins. Equally Kayama's assumption that Asato was "prepared" was an affirmation of his Japaneseness, as he prepared to die for having betrayed "his" nation. This provided Kayama with the rationale (*riyū*) for carrying out the execution: Asato's traitorous act. However, it also presents an intrinsic paradox, one that has continued to vex writers on Okinawa since the end of World War II: To defend the people, to what extent must those being "defended" suffer, even suffer annihilation, at the hands of their "defenders"? It also raises important questions about the nature of identity: In executing an Okinawan as a Japanese traitor, was Lieutenant Kayama acknowledging Asato's Japaneseness in the first instance and taking action on that basis? Legally, that is what he did. However, was not this action taken against an Okinawan civilian an act justified by cultural and linguistic difference—that is, the difference between Japanese and Okinawan? The action itself occurred within a climate different from that on the home islands and the legal rationale for his actions was to be found in an edict that actively discriminated against Okinawans (and implicitly labeled them as "outside" Japan—i.e., the "spy" edict). Is this not evidence of the most elemental recognition of difference between Okinawans and Japanese? In the act of not trusting, differentiation is explicit, and identity implicit. In carrying the distinction to the point of execution, there could be no clearer divide.

Meanwhile, Kayama continued to launch an all-out search for "spies" among the ten thousand Kumejima citizens. As we have seen, on 29 June, Kayama executed nine people as "spies." He could only do so in the immediate postwar environment because he still held authority, even though the Americans had arrived on Kumejima. Such a small number of armed Japanese troops would not have been able to maintain control of the island without support from the people. Still, it is impossible to tell what combination of terror, routinization within the structures of Japanese military training, or loyalty to Japan enabled Kayama to maintain authority over the hundreds of Kumejima people who hid in the mountains during the weeks that followed Japan's surrender.[51]

By early July, he had issued a further edict threatening to execute anyone who left the mountains or returned to their villages for any reason. This was followed a day later by an American order that people in the hills should come down to their houses, now that the war was over.[52] Those who sought to return home were open to harsh and immediate reprisals.

A WOLF AT THE BACK GATE

The massacre of the Tanegawa family occurred on 20 August 1945, five days after Japan's formal declaration of surrender (15 August). As word spread by mouth about the atrocity, villagers from both districts made a pact to hunt down the Japanese troops and deliver them to the Americans.[53] By early September, local people had captured most of Kayama's men. Lieutenant Kayama and the troops who had evaded locals' attempts to capture them formally surrendered on 8 September to the head of the American delegation on the island.[54] Thus, Kayama, who had subjected Okinawans to execution at the slightest hint that they might surrender, turned himself in to American forces.

The Tanegawa tale with the themes of injustice, incomprehension, and barbarism is an oft-told tale. While the storytellers emphasize the demonic actions of the army, and Lieutenant Kayama in particular, and the ruthlessness of the killings, less effort is expended on developing the characters of the family. Indeed, some retellings do not even mention the family by name, referring instead to "the Korean family."

From the end of June, the American military had dropped supplies of food to the islanders.[55] Kayama and his men had decreed that anyone who touched the supplies would be executed for treason. He assured the islanders that the food was poisoned, in any case.[56] Kayama's outrageous demands on starving people had set the Japanese troops in direct confrontation with the villagers.[57] In desperation, operating under cover of darkness, groups of householders together defied Lieutenant Kayama's injunction and surreptitiously recovered the supplies in order to feed themselves. In mid-August, the head of the Tanegawa household was seen by one of Kayama's soldiers dragging a box of supplies from the sea near his home. The incident was reported to Kayama, who executed all the members of the family. A former primary school teacher, who was a thirteen-year-old boy at the time, recalls the event:

> It's still not clear to me how the Korean family could have been labeled spies. There were quite a few Koreans living on the island. Must have been 80 or so.[58] Their Japanese language was very good. There were three adults and five children living in one house not far from here. It was an old, run-down place. Everyone was always doing repairs and contributing money to them, and eventually they had given it a new lease on life. Generally they hunted wildlife for food at night, wandering around Gushikawa. Occasionally they also turned their hands to farming. They grew a little rice at one stage, but they never had much to eat.
>
> Anyway, they were caught eating some of the American supplies. All eight of them were taken outside by Kayama and executed one night. The youngest victim was just one year old. In fact the five children were all under fourteen years of age. It was tragic.[59]

Like other accounts, Motonaga's emphasizes the injustice of the killing and the human tragedy of the act. His tale differs slightly from others in that he says that the Tanegawas were executed for eating American goods—that is, for explicitly disobeying orders. Other accounts[60] state that the family was executed because the father was charged with profiteering by selling the American goods. Regardless of the accuracy of the accounts on this detail, the act of the killing and the vengeance against an entire family are beyond dispute.

Motonaga's story also provides more context in which to understand what took place. In describing the circumstances of the Japanese occupation of the island, he matter-of-factly reveals the violence exerted over the islanders by a small number of soldiers:

> While I was at school I was selected with a group of 11 other kids by Kayama to be messengers for the army. He came down from the mountains especially to select the fastest runners. The idea was that we'd be responsible for delivering important messages from the observation points on the coast to the mountain headquarters, and vice versa.
>
> It was a long way to run—nearly eight miles—especially if you had to deliver something to the mountain by a certain time. The Japanese officers always harassed us, accusing us of being lazy, stupid and incompetent if we were at all late. They'd beat us about the head, punching our ears.
>
> Those officers would also make demands on the girls in the villages. They'd see a nice-looking 16 or 17-year-old working in the fields, or somewhere. Then they'd summon her to come to the headquarters in the mountain, where they'd use her for sex and then send her home in shame, her reputation ruined. They were pigs.[61]

As Ōta Masahide[62] has observed, the Japanese army resembled an army of occupation, rather than an army of defense. Motonaga's narrative provides vivid examples of ways in which the Japanese army on Kumejima treated the islanders as though they were part of an occupied land. Indeed, the parallels between the Japanese military's behavior on Kumejima and its behavior in occupied China and Southeast Asia are striking.

Motonaga introduces another important theme on the question of language and spying, which reinforces the problem of identity and difference:

> Because you could be executed if you were found to be different in the way you spoke—that is, you spoke dialect—the people became very careful about *not* talking in public. There were other groups who were also immediately on the suspect list. I've already mentioned the Koreans. There were also those immigrants who went to South America and parts of North America in particular, who, when they returned home were identified by their strange Japanese. They were isolated as spies and executed. I've heard many of those stories.[63]

Those who had returned to Kumejima from overseas were mostly the victims of anti-Japanese policies and expulsion orders imposed in the 1940s in South America. When they returned, they were immediately noticeable by their accent and were often suspected by Japanese forces of harboring sympathy for the Americans. They were neither wanted in the countries they had originally escaped to nor desired in their own land; they were literally displaced people. Their status, on the margins of an already marginal people, was highly conspicuous, and as a group they suffered disproportionately at the hands of the Japanese. Ironically linked by their marginality in Japanese society, returned immigrants, Koreans, and Okinawans were perceived as belonging to groups of liminal "others" in the Japanese order of things. This is consistent with Amemiya's understanding of the status of Okinawans within Japan: "As a people [Okinawans] have never been fully accepted into the Japanese mainstream, but have been kept at the periphery—in terms not only of geography, but in politics, the economy and social life as well. I call them, therefore, 'peripheral Japanese.'"[64]

The ambivalence of the status of Okinawans in Japanese eyes strongly influenced a number of critical decisions that were taken on Kumejima in 1945, as we have seen. Of equal importance in this dialogue, however, is how Okinawans saw themselves. Amemiya maintains that Okinawans used the war as an opportunity to demonstrate their loyalty to Japan, thereby attempting to transform themselves from "peripheral Japanese" to "mainstream" Japanese in both their own eyes and the eyes of Tokyo.[65] Such attitudes probably did not apply to all Okinawans, but even if some Okinawans did attempt to become "Japanese," as the Battle of Okinawa reveals, their efforts were far from being rewarded. Subjected to a form of legal violence by others who named themselves Japanese, Okinawans were treated in a manner that reinforced their status as suspect semi-peripheral outsiders.

Lieutenant Kayama applied the most violent sanctions as a warning to islanders of the dangers of disobeying military orders. Islanders were subjected to what amounted to a reign of what Walter Benjamin has referred to as "lawmaking violence": the violence of the Japanese directed against Okinawans and others in a desperate effort by the military to control the population. These factors point to a recurrent theme in the Japanese-Okinawan relationship: distrust.

In Kayama's tortured logic, Okinawans and Americans were reconstructed to be seen as sharing attributes that made them both potential enemies. His testimony at the War Crimes Tribunal, at which he was exonerated from any wrongdoing, is revealing:

> Unless we took firm measures, we would have been killed by the local residents before being killed by the Americans. My troops consisted of a mere thirty or so soldiers while there were ten thousand residents. So, if the residents had turned on us and sided with the Americans, we would have been finished right away. . . . We needed to take firm measures. So I conducted executions in order to keep the civilian residents under our control.[66]

Ōta argues that this use of violence to reinforce the military's control was predicated on the Japanese army's suspicion of Okinawans' loyalty. In the Kumejima case, Lieutenant Kayama feared the population would turn against him. He had so little belief in the efficacy of ideology to win the support of Okinawans that he assumed they would support the Americans as soon as they landed. Such distrust almost certainly would not have been directed at Japanese in the home islands, and on Kumejima it was based on no evidence. Underlying such discourse is the hierarchy of relations between Japan and not-Japan, notwithstanding Okinawans' formal status as citizens of Japan and the desire of many Okinawans to be full Japanese. "We had a tiger at the front gate and a wolf at the back."[67] This phrase, often spoken by Okinawans, and commonly seen in the literature on Okinawa during the Pacific War, has a series of appropriate cadences in the context of war and memory.

WAR, MEMORY, AND IDENTITY

This point raises issues, then, about how such actions are perceived today and brings us back to the "living history" program, mentioned at the beginning of this chapter. By displacing the responsibility for the illegitimate and horrific killings from "Japanese" or "the Japanese military" to the individual responsible for the massacres—Lieutenant Kayama—Kume Islanders are able to come to terms with their choice of contemporary political control. But, unlike generations educated before the war within the Japanese Imperial system or those educated during the time of the American military government, current generations now have the opportunity to critically reassess the nature of the Battle of Okinawa and the impact that war had on the lives of those around them.

School textbooks more than half a century later are still reticent about the Battle of Okinawa, despite recent controversy over the way the Okinawan "mass suicides" and massacres were reported. In Nakazato, the "class for young and old" produces discourses of unsettling honesty in appraising the impact of war on a people. Transmitted as stories, reinforced by place (visits to important memorial sites, the sites of executions, air raid shelters, etc.), a highly critical and personal series of accounts informs children of their heritage. Such stories are related passionately. In response, not only did the children display the attention necessary to be converted into storytellers, but many have made a commitment to remember the stories and to pass them on to future generations. This is consistent with outcomes predicted by Walter Benjamin: "The more natural the process by which the storyteller forgoes psychological shading, the greater becomes the story's claim to a place in the memory of the listener, the more completely is it integrated into his own experience, the greater will be his inclination to repeat it to someone else someday, sooner or later."[68]

Constructing an environment in which the spoken word is the ultimate authority had the effect of bringing the children within the thrall of the storytellers' spells. From their essays it was clear that they were not only shocked by the conditions in which their relatives had lived and died but also deeply affected by the conflict-ridden relations between the Japanese army and Kume Islanders. Perhaps, more important still, in their writing emerges a powerful theme that wars must never happen again; it is as if there is no need to point a finger at any group today but rather to remember what happened during the war as a consequence of the horror of war itself. While younger generations of Kume Islanders may no longer feel a need to demonize Japan, ample reasons exist to reassess the past in the context of the current political circumstances in Okinawa. Moreover, it has become important to the students of the *nen warabi gakkyū* to pass on the content of stories that affected them deeply and, in some cases, devastatingly.

Spared the massive dislocations suffered by those on the main island of Okinawa, the people of Kumejima experienced instead a particular, personalized violence in the form of Lieutenant Kayama's reign of terror. As representative of the Japanese state, and as the commander of the island during the battle, his actions were subsequently seen as "legitimate" by the High Court of Japan in 1972.[69] The islanders were presented with confused messages about loyalty and protection, however. While the military distrusted Kume Islanders, the islanders played their part as loyal citizens of Japan, and followed the directions of Kayama for the most part. Only when faced with starvation and with an American marine contingent did citizens covertly begin to defy military orders. The massacre of the Tanegawa family provided a catalyst for islanders to finally resist the Japanese military on the island. Tomiyama[70] cites Yoshihama Tomokai's diary of events to show that while the massacres were taking place, islanders were discussing the fact that the war was lost and that they must take action to resist the violence of the Japanese army and to survive. It was this decision, based on the idea that the actions of the army were illegitimate, and specifically that Kayama and his troops had betrayed *them*, that led to locals capturing the remaining soldiers.

However, the issue of why the Japanese military distrusted Kume Islanders has most relevance to the idea of identity. The rhetoric of distrust on the part of the Japanese army revolved around perceptions of Okinawans as different, outsiders, beyond Japan, far more than it did around any evidence that Okinawans were prepared to betray Japan. The actions of the military, not just on Kumejima but also on Okinawa Island, demonstrate that in the futile battle in which both Japanese troops and Okinawan civilians were sacrificed, it was not the Okinawans who were "untrustworthy" but the Japanese army and government leaders who were deceitful, ultimately betraying Okinawans' trust that they would be protected. While housed within the rhetoric of the nation-state of Japan, in practice Okinawans were designated a "disposable people"—indeed, an unreliable "other," different from other Japanese.

Clearly the Battle of Okinawa had a deep impact on Kume Islanders' lives. Yet faced with reconstructing the remnants of their society and their lives, many shrugged off their experience with the Japanese military and the postwar "sellout" by Japan, concentrating instead on rebuilding society under American administration. At the personal level, the experiences of life under the Japanese during the war were retold within families, between friends, in age associations, and even at school.

What surprises a contemporary observer is the absence of acrimony directed at either Japan or the United States by both those who experienced the war and those who have been taught about it through stories. It is war itself, rather than either Japan or the United States, that is perceived as the enemy. On Kumejima, the nationality of Kayama as Japanese is always understood, but the military's outrageous actions on the island are commonly expressed as the actions and orders of the commander alone. In this sense, islanders have displaced "Japan" with "Kayama" in allocating responsibility for what transpired.

Such a position, which effectively eschews assigning responsibility for what took place on the island to Japan, could be seen as a means for people to deal with their identity as not-quite Japanese in the new millennium, while not appearing disloyal to Japan. Certainly, the stories cited earlier could be seen to illustrate the ultimate futility of Okinawans attempting to become "proper Japanese" in the wartime and prewar periods of Japanese control, regardless of the state's rhetoric that they were Japanese. Unable to join the "inner circle" of Japan proper, Okinawans lived on the discursive, cultural, and geographic semiperiphery of the empire, attempting to accommodate the structures of polity, economics, identity, and mobilization imposed from above. Tomiyama describes the processes that gave rise to this state during the Pacific War:

> As people became trapped in an existence as labor power, lifestyle reform gave birth to labor discipline. But this disciplinization was experienced and articulated as related to an identity, to becoming "Japanese." This operation created the kind of ambivalent identity described by Homi Bhabha in which the Other—here the "Okinawan" who is not "Japanese"—is formed within the Self.[71]

Tomiyama goes on to say that this ambivalent identity also gives rise to identity politics.[72] If ever there was a pertinent example of how a nexus, a "dangerous moment," to employ Benjamin's phrase, can create ripples in the universes of meanings of identity, the confounding of Okinawan identity in that moment of a couple of months at war's end was one. Memories of the massacres and the era of Japanese military government are shrouded in ambivalence about identity and about the pragmatic difficulties for islanders that this situation generated. Educated to be Japanese and to expect the Japanese military to protect them, islanders were betrayed by a Japanese commander who was prepared to go to extreme lengths to maintain his own control over the islanders, regardless of the collateral damage he inflicted. They were, then, caught between a fanatical Japanese commander, who seemed unable to face the reality of losing the war, and the perceived mercilessness and power of the U.S. Army. Islanders faced two enemies, a situation that was exacerbated by their status on the semiperiphery of the empire. The often-reiterated comments about wolves and tigers are evidence of this state. So how does the memory of war influence the nature of contemporary identity and the relations between Japan and Okinawa?

Distinguishing itself from mainstream Japan, Okinawa presents itself in the new millennium as a region (in the performative sense that Bourdieu[73] uses the term) that has been victimized by war. Like Nagasaki and Hiroshima within Japan, Okinawa, too, has championed the peace movement, drawing on the human experience of suffering as the means of communicating the evils of war. All three sets of representation as victims have at their core the broader sense of warfare, rather than the specific sense of Japanese empire building, and its consequences. While all three sites today display artifacts of their wartime experiences (the Peace Parks in Okinawa, Hiroshima, and Nagasaki are vivid visual reminders of the devastation of war), Hiroshima and Nagasaki are portrayed as victims of atomic and, implicitly, American acts. In Okinawa today, the damage of war is remembered not only as the physical destruction wrought by the American "typhoon of steel" but also, and more powerfully in both the narratives of Kumejima and the main island, as the psychological and personal damage wrought by the Japanese army. In this sense, the distinction between Okinawan victims and the victims of the atomic bombings is clear.

The Nakazato Board of Education has created opportunities for children to reassess the past through stories told by survivors of the war. The *nen warabi gakkyū,* designed to teach young people who they are and where they come from, has successfully introduced the junior high school students to the personal experiences of war and rendered war an evil, though largely incomprehensible, thing with a public and historical face—that of Lieutenant Kayama. While no Japanese children learn much about the ideology of war, the Nakazato board was convinced that Okinawan children's identity—their roots—was more profoundly and tragically overlooked. The *nen warabi gakkyū* is attempting to address that absence today. By reopening discussion about the Battle of Okinawa, the *kyōiku iinkai* has created a new nexus for reconsidering the ambivalence underscoring contemporary Okinawan identity, and in so doing it has provided a direction for the emergence of a reimagined community. Seen in this light, the story workshop provides new and revived forms of discursive resistance to the normalizing and homogeneous rhetoric of the integrated Japanese state, while at the same time reinforcing the idea that history and identity are endlessly negotiable values, contingent on how the past is presented and re-presented.

NOTES

This chapter was first published in Matthew Allen, *Identity and Resistance in Okinawa* (Lanham, Md.: Rowman & Littlefield, 2002) and is used with permission.

1. Ōta Masahide, "Re-examining the History of the Battle of Okinawa," in *Okinawa: Cold War Island*, ed. C. Johnson (Cardiff, Calif.: Japan Policy Research Institute, 1999); Tomiyama Ichirō, "'Spy': Mobilization and Identity in Wartime Okinawa," in *Japanese Civilization in the Modern World XVI: Nation State and Empire*, ed. T. Umesao, T. Fujitani, and E. Kurimoto, Senri Ethnological Studies, no. 51 (Osaka: National Museum of Ethnology, 2000).

2. Fukuchi Hiroaki, *Aigō: Chōsenjin no Okinawasen* (The Horror: Koreans in the Battle of Okinawa) (Naha: Gekkan Okinawasha, 1986).

3. Tomimura Junichi, *Aigō! Akiyō! Tennō!* (The Horror! We've Had Enough! The Emperor!) (Tokyo: private publication, 1974); Watanabe Norio, *Nigeru tsuwamono* (Runaway Soldiers) (Tokyo: Bungeisha, 2000).

4. Tomiyama, "'Spy.'"

5. Sakuda Isamu, interview, 2000.

6. Kume Island (Kumejima) is divided into two districts: Gushikawa and Nakazato. Each administration produces a *sonshi* (district history) at different historical junctures. Nakazato's most recent edition was in 1997, while Gushikawa's was 1976.

7. Tomimura, *Aigō! Akiyō!*; Watanabe, *Nigeru tsuwamono*; Fukuchi, *Aigō: Chōsenjin*; Tomiyama, "'Spy'"; Ōta, "Re-examining the History"; Ōta Masahide, *Essays on Okinawa Problems* (Gushikawa City: Yui Shuppan, 2000).

8. The United States was largely omitted from this set of memories; it was the troubled relationship between the Japanese military and the islanders that became the focus of the forum. When reference was made to the United States, it was to "the enemy" as described by the Japanese army, in contrast to the enemy in the midst of the islanders. The United States' involvement in the Battle of Okinawa is recognized as historically and factually noncontroversial—the United States and Japan were at war—whereas the Japanese army's involvement in Okinawa has been contentiously reconstructed in memory.

9. The elderly people who tell stories about their personal experiences during the war are experiential storytellers—they authorize their accounts with personal anecdotes but situate their discussions within the structure of the overall program.

10. Sakuda, interview, July 2000; The *kyōiku iinkai* (board of education) was the major motivator in establishing this program. While the men from the *kyōiku iinkai* are influenced by their perception of history, culture, politics, and current events, the organizers of this program are in their twenties and thirties and have no personal

experiences of war. Nevertheless, the post–Cold War environment, which saw the emergence of a flurry of activities that questioned memories of the war years, may have influenced the development of the program, which began only four years after the fiftieth anniversary of the end of the Pacific War.

11. Sakuda, interview, July 2000.

12. Sakuda, interview, August 2000.

13. Nakazato kyōiku iinkai, *Nen warabi gakkyū* (The Class That Spans Years) (Nakazato: n.p., 2000), 1.

14. Nakazato kyōiku iinkai, *Nen warabi gakkyū,* 1–2.

15. Gushikawa-son, *Gushikawa sonshi* (Gushikawa District History) (Naha: Shinsei, 1976), 440–75.

16. Michel Foucault, *Power/Knowledge: Selected Interviews and Other Writings, 1972–1977*, ed. Colin Gordon (London: Harvester, 1980).

17. Why didn't they know more? Some reasons include the fact that more than two generations have been born since the war, the fragmentation of the three-generation family, the pain of remembering such events, and the perceived irrelevance of the war to young people's lives. Moreover, the war crimes investigations mounted by the United States in the late 1940s dealt with many of the complaints. As one Gushikawa villager in her nineties said, "Leave it be. There's no need to dwell on what happened in those days. It was like a different world" (Asato Junichi, interview, July 2000).

18. Tomiyama, "'Spy.'"

19. Okinawa-ken kyōiku iinkai, *The History and Culture of Okinawa* (Naha: Yugen kaisha Sun, 2000), 45.

20. It is uncertain how many Okinawans either enlisted in the Japanese army or were conscripted, but Ōta states that twenty-five thousand civilians were drafted into the army in 1945 to supplement their insufficient troop numbers ("Re-examining the History," 44). This number does not include the Okinawans who had joined the Japanese army earlier in the conflict. As the war neared, the Okinawa Prefecture *kenshi* (Prefectural History) estimates that more than four hundred thousand people were mobilized to help in the war effort (1997).

21. Ōta, *Essays on Okinawa.*

22. Ōta, *Essays on Okinawa.*

23. Ōta, *Essays on Okinawa.*

24. Ōta, *Essays on Okinawa.*

25. Herbert Bix has written a damning account of Japanese military strategy at the end of World War II that highlights the inefficiency of the High Command's decision-making structure. Bix emphasizes the institutional myopia of those in power, decrying decisions taken to prolong the war. Herbert Bix, "Japan's Delayed Surrender: A Reinterpretation," in *Hiroshima in History and Memory*, ed. M. Hogan (Cambridge: Cambridge University Press, 1996), 80–115.

26. Hand grenades were to be used by civilians not to attack the enemy but to commit group suicide.

27. Shigeaki Kinjō, "Now They Call It Group Suicide," in *Japan at War: An Oral History*, ed. H. T. Cook and T. F. Cook (New York: New Press, 1992).

28. Ōta, *Essays on Okinawa*, 64.

29. Tomiyama, "'Spy.'"

30. Ōta, "Re-examining the History"; Tomiyama, "'Spy'"; Gushikawa-son, *Gushikawa sonshi.*

31. Ōta, "Re-examining the History," 29–30.

32. Ōta ("Re-examining the History") has denied that Okinawans in any way attempted to betray the Japanese government (instead arguing that they were deluded by false expectations of protection).

33. Ōta, "Re-examining the History," 29.

34. Ōta, "Re-examining the History," 34.

35. Not all Okinawans, or, for that matter, all Japanese soldiers, agreed with this requirement that all should fight to the death.

36. In Cook and Cook, eds., *Japan at War,* there are three poignant accounts of how individuals survived during the onslaught. Not prepared to sacrifice their lives for the Japanese state, their stories are epics of courage and survival in the face of overwhelming odds. Tomiyama, too, has demonstrated that Okinawan language was employed on the battlefield as a form of resistance to Japan ("Spy,'" 130). Some villagers cried "*Rika shimankai!*" (Let's go home!) instead of participating in the mass suicide required of them. They used Okinawan when criticizing Japanese soldiers. Not all Okinawans resisted Japanese orders. As we have seen, many did follow the orders to commit suicide.

37. The U.S. Marines were ordered to clear all resistance from fortified areas, which included the caves in which many civilians hid—as "Japanese," Okinawans were perceived as the enemy.

38. Tomiyama, "'Spy,'" 128.

39. Tomiyama notes that during the "lifestyle reform" of the early twentieth century in Okinawa, the image of an idealized "Japanese" was presented to Okinawans for consumption but that this was an unattainable identity for Okinawans. "The 'Japanese' of the lifestyle reform existed only as an imaginary entity within the self-discursive practices of daily life" ("'Spy,'" 127).

40. Tomiyama, "'Spy,'" 127.

41. Gushikawa-son, *Gushikawa sonshi.*

42. Ōta, "Re-examining the History"; Tomiyama, "'Spy.'"

43. Tomiyama, "'Spy,'" 130.

44. Most of the island's elderly population in 1945 spoke little Japanese, but unlike people from other islands in the archipelago, there was also a sense of pride in the academic achievements of Kume people, which included positive efforts to speak *hyōjungo* "properly." As a result, most young adults were fluent in both dialect and Japanese, speaking Japanese in public and dialect at home, according to one local historian (Yamazato, interview, July 1997).

45. Gushikawa-son, *Gushikawa sonshi,* 650.

46. Gushikawa-son, *Gushikawa sonshi.*

47. Motonaga Shungen, interview, August 2000.

48. Gushikawa-son, *Gushikawa sonshi,* 679.

49. Okinawa-ken kyōiku iinkai, *The History and Culture of Okinawa,* 7.

50. Watanabe, *Nigeru tsuwamono,* 259–60.

51. Okinawa's mobilization had led to a radical restructuring of accountability within society. The very structure of villages and hamlets was reorganized to situate people within the gaze of the military state and its representatives. Storytellers

emphasize the loyalty they felt toward Japan even during the events of 1945; there was no alternative polity. In this context, the actions of the army were even more shocking and inexplicable.

52. Yoshihama, 1945, quoted in *Nakazato-son*, 1976.

53. Yoshihama Tomokai, *Nikki: Kumejima sensōki* (Diary of Kumejima during the War) (Okinawa Prefectural Archives, 1945); Tomiyama, "'Spy.'"

54. While Kayama's surrender was greeted with relief by islanders, it leaves some important questions unanswered. Why did Kayama surrender? Why did he not commit suicide, as would be expected of such a "loyal" officer? Could he be construed as a "bad officer" in light of his surrender? (Gushikawa-son, *Gushikawa sonshi*, 664).

55. Okinawa-ken kyōiku iinkai, *Okinawa kenshi*, 40.

56. It is quite possible that Kayama believed that the food was poisoned.

57. Gushikawa-son, *Gushikawa sonshi*, 655–57.

58. This number of eighty Koreans living on the island during the war is supported by population statistics generated by both districts on Kumejima. Today, officially, there are no people of Korean nationality or descent living on Kumejima. Municipal officials assured me that all the Koreans on the island were repatriated after the hostilities were over (Gushikawa municipal officials, interviews, September 1999; August 2000).

59. Motonaga, interview, July 2000.

60. Sakuda, interview, 2000; Nakazato kyōiku iinkai, *Nen warabi gakkyū*; Gushikawa-son, *Gushikawa sonshi*.

61. Motonaga, interview, July 2000.

62. Ōta, "Re-examining the History"; Ōta, *Essays on Okinawa*.

63. Motonaga, interview, July 2000.

64. Amemiya Kozy, "Being 'Japanese' in Brazil and Okinawa," in *Okinawa: Cold War Island*, ed. C. Johnson (Cardiff, Calif.: Japan Policy Research Institute, 1999), 161–62.

65. Amemiya, "Being 'Japanese,'" 162.

66. Quoted in Ōta, *Essays on Okinawa*, 58.

67. Motonaga, interview, July 2000.

68. Walter Benjamin, *Illuminations*, trans. Harry Zohn (London: Fontana, 1973; originally published 1955), 90.

69. Tomimura, *Aigō! Akiyō!*

70. Tomiyama, "'Spy,'" 130–31.

71. Tomiyama, "'Spy,'" 127.

72. Tomiyama, "'Spy,'" 127.

73. Pierre Bourdieu, *In Other Words: Essays towards a Reflexive Sociology*, trans. Matthew Adamson (Oxford: Polity, 1990).

3

Waging Peace on Okinawa

Gerald Figal

OKINAWA AS "FORTRESS OF PEACE"

The ubiquitous conversion of war experience into peace mobilization in Okinawa finds no better expression in contemporary popular culture than in pop singer Kina Shoukichi's White Ship of Peace Project. Inverting the image of Commodore Perry's "Black Ships" (*kurofune*), which he identifies with the forceful introduction of a war-prone modernity and the threatening presence of U.S. military bases in Japan, Kina's metaphorical "White Ship" (*shirofune*) aimed "to reciprocate the visit by Perry's Black Ships" in 1853 and "bring to the USA a message of peace for the future."[1] Kina and company—forty Okinawans, several "Native Americans and enlightened Caucasians," and an additional ninety Japanese (including several Buddhist monks and three Ainu) who later joined the group in New York City—realized this trip in the form of a musical peace caravan that began on 23 November 1998 at the University of California, Berkeley ("historical place for many civilian movements"), and ended at the Onondaga Iroquois Nation in upstate New York on 11 December. Along the way their bus stopped at Alcatraz Island for an "Unthanksgiving Day" gathering, the Ute Reservation in Utah, the Pine Ridge Reservation/Wounded Knee in South Dakota, various peace activist centers across the Midwest, and the United Nations, where on 9 December Kina promoted the White Ship's slogan—"Lay down your weapons, take up musical instruments" (*subete no bukki o gakki ni*, from his book of the same title)—by presenting the representative of the UN secretary-general with a *sanshin*, as if to suggest that true UN peacekeeping missions should arm their troops with this traditional Okinawan instrument rather than rifles. In Kina's vision of an idyllic Okinawa, which is formed around an imagined premodern indigenous spirit of peace among neighbors, the military personnel stationed in Okinawa would turn into musicians, practicing live music rather than live artillery firing. (For more on Kina, see Roberson's chapter in this volume.)

Kina is not alone in employing tropes of conversion when campaigning for peace in Okinawa and beyond. The White Ship of Peace is but one playful manifestation of the very serious business of constructing what was described at the Second National Symposium for War Ruins Preservation (Sensô iseki hozon zenkoku shinpojiumu) as a "fortress of peace" in Okinawa. This symposium, held on 21 June 1998 in the southern Okinawan town of Haebaru and attended by approximately three hundred participants from throughout Japan, concluded that it was important to preserve old battle sites as "not merely symbols for the recollection of war" but as "symbols of peace."[2] As a representative of the Okinawa Peace Network put it, preserved battle sites will be the "'living witnesses' that pass on local war experience in place of the Battle of Okinawa survivors who are quickly passing away."[3] Indeed, preservation activity has surged over the last decade upon the realization that indiscriminate development since reversion (1972) has reduced the number of battle site ruins to about 100 according to an Okinawa Peace Network survey. This statistic can be appreciated by recognizing that virtually the entire main island of Okinawa was turned into one big battle site during the three-month campaign (late March to July 1945) that resulted in over two hundred thousand deaths, including about ninety-four thousand Okinawan noncombatants.[4] This preservation effort, supported by the teaching and practice of "battle ruin archeology" (*senseki kōkōgaku*), has paralleled systematic training and mobilization of a younger generation of "peace guides" (*heiwa gaido*) in Okinawa to replace the "war experience storytellers" (*sensō taiken kataribe*), who will represent only about 5 percent of the population in Okinawa Prefecture by 2005.[5]

This chapter reflects on the ways in which war-related tours conducted by volunteer peace guides and catering primarily to mainland high school study tours have been framed in relation to history education and peace discourses, on the one hand, and popular commercial battle site tours and veterans' group pilgrimages, on the other.

My interest is not only in how "war tourism" is reconfigured as "peace tourism," à la Kina's transformation of Black Ships into White Ships and guns into *sanshin*. At the intersection of concerted Okinawan peace promotion—a politicized reaction to the wartime past as much as it is hailed as the universal hope of the future—and general tourism—an industry that many in Okinawa are betting their economic futures on—tensions strain beneath the seemingly serene surfaces. While providing an overview of the peace courses and discourses in which Okinawa's peace guides find themselves situated, I want to highlight the contests over representations of the war past that gave rise to this form of war (peace) tourism program and that continue to provide much of its impetus. A controversy that broke out over the exhibit content of the new Prefectural Peace Memorial Museum before it opened to the public on 1 April 2000 (the fifty-fifth anniversary of the U.S. invasion of the island) is testimony to ongoing "peace wars" in Okinawa and is very much a part of the historical, political, and pedagogical contexts of peace guides. I will thus end with a brief report on this issue—one that emerged, in a sense, as an Okinawan version of the "history wars" fought at the Smithsonian's Air and Space Museum in 1995 between candid historical representation and selective patriotic commemoration of the atomic attack on Hiroshima carried out by the B-29 *Enola Gay*.[6]

The Okinawan battle over the representation of the Battle of Okinawa pits not a putatively "Japanese" (or "Okinawan") version against a putatively "American" version of events. Rather, it focuses, in general, on the scale of civilian loss in the only land battle of the war fought on the home islands (despite Okinawa's peripheral status therein) and, in particular, on the issue of discrimination and violence against Okinawans by "friendly" forces during the war, even as many Okinawans were striving to prove themselves loyal Imperial subjects. While not ignoring the violence Americans brought to the island, it is this focus on Japan–Okinawa relations that intimates the present stakes involved in wars over Okinawa's recent past, wars that find their expression on the front lines of memorial epitaphs, textbooks, tours of battle site ruins, and locally produced narratives. One goal is to "set the historical record straight" by paying attention to "Okinawan voices." A more specific issue is that of past Japanese discrimination and violence against Okinawans, which is bound up with contemporary discrimination and violence resulting from an overwhelming U.S. military presence on Okinawa. The widely held but by no means monolithic Okinawan viewpoint is that the Japanese government has been far too willing to embrace the "security" arrangement with the United States ever since that fateful "Day of Shame" (8 September 1951) when Japan signed the San Francisco Peace Treaty to end the U.S. occupation of the mainland at the cost of extending it in Okinawa indefinitely.[7] In practical terms then, "waging peace on Okinawa" means engaging in present-day political and economic struggles even though the effort ostensibly deals only with promoting historical knowledge of the past.

PEACE DISCOURSES, SOUTHERN-STYLE

Since the March 1954 *Lucky Dragon* Incident,[8] peace movements in postwar Japan have been closely associated with antinuclearism, which in turn has defined the city of Hiroshima (and to a lesser extent Nagasaki) as the epicenter of Japanese peace discourse.[9] As many commentators have noted, this association of peace with the horrors of atomic warfare has tended to sustain a victim consciousness (*higaisha ishiki*) in Japan that for some has served to sidestep critical self-appraisals of Japan's role as aggressor in the Asia–Pacific War.[10] While certain commentators in the United States have played up the structure of denial built into a Hiroshima-centered peace discourse (often with unintended help from a minority of outspoken Japanese right-wing activists and government officials who provide "proof" that "the Japanese" are forever in deep denial about Japan's aggression), critical self-appraisals of Japan's colonial past and wartime aggression among Japanese have in fact existed throughout the postwar period and, since Emperor Hirohito's death in 1989, have become more frequent, and perhaps they are now shared by the majority of the population.[11] Nonetheless, peace discourses derived from Okinawan war experiences (which when recounting civilian deaths at the hands of both Americans and Japanese understandably invite their own version of victim consciousness) have remained peripheral to mainstream Japanese peace movements despite their centrality in Okinawa, perhaps because of their capacity to render Japanese victim consciousness problematic. On the other hand, Okinawans involved in peace promotion—from private groups and individuals to prefectural government officials—have not made it their goal to assimilate wholeheartedly and unreflectively to mainland (*hondo*) or "Yamato" discourses. Conscious efforts have indeed been made by local officials and some peace activists to connect (the Battle of) Okinawa with (the atomic bombings of) Hiroshima and Nagasaki as peace centers built on war ruins, but as we will see, equally conscious efforts have been exerted to maintain a difference from mainland peace practices.

The conspicuous outbreak of reinvigorated peace promotion in Okinawa over the last decade is built on well-developed Okinawan peace discourses constructed throughout the postwar period primarily from war experiences (and their constant reminder, U.S. military bases) and secondarily from a real or imagined pacifist premodern history. Calls for rebuilding Okinawa as a "cornerstone of peace" (*heiwa no ishizue/ishiji*) date back at least to the early 1960s, prefiguring the memorial of the same name that was unveiled in June 1995 and discussed later.[12] More recently, peace promotion was catalyzed by the end of the Cold War and the fiftieth anniversary of the end of the Asia–Pacific War and publicly galvanized under former prefectural governor Ōta Masahide and his struggles with Tokyo and Washington over the removal of U.S. bases from Okinawa. Both sources—war memory and idealized history—draw comparisons with their mainland counterparts and form the twin pillars of what sociologist Ishihara Masaie identifies as Okinawa's distinctive "philosophy of peace" (*heiwa no shisō*), a kind of habitual way of life born of Okinawan historical experience. Ishihara's observations are based on his own experiences as a recorder of oral histories related to the Battle of Okinawa and as a public intellectual involved with peace education. (He specializes in peace studies at Okinawa International University and has been at the center of various peace promotion activities.)[13] As he sees it, memories and ruins of the Battle of Okinawa, the prolonged "undemocratic American military occupation" from 1945 to 1972, and the continued heavy concentration of military bases in Okinawa have led to high public awareness of the war and to widespread public participation in recording its history for purposes of peace promotion. "It may be argued," Ishihara suggests, "that memories of war have become an integral part of Okinawan thought and culture" in a way unknown on the mainland.[14] Ishihara and others have warned against Okinawans dwelling exclusively on their own victimization—especially at the hands of Japanese Imperial Army soldiers—without acknowledging Okinawan complicity in imperial Japan's colonial aggression. Yet, he argues for a defining difference between Okinawan and mainland Japanese attitudes toward the war and, consequently, in their respective attitudes toward peace, because Okinawans experienced the only combat in Japan proper and witnessed "Japanese troops killing and massacring their own countrymen."[15]

As reflected in much Okinawan peace (and tourist) promotion literature, Ishihara's argument for this reaction to war experience is held to be a manifestation of the "peaceful spirit of Okinawa," supposedly nurtured since the "Golden Age of Trade" (from the late fourteenth century to the sixteenth century) "when men from the tiny Kingdom of Ryūkyū traveled without weapons, armed only with words, consideration, and good nature, and maintained peaceful relations with peoples throughout East and Southeast Asia."[16] The guide pamphlet for the original Prefectural Peace Memorial Museum likewise defines this fundamental "*Okinawa no kokoro*" (Okinawan spirit) as consisting of "a deep regard for human life, a categorical rejection of war related acts, the pursuit of peace, and a love of culture that manifests our humanity." Although this essentialist view of Okinawa's Ryūkyū Kingdom past (and present) is arguably as romanticized as mainland Japanese views of Okinawans' patriotic defense of the homeland during the Battle of Okinawa, the emphasis on Okinawa's historical connections to the rest of Asia is not insignificant in contemporary efforts to carve out a distinctive Okinawan identity that can be deployed in various political, economic, and cultural contexts. Whether protesting the presence of U.S. bases, encouraging the revival of regional foreign trade and investment independent of Tokyo, advertising an exotic tourist destination for mainlanders, or one-upping them in peace promotion, this cultivation of transnational, transethnic, transhistorical tropes has served to create a real and rhetorical space in which Okinawans might act independently of the mainland.

The activities marking the unveiling of the Cornerstone of Peace (Heiwa no ishiji) memorial (figure 3.1) on the weekend of 23–25 June 1995 expressed Okinawa's connections with and differences from Japanese mainland peace practices. This event was Okinawa's contribution to the memorializations that took place worldwide to mark the fiftieth anniversary of the end of World War II. The memorial itself was advertised as unprecedented and distinctive in its design concept: Engraved on waves of marble walls are the names of over 240,000 war dead, "without regard to nationality or ethnicity." Compared to other memorials worldwide, the Cornerstone of Peace does stand out for breaking the usual nation-bound and patriotic modes of memorialization. Friend and foe, combatants and noncombatants of the Battle of Okinawa are included on an apparently equal basis within the same space, although that space is in fact (contrary to claims that nationality and ethnicity are of no regard) subdivided by nationality/ethnicity. Okinawan victims are also accorded special status

Figure 3.1. The Cornerstone of Peace and Mabuni Hill viewed from the new Peace Memorial Museum.

Source: Photo by Gerald Figal, March 2001.

in several subtle ways, not the least of which is that they include all Okinawans who died in war-related contexts from the 1931 Manchurian Incident to one year after the official surrender of Japanese forces on Okinawa that took place on 7 September 1945. Okinawans dying as a result of the atomic bombings of Hiroshima and Nagasaki are exempted from this time limit. The inclusion of Okinawans who died in circumstances outside the Battle of Okinawa accounts for the memorial's total number of names (236,095 at the time of unveiling; 238,480 as of June 2002) exceeding the number of documented dead from the Battle.[17]

Just when the Cornerstone of Peace and the rhetoric surrounding it were highlighting difference, the city of Naha used the occasion of this memorial's opening to forge explicit links with Hiroshima and Nagasaki in a triad of peace sites. The Peace Flame (*Heiwa no hi*) at the Cornerstone asserts this association through its identification as one of the four "eternal flames" in Japan. (The other three are Hiroshima's "Peace Torch," Nagasaki's "Oath [of Peace] Flame," and the so-called "Battle of Okinawa Flame," which is located on Akajima, the tiny island among the Kerama island group west of the main island of Okinawa where U.S. troops first made landfall on Okinawan [Japanese] soil, 26 March 1945.)[18] Situated at the focal point of the waves of walls, on one side, and opening out to the world over the Pacific, on the other, this new eternal flame trumps the others in the universalizing effect of its spatial and rhetorical orientation even as it is particularly identified with the Battle of Okinawa by its location among the conflict's final battlegrounds. The flame's alignment, along the central axis of the memorial grounds, also recalls the most popularized end date of the Battle of Okinawa through its orientation to the sunrise over the Pacific Ocean on 23 June, Okinawa's Memorial Day (*Irei no hi*).[19] To drive home the association of Okinawa itself with regional and global peace, the bottom of the pool in which the flame sits is inscribed with a map of Pacific Asia, with the flame marking Okinawa's location (figure 3.2).

Two days after the flame's first lighting, the city of Naha hosted a summit at which the mayors of Naha, Hiroshima, and Nagasaki announced the formation of a "Peace Triangle" (*Pīsu toraianguru*) among their cities. A month and a half later, Emperor Akihito sanctioned this relationship by touring each site in succession as part of a "Memorial Tour" (*Irei no tabi*). The front pages of the two major Okinawan dailies featured photos of the imperial couple inspecting the Cornerstone of Peace with the guidance of the prefecture's vice governor and the emperor's key, albeit vague, comment: "You have done a good thing" (*Yoi koto o sareta*).[20] Since the Peace Triangle's founding, the three cities have organized various exchanges and joint projects. The activities for 1998, for example, included the following:[21]

Figure 3.2. Okinawa as Peace Flame.
Source: Photo by Gerald Figal, 23 June 1999.

- A joint tour of battle sites by eighty elementary and middle school students from Nagasaki and eighty elementary and middle school students from Naha, followed by "exchanges of friendship and peace for the future"
- A nationwide four-day "Youth Peace Forum" sponsored by the city of Nagasaki "to heighten peace awareness and promote mutual understanding," attended by four boys, four girls, and two teachers from Naha's Kinjō Middle School
- A "Hiroshima-Okinawa Peace Campus" at which twenty university students and graduates from Hiroshima and Naha and ten (unspecified) Asian foreign exchange students studying in Hiroshima and Okinawa met to "learn the facts of war and the atomic bomb, enhance their historical awareness, and discuss the role youths must take on to realize world peace"
- A "Naha-Hiroshima-Nagasaki Storytellers Meeting" in Naha at which survivors related war and atomic bomb experiences and made appeals for peace and nuclear disarmament to a public audience

This kind of association with Hiroshima and Nagasaki is double-edged for Okinawa. On the one hand, links to the famed atomic bomb sites raise the profile and public awareness of the Battle of Okinawa and the contemporary protest against U.S. military bases. Thus, Okinawa war experiences and peace promotion are brought from the periphery to the center of Japanese and international attention. On the other hand, some Okinawans have expressed concern that the very difference in memorial practices and peace discourses that Okinawa represents will succumb to two separate problems: a "Hiroshima-Nagasakification" and "Yasukunification." The former term refers to the perceived superficiality and commercialized aspect of Hiroshima and Nagasaki tours that are conducted by large tourism companies.[22] "Yasukunification" refers to the deification of the war dead, in general, and, more specifically, to the glorification of (the) war as expressed in the siting of memorials erected in Okinawa by mainland Japanese prefectures and veterans associations, the attention given to them, and, especially, the epitaphs inscribed on them.[23] While Yasukunification has in recent years become a focus of criticism that takes on overtones of local autonomy versus mainland centralization/nationalization, it should be pointed out that during the 1960s the identification of the Okinawan war dead with Yasukuni Shrine, especially through the efforts of the Okinawa Bereaved Families Association, was a powerful component in the growing reversion movement and was not viewed as particularly problematic. Only after the emergence of postreversion disillusionment with Tokyo since the early 1980s has Yasukunification acquired its current critical edge. I address later how Okinawans have attempted to avoid the fate of Hiroshima and Nagasaki in the construction of their own "peace courses," but let's look first at the issue of Yasukunification.

The authors of *Kankō kōsu de nai Okinawa* (The Okinawa Not on Sightseeing Tours) point out that in relating war experiences to future generations, Okinawa's battle sites and memorials are inscribed in two very different ways: to serve as a source for peace education and to mark where the meritorious deeds of the Imperial Army were manifested.[24] Those who tour the major sites are bound to come away with a mixed message. This is the product of a conflict, which has grown since reversion in 1972, between local (Okinawan) civilian representations of war experience, memory, and history, on the one hand, and national (mainland) representations, on the other.[25] While the former emphasize appeals to peace in response to the slaughter and sacrifice of innocents who were caught in cross fire, coerced into suicide, or killed outright by Japanese soldiers, the latter highlight the selfless heroism of loyal soldiers (and in some instances, of civilians) in the defense of the homeland. One survey indicated that the vast majority of memorials built before the 1960s include epitaphs that indicate in a subdued fashion the circumstances of death and/or of the building of the memorial without expressions of patriotism or glorification of war. In contrast, of the sixty-six memorials erected in the 1960s—the decade that saw the highest concentration of new prefectural memorials—forty-five contained expressions glorifying the war.[26] The set phrase "glorious spirits and manifest merits of the war dead" (*eirei kenshō*) sums up the message of the epitaphs found on the prefectural memorials lined up on "memorial hill" above the Peace Park in Mabuni (figure 3.3) and on monuments put up by veteran associations (*senyūkai*) at scattered locations on the island. Several epitaphs quote or paraphrase lines from General Ushijima's final order, which speaks of "the brave and heroic fight" of those who died and now "live on in eternal righteousness." These inscriptions have sparked the "epitaph issue" (*hibun mondai*), a prime focus of the critique of "Yasukunification" (i.e., the patriotic nationalization) of memorials in Okinawa.

This controversy marks these memorials as one medium, alongside museum displays and national history textbooks, through which contests over the definition and scope of citizenship—for now and the future—are fought. Their appearance in Okinawa makes for particular complexities given the historical treatment of Okinawans as second-class citizens within Japan and in light of contemporary Okinawan initiatives to nurture regional economic, cultural, and political ties that go beyond anything that Tokyo has had the political will or imagination to conceive.[27] That the majority of patriotic memorials in Okinawa appeared during the

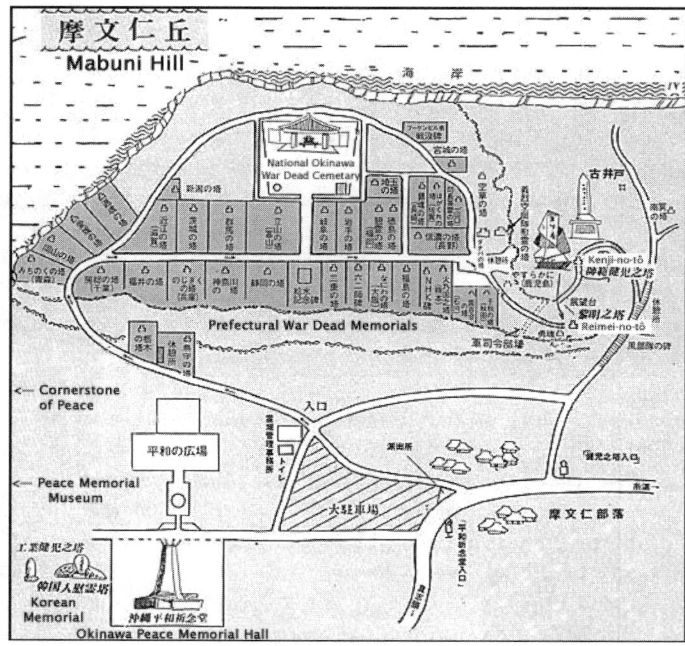

Figure 3.3. Map of Mabuni Hill and Peace Park.
Source: Aruku, miru, kangaeru Okinawa, adapted courtesy of Okinawa jiji shuppan.

1960s could be seen as an assertion of newfound Japanese national pride in the wake of postwar economic recovery and as a prelude to the Japanese reterritorialization of Okinawa that would come with reversion in 1972. In addition, these memorials came in the wake of the struggles in the 1960s to revise the U.S.–Japan Security Treaty and amid escalation of U.S. involvement in Vietnam, which in turn exacerbated vigorous antiwar and proreversion protests in Okinawa, a major staging and "R&R" area for U.S. military operations. In this context, patriotic Japanese memorials in Okinawa appear—in a twisted and ironic way—consonant with the goals of the Japan–U.S. Security Treaty. Under these conditions, the scope of citizenship implied in textbook and epitaph battles in Okinawa is especially important because Okinawans variously identify with a past that idealizes peaceful regional relations with other Asians while problematizing relations with "Yamato." At the same time, they envision a future that places Okinawa at the crossroads of a regional economy and as a "cornerstone of peace" for building rapprochement with Asians brutalized by past Japanese aggression. This self-definition also implies a commitment to the removal of U.S. military (and Japanese Self-Defense Force) bases, however unrealistic that goal might be for the near future, especially in light of America's new "war on terrorism" after 11 September 2001.[28] From this perspective, critiques of war glorification inscribed in memorial epitaphs, renewed peace promotion efforts, and concerted campaigns for base removal under former governor Ōta Masahide's administration (1990–98) are not just developments of previous movements in Okinawa. These efforts are also responses—counterdiscourses—to long-standing U.S.–Japan hegemony over Okinawan space (physical and discursive), made more thinkable and publicly speakable since the dissolution of the Cold War rationale for the Security Treaty and Okinawa's place in it.[29]

Several independent sites outside of the Peace Park speak to the issue of the Yasukunification of local memorials, but one example, the site where the Mange-no-tō is located, will suffice to suggest the particular ways in which this phenomenon has taken place. Erected in August 1951, the Mange-no-tō is a good example of the pattern of early memorials founded as the result of bone collection carried out by survivors across battle sites, in this case, Makabe Village in Itōman City. Remains of 19,207 unidentified civilian Okinawan refugees, Japanese soldiers, and American soldiers were entombed within a concrete block crowned with a stone cross. The civilian dead constitute the majority. Many memorials erected during the 1950s were adorned with crosses, and at least two—not mutually exclusive—explanations for the use of this Christian symbol exist. One is that it was placed out of deference to American soldiers who were occupying Okinawa at the time and whose countrymen's remains are included in these types of mass burials.[30] The grislier explanation is that it was a "means of last resort" to try to persuade American soldiers to stop taking Japanese and Okinawan skulls for souvenirs.[31] Off to the side of the Mange-no-tō is the mouth of the Sennin-gō ("thousand-person cave"), one of many caves on Okinawa where civilian refugees sought shelter alongside soldiers who forced them to "silence" crying children by killing them. As if to counter the emphasis on the tragedy of such civilian losses and their implications, in 1966 the veterans' association of the First Regiment Combined Field Artillery erected right beside the Mange-no-tō its own memorial, the Hōhei Yamabuki-no-tō, for the repose of the souls of 739. Its epitaph sings the praises of the "brave and heroic fight" and includes a poem by Emperor Meiji entitled "Loyal Soul" (*chūrei*), a common motif on patriotic memorials. Both Mange-no-tō and Hōhei Yamabuki-no-tō are lined by artillery shells of the type that the regiment used during the battle. As one commentator put it, this pair presents the "classic contrast" among Okinawa's battle site memorials.[32]

This contrast between subdued civilian-centered memorials, which often carry only explicit messages of peace, and those that honor the military war dead in ornate patriotic language while also offering prayers for peace is part of a wider tension between locally and nationally oriented memorial practices. This tension is most clearly evident in the Peace Memorial Park area in Mabuni and in its historical relationship to the Konpaku-no-tō, the earliest memorial to war dead of the Battle of Okinawa.[33] Initially developed from 1965 within a Government of the Ryūkyū Islands (GRI)–designated "Battlefield Park Special Zone" that spread (and still spreads) across a large swath of the southernmost portion of Okinawa Island, the Peace Park area has taken shape at the foot of Mabuni Hill since the mid-1970s. On top of the hill is a phalanx of prefectural war memorials capped by the Reimei-no-tō, the striking memorial to Commander Ushijima Mitsuru and his chief of staff Chō Isamu, near where they committed suicide (figure 3.4). The hill is also the site of the National Okinawa War Dead Cemetery—Japan's only national cemetery—and down the slope below the Reimei-no-tō is the popular Kenji-no-tō, dedicated in March 1946 to the students of the Okinawa Normal School who fought alongside Ushijima's forces as they retreated to Mabuni. While a part of the Peace Park, the hill area is administratively separate. The area spreading from the base of Mabuni Hill features the now empty former site of the original Prefectural Peace Memorial Museum (1975), the Korean Memorial (1975), the Okinawa Peace Memorial Hall (1978), and the Cornerstone of Peace (1995) (figure 3.5). The new Peace Memorial Museum, a massive complex compared to the old building, opened in the park in April 2000.

Before this onslaught of postreversion development, the Konpaku-no-tō, founded in February 1946 in Komesu a couple miles to the west of Mabuni, had been considered the spiritual center of annual memorial observances on 23 June. Many old-timers and peace activists still treat this

Figure 3.4. School study tour group at Reimei-no-tō, the memorial to Ushijima and Cho, near their suicide spot on Mabuni Hill.
Source: Photo by Gerald Figal, 23 June 1999.

Figure 3.5. Central Peace Park area from Mabuni Hill. The new Peace Memorial Museum (right) and Peace Hall (left) loom over the Cornerstone of Peace.
Source: Photo by Gerald Figal, 23 June 1999.

"tomb of the unknowns" as such, and it is customarily viewed as Okinawa's prefectural memorial. Ten prefectural memorials, including that of Hiroshima, are also clustered here rather than on Mabuni Hill. Like the Mange-no-tō, Konpaku was the product of a bone collection campaign, this one organized by Kinjō Washin, the head of Mawashi Village, whose 4,300 citizens had been ordered by Occupation authorities to relocate to Komesu. There they found tens of thousands of unidentifiable remains littered about.[34] Approximately thirty-five thousand remains were originally interred under an unadorned and (save the simple marker "Konpaku") epitaph-less earth, concrete, and coral mound (figure 3.6). In February 1979, most of the remains were transferred to the National Cemetery on Mabuni Hill. Today, only one symbolic bone rests at Konpaku.[35] In other words, as in the case of several central bone repositories in Okinawa, the remains of the dead were moved from a subdued, functional, and locally constituted site to a newly anointed national "sacred ground" that includes prefectural monuments that enshrine (*gōshi*) the remains of all Japanese soldiers who died in the Pacific War—not just those who died at the Battle of Okinawa. The construction of the Cornerstone of Peace has, in a sense, completed this shift of ceremonial center from Komesu to Mabuni, but crowds still flock annually to Konpaku to present

Figure 3.6. Konpaku-no-tō, the original focus of war memorialization on Okinawa.
Source: Photo by Gerald Figal, 23 June 1999.

flowers, food, prayers, and chains of paper cranes before, after, or instead of going to the official ceremonies at the Peace Memorial Park. For example, outspoken Naha City assemblywoman Takasato Suzuyo and other activists boycotted the official ceremonies at Mabuni on 23 June 1999 and instead held a rally at a spot between the Konpaku-no-tō and the nearby Hiroshima-no-tō. Their aim was to protest what they saw to be the sellout of former governor Ōta's base removal initiatives to Tokyo interests by Inamine Keiichi, the newly elected LDP governor of Okinawa Prefecture. The modest gathering of one hundred to two hundred people featured speeches against the U.S.–Japan security arrangement and military bases, as well as traditional music performed by youth organizations and the testimony of students who had participated in peace study programs.

Taken as a whole, the Mabuni Hill/Peace Park area exhibits an astounding juxtaposition of war/peace discourses. On a general level, the setting off of certain individual deaths, such as those of Ushijima and Chō at the apex of Mabuni Hill, as more significant than any other is countered by the inscription strategy of the Cornerstone of Peace, which strives to accord equal treatment to all. The names of Ushijima and Chō are inscribed in the same fashion as the rest and are located in their respective home prefecture sections alongside common recruits with no special mark or title; none are enshrined as deities. Both practices, however, have raised complaints. Some resent the spotlight on Ushijima and the generally heroic tone of the prefectural memorials for the military dead in light of the greater number of total civilian deaths. Others have questioned the appropriateness of giving equal treatment to individuals who held different degrees of responsibility in the prosecution of the war, whether between commander and foot soldier or combatant and noncombatant. Of course, including the dead of the enemy and of colonial subjects in the Cornerstone of Peace presents another source of complaint and contrast to the nationalized space on the hill just above. Whether consciously planned or not, such contrasts work to associate "national" with "martial" and "international" and "local" (i.e., "Okinawan") with "peaceful." The Peace Memorial Hall, the tower of which visually anchors the side of the park opposite Mabuni Hill, reinforces this alignment as it offers a discursive counterpoint to the prefectural memorials. Its seven sides symbolize the seven continents; the dais of the forty-foot cannon-like "Peace Memorial Statue" contains peace messages from around the world; and the walls display multicultural paintings on the theme of peace. Okinawa, promoted in this space as a global cornerstone of peace, is associated with the international qua peaceful as if to counterbalance the burdens of the national war history enshrined on the hill.

The heroic epitaphs of Mabuni Hill even more palpably grate against the Korean Memorial and the printed testimonies that fill one room of the

Peace Memorial Museum. Completed in August 1975, the Korean Memorial (Kankokujin irei-tō) seems to have avoided the kind of controversy among resident Koreans over its siting and inscription that Lisa Yoneyama has described with respect to its counterpart at the Hiroshima Peace Memorial Park (completed in 1970), but this point requires further investigation.[36] Unlike the Hiroshima monument, Okinawa's memorial to the estimated ten thousand Koreans who suffered and/or died in Okinawa is within the Peace Park and is not easily avoided given its location next to the Peace Memorial Hall on one side and a taxi stand across from the back of the Peace Memorial Museum on the other. The frankness of its epitaph (inscribed in Japanese, English, and Korean) is highlighted in virtually all popular guidebooks designed for high school study tours. The English (which closely follows the Japanese and Korean versions) reads:

> When the war in the Pacific region broke out in 1941, the young people of Korea were pressed into service by Japan and stationed at various fronts on the Continent and in the South Seas. Thus conscripted and drafted, they suffered innumerable hardships, and some of them were killed in battle and even slaughtered [*gyakusatsu*] here in Okinawa. These pitiful victims of the war were as many as ten thousand.
>
> The sorrowful spirits of those who failed to return home will be wandering in the alien skies above these rough seas, buffeted by the rain and the wind. In order to console the lonely spirits, here we erect a monument in the name of the whole Korean people, hoping devoutly that the spirits of the departed rest in peace.
>
> Dedicated by the Committee for the Construction of the Korean Monument in Okinawa, August of the Year One Thousand Nine Hundred and Seventy-five.

The key word here is "slaughtered" (*gyakusatsu sareru*), which appears on only one other epitaph in Okinawa—the Tsûkonhi on the outlying island of Kumejima where twenty civilians were massacred by Japanese soldiers—although it is liberally used in other printed Okinawan accounts of Japanese soldiers killing Okinawan civilians. Despite the lack of a named actor in this circumlocution, the intended meaning (Koreans massacred by Japanese) is clearly understood given the long-standing controversy over the use of *gyakusatsu* to characterize violence by Japanese forces. Use of the word in textbooks depicting the Battle of Okinawa has been, for example, one point of contention in historian Ienaga Saburō's lawsuits against the Ministry of Education. The issue at this memorial is particularly jarring after a visit to the prefectural memorials across the park.

The tension the Korean Memorial epitaph creates vis-à-vis those of the nearby prefectural memorials is enhanced by the war testimonies on display at the Peace Memorial Museum, which originally was literally in the shadow of Mabuni Hill. While they generally do not go out of their way to focus specifically on Japanese atrocities, some testimonies do mention them and the general content and tone of these tragic accounts are anything but expressions of the righteousness of the "brave and heroic fight." Cases of so-called group suicide (*shūdan jiketsu*), an iconic image in the representation of the Battle of Okinawa, present another point at which representations and interpretations conflict. Much of the debate has boiled down to the question of exactly how voluntary such self-inflicted deaths were among civilian refugees hiding in caves alongside soldiers who urged such action. Many argue that even civilians who ostensibly chose death without any direct coercion by Japanese soldiers did not act freely, given the wider context of war propaganda and education aimed to produce loyal Imperial subjects who would die for the emperor and the country. Some critics reject the term *shūdan jiketsu*, which implies the valiant self-determined sacrifice among Okinawans that Ministry of Education textbook censors, nationalist advocates, and mainlanders who romanticize images of the Battle of Okinawa work to perpetuate. They have opted rather for the more neutral "*shūdan shi*" (group death) if not the more pointed "group murder" or "massacre." Norma Field's suggestion of "compulsory group suicide" is I think a more accurate description of what actually happened in these cases, which accounted for at least one thousand civilian deaths.[37] Combined with gritty displays and graphic photos in adjoining rooms, these survivor testimonies at the museum, even when read in the most forgiving interpretations, form an affecting, earthy counterweight to the lofty abstractions on the hill. This is the one place, many peace educators stress, where all groups touring the southern battle sites should stop to learn about the harsh reality of the battle and to reaffirm commitments to peace. Precisely because most commercial tours bypass the museum on the way down from Mabuni Hill, concerned Okinawans have taken the initiative to develop their own war history tours for peace education, programs that directly engage today's battles over the extent of Okinawan historical and contemporary self-representation and "voice" within Japan and indirectly engage the issue of Okinawan political and economic self-determination vis-à-vis Tokyo. Here, too, one of the most contentious points is the presence of U.S. military bases occupying premium Okinawan land fifty-seven years after the end of war, fifty years after the end of mainland occupation, thirty years after reversion, and more than a decade after the end of the Cold War.

PEACE COURSES: WALKING THE TALK

Critique of the "*Nanbu senseki kankō kōsu*" (southern battlefield sightseeing course [tours]) packaged for mainland visitors began not too long after such tours became popular in the late 1960s and early 1970s during the transition from American to Japanese rule over Okinawa. Catering to Japanese veterans and families of the war dead who could more easily visit old battle sites and memorials after travel restrictions were relaxed and domestic air service developed after reversion, these bus tours typically honored the heroic exploits of the military and the sacrifices of loyal civilians. Their content served largely to redeem the dead from a meaningless death and reclaim a national(istic) history that had been suppressed during direct U.S. administration of Okinawa. Features of such tours included the Thirty-second Army Headquarters Cave site, the Naval War Dead Memorial, and the bunker complex below it (excavated and turned into a sightseeing spot in 1969); suicide spots of top commanders; the prefectural memorials and Kenji-no-tō in Mabuni; the prefectural memorials clustered around the Konpaku-no-tō in Komesu; and the nearby Himeyuri Memorial dedicated to the famed student nurses whose dramatic story has, through popular literary and film treatments, become emblematic of loyal Okinawan sacrifice and remains a principal mainland image of the Battle of Okinawa.[38] (See Angst's chapter in this volume.)

Lacking the financial resources that mainland organizations enjoyed, pre- and postreversion Okinawa could little compete in the creation of war-related sightseeing courses that might present a counterdiscourse. Moreover, many Okinawan and Japanese investors sought to develop Okinawa as "Japan's Hawai'i" for domestic leisure tourism, relying on the improved infrastructure and tourist promotion that postreversion development aid from Tokyo would supposedly bring.[39] However, some Okinawans monitored and critiqued battleground bus tours, providing early on the foundations for what has become a cottage industry in Okinawa peace study courses. Ishihara Masaie, for one, accompanied bus tours in the early 1970s and recorded the content of their narratives, which he thought sanitized ugly aspects of Okinawan war experience.[40] Okinawa Prefectural Diet Member Itokazu Keiko, a prominent spokesperson for a women's anti-military coalition, actually worked as a bus tour guide for twenty years before entering politics and becoming an instrumental promoter of locally organized peace guides in the mid-1990s. Mainland Japanese high school demand for these peace courses has strained the supply of guides trained to give them, although that demand has dropped dramatically after 11 September 2001.[41]

Serious Okinawa study tours, which are now positioned as a corrective to commercial bus tours and conducted under the banner of "peace learning," stemmed from earlier grassroots efforts to organize peace education programs for Okinawan schoolchildren, which continue to this day. By 1982, for example, the Okinawa High School Teachers' Union Educational and Cultural Materials Center had published practical guides to peace education that included student-conducted fieldwork on "Okinawa [Kōza] City's Black [African-American] Street" and interviews with surviving Himeyuri women.[42] In 1983, a teacher at Haebaru High School organized students to conduct door-to-door surveys of area residents to compile statistics on wartime households and deaths they suffered during the battle. He is credited with inspiring similar surveys in other areas and leading the way for the establishment of the Haebaru Culture Center where a portion of the Haebaru Army Hospital Cave has been re-created with items excavated from the actual site. This kind of hands-on approach to teaching war history—developed to a high degree in Okinawan schools—reflects recent trends in other parts of the world.[43] As one site of the Himeyuri student nurse story, the town of Haebaru had the remains of the Haebaru Army Hospital Cave designated a Cultural Property in 1990, the first battle site in Japan to be so designated.[44] It is now a regular stop on full-day study tours for students. These types of local initiatives have paralleled the research on the Battle of Okinawa undertaken by professionals over the past twenty years, much of which has involved the collection of war experience narratives, surveys of casualties, and the preservation of battle ruins—the raw material for peace guide tours.

Peace guide tours have emerged as the backbone of study tours, and the Okinawa Peace Network, founded in 1994 by Murakami Akiyoshi, has become their de facto nerve center. After coming to Okinawa from Tokyo in 1973, Murakami became involved in peace movement activities and formed the network's predecessor, the Okinawa Heiwa Gaido no Kai (Okinawa Peace Guide Association) in 1987. He has also contributed, with Okinawa historians such as Aniya Masaaki and Arasaki Moriteru, to guidebooks and instructional material recommended for use on Okinawa study tours. As of June 2001, nine volunteer groups participated as peace guides, including the Okinawa Peace Network. Most of the others are city-administered programs founded in the mid-1990s, sparked by the establishment of the Cornerstone of Peace. One exception is the Prefecture Sightseeing Volunteer Guide Friends Club, which was established in early 1997 by the Okinawa Tourist Convention Bureau (OTCB), the principal organ for commercial tourist promotion in Okinawa. It is easy to view the OTCB's jump onto the peace guide bandwagon as a cynical attempt to exploit a trend for commercial gain, but it is probably best to view this initiative as a reflection of the success of the Okinawa Peace Network in developing and promoting the concept of peace guides. It reported a total number of 878 school study trips (140,000 students) from the mainland from October 1995 to September 1996 (4 percent of all tourism), one-third of which participated specifically in peace learning programs. The OTCB no doubt recognizes that these are significant numbers and sees the advantages of increasing cooperation between volunteer and commercial tour groups. Members of the Peace Network led the first group of seventy Sightseeing Volunteer Guide trainees on the fieldwork tours in March 1997, covering what might be called a classic peace guide course: the Thirty-second Army Headquarters Cave, Itokazu Cave, the Cornerstone of Peace and Prefectural Peace Memorial Museum, Konpaku-no-tō, and Himeyuri-no-tō, among other sites.[45]

Aruku, miru, kangaeru Okinawa was the first of the many guidebooks for Okinawa peace courses expressly designed for use in the field by students. First published in 1986 in the context of organizing the original Okinawa Peace Guide Association, this book was compiled by a peace education research committee that included Ishihara Masaie and Murakami Akiyoshi and was revised in 1997 by the Okinawa Peace Network. It is printed on sturdy card stock, bound in loose-leaf notebook form, filled with detailed maps, photos, and clearly written historical explanations of important battle sites and U.S. bases. It also offers a menu of "Course Plans," model routes to follow based on various interests, themes, modes of transportation, and time allotments. The three full-day feature courses—"battlefield course," "bases course," and "battlefield and bases course"—are dubbed "peace learning courses" while their half-day counterparts are "introductory courses." The seven shorter special theme courses are: "Civilian Shelters," "Himeyuri Student Corps," "Shiraume Student Corps," "Thinking About Epitaphs," "Nuclear Bases," "Communications Bases," and "Listening to the Voices of Antiwar Landlords."[46] Although the topic of U.S. bases is an important one for peace education tours, I will limit myself here to pointing out a few details of model battle site tours, which are the most heavily subscribed.

The must-see core sites of the battlefield courses suggested in the original *Aruku, miru, kangaeru Okinawa* are Itokazu and Garabi caves, the Mabuni Hill/Peace Park area, Konpaku, and Himeyuri, in that order. Expanded tours suggest starting at Kakazu Bluff in the central part of the main island from which to gain an elevated view of the spot of the 1 April land invasion by U.S. forces, and then progressing south to the 32nd Army Headquarters Cave and the Haebaru Army Hospital before picking up the core segment and swinging back north to end with several other memorials in the Itoman area, including the Shiraume-no-tō and the Mange-no-tō (figure 3.7). The sample full-day "peace learning course" advertised on the Naha *Heiwa Gaido* Internet home page follows the same basic route from Kakazu to Himeyuri/Konpaku, but, interestingly, bypasses the Peace Park and Mabuni Hill.[47] This is possibly done to allow more time at the other sites that require greater guided explanation, his-

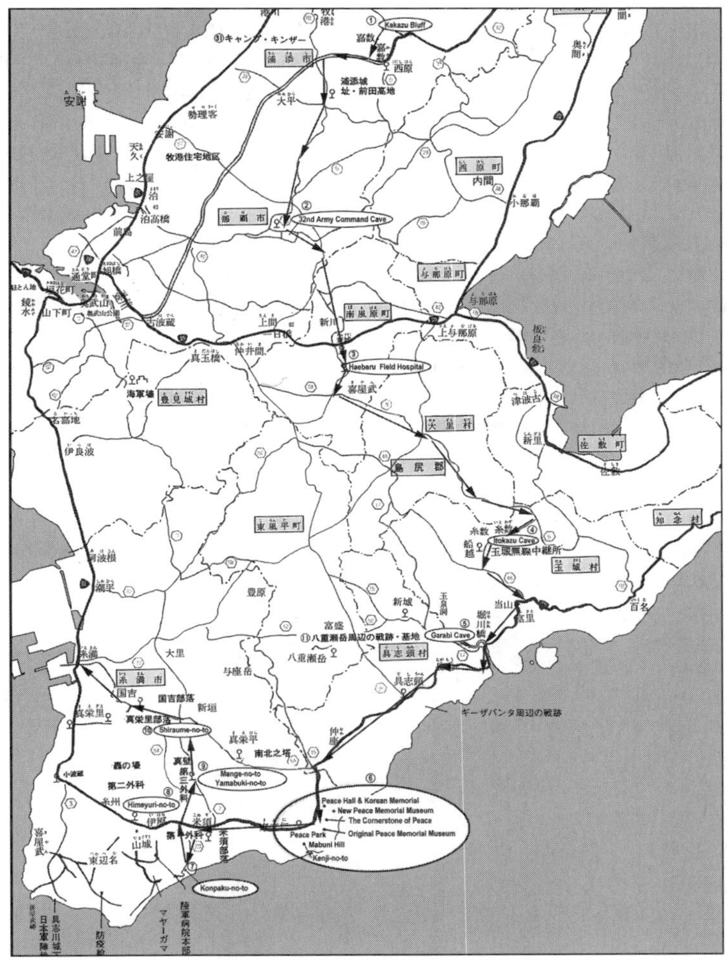

Figure 3.7. Battle site course map.

Source: Aruku, miru, kangaeru Okinawa, adapted courtesy of Okinawa jiji shuppan.

torical narration, and careful spelunking. Naha's half-day sample course is whittled down to Itokazu Cave, Himeyuri, and Konpaku.

Since its inception, Naha's program alone has seen a sharp increase in the annual number of participating mainland schools: 49 schools (8,200 students) in 1996; 133 schools (29,500 students) in 1997; 158 schools (31,400 students) in 1998.[48] The rising popularity of these programs since 1995 is likely the result of several factors: the general rise in Japanese public reflection on the Pacific War that accompanied the fiftieth anniversary; the active promotion of peace education on the part of public and private Okinawan organizations after the Cornerstone of Peace opened; and the media exposure Okinawa received because of the September 1995 rape of a twelve-year-old Okinawa girl by three U.S. Marines. Progressive mainland teachers also choose peace guide tours to supplement (and circumvent) state-approved history textbooks that in their opinion (like that of most Okinawans) do not go far enough in portraying the full extent of Japanese ill treatment of Okinawans during the Battle of Okinawa.

Itokazu Cave (and to a lesser extent Garabi Cave, which is seeing fewer visitors now because of safety concerns) has become the highlight of Okinawa's peace courses. Not only has it been described as "a representative cave for the purposes of peace study in Okinawa"; going down into the cave is a big hit with students (figure 3.8).[49] True to form, *The Okinawa Not on Sightseeing Tours* criticizes commercially promoted battlefield sightseeing tours that bypass Itokazu and Garabi Caves to stop at nearby Gyokusen Cave, a beautiful stalactite-filled cavern billed as "the most spectacular natural cave site in Asia."[50] While a part of the wider battlefield, Gyokusen Cave is advertised to general tourists as a stand-alone natural sightseeing spot, and its importance as a battle site pales in com-

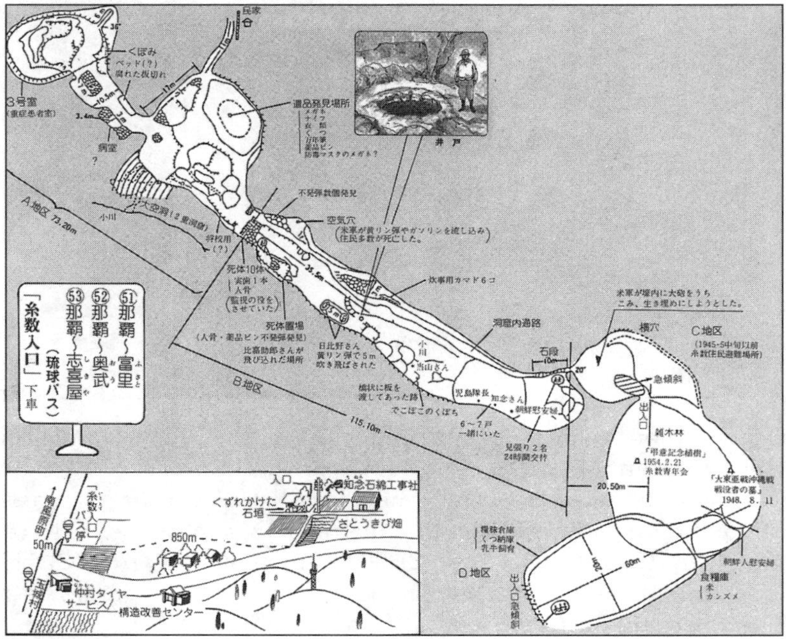

Figure 3.8. Map of Itokazu Cave (Abuchiragama).
Source: Aruku, miru, kangaeru Okinawa, adapted courtesy of Okinawa jiji shuppan.

parison to that of the other caves. Itokazu Cave is presented in school field trip guides (in composite paraphrase) as follows:[51]

> The sprawling 270-meter Itokazu complex was outfitted by the Japanese army for the long haul: it contained six ovens, air shafts, a well for drinking water, storehouses for food and gear, beds, and hospital facilities. The body of a Korean "comfort woman" was even found there during postwar excavations. In late April 1945, a branch of the Haebaru Army Hospital, accompanied by two doctors, many soldiers, nurses, and sixteen Himeyuri student nurses, was moved here until given the order on 25 May to evacuate farther south to the Kyan Peninsula. At the time, nearly one thousand wounded filled the cave along with civilian refugees. Those who could not easily be transported were provided with grenades and cyanide with which to kill themselves before capture by the enemy. When U.S. troops overran the area in June, the wounded who could not bring themselves to commit suicide joined fleeing soldiers and civilians in the back of the cave, where steadfast troops blocked any attempts at surrender. Subsequently, the Americans used gasoline and phosphor bombs at cave openings to asphyxiate the people within. In the meantime, civilians who had been taken prisoner outside of the cave and placed in a nearby shelter, wandered back into the cave right after the 15 August surrender in search of food. Loyal Imperial Army soldiers still in the cave, not believing Japan had surrendered, took these civilians as spies and murdered them one by one. The soldiers and the other civilians, surviving in the far reaches of the cave among filth and rotting bodies, did not emerge until 22 August.

Itokazu Cave represents a microcosm of Okinawan war experience and is thus showcased on locally produced peace guide tours, study trip primers, and field guidebooks.[52] These materials include conspicuous mention of Japanese-on-Okinawan (and Japanese-on-Korean) violence despite the greater number of deaths caused at the hands of the U.S. military by equally inhumane methods of killing, even in wartime (flame throwers, gasoline, and phosphor bombs). Anti-Americanism per se is not an issue in tour content; rather, the message is antimilitarism of all stripes and the waste of life and land that war brings. In any case, no one disputes that the U.S. military brought massive death to the island in 1945; in fact, it is accepted that this was their expected mission. What is at issue is the extent to which Japanese wartime policies and defensive strategies for the homeland and Japanese treatment of Okinawans was responsible for the unnecessary loss of Okinawan life. While the source and motivation for *shūdan jiketsu* might be ambiguous and therefore contested, documented killings of Okinawans by Japanese soldiers are impossible to recast in a favorable light and thus open up doubts about official Japanese interpretations of group suicides and, indeed, of the overall actions of Japanese war planners vis-à-vis Okinawa. The relatively small number of such killings (perhaps a couple hundred of ninety-four thousand total noncombatant deaths) was the principal fact that the Ministry of Education cited in arguing that Ienaga Saburō's textbook depiction of the battle placed too much emphasis on these instances without highlighting the greater number of deaths by *shūdan jiketsu* (implicitly interpreted by the ministry censors as heroic self-sacrifices demonstrating Okinawan loyalty to the Japanese state). This official downplaying of clear instances of Japanese violence and discrimination against Okinawans is precisely what drives the counterdiscourse Okinawans and their sympathizers have constructed through peace guide courses and other forms of war-related peace education. Again, on one level they are setting the historical record straight from a neglected and undervalued perspective; on another level, however, a peace guide trip to Itokazu cave is part of a proxy war being fought over the political and economic future of the prefecture within the Japanese polity. In other words, this form of peace promotion—while no doubt founded in part on universal humanitarian ideals—stems from historical and contemporary grievances addressed to the Japanese government as the party most responsible for Okinawa's predicament, even if the concrete manifestation of the problem, at least for most residents, is the continued and concentrated presence of U.S. bases.

This plot line of peace study courses, like that of Okinawan peace discourses, contrasts predictably with battle site tours that cater to mainland veterans and bereaved families. But at the same time it also clashes with the sightseeing trips packaged for the general mainland tourist vacationing on Okinawa's beaches. With war experience and history so much a part of contemporary Okinawan "thought and culture," as Ishihara would have it, the problem becomes how, if at all, to represent that aspect of Okinawan identity to those seeking to experience "Okinawa" or to know its modern history. On this point, peace guide programs are waging a two-front war; they are clearly fighting against whitewashed war history emplotted as heroic—if tragic—epic, on the one hand, and against the ignorance or indifference of the sunbathing beachcomber, on the other. One strategy that often emerges from Okinawa study tour literature is to combine the grisly war history lesson with a turn to the natural and cultural assets of the Ryūkyū Islands qua Okinawa (much as general tourism promotion does) and embrace the juxtapositions this move entails as another part of the area's fascinating difference, diversity, and distinctiveness. Okinawa, like other global tourist spots that combine natural/cultural beauty with histories of devastation, then appears to the mainlander as a mystery to discover, something that requires serious study to understand and appreciate fully. It is not simply the place of the Himeyuri Student Nurses Corps story; nor is it simply the source of Okinawan pop singer Amuro Namie's—and the would-be sunbather's—tan.

The introduction to the recently revised *Okinawa shūgaku ryokō hando bukku* (Okinawa study tour handbook, 1997–1999) demonstrates this approach as it attempts to appeal to the student assigned to read it before visiting Okinawa. Its first paragraph could be straight out of a tourist brochure:

> Okinawa—blue sea, white-sand beaches. A southern island, Okinawa awaits you. Okinawa's sea is a sea of world-renowned coral reefs. Marine sports are at their best. Beautiful flowers of primary colors indeed say "Okinawa." Strolling and shopping International Street also promises a good time.
>
> Okinawan culture is not just that of the Japanese mainland. It was born from numerous exchanges with China, Korea, and Southeast Asia intertwining with its own unique environment. Shuri Castle of the Ryūkyū Kingdom, which was burnt to ashes in the flames of war, has been restored and conveys to the present the culture of the past Sho Dynasty. This kingdom fell under the control of Satsuma domain in 1609, and in 1879 was dissolved under the Meiji government's "Ryūkyū disposal" program. However, the culture of the people of Okinawa pulsates, even now.
>
> The Battle of Okinawa at the end of the Pacific War turned into a fierce land battle that enveloped the entire population. Many youths were called up to the battlefront, and one-quarter of Okinawa prefecture's population was sacrificed. Moreover, in postwar, too, Okinawa was occupied by the U.S. military, and the land of residents was illegally taken from them and turned into huge U.S. base complexes. Even after Reversion to the mainland in 1972, numerous U.S. military bases have remained as is, all the way to the present.
>
> So, let's *really* learn more about Okinawa.[53]

Learning more about Okinawa is presented here as a way to push the presumably young reader beyond the travel-poster image of coral reefs and bikini-clad women on white-sand beaches, although this stereotype of Okinawa as a marine sports haven and tropical, exotic, and erotic paradise provides the hook. Okinawa's differences from the mainland are highlighted and advertised as basic to Okinawan identity: Its culture is not limited to that of Japan, it was a latecomer to the Japanese polity, its war experience was harsher, its postwar foreign occupation longer, and its post-postwar has not yet arrived. This text does not urge assimilation with the mainland but rather exploits well-circulated albeit shallowly exoticized differences to educate the reader about deeper ones. If anything, the text works to earn not equality for Okinawa with the mainland (whatever that might mean) but rather respect for Okinawa through an explication of the trials and tribulations at the heart of its differences from the mainland.

The rest of this sixty-page handbook contains chapters on "The Nature, Culture, and History of Okinawa," "The Battle of Okinawa," "U.S. Military Control and Land Struggles, Reversion Movement," and "Okinawa,

Island of Bases." The chapter on the battle features descriptions of the primary peace course stops: Kakazu Bluff, the Thirty-second Army Headquarters Cave site; the youth-related Himeyuri, Shiraume, and Kenji-no-tō; Itokazu and Garabi Caves, as well as the more recently excavated *shūdan jiketsu* cave, Chibichirigama; Konpaku-no-tō; the Cornerstone of Peace and Peace Memorial Museum; and the Korean Memorial. Although it includes a map of the Mabuni Hill/Peace Park area, it astutely avoids any description of the prefectural memorials and the Reimei-no-tō. Rather—like some other study tour guides—it goes out of its way to give the out-of-the-way Nanboku-no-tō a photo and a description of the story attached to it. Japanese soldiers of the Twenty-fourth Regiment who were seeking shelter forced civilian refugees out of a cave near the present memorial's spot and into the "typhoon of steel" of American heavy guns, where 551 of the 900 residents of Maehira Village alone died. Dozens of civilians reportedly were also killed directly by Japanese soldiers. The name *Nanboku,* however, derives from the inscription provided in 1966 by Teshi Yoshiji, an Ainu veteran of the Twenty-fourth Regiment. Teshi and several other Ainu recruits from the Twenty-fourth—discriminated against as an ethnic minority within the army—are said to have saved local residents from Japanese soldiers. The memorial's name alludes to the people from South (Okinawa) to North (Hokkaidō) who rest together at this spot. The small epitaph attached simply reads "Kimun Utari" (Ainu for "people of the mountains") and "Maehira Kumin" (residents of Maehira) to mark the relationship between the locals and the Ainu recruits.[54] This is one example of linkages between Okinawans and Ainu as groups historically discriminated against within Japan, linkages that in recent years have continued on a small scale. Kina Shoukichi, for example, has been explicit in associating Okinawans with Ainu in his musical experimentation and his White Ship of Peace project.

Nanboku-no-tō, Itokazu Cave, and other sites, when joined with the Korean Memorial, provide peace courses with ample material for lessons about Japanese colonial aggression, ethnic discrimination, and Okinawan visions of an implied future; when juxtaposed with patriotic memorials to the war dead, they comment on the chauvinism that warfare incites, as well as on the need to account for losses in some way. It is unclear to what extent, however, these points are emphasized on actual tours in comparison to the treatment they receive in model courses and their supporting materials. One wonders, too, how many beachcombers dare to venture from their resort compounds and packaged tours to have their peaceful vacations ruined by peace courses. These are issues for future fieldwork. Still, it is significant to underscore here that the configuration of these model peace courses manifests Okinawan inflections in peace discourses in Japan. They strive to maintain history, memory, and peace promotion as active processes that ceaselessly engage individuals and the state in a critical awareness of the past for present and future social existence. Ritualized chants of "*heiwa*" and equally ritualized memorial practices—in Japan, in Okinawa, in Germany, in the United States, everywhere—run the risk of relieving states and individuals of the burdens of the past and present that are often best walked through (mentally, sometimes even physically) rather than dropped off with a wreath at a monument or expiated with a pledge at a rally. Okinawan peace courses and discourses, however, are difficult to dismiss as simply familiar rhetoric motivated by unreflective and parochial victim consciousness, even when the peace talk of Hiroshima and Nagasaki seems dangerously jaded, as it does to some Okinawans. Peace education advocates in Okinawa, especially peace guides, are walking that talk down different paths.

That path, though, might be leading to a third front in Okinawa's peace wars if the controversy that broke out in August 1999 over the construction of the new Prefectural Peace Memorial Museum is any indication. In addition to the patriots on the one side and the resort tourists on the other, peace educators and activists now must contend with the administration of the new governor, Inamine Keiichi. On 11 August 1999, the *Ryūkyū Shimpo* reported that exhibit content for the museum, slated to open in April 2000, had been changed without the knowledge of the committee of experts who had been assigned in September 1996 to draw up guidelines for the designs and captions of exhibits. Committee members, including Ishihara Masaie, first became aware of the changes when visiting the site to inspect progress in July. The plans for the section "The Battle of Okinawa and Civilians" included a scene from a cave diorama entitled "Daily Life of Civilian Refugees" that, according to a summary outline dated 23 March 1999, was to depict "a Japanese soldier ordering a mother at gunpoint to cover her [crying] child's mouth." In the diorama under construction, the gun was removed. Another cave scene called "Nursing Wounded Soldiers and Coercing Suicide" was supposed to depict a Japanese soldier handing cyanide-laced condensed milk to a wounded soldier. The completed diorama contained no such Japanese soldier.[55]

Then, on 28 August, the same newspaper broke the story that the prefecture's Culture and International Office, without the knowledge of the exhibit committee, had issued an "alteration guide" directing the exhibit construction crew to change the depiction of civilian massacres and atrocities committed by Japanese soldiers. It instructed exhibit workers, for example, to change the word *gyakusatsu* (massacre) to *gisei* (sacrifice), *sute-ishi sakusen* (the "sacrificed stone strategy," a reference to a strategy in the game of *go* that is commonly applied to describe Japanese war planners' strategy to defend Okinawa just long enough to buy time for full fortification and defense of the mainland) to *jikyūsen* (war of attrition, implying a full defense of Okinawa), and *Jūgo-nen sensō* (The Fifteen Years War, which encompasses Japanese invasions of north China from the 1931 Manchurian Incident and thus emphasizes Japan's aggressive colonial enterprise in which Okinawa too was implicated as both the colonized and colonizer) to *Ajia-Taiheiyō sensō* (Asia–Pacific War, which starts the war at the 1937 China Incident and skirts the issue of earlier colonial aggression). The guide also called for the removal of a map of "comfort stations" and the deletion of anti-Okinawan sentiments by Japanese soldiers. None of the points for revision were unusual in the literature on the Battle of Okinawa, and many in fact were used in displays at the original Peace Memorial Museum. The high public profile of the new museum combined with the return of a more conservative LDP-led prefectural government, however, has created a new context and therefore new meanings and reactions to these well-used words and visuals.

The exhibit committee called these changes "a whitewashing of the facts of the Battle of Okinawa." Ishihara was one of the most vocal in denouncing these machinations, pointing out that during the textbook controversy in 1982 the central government had tried to hide the facts of civilian massacres, but now such distortions were originating in Okinawa itself.[56] From where in Okinawa was at first not exactly clear, but later reports and hearings held in October intimated that Inamine himself initiated the changes after seeing the original proposal for the first time last March. As this controversy over museum content unfolded in the Okinawan media during the fall of 1999, the Okinawa Peace Network responded by mobilizing its forces and framing the issue in terms of "truth" and "peace" in the name of the (Okinawan) people. In a symposium the network and its allies put together on 18 September on the theme "How Do We Relate the Truth of the Battle of Okinawa?" critics repeated the charge that the changes ignored or watered down (*honenuki*) the "actual facts" and "full scope" of the battle (especially the Japanese-on-Okinawan violence that to many commentators constitutes one of its defining traits). They also circulated the view that if the new museum, and by extension Okinawa, is to exist—as it has been widely advertised in promotional literature—as a "place of dispatch for peace" (*heiwa no hasshinchi*), the Inamine administration should accept the general will of the people, not make unilateral decisions behind closed doors.[57] Placing the burden of peace, so to speak, on Inamine was a tactic to force him to walk his talk when he utters the H-word in public.

After defending the clandestine changes on the grounds that "many different interpretations" exist of the battle's events, the Inamine administration finally bowed to public pressure and negotiated the reinstatement of most of the original display plans, but with compromises. For example, the soldier offering the cyanide-laced milk was returned but placed in the background mixing the poisonous concoction while a student nurse attended to the wounded soldier. Likewise, the scene of the soldier threatening mother and child at gunpoint was completed, but with his bayonet-tipped rifle pointed not at the refugees but instead angled over them, as if protecting—not threatening—them (figure 3.9). However, Ishihara—one of the harshest critics—voiced his approval of the new museum's content upon opening, although others thought much material was still needed.[58]

In any case, this new public debate concerning how and why the Battle of Okinawa should be represented, and who should have a say in constructing that representation, speaks to the high level of commitment among Okinawans to fill in censored gaps of the past for future generations. But, more important, it reminds us how history making in its many manifestations—memorial epitaph, museum display, school textbook, TV documentary, professional monograph, amateur memoir, sightseeing narrative—involves a dialectic between past and present that is directed toward the future. At least in Okinawan public discourse, to engage in the history and memorialization of the battle is—whether intended or not—to engage in (the politics of) peace promotion. These politics inevitably raise the issue of U.S. bases regardless of one's position on them

Figure 3.9. Japanese soldier threatening or protecting Okinawan refugees as mother silences/smothers her child. Diorama at Okinawa Peace Memorial Museum.
Source: Photo by Gerald Figal, 23 June 2001.

(the bases ensure peace/the bases jeopardize peace; the bases aid Okinawan economic development/the bases stunt Okinawan economic development). And this in turn has everything to do with past, present, and future relations between Okinawa and the central Japanese government that has presided over a history of invasion, annexation, subordination, devastation, and occupation of the Ryūkyū Islands. Imagining a future without bases (and without the subsidies from Tokyo that implicitly come with them) is, like peace studies, a cottage industry in Okinawa, but should that base-free future come to pass, it will inevitably affect peace studies, history education, and the prefecture's livelihood.

NOTES

This chapter is a revised version of an essay published in *Critical Asian Studies* 33, no. 1 (March 2001) and is used with permission. I owe special thanks to Ishihara Masaie of Okinawa International University; Aguni Chieko, formerly of the Peace and International Exchange Office of Naha City; Kawamitsu Akihiro of Okinawa Jiji Shuppan; former governor Ōta Masahide; Moe Yonamine; Linda Angst; Julia Yonetani; and Sigrid Hofmeister for providing materials and information that greatly facilitated the research for the original essay and aided follow-up research for the present version. I am also grateful to Ms. Yonamine for introducing me to Naha City assemblywoman Takasato Suzuyo and other peace activists on a very hot and humid Okinawan Memorial Day in 1999. Laura Hein, Mark Selden, and Tom Fenton were instrumental in shaping this article for publication in *Critical Asian Studies* 33, no. 1 (March 2001) (where additional related images may be seen), and in the present volume. Without their editing and encouragement, this work would still be unorganized notes on my hard drive.

This research was initially supported by a General University Research Grant from the University of Delaware. A subsequent Japan Foundation Research Grant for a broader project on Okinawa tourism allowed me to update information and photographs during my stay in Okinawa during the spring and summer of 2001.

1. The White Ship of Peace website, ryukyu.ne.jp/~champloo/english/whiteship/PURPORT.html, June 2001. This page has been removed. A discussion of the tour's aim appears at www.towardfreedom.com/1998/aug98/whiteship.htm.
2. "Senseki o heiwa no shinboru ni," *Ryūkyū Shimpo Internet Newswire*, 22 June 1998, www.ryukyushimpo.co.jp/news01/1998/9806/980622a.htm.
3. "Senseki hozon e uneritakamaru," *Ryūkyū Shimpo Internet Newswire*, 17 June 1998, www.ryukyushimpo.co.jp/news01/1998/9806/980617ea.htm.
4. The most frequently cited battle death statistics from Okinawa Prefectural sources list 94,000 Okinawan noncombatants, 28,228 Okinawan conscripts, 65,908 Japanese troops from outside Okinawa Prefecture, and 12,520 U.S. troops, for a total of 200,656. Deaths among Korean and Taiwanese colonial subjects (including labor conscripts, combatants, and "comfort women"), probably in the thousands, are difficult to calculate because of a lack of accurate records and are rarely noted

in popularly published statistics although they have become a focus in peace tours. Eighty-two British war dead are also recognized at the Heiwa no ishiji (Cornerstone of Peace) monument.

5. "Senseki hozon he uneritakamaru."

6. On the controversy stirred by the *Enola Gay*, see Edward T. Linenthal and Tom Engelhardt, eds., *History Wars: The* Enola Gay *and Other Battles for the American Past* (New York: Metropolitan Books, 1996); Laura Hein and Mark Selden, eds., *Living with the Bomb: American and Japanese Cultural Conflicts in the Nuclear Age* (New York: Sharpe, 1997).

7. Imputing a single "Okinawan" voice on what is a diverse field of opinion in Okinawa Prefecture would be folly; even the label "Okinawan" is fraught with complications given the disparate historical experiences among the prefecture's many islands, the existence of a substantial Okinawan diaspora, and the participation of many non-Okinawa-born Japanese in the discourse on Okinawa's plight.

8. The *Lucky Dragon* Incident, in which the crew of a Japanese tuna boat was irradiated by fallout from a U.S. hydrogen bomb test in the South Pacific, awakened public consciousness about potential atomic attacks on Japan as a Cold War ally of the United States. In this context, "peace" came to mean not only antiwar in general but antinuclear and anti–U.S.–Japan Security Pact (ANPO) in particular. The United States used bases in Japan—Okinawa in particular—as staging areas for military operations in Vietnam.

9. For an analysis of the configuration of Hiroshima as peace site, see Lisa Yoneyama, *Hiroshima Traces: Time, Space, and the Dialectics of Memory* (Berkeley: University of California Press, 1999).

10. Hein and Selden, *Living with the Bomb*. In addition to his contribution to that volume, John Dower has written variously on the atomic attacks in the context of postwar "peace and democracy."

11. Two prominent examples are the reportage of Honda Katsuichi, whose writings on the Rape of Nanjing have recently appeared in English, and Ienaga Saburō's lawsuits over Ministry of Education censorship of textbooks. Amateur "self-histories" (*jibunshi*) written and published on a small scale by ordinary citizens also sometimes reveal surprisingly critical edges. See Gerald Figal, "How to *Jibunshi*: The Making and Marketing of Self-histories of Shōwa among the Masses in Postwar Japan," *Journal of Asian Studies* 55, no. 4 (November 1996).

12. The phrase *heiwa no ishizue* appears, for example, in articles appearing during the 1960s in *Wakatake*, the publication of the Youth Division of the Okinawa Bereaved Families Association. In the case of the like-named memorial, the Okinawan word for *cornerstone* (*ishiji*) is used instead.

13. Ishihara's publications include *Gyakusatsu no shima: Kōgun to shinmin no matsuro* (Tokyo: Banseisha, 1978), *Daimitsubōeki no jidai: Senryō shoki Okinawa no minshū seikatsu* (Tokyo: Banseisha, 1982), *Shōgen, Okinawa-sen: Senjō no kōkei Dai 1-han* (Tokyo: Aoki Shoten, 1984), *Sengo Okinawa no shakaishi: Gunsagyō, senka, daimitsubōeki no jidai* (Naha: Hirugisha, 1995), *Okinawa no tabi: Abuchiragama to Todoroki no gō* (Tokyo: Shueisha shinsho, 2000).

14. Ishihara Masaie, "War Experience of the People of Okinawa and the Development of the Okinawan Philosophy of Peace," *Okinawa Kokusai Daigaku Bungakubu Kiy*, no. 1 (December 1995): 13.

15. Ishihara, "War Experience of the People of Okinawa," 14–15.

16. Ishihara, "War Experience of the People of Okinawa," 16.

17. For a more detailed analysis, see Gerald Figal, "Historical Sense and Commemorative Sensibility at Okinawa's Cornerstone of Peace," *positions: east asia cultures critique* 5, no. 3 (Winter 1997).

18. Arasaki Moriteru et al., *Kankō kōsu de nai Okinawa: senseki, kichi, sangyō, bunka* (Tokyo: Kōbunken, 1998), 132.

19. On 23 June 1945, the Japanese commander Ushijima Mitsuru committed suicide, effectively marking the end of organized resistance, but several other days (19, 21, and 22 June; 7 July; and 7 September) are equally viable candidates for marking the end of the battle. Ushijima's final order explicitly urged a fight to the end; in other words, he implied that his death should not be interpreted as the end of the battle. See Figal, "Historical Sense and Commemorative Sensibility"; Arasaki et al., *Kankō kōsu de nai Okinawa*, 120–22; Masahide Ōta, "Re-Examining the History of the Battle of Okinawa," in *Okinawa: Cold War Island*, ed. Chalmers Johnson (Cardiff, Calif.: Japan Policy Research Institute, 1999), 13–15.

20. "Heika: 'Yoi koto o sareta'," *Ryūkyū shimpo*, 3 August 1995, 1.

21. Naha-shi sōmu-bu heiwa to kokusai kōryū-shitsu, "1999 nendo yosan iinkai shiryō" (Naha, February 1999 meeting), 2.

22. The Okinawa Peace Network seems particularly determined to prevent peace studies and battle site tours in Okinawa from going the route of their Hiroshima and Nagasaki counterparts. See "Heiwa gakushū to kyōshi no sekinin," *Ryūkyū shimpo Internet Newswire*, 28 June 1997, www.ryukyushimpo.co.jp/kinkou/kin/k970628.htm.

23. The term *Yasukuni-ka* is part of peace memorial discourse in Okinawan newspapers and other published sources. See, for example, Arasaki, *Kankō kōsu de nai Okinawa*, 105.

24. Arasaki, *Kankō kōsu de nai Okinawa*, 167.

25. While colonial subjects generally have been considered among the noncombatant victims, this polarization (and in the battle site tours I have examined) obscures the many willing and patriotic Okinawan combatants.

26. Cited in Ōta Masahide, *Okinawa-sen senbotsusha o matsuru irei no tō* (Naha: Naha shuppansha, 1985), 38.

27. Laura Hein and Mark Selden incisively delineate the present stakes involved in battles over national textbooks and the limitations of Japanese conceptions of citizenship in "The Lessons of War, Global Power, and Social Change," in *Censoring History: Citizenship and Memory in Japan, Germany, and the United States*, ed. Laura Hein and Mark Selden (Armonk, N.Y.: M. E. Sharpe, 2000), 3–50.

28. John Purves's online text "Island of Bases: A Contemporary Political and Economic History of Okinawa" offers insightful discussion of Okinawan postwar development issues, especially related to the bases; see www.niraikanai.wwma.net/pages/base.html.

29. Hein and Selden point out in *Censoring History* that with the end of the Cold War, "in the 1990s other Europeans and Asians [other than Germans and Japanese] gained new leverage to insist on recognition of their perspectives in German and Japanese historical memory, and specifically in textbook narratives of history," "The Lessons of War," 15. Okinawans should be considered as a special case

under this rubric, as briefly discussed in Nozaki Yoshiko and Inokuchi Hiromitsu, "Japanese Education, Nationalism, and Ienaga Saburō's Textbook Lawsuits," in *Censoring History*, 116–19.

30. Arasaki, *Kankō kōsu de nai Okinawa*, 106.

31. Okinawa-ken kōtōgakkō kyōshakuin kumiai nambu shibu and Heiwa kyōiku kenkyū iinkai, eds., *Aruku, miru, kangaeru Okinawa* (Naha: Okinawa jiji shuppan, 1986), memo in section 21.

32. *Aruku, miru, kangaeru Okinawa*, section 21.

33. If American memorials are taken into account (which they are not in Okinawan reckonings), the first Battle of Okinawa memorial would be the Ernie Pyle Memorial erected by the 1118 Engineer Combat Group on 21 June 1945 at the site on Iejima where the famed war correspondent was shot dead by sniper fire.

34. Kinjō Washin also led the efforts to establish the two other important early memorials, the Kenji-no-tō (March 1946) and the original Himeyuri-no-tō (April 1946). His two daughters were among the Himeyuri student nurses; the youngest one died in the Third Surgery Cave. Arasaki Moriteru et al., *Okinawa shūgaku ryokō* (Tokyo: Kōbunken, 1999), 65. See also Ōta, *Okinawa-sen senbotsusha o matsuru irei no tō*, 30–31.

35. *Kankō kōsu de nai Okinawa*, 138–41.

36. See Yoneyama, *Hiroshima Traces*, chap. 5.

37. Norma Field, *In the Realm of a Dying Emperor: Japan at Century's End* (New York: Vintage, 1993), 61. See also Koji Taira's analysis of the use of the term *shūdan jiketsu* in "The Battle of Okinawa in Japanese History Books," in Johnson, *Okinawa: Cold War Island*, 39–49. Statistics for *shūdan jiketsu* are difficult to state with precision and are usually categorized separately from documented cases of outright killings of civilians by Japanese soldiers, but see Arasaki, *Kankō kōsu de nai Okinawa*, 150.

38. Linda Angst, "Gendered Nationalism: The Himeyuri Story and Okinawan Identity in Postwar Japan," *PoLAR: Political and Legal Anthropology Review* 20, no. 1 (May 1997): 100–13.

39. Besides money funneled through the Okinawa Development Agency (ODA), Tokyo had also promised previous to Reversion to encourage Japanese tourism to Okinawa by supporting the Marine Expo '75 there. Economically speaking, the Expo was largely a bust for Okinawan interests because of overinvestment and lower-than-expected attendance. Mainland-based construction and travel companies profited most from this venture. Since then, beach resort development in Okinawa—marketed to Japanese who are 95 percent of all tourists—has boomed, but with mixed results for the local economy. Attempts have been made recently to attract other Asian tourists, but most American tourists in Okinawa are in the military community, which has exclusive access to several beaches. These issues are the subject of my ongoing research.

40. Interview, 22 June 1999. Ishihara also related the story of mainland historians coming to Okinawa to learn from detailed battle site tours put together by local researchers.

41. Aguni Chieko, former senior manager of the Peace and International Exchange Office of Naha City, stressed in an interview on 24 June 1999 that because guides are all city workers who have to take time out of regular work to conduct

tours, the city hasn't been able to keep up with recent demand and now full-day tours are frequently scaled down to half-day tours.

42. "Heiwa kyōiku: Sedai kōdai no jiki otozureru; wakai kyōshi wa jikō-sakugō," *Ryūkyū shimpo Internet Newswire*, 16 June 1999, www.ryukyushimpo.co.jp/special/kyouiku/html/k990616.html.

43. See, for example, the beyond-the-textbook teaching strategies discussed by Gregory Wegner, "The Power of Selective Tradition: Buchenwald Concentration Camp and Holocaust Education for Youth in the New Germany," and Kathleen Woods Masalski, "Teaching Democracy, Teaching War: American and Japanese Educators Teach the Pacific War," in *Censoring History*, ed. Hein and Selden.

44. *Okinawa shūgaku ryokō*, 41–42.

45. "Heiwa gaido yōsei de 70-nin ga fīrudowāku," *Ryūkyū shimpo Internet Newswire*, 17 March 1997, www.ryukyushimpo.co.jp/news/970317ja.htm#jnews_1.

46. *Aruku, miru, kangaeru Okinawa*, leaf 3. My discussion here is of the original 1986 publication.

47. "Naha-shi shūgaku ryokō heiwa gakushū gaido no go annai," www.city.naha.okinawa.jp/heiwa/gaid/gaid3.htm.

48. Naha-shi sūmu-bu heiwa to kokusai kōryū-shitsu, "1999 nendo yosan iinkai shiryō," 1.

49. Arasaki, *Okinawa shūgaku ryokō*, 42.

50. *Kankō kōsu de nai Okinawa*, 90.

51. Taken principally from *Okinawa shūgaku ryokō*, 43–44; *Aruku, miru, kangaeru Okinawa*, leaf 9.

52. Part of the re-creation of this experience at Itokazu is the "pitch black experience" whereby all illumination in the cave is extinguished for several minutes. For a very nice online presentation of one of Ishihara Masaie's seminar trips to Itokazu Cave, see www.asahi-net.or.jp/~nj4y-tkdt/oki/11/oki11.htm.

53. Aniya Masaaki, dir., and Heiwa kokusai kyōiku kenkyūkai, ed., *Okinawa shūgaku ryokō hando bukku* (Tokyo: Heiwa bunka, 1999), 3.

54. Masaaki, dir., and Heiwa kokusai kyōiku kenkyūkai, ed., *Okinawa shūgaku ryokō hando bukku*, 32. See also *Aruku, miru, kangaeru Okinawa*, leaf 20; *Kankō kōsu de nai Okinawa*, 102–4.

55. "'Gama de no sangeki' nihonhei kieru," *Ryūkyū Shimpo Internet Newswire*, 11 August 1999, www.ryukyushimpo.co.jp/news01/1999/9908/990811a.html.

56. "Zangyakusei usumeru yō shiji," *Ryūkyū Shimpo Internet Newswire*, 28 August 1999, www.ryukyushimpo.co.jp/news01/1999/9908/990828a.html.

57. Reportage of the symposium appears in *Ryūkyū Shimpo Internet Newswire*, 19 September 1999, www.ryukyushimpo.co.jp/news01/1999/9909/990919a.html.

58. The new website for the new Peace Memorial Museum (www.peace-museum.pref.okinawa.jp) features a database of visitors' responses—scanned from the actual handwritten copies—which is searchable by age, gender, occupation, and home area. At the time of this writing (27 June 2002), it contained a total of 3,547 responses and would make interesting material for analysis of public reaction to the displays.

4

Memories of Okinawa

Life and Times in the Greater Osaka Diaspora

Steve Rabson

This chapter is a study of people who have migrated from Okinawa to greater Osaka and their descendants. *Okinawans* are defined as individuals with at least one grandparent or two great-grandparents from Okinawa, including those who moved to greater Osaka between late 1945 and early 1972 when Okinawa was officially called "The Ryukyu Islands"[1] by its American military occupiers.[2] From July 1999 until June 2001, I administered a survey questionnaire to 313 respondents, interviewed more than 100 individuals, collected writings by and about Okinawans in greater Osaka, and attended their social functions, performance events, and informal gatherings. Throughout the two years of this study, I lived among Okinawan neighbors in the largest residential community of Okinawans in greater Osaka, which is located in Taishō Ward of Osaka City. This chapter summarizes the history of Okinawan migration to greater Osaka; presents interviews and writings that describe, in particular, their experiences residing in what Okinawan scholars have called "ethnic communities"[3]; examines the role of prefectural associations and other organizations of Okinawans in greater Osaka; and discusses the ways in which individuals in this diaspora remember Okinawa or view their relationship with an ancestral homeland where many of them have never lived.

WHY THEY CAME TO GREATER OSAKA

Okinawans started moving to greater Osaka in significant numbers, mostly for temporary sojourns, around 1900, the same year commonly cited as the start of Okinawan emigration abroad. Most came either to work in factories or to sell Okinawan products, such as sugar, *awamori*, and textiles, after regular boat service was established between Naha and Osaka. During this period, Osaka was becoming known as "the Manchester of the East" for its many textile mills that recruited large numbers of workers, mostly women, including many from Okinawa and Korea as well as rural areas on the mainland. Families in Okinawa usually received a lump-sum payment for contracts negotiated through recruiters, and the factories provided their children, often girls as young as thirteen, with gainful employment, regular meals, dormitory lodging, and wages that helped support the household back home.[4]

Unlike the vast majority of women from Okinawa who emigrated abroad either to join their families or marry male emigrants, women and girls who went to work in mainland textile factories earned an independent income. Looking back decades later, many recall that, despite horrendous working and living conditions that were exacerbated by prejudice and discrimination, they felt proud to be earning money to help support their impoverished families and finance educations for their brothers. Retrospective accounts of this experience show a striking diversity of memories. In contrast to the firsthand accounts of exploitation and discrimination (quoted later) in Fukuchi Hiroaki's 1985 book *Okinawa jokō aishi* (The Tragic History of Okinawa's Women Factory Workers), Higa Michiko published a series of interviews ten years later in the *Okinawa Times* quoting women who remember spinning factories as "good places where, as long as you could work, you could eat three meals a day. Even orphans could make a living."[5] Such memories remind us of desperate conditions in Okinawa, especially during the 1920s and 1930s when many families were short of food.

For mainland Japan, however, World War I brought enormous economic benefits. Besides adding former German concessions in China and German territories in the South Pacific to its empire after Germany's defeat, Japan gained a huge export market, which greatly stimulated its domestic industries. Manufacturers were deluged with orders for munitions and supplies as they displaced American and European manufacturers in large sectors both of the domestic consumer market and Asian markets.

The rural economy in Okinawa, already languishing, was devastated by the collapse of world sugar prices in 1921, compelling more Okinawans to leave for South America, Hawai'i, and the Philippines; however, the largest number moved to mainland Japan. Meanwhile, expansion of the industrial and consumer economy on the mainland that started during the "World War I boom" intensified competition for workers among recruiters and employers. This not only resulted in better wages for women and men working in factories but also made possible access to more prestigious jobs, especially for women, some of whom were now able to leave the spinning factories for work as department store clerks and telephone operators.[6] New factories in Osaka and its environs brought a rapid increase in the city's textile, construction, metal processing, and lumber industries. Shipbuilding firms also opened assembly plants in what was then the city's Minato ("Harbor") Ward where Osaka's largest Okinawan community settled in the eastern portion that split off in 1932 to create Taishō Ward.

By late 1914, when Okinawan communities had begun to form, two-fifths of the population of Osaka's Kita Okajima Precinct (part of Taishō Ward after 1932) was estimated to be from Okinawa.[7] Of the approximately twenty thousand who came to the mainland from Okinawa every year during the 1920s and 1930s, nearly half worked as manual laborers in the factories of greater Osaka. In 1925, for example, of 19,926 Okinawans moving to the mainland, 8,994 came to the Osaka-Kobe area. The recorded population of Okinawans residing there grew from 1,575 in 1920 to 8,994 in 1925 and 20,356 in 1930, declined to 16,929 in 1935, and grew again to 53,678 in 1940. During this same period for the mainland as a whole, the resident population grew from 9,626 in 1920 to 19,926 in 1925 and 43,150 in 1930, declined to 32,335 in 1935, and grew again to 88,319 in 1940.[8] By 1940, the population of Okinawans on the mainland was approaching 15 percent of the total population of Okinawa Prefecture itself, some six hundred thousand at the time.

In contrast to Osaka, known as a "labor market," Okinawans thought of Tokyo as a "center of arts and culture" where young people went to attend school and begin careers in such fields as literature, journalism, and painting, as well as business. A popular saying in Okinawa at the turn of the twentieth century was "The rich emigrate abroad, the students go to Tokyo, and the poor go to Osaka."[9] In reality, of course, students also went to schools and colleges in Osaka and Kyoto. And, despite this "working-class" image of Osaka, many Okinawans in professions such as medicine, pharmacy, law, and education settled there after completing their schooling on the mainland. Okinawans in Osaka worked on the prefectural police force, in the city hall, on newspapers as reporters, and in local hospitals as physicians. By 1910, Osaka had approximately sixty Okinawan schoolteachers and thirty firefighters. Okinawans also worked in banks, shipping companies, and retail stores, managed restaurants and clothing stores, and owned small businesses in the city.

Yet in Okinawa today, there is a tendency to heroicize Okinawan emigrants abroad, especially those who have achieved prestigious social status, and to minimize discussion of Okinawan communities in greater Osaka which are still associated with poverty, day labor, unemployment, and slum conditions that no longer exist.[10] To be sure, there are Okinawans in greater Osaka working in factories and on construction sites, but I also interviewed company presidents, a middle-level executive in a nationwide pharmaceutical company headquartered in Osaka, a woman sales manager in the local branch of one of Japan's largest insurance carriers, the minister of a Christian church, teachers in public and private schools, university professors (one specializing in the *Manyōshū* and another in Shakespeare), and a magazine journalist who had just written her first novel. Commemorative volumes published by Okinawa prefectural associations in greater Osaka accentuate Okinawan residents in high-status occupations at least partly to counter negative stereotypes in Okinawa and among mainlanders.

When discussing Okinawan migration, mainlanders invariably refer to the "palm tree hell" (*sotetsu jigoku*). This ironic phrase is commonly used to describe economic conditions in Okinawa during the years following the collapse of world sugar prices in 1921. The devastating shock, felt first by farm families, spread rapidly to related businesses and banks that failed one after another. Employers could not meet their payrolls, and even the Okinawa Prefectural Government, unable to collect taxes, went bankrupt.[11] As in times of famine in the former Ryūkyū Kingdom, people resorted to eating the seeds and lower stalks of Japanese fern palm (cycad) plants that provided nourishment, but required careful cooking to avoid food poisoning. Okinawans, however, criticize the term "palm tree hell," noting that it sounds like some kind of natural disaster, obscuring the responsibility of the Japanese government for its discriminatory policies toward Okinawa where, before World War II, people paid higher taxes and received fewer social services than in any other prefecture. Okinawans also note that, far from protecting the local sugar industry, the Japanese government abandoned it in favor of an intense program to develop sugar plantations in Taiwan, Japan's colony acquired as one of the spoils of victory in the Sino-Japanese War of 1894–1895.[12]

With Okinawan migration to greater Osaka increasing thirteenfold between 1920 and the early 1930s, the national government dealt with depression-era conditions in Okinawa by rejecting proposals for relief and, instead, sending fifty-six thousand Okinawans as emigrants to Japanese island territories in the South Pacific where by 1940 they outnumbered local populations.[13]

Okinawan residents of greater Osaka today include people who came to rural areas of the mainland initially in the massive evacuation that began in late 1944 and others who barely survived the battle in 1945. Memories of the evacuation, the battle, and the firebombing of Osaka in 1945 comprise an important legacy of the Pacific War in the Okinawan community. A former resident of Motobu in northern Okinawa Main Island who migrated to Osaka in 1978 recalled his experience as a teenage survivor of the battle in a September 2000 interview:

> I was drafted at sixteen for construction labor on the airfield at Kadena. The Imperial Army soldiers had plenty of food, but for meals they gave Okinawan workers only one brown-rice ball (*nigiri*) apiece. We were housed in Kin Village and, when it was bombed, I was the lone survivor on our block, and had to take the bodies of my neighbors to their relatives. By this time our rations had dwindled to almost nothing, so we chewed sugar cane leaves and filled our stomachs with river water. After evacuating back to northern Okinawa, I found Motobu in ruins and was wounded slightly in the head and leg by shrapnel from an exploding shell nearby. I couldn't find any of my relatives, so I stayed with a family we had known well. The father fished for food in the bay off Sesoko Island where he also swam to pick up leftovers that had been thrown away by crews on U.S. warships. The American soldiers put us in a refugee camp, but I escaped and fled back to Motobu, hiding inside caves and tombs along the way.
>
> After the war I was ill for a time from malnutrition.

In published reminiscences, Miyagi Masako, who later migrated to Amagasaki in Hyōgo Prefecture, remembered the battle from when she was eight years old.

> We had dug an air raid shelter under our house, but when the bombing and shelling got heavy, it was too dangerous and we had to leave. . . . We stayed for a while inside the family tomb, but couldn't get any food there. . . . After one of my cousins died of starvation, we decided to set out for evacuation to northern Okinawa. . . . What I remember most after that is stepping over dead bodies and drinking water full of mosquito larvae. I tried not to look at the bodies, but they lay everywhere, swelling up grotesquely as days passed. I got so thirsty that I scooped up rain water with my hands from wash-tubs where baby mosquitoes were swimming. Finally, with no food or water and exhausted from walking, we became prisoners-of-war and ended up in the refugee camp at Koza.[14]

When the war finally ended, many Okinawans who had lived on the mainland or evacuated there before the battle were unable to return during the period Okinawans call "*kaosu*" (chaos) stretching into the aftermath of massive destruction in which whole families were annihilated, villages were obliterated, property was demolished, and the landscape was altered irrevocably. Thousands were finally able to go back, at least temporarily, beginning in 1946, but travel to and from Okinawa was strictly controlled under the U.S. "military government" which began requiring that people wanting to return provide family registers that had also, in many cases, been destroyed in the battle. Those wanting to go to Okinawa included Okinawan soldiers returning from military service abroad or from prisoner-of-war camps in the USSR, as well as civilians. Occupation authorities on the mainland first established an office in Fukuoka to provide alternative documents, but many people were unable to obtain them. Later, U.S. occupation authorities in Okinawa issued what were euphemistically called "passports" for travel between the mainland and Okinawa but were really more like the old Soviet exit visas, obtainable only after what were sometimes lengthy investigations. Those who did manage to return in the early postwar years often arrived to find their families decimated, their homes in ruins, little prospect for employment, and, in some cases, their lands seized, without compensation, for U.S. military bases. As a result, many had to make U-turns back to the mainland. Kinjō Isamu recalls his family's U-turn:

> Both my parents had come to Osaka when the war started. My father got a job hauling military supplies, and my mother worked in a cotton-spinning factory. They fell in love, got married, and a daughter was born just as the war ended. But there wasn't enough food in the place where they'd evacuated, and she died of malnutrition. They returned to Okinawa, where I was born, but couldn't make a living there, so they took us back to Osaka. . . . Carrying our "passports," the family—my parents and us five children—rode the boat over rough seas for three days and nights. . . . The first thing I remember about arriving in Osaka in 1954 at the age of three is that it was cold.[15]

A woman in her mid-fifties, born in Taishō Ward, commented on her questionnaire that "a month before I entered high school [in 1959], my parents took me for my first visit to Okinawa. It seemed so strange to me that we had to get a passport for traveling to what had been my parents' home prefecture in Japan. I loved the beautiful scenery, but was shocked by all the military bases there, and it hurt me to see how many people were poor."[16]

Having sacrificed 147,000 Okinawan lives in the 1945 war of attrition,[17] the Japanese government continued to treat Okinawans as expendable after the war by agreeing in the 1951 San Francisco Peace Treaty not only to relinquish its colonies and territories but also to hand over the Ryūkyū Islands to the U.S. military in exchange for regaining Japanese sovereignty on the mainland. Many argue that the Japanese government's discriminatory treatment of Okinawa continues today with postreversion economic polices aimed at keeping the U.S. military presence concentrated in Okinawa by vastly increasing the "rents" paid Okinawans whose lands are still occupied by the bases and by establishing a large "sympathy budget" (*omoi-yari yosan*) to fund construction in surrounding communities. The comparatively high unemployment rate (often twice the national average) resulting from this distorted economy still compels many in Okinawa to seek "work away from home" (*dekasegi*) on the mainland.

WHERE THEY SETTLED: GROWTH, MOVEMENT, AND CHANGING CONDITIONS IN THE GREATER OSAKA DIASPORA

Kansai, the mainland region with the largest number of migrants, encompasses Osaka, Hyōgo, and Kyoto Prefectures, but it can also refer, along with Kinki, to a wider area including Mie, Nara, Shiga, and Wakayama Prefectures. Okinawans reside throughout this region, but by far the largest numbers live in Osaka and Hyōgo, the only prefectures in Kansai with Okinawan residential communities. This is why, for the sake of convenience, I refer to Osaka and Hyōgo Prefectures as "greater Osaka." Residential communities of Okinawans can still be found elsewhere on the mainland in Yokohama and Kawasaki, while in Fukuoka, Nagoya, Hiroshima, and other cities, where such neighborhoods existed in the past, Okinawan migrants and their descendants have now largely dispersed, a process that occurs among migrant and immigrant diaspora in many countries. Such dispersion has also occurred in greater Osaka where Okinawans have settled in other neighborhoods and may have little or no connection with the residential communities.

Precise figures for Okinawans now residing on the mainland are not available. Until 1940, such statistics were compiled periodically from official family registers (*kōseki*) by the prefectural police in Okinawa. However, since the war, family registers of most Okinawans born in greater Osaka have indicated domiciles on the mainland, not in Okinawa. And many migrants established new family registers on the mainland after their official records were destroyed during the Battle of Okinawa. Prefectural associations have compiled estimates based on their membership lists, but, until recently, these have enumerated households, not individuals, and do not include nonmember households. A more comprehensive, though imprecise, mainland-wide survey was published by the Hyōgo Okinawa Prefectural Association (Okinawa Kenjinkai Hyōgo-ken Honbu) in November 2000. It estimated that the two largest populations by far were 36,500 in Yokohama City and 70,000 in Osaka Prefecture. Other sources estimate the population of Okinawans in Osaka City's Taishō Ward at nineteen thousand,[18] by far the largest in Kansai.[19]

Like migrant and immigrant communities elsewhere, Okinawan communities in greater Osaka formed near where jobs were available and where other Okinawans already lived who could provide support and contacts, especially important for newcomers. Many Okinawans also preferred an environment for daily life where it was possible to speak the dialects, eat the food, practice the religious observances, and maintain other social and cultural customs of the homeland to the extent possible in what were, for most, unfamiliar urban conditions. And, like migrants and immigrants in many places, people from Okinawa chose to live in such communities in order to cope with prejudice and discrimination, including denial of lodging and employment, that they encountered because societies at large have often tended to look down on or exclude people with differences, real or imagined. Relentless pressures to "assimilate" (*dōka*), coming both from mainlanders and from Okinawans themselves, caused many to abandon much of what was distinctively Okinawan when they stepped outside the community, but inside it people could still live, in many ways, as they had before coming to the mainland. In 1996, Kinjō Isamu recalled his early childhood in Taishō Ward shortly after his family moved there from Okinawa in 1954. By this time, Okinawans had been settling there for some three decades, and his childhood memories are far more positive than those of people who had migrated in the 1920s when the community was still going through its early growing pains. (See Oyakawa Takayoshi's reminiscences presented later.)

> My parents maintained our Okinawan lifestyle so completely that sometimes we forgot we were in Osaka. We always spoke in Okinawa dialect and, since we were among many other Okinawans in the Manzai-bashi section of Kita Okajima Precinct, it was easy to live this way. My father raised pigs [for the many cuts of pork used in Okinawan cuisine] and grew *gōyaa* [bitter gourd] in a vacant lot, and he made brown sugar candy. My mother had her weaving implements sent from Okinawa, and wove [Okinawan style] *kasuri* splash-patterned cloth. We conducted all the annual religious observances strictly by the old lunar calendar, including the spring *shiimii* festival of feast and prayer when relatives gather to honor departed ancestors, and the summer *o-bon* festival [when spirits of the ancestors are said to return to this world for a brief visit].

The distribution of the Okinawan population in greater Osaka has changed over time with shifting labor and consumer demands as old factories closed and new ones opened. The Okinawan community in Wakayama, a center of the prewar textile industry, virtually disappeared after World War II as many of its residents moved to the growing Okinawan community in Amagasaki where small and medium-sized metalworking shops were opening. Such shops can be found as well in Taishō Ward of Osaka, where community residents also work in the two large metal parts factories, Kubota and Nakayama. Other Taishō residents work as proprietors or employees in stores, selling mostly consumer goods and services, including those that line the three-block long shopping arcade (*shōten-gai*) in Hirao Precinct, and also as professionals in real estate, pharmacy, medicine, dentistry, and teaching. Many single male residents in Taishō Ward work for local private contractors at construction sites, while, as elsewhere in Japan, there is a large and growing population of retirees.

Major movements of population have also occurred within localities, particularly starting in the late 1950s when families of Okinawans, as well as many mainland Japanese, moved from houses or tenements to apartment blocks (*danchi*) being built in large numbers at the time. This movement, however, was not always voluntary. In Taishō Ward, for example, residents of makeshift houses and barrack-like tenements in a low and often-flooded riverbank area of Kobayashi Precinct that Okinawans called "the hollows" (*kubun-gwa* in Okinawa dialect) were relocated by the city of Osaka to newly constructed municipal apartments nearby in the late 1960s and early 1970s. This was part of a citywide "slum clearance" plan that targeted this area of marshy, unclaimed land officially deemed unsanitary and unsafe. Okinawans had begun living there in the chaotic period just after World War II, which had left much of greater Osaka devastated from firebombings. On what had been unclaimed land they constructed dwellings from tar paper, tin, cardboard, plywood, and scrap lumber without official building permits. Interviewed in 1999, a former resident described the origins and growth of the hollows:

> Many poor people began living there shortly after the war. When one person put up a house, others followed, building houses, moving in, and starting families. In the aftermath of recent bombings, there were always big puddles everywhere. Around 1950 people began putting up barrack-like tenements using lumber, tarpaper, and cement. Landlords living elsewhere also built tenements they rented.
>
> There was electricity in the hollows, but the puddles slopped over with what seemed like sewer water. They were pumped out occasionally, but most of the time people had to put down boards for walk-paths to avoid sloshing through them.[20]

Kinjō Isamu recalled the hollows from the 1950s:

> About one-third of the people there were Okinawans, with many of the others from Kyūshū and Shikoku. When new people moved in from Okinawa, their friends and relatives would come to help put up a house using

discarded lumber and other materials. No one owned most of the land, so it was squatters' rights for the first to claim an open space. My father built his first house this way with help from other Okinawans. Instead of paying them, he served food and drink afterwards. This was one of the ways the *yuimaru* (cooperative labor) system, used in Okinawa for such hard work as cutting sugar cane, also came to be applied in Osaka.[21]

Though called by the media at the time an "Okinawa slum,"[22] some of the approximately 1,500 Okinawan migrants and their descendants who lived there recall the hollows wistfully as a place with "a spirit of community cooperation" (*kyōdō-tai seishin*) where people helped build dwellings by *yuimaru* and loaned money to each other under the co-op system, called "*moai*" in Okinawa, of pooling funds among relatives and close friends that is also practiced elsewhere in Asia. In addition, they made room in their homes for displaced neighbors, especially during such troubled times as when typhoon Jane leveled many dwellings and flooded the area in 1950.[23] But other former residents call nostalgia for the hollows a romanticization of the past, and recall freezing winters, sweltering summers, flooding waters where sewage floated, swarming mosquitoes, devastating fires that fed on tar paper, and taxi drivers who would refuse to take passengers to Taishō Ward for fear of soiling their vehicles in mud puddles or damaging their tires in potholes.[24] Kinjō Isamu recalled that

> [c]onditions there were much worse than in the neighborhoods of soggy old houses crammed together that we saw in a documentary film shown by one of our teachers at school with a passionate interest in the "Buraku problem." I realized then that, like Buraku people, many Okinawans were hired only for grueling, dirty jobs, but that, in a way, we faced worse discrimination because, unlike them, we needed "passports" to visit our hometowns [in Okinawa under U.S. military occupation].[25]

In 1996, Kakinohana Yoshimori remembered his first impression of the hollows from the early 1970s, shortly after he had moved to Osaka from Miyako Island:

> Now people in Taishō Ward dress neatly, wearing the latest fashions, but in those days laborers walked the streets in baggy work fatigues. On the one hand, I was relieved to be among other Okinawans, but the place was depressingly poor. When I first saw the hollows, before the relocation, I was appalled, wondering if this was how Okinawans on the mainland had to live. It truly was a slum, though people from there would be angry to hear me say that today. But it's the truth. One glance at the outdoor sinks and toilets, the maze of alleys, the houses patched together with boards and tin, and anyone would have to agree.[26]

The current fascination among mainland Japanese with things Okinawan, which includes Okinawan communities on the mainland, could explain, in part, why a place commonly called a "slum" in the past has become the object of recent nostalgia in Japan for the early postwar period and of admiration for the resourcefulness of its residents in the face of adversity. This trend could also explain why it has come to acquire a more positive image in the current memories of some Okinawans and why published interviews and writings like those quoted in this chapter have been appearing recently. In May 2001, the Kansai Okinawa Bunko (Culture Center) presented a four-day exhibition of work by Okinawan photographers who had been longtime residents of Taishō Ward. Advertised as "photographs of the hollows," it drew a steady stream of visitors, mainlanders and Okinawans alike, as well as coverage by the greater Osaka media.

Still, whatever "narrative" of the hollows one accepts today, for most residents it was their one and only home when Osaka City targeted it for "clearance" in 1969. Okinawan student leaders organized protests, applying such tactics as sit-ins at municipal government offices learned from local Buraku activists. Protracted negotiations with the city dragged on until most residents agreed to move, with negotiated rent subsidies, to new municipally owned apartment buildings (*shi-ei danchi*) in the early 1970s. The smaller number of people living in the hollows with deeds to their land were offered alternative lots, though of somewhat smaller size, in nearby precincts.[27] Interviewed in 1999, one former resident recalled that "the compensation money the city was offering us to evacuate didn't amount to a sparrow's tear. They built fine apartments at the places we were relocated, but moving there put us all deeply in debt. I can still remember how worn out with worry members of the tenants' association were as they ran around every day trying to scrape up the money for moving expenses."[28] The last tenant to hold out, an elderly woman, finally moved to a municipally owned apartment in 1979. "She was the last one to stay and fight the city's evacuation order," longtime Taishō Ward resident Kinjō Kaoru recalled in 1996. "Her life had been hard since she was a child. She couldn't read and had no marketable skills. I once saw her walking alone through the pouring rain back to the hollows. She looked so lonely, though she never showed her sadness when she was with other people."[29]

After that, the hollows was sunk underwater, flooded deliberately for the artificial expansion of Osaka Bay. Meanwhile, some mainland Japanese living elsewhere in Taishō Ward voiced resentment because they were not offered relocation rent subsidies in the new apartments or alternative parcels of land. Today, nothing of the hollows or anything like it remains in Taishō Ward. Apartment buildings, large and small, and one-family houses predominate, along with residences storekeepers have built above or behind their shops. The Okinawan community there is now a modestly prospering, though far from affluent, neighborhood of merchants and working people roughly comparable in cultural distinctiveness and economic circumstances to Brooklyn's ethnic neighborhoods in Williamsburg (Italian) and Greenpoint (Polish). As for land, virtually no vacant lots or open spaces remain today like those still available when Kinjō Isamu's family moved to Taishō in 1954, so Okinawans can no longer raise pigs. However, many families still maintain small gardens of *gōyaa* that are so numerous on one street in Kobayashi Precinct that it has come to be known as "*gōyaa dōri*." Okinawan foodstuffs for preparation at home and in restaurants are sold in many neighborhood stores, including some run by mainlanders. Forty-six percent of the respondents to my questionnaire indicated that they ate Okinawan food regularly; 40 percent indicated that they observed Okinawan religious practices; and 60 percent indicated that they perform or listen to Okinawan folk music, which one can often hear walking along neighborhood streets in the evening.

HOW THEY COPED: ADJUSTING TO DIFFERENCES AND RESPONDING TO PREJUDICE AND DISCRIMINATION

People from Okinawa have encountered hardships on the mainland because of differences that are real but more often imagined or exaggerated in the minds of mainlanders. A proportionally larger population from Southeast Asia and the Pacific Islands settled in the Ryūkyū Islands in prehistoric times than in what is now mainland Japan.[30] As a result of this early migration, physiological characteristics distinguishing Okinawans from mainland Japanese include shorter average stature, darker skin, fuller chests, and rounder eyes. Yet many Okinawans are physically indistinguishable from a majority of people on the mainland where there is also significant individual and regional variation to the extent that some mainlanders are even said to "look Okinawan." Mainlanders have tended to exaggerate or invent "differences," cultural as well as physiological, fostering stereotypes that are likely to be activated when someone is *thought* to be Okinawan. Furthermore, people who are said to "look Okinawan," like Okinawans themselves, have been ridiculed for features that are, in fact, envied by many on the mainland. In what is one of the most popular cosmetic surgical procedures in the country today, women have tissue removed to enlarge their eye openings. And the beaches in Okinawa are crowded year-round with women and men from the mainland assiduously darkening their skin, suntans acquired in the pursuit of leisure being a mark of wealth and sophistication often associated with travel abroad.

While their physical features have often attracted unwanted attention, language differences have posed more serious problems for Okinawans on the mainland. Again, both real and imagined differences are involved. During the U.S. military occupation of Okinawa, mainlanders sometimes asked people from Okinawa whether they spoke English at home. As for actual differences, the dialects of mainland Japan and the Ryūkyūs are closely related structurally, and they are said to have diverged from a single "mother dialect" in a process thought to have occurred between the second and seventh centuries A.D.[31] Today Ryūkyū dialects have come to be the most divergent among all local dialects in Japan, a distance that has been compared to the difference between French and Italian.[32] And, like dialects in northern Honshū and southern Kyūshū today, the dialects of the Ryūkyū Islands, some of which are mutually unintelligible, are not understood by people in other parts of the country unless they make a special point of studying them. On the other hand, for more than a century, since the middle of the Meiji Period (1868–1912), "standard" Japanese has been promoted by the media in Okinawa and required—at times punitively—in local schools. With daily discourse among those under fifty now conducted almost entirely in "standard" Japanese, the dialects of Ryūkyū are gradually dying out despite recent efforts at preservation in the arts and education.

Nevertheless, many Okinawans on the mainland, especially those migrating after early childhood, have struggled, at least to some extent, with "standard" Japanese. Even younger migrants who have mastered it in Okinawa as their first language often retain a distinctively "Okinawan accent" and may be unfamiliar with certain local idioms, resulting in ridicule and a self-consciousness that hinders their ability to express themselves fully. An "Okinawan accent" includes a more fluctuating intonation (as opposed to a flatter mainland intonation) along with the occasional lengthening and shortening of vowels contrary to the mainland standard (*Amagasaki* pronounced as "Amagasaaki" and *Osaka* pronounced as "Osuka").[33] A woman in her late fifties who had come to Osaka in 1953 reported that one reason she had become active in the local Okinawa Prefectural Association was so that "I could feel comfortable about speaking with others in an Okinawa accent (Okinawa-*namari*)."[34] When speaking to each other in Osaka, first-generation migrants from Okinawa often mix words and phrases from Okinawa dialect with Kansai Japanese. In an ironic reversal, the recent "boom" of interest in Okinawan culture has given the dialect a "trendy" status in Japan today so that mainlanders are now picking up expressions like *chura* (pretty girl or handsome boy), *waji-waji* (angry), and *kūsu* (*awamori* aged at least five years), as well as learning the words for such Okinawan cuisine as *gōyaa* (bitter gourd), *mimi-gaa* (pickled pigs' ears), and *saada-andagi*i (spherical donut).

Among Okinawans interviewed for this study who recalled struggles with language on the mainland was a woman in her fifties who had moved to Osaka from Nago in the early 1960s. After finally receiving her "passport," she arrived in Osaka and was hired in an office where she had to answer the telephone and take messages. She often needed to ask callers to repeat information because she could not understand it the first time or worried that her reply was not being understood by the caller. At such times she would apologize, explaining that she had arrived only recently from Okinawa.[35]

A woman in her mid-forties who had come to greater Osaka in the mid-1970s told in a June 2001 interview of a coworker from Okinawa at a supermarket who was harassed relentlessly by his supervisors because he couldn't adjust immediately to local customs of repeatedly greeting and thanking customers with the correct phrases of Osaka dialect. And, in a case that became a cause célèbre in the Taishō Ward community, a nurse trainee from Okinawa was fired in 1977 by a local hospital for alleged "inefficiency" because, her supervisor said, she spoke with an Okinawa accent. Despite intimidation by *yakuza* thugs, her supporters lodged a formal protest with the hospital director and the young woman's dismissal was rescinded. She subsequently resigned her job, received compensation from the hospital as part of a settlement, and returned to her home on Iheya Island.[36]

Interviewed in April 2000, a forty-eight-year-old neighbor of mine who had migrated to Osaka in the early 1970s and remains single gave struggles with language as the main reason he never dated women born and raised on the mainland, though he had been approached a number of times over the years, including on two occasions during my residence there, by such women who said they found him attractive. And a woman from Nago in her early thirties who had migrated as recently as 1985 reported that "I had real trouble with language when I first arrived, especially because idioms and intonation were different. I felt depressed because I was often unable to express myself or understand completely what others said. Even today, I have occasional problems."[37]

It is important to note, however, that Okinawans are not the only people from local areas of Japan to struggle with language. As mentioned earlier, some dialects spoken on the mainland, especially in northern Honshū, southern Kyūshū, and other mountainous or rural areas, are also largely incomprehensible outside their localities of use. People from these areas have also encountered language problems when they left home for work in Osaka and elsewhere in Japan. Even today, people from other places on the mainland who live in Osaka are said, often disparagingly, to speak with "a Kyūshū accent" or "a Shikoku accent." Speaking Japanese with an accent or lacking immediate mastery of local greetings hardly justify the mistreatment Okinawan workers have suffered at the hands of mainland employers who have sometimes sought to exclude them altogether.

Aside from language, other differences exaggerated or invented have spawned prejudices and discrimination in their most virulent forms. Japanese who traveled or worked in Okinawa early in the Meiji Period initially conveyed stereotypes that were already widespread and deeply rooted in Japan by the turn of the twentieth century. Perhaps the most blatant (and subsequently most studied) manifestation of these attitudes was the notorious 1903 "human pavilion incident" at the Fifth World Trade and Industrial Exhibition, held that year in Osaka. The so-called scientific human pavilion (*gakujutsu jinrui-kan*) was not one of the official, government-sponsored exhibits but designed and constructed as a private business venture in consultation with Tsuboi Seigorō,[38] known as "the founder of Japanese anthropology." What has subsequently been described as a "freak show" was located just outside the main entrance to the exhibition grounds where it could easily attract some of the estimated 5,300,000 visitors to what was Japan's largest yet international exhibition. Scheduled to open on 10 March, it was to feature twenty-one highly exoticized "representatives" of "eight peoples": five Ainu, four Taiwanese, two Koreans, three Chinese, three (Asian) Indians, one Javanese, one Bulgarian, and two Okinawans, all dressed in their "native" (*genjū-min*) clothing and displayed in cubicles that were later compared to animal cages at circuses.[39] Protests from the Chinese Embassy and from Koreans in Osaka led to cancellation of exhibits from these countries (Korea was "annexed" by Japan as a colony seven years later in 1910), and protests from Okinawa, such as an angry editorial in the 7 April 1903 *Ryūkyū Shinpō* declaring, "We must never tolerate such humiliation," led to removal of the "Ryūkyū" exhibit in May after two months of display.

Poet Yamanokuchi Baku (1903–1963), born in Naha, who spent virtually all of his adult life on the mainland, poignantly evoked mainland stereotypes of Okinawans. In his short story "Mr. Saitō of Heaven Building,"[40] the narrator recalls the experience "of living in Tokyo as a man from 'Ryūkyū' for the past sixteen years. I've run into people wherever I go who . . . stare at me strangely—as if I'm not even human. And in those stares I can hear their questions. Is Ryūkyū in Okinawa Prefecture? Do the people there eat rice?"[41] More recently, during the U.S. military occupation when far fewer mainlanders than now made visits to Okinawa, which then required passports and entry permits, people from

Okinawa on the mainland were asked such questions as whether they lived in a jungle, wore grass skirts, or ate with knives and forks.[42]

Moving from Okinawa to Osaka in 1925 at the age of nine, Oyakawa Takayoshi recalls his first few weeks in school on the mainland: "Some of the other students would look at me derisively, calling me 'Ryūkyūan.' . . . I was shocked, having no idea why they made fun of me because I was from Okinawa. . . . It got so bad I couldn't stand it, and stopped going to school for about a week. My parents understood what was happening, though, and didn't scold me."[43]

Drafted into the Imperial Japanese Army in 1937, Oyakawa writes, "the first unit I was assigned to was all Okinawans because, it was explained in the company briefing, soldiers from each prefecture were trained in separate units. But the company commander made fun of us, saying it was really because 'Okinawa is thirty years behind the mainland.'"[44]

Okinawans have encountered prejudice on the mainland whether, like Oyakawa, they settled there or came temporarily for "work away from home." Kinjō Tsuru went to work in 1919 at the Fukushima Spinning Factory in Shikama, Hyōgo Prefecture.

> My contract was for three years, but I ran away after working for only one. . . . I just couldn't stand it anymore, always being made fun of because I was from Okinawa.
>
> I was taunted especially by the woman of about fifty who was in charge of our rooms in the dormitory. Whenever she talked to me, she would yell out scornfully, "Hey, you, Ryūkyū" or "Listen here, Ryūkyū."
>
> I'm no weakling, though, and yelled back at her. . . . "So what's wrong with being from Okinawa?" or "Didn't you also come out of a womb?" . . .
>
> We Okinawan women formed a group that stood up to her, and there were a lot of big arguments. I remember Ms. Yonamine especially. She was about forty and really told that room manager off. "We might be under contract here," she said, "but we haven't sold our lives to you." I'll never forget how good that made me feel. . . .
>
> If we were late getting back for the five-o'clock curfew, we'd be called into the office the next day for a bawling out of "you Ryūkyū girls." Only one person there, a man working in the kitchen, treated us well because, he said, we had come from so far away. We called him Dad.[45]

Besides barbs and insults, the problems people faced on the mainland simply because they came from Okinawa manifested themselves in material ways that directly affected their lives and livelihoods. Starting in the 1920s, some employers and landlords posted signs in front of factories, employment offices, and lodging houses announcing "Koreans and Okinawans prohibited" (Chōsen-jin Ryūkyū-jin o-kotowari). In explaining such exclusion, employers sometimes complained that Okinawans tended to change jobs if they were offered better conditions elsewhere, and landlords claimed that Okinawans tended to live with too many relatives in lodgings meant for fewer tenants. It is true that people who traveled long distances to "work away from home" often lived with relatives, at least temporarily until they got settled. But Okinawans were certainly not the only ones coming from remote rural areas of Japan to lodge with relatives in cities like Osaka, especially during the acute prewar housing shortage. Furthermore, large families that often included in-laws and grandparents were still the norm in Japan at this time. And, while it is true that Okinawans would change jobs for higher wages, especially since they had to send at least part of their earnings back to their families, they were surely not the only workers in Japan leaving one workplace for better conditions at another.[46]

In fact, Okinawans might have been motivated, at least in part, to change jobs because employers seem to have considered it smart business practice to offer them lower wages and inferior working conditions. Extensive statistical records from the 1920s and 1930s reveal a pattern of discrimination in employment contracts, housing, and even workplace safety measures. Tomiyama quotes published interviews of company officials who recalled that, seeking workers at low wages, "we made a special effort to recruit factory women from among Koreans, Okinawans, and Burakumin."[47] Employers at mainland cotton spinning factories in particular assumed that "'Ryūkyūans' could be paid lower wages, would put up with abusive working conditions, and did not require compensation for fires or accidents. This discriminatory attitude manifested itself in a number of management policies, such as housing Okinawans separately and giving them different meals from mainland workers."[48]

Statistics also show that women from Okinawa were disproportionately assigned the most dangerous and arduous jobs in spinning factories.[49] Arakaki Kaeko, who worked in 1927 at the Fukushima Spinning Factory, in Hyōgo Prefecture, describes one of several successful protests against discriminatory treatment of workers from Okinawa:

> They deducted 15 sen from our monthly wages for meals, but served only leftovers to the Okinawans. The mainland workers got warm rice, while ours was always cold. It was clearly discrimination.
>
> Finally, we couldn't stand it anymore, and six of us Okinawan factory women decided to take action in protest. "The hell with this," we told them.
>
> "You deduct all this money from our pay, and give us nothing but leftovers." Then, as soon as they served us the food, we hurled it back in their faces and knocked the serving trays down on the floor.
>
> This really shocked the company, and after that we got the same food as the mainland workers.

Also, among other insults, our supervisors were always telling us that "Okinawans are dirty because you eat garlic and pork, like Koreans who eat red pepper."

So one day all the Okinawans gathered for a protest in the factory yard. We sat down on the ground and refused to work or eat in what today would be called a hunger strike. Then, maybe after the company contacted him, the president of the prefectural association, Mr. Kinjō, arrived in a hurry to check out the situation. "We can't work any more in a place like this," we told him. "Please get us the money for our return fares."

At last the factory manager showed up and apologized to us, and since the supervisors had to go along with him, our treatment suddenly improved.[50]

As recalled in interviews, these experiences from the spinning mills indicate, first, that Okinawans did not necessarily accept prejudice and discrimination passively and, second, that mainland coworkers and supervisors were responsive at times to their protests. Blatant discrimination persisted well into the postwar years despite the fact that it was now illegal. Two people I interviewed for this study reported seeing signs in front of apartment buildings in Taishō Ward as late as 1973 announcing, "Okinawans and members of Soka Gakkai not admitted" (Okinawa to Soka Gakkai, nyūkyo o-kotowari), and a local community leader reported in 1987 that some landlords in the city were still refusing to rent to Okinawans.[51] A woman interviewed in April 2000 said she was told by landlords that Okinawans tend to live with too many relatives, the same excuse given in earlier decades, and that members of Soka Gakkai, a Buddhist sect that actively recruits and proselytizes, tend to hold crowded, noisy prayer meetings at night. Signs excluding Okinawans on taverns and restaurants in Tokyo and Yokohama have been observed as late as the mid-1980s and were given by one interviewee in March of 2001 as a major reason for moving from Yokohama to Osaka.

Protests by women mistreated in textile factories and by supporters of the nurse fired in 1977 for speaking with an "Okinawan accent" represent some of the many ways Okinawans on the mainland have responded to these injustices. Considering that the source of prejudice and discrimination is often psychological—presumptions of superiority by a majority over a minority—many Okinawans have sought to associate themselves in mainland minds with the majority by undertaking prodigious efforts to "assimilate." Throughout the prewar and wartime years, and during the U.S. military occupation, Okinawans have often identified themselves with this majority by vigorously emphasizing their Japanese nationality. Published reaction from Okinawa in 1903 to the "human pavilion" at the Fifth World Trade and Industrial Exhibition in Osaka did not criticize the inhumanity of such a display but its inclusion of Okinawans with Ainu and Taiwanese. A 7 April editorial in the *Ryūkyū Shinpō* declared that "it is a great insult for people of our prefecture to be singled out for inclusion with Taiwanese tribesmen and Ainu. . . . Our prefecture is making rapid strides today in education and in conforming with (*itchi suru*) other prefectures in all matters, such as styles of dress for men and women." The writers objected not to the exhibit in principle but to its inclusion of "Japanese citizens of Okinawa Prefecture," and complained that "lining up citizens of Okinawa Prefecture with Taiwanese barbarians (*seiban*) and Hokkaido Ainu is to view Okinawans . . . as one of these." With heavy overtones of scapegoating, the editorial described this "humiliation" as the result of "being portrayed as an 'inferior race' (*rettō shuzoku*)."

This attitude has been characterized as the victims of discrimination becoming its perpetrators, and it was also observed among women factory workers in Osaka from Okinawa and Korea who are said to have hurled the derogatory epithets "Korean whore" (*Chōsen pii*) and "Ryūkyū pig" (*Ryūkyū buta*) at each other during arguments.[52] Furthermore, Okinawans sometimes assign high and low "status" among themselves. A first-generation migrant from Miyako Island, interviewed in April 2001, reported that some migrants to Osaka from Okinawa Main Island (*hontō*) have tended to look down on people from the outer islands (*ritō*). Protesting "the evils of discrimination" with a more positive appeal to shared national identity, Okinawan novelist Kushi Fusako pointed out in 1932 that "[l]ike mainlanders, Okinawans serve in the military and perform their other duties as citizens."[53]

Okinawans who emphasize their Japanese nationality have often, but not always, deemphasized their Okinawan ethnicity. Their efforts to "assimilate" culturally with majority Japanese (*Yamatun-chu*) have included not only practicing mainland customs of dialect, diet, dress, interpersonal formalities, and religious observances, at least outside the home or neighborhood, but also rejecting traditional Okinawan religious practices and such art forms as classical dance (*ryūbu*) and folk songs (*min'yō* or *shima-uta*), or performing them in private, away from the eyes and ears of *Yamatun-chu*. Oyakawa Takayoshi recalled that, after moving to Osaka in 1925 as a child, he developed a strong aversion for things distinctively Okinawan.

> I hated Okinawan dance and *sanshin* [Okinawan *shamisen*] music. . . . and despised the word "Ryūkyū."[54] . . . In Chitose Precinct there was an open field where performers erected a lean-to stage, set up a booth for collecting admission, and put on Okinawan plays. Mainlanders would gather to watch in fascination, but they made fun of Okinawans in loud voices and I felt ashamed.
>
> Another thing I hated was when people riding the trains or walking down the street spoke in Okinawa dialect. I thought that in public they should always use standard Japanese or Osaka dialect.[55]

Perhaps the most conspicuous way Okinawans on the mainland have sought to deemphasize or conceal their ethnicity has been changing the pronunciations, and sometimes the Chinese characters, in their distinctive Okinawan names. This trend started in Okinawa itself after Japan's victory in the Sino-Japanese War of 1894–1895 when more and more Okinawans wanted to identify themselves with a nation rising in wealth, power, and status. Name changing is, of course, an expedient familiar to many Americans, like myself, whose names were changed from those of recognizably Irish, Italian, or Jewish origin to inconspicuous "Anglo" alternatives. My grandfather, who emigrated from Russia to the Lower East Side (then a Jewish ethnic community) of Manhattan in 1900, agreed somewhat reluctantly when his children changed the legal family name from the obviously Jewish Rabinowitz (meaning rabbi's son) to "Rabson" during a time of widespread anti-Semitism in the 1930s. (Despite the legal change, he never used "Rabson.") Okinawans changed their family names around the same time in mainland Japan so that Kinjō became "Kaneshiro," Higa became "Hiyoshi," and Kabira became "Kawahira"; and men also changed their personal names from, for example, Shin'yū to "Masahiro," Ryōmei to "Yoshiaki," and Shōtoku to " Masanori."[56] In Japan before 1945, changing one's name to characters or their readings more common on the mainland was a relatively easy procedure and even officially encouraged at a time when the Japanese government was also endeavoring to "assimilate" residents of colonies in Taiwan and Korea as "imperial subjects." In fact, such changes were made mandatory in Korea by the notorious "Name Order" of 1939 requiring Koreans to adopt Japanese names.

Yet even during the prewar years when pressures to assimilate were at their peak, some Okinawans on the mainland opposed tendencies to reject their traditional culture, vigorously asserting its value. In 1927, *sanshin* performer Fukuhara Chōki founded a record company in Osaka devoted to Okinawan folk music; and Kushi Fusako wrote five years later, "I do not believe that our customs that differ from those on the mainland should be despised or discarded. [They] have deep roots in our culture [and] natural environment."[57] Interviewed in 1996, Kinjō Kaoru, who immigrated to greater Osaka as a small child in 1954, asserted that "people being different doesn't make them better or worse. I think it's been a mistake for us to try to become Japanese to the extent of destroying our own ethnicity."[58] Published in 1996 during a nationwide "boom" of interest in Okinawa, such affirmations of the value of Okinawan ethnicity could well have had more resonance among readers in contemporary Japan than Kushi's affirmations would have had in 1932 when government policy and popular trends for assimilation were intensifying after the Manchurian Incident the previous year.

HOW THEY ORGANIZED: CHANGING FORMS AND AGENDAS OF THE OKINAWA PREFECTURAL ASSOCIATIONS

Along with the sometimes-painful efforts to "assimilate" with mainland Japanese, migrants from Okinawa have had notable successes organizing for their mutual benefit and advocacy as Okinawans. This organizing, crucial to survival for people dealing with poverty, cultural differences, and discrimination, began informally with the first "pioneer" migrants who provided material assistance and networks of contacts for housing, employment, and even marriage, to friends, relatives, and fellow villagers moving to the mainland. The first formal organization in greater Osaka was the Kansai Okinawa Prefectural Association (Kansai Okinawa Kenjin-kai), founded in 1924. The association's newspaper *Dōhō* (Comrades) explained:

> Our prefecture is under the same government as the rest of Japan, but, because we are in a remote location and have a different history and economic structure, we encounter unexpected misunderstandings and insults from the people of other prefectures. If we are to overcome the many obstacles imposed only on our prefecture and advance, socially and economically, to the status of people in other prefectures, we cannot possibly rely on the strength of disparate individuals. . . . It is through one organization that we must move into society.[59]

The authors of this article go on to support their call for organizing with comparisons that pose discrimination in global terms but are sure to raise eyebrows today:

> As individuals, the Jewish people have produced great numbers of outstanding individuals compared with other peoples of the world, and, it is fair to say, have been praised and honored since ancient times as being truly the highest among races in human society. Yet, the reality of their daily lives is precisely the opposite. In Europe and America today, Jews are subjected to outrageous insults. This is because their strength as individuals is dispersed and they have not organized as a group. . . . In the reverse phenomenon, the Burakumin have not produced outstanding individuals of world-renown, but, in less than four years time, they have built an organization and forged an ethnic solidarity that have made them the largest and most powerful social movement in Japan.[60]

Despite a founding statement that contained apparently unintended slights of Burakumin and factual errors (there were numerous Jewish organizations in Europe and America in the 1920s), the Kansai Okinawa Prefectural Association built on appeals for ethnic solidarity to establish numerous local branches and subdivisions. The association has subsequently gone through one dissolution and rebirth as well as several reorganizations. Meanwhile, separate associations have been formed in the other prefectures of greater Osaka, the largest and most active today being the Hyōgo Okinawa Prefectural Association, founded in 1946. People have also organized into groups from local areas of Okinawa, and today there are hometown friendship associations (*kyōyūkai*) of migrants and their descendants for Nakijin, Haneji, Haibaru, Kochinda, and other localities from which large numbers of people have moved to greater Osaka.

The roles of the prefectural associations have, of course, differed from each other and changed over time. In the early years, they provided essential support systems, including loans and temporary housing, to new arrivals and, unlike today, they led the movement for improved conditions among Okinawan factory workers. While they have continued to aid new arrivals from Okinawa, they function more as social and cultural facilitators today, presenting concerts and Okinawan products expositions, arranging and providing venues for classes in Okinawan performing and design arts, and organizing regular gatherings of community members. While they cooperate with each other in a wide range of ways, disagreements have arisen from time to time within and among prefectural associations over, for example, whether and how to become involved in political issues.

The first incarnation of the Kansai Okinawa Prefectural Association was led by activists committed to Marxist ideals and organized on the model of a political party. Established in 1924, it was deeply involved in labor union efforts to improve the wages and working conditions of factory workers in Osaka, many of whom came from Okinawa. However, within two years, this organization was virtually decimated by arrests of its leaders following brutal government suppression in 1926 of a strike by Okinawan workers that association leaders helped organize at the Tōyō Cotton Industries' Sangenya factory, located in the present Taishō Ward of Osaka. On 11 August, union members submitted a fifteen-point written petition to company officials seeking compliance with factory labor laws, freedom to leave the company grounds, an end to mandatory transfers of workers' earnings to their families in Okinawa, equalization of wages, and reforms of other discriminatory practices. The company responded by firing forty of the petitioning union members. A strike began in the early morning of 14 August with two hundred factory women from Okinawa leaving the dormitory. The police were quickly mobilized to drag them forcibly back to the factory grounds where many were beaten, kicked, and thrown in the mud by company supervisors. Now the police arrested more than fifty labor activists in the Kansai Okinawa Prefectural Association on charges of inciting a riot, and jailed many of them. Two years later the labor organizing activities of the association were effectively shut down by the massive police roundups of "leftists" and others viewed as dissidents on 25 March and 16 April 1928, and continuing government suppression resulted in an end to all the association's activities in the late 1920s.[61]

This experience has loomed large in the memories of older Okinawans in Osaka, and it was cited by Okinawan sociologist Shingaki Masami as one reason that the current leadership of the Osaka League of Okinawa Prefectural Associations (Osaka Okinawa Kenjin Rengō-kai), established in 1946, a successor organization to the Kansai Prefectural Association, has been reluctant to pursue an active agenda on social and political issues today.[62] When the Kansai Okinawa Prefectural Association was reestablished in 1931, the labor activists were gone and its new leadership was composed of professionals with university degrees who turned away from labor activism.[63] In place of the former political party structure, the leaders recentered the organization on the hometown friendship associations of people from local areas of Okinawa. Though debate resumed over the relative merits of assimilating or living as Okinawans, leaders called for Okinawans to speak "standard Japanese," associate more with people from other prefectures, minimize the practice of Okinawan customs, and abandon Okinawan religious practices in favor of mainland Shintō. This was, of course, a highly repressive period of growing militarism in Japan when the government was compelling the worship of state Shintō and banning indigenous religious practices as part of the "policy to make imperial subjects" (*kōminka seisaku*) in Okinawa, as well as in Japan's colonies and territories.

Since World War II, the leaders of prefectural associations have continued to disagree on how to respond to pressures for assimilation and whether or how to advocate on political issues. However, as in Okinawa itself, overwhelming support developed among members for reversion, particularly after U.S. seizures of private land for military bases brought many involuntary "migrants" to greater Osaka. Okinawans there felt increasingly cut off from their homeland after what they called the "disappearance of Okinawa Prefecture" in 1945 and the Japanese government's agreement to a Peace Treaty that "severed Okinawa from Japan" in 1952.[64] Overcoming initial reluctance among leaders of the Osaka League, prefectural associations in greater Osaka and elsewhere on the mainland went on to play a major role in the reversion movement. They organized large demonstrations in 1956 that featured speakers from Okinawa as part of the "land struggle" (*tochi tōsō*) protesting U.S. seizures of land for military bases in Okinawa and occupation rule generally. Subsequent protests calling for reversion drew many participants, including a demonstration by more than ten thousand in Osaka

City on 1 October 1966 during which a petition was presented to visiting Prime Minister Satō Eisaku.

Large numbers of mainland Japanese joined the struggle for reversion, though Okinawans sometimes complained about ulterior motives among those on the right who seemed interested mostly in recovering territory lost in war and those on the left who seemed intent on using "the Okinawa problem" as a political football to attack the conservative government.[65] Nevertheless, achieving reversion was crucial materially and psychologically for the entire Okinawan diaspora, removing the stigma of Okinawans as "an occupied people" and freeing the flow of communication, information, and travel. Japanese citizens no longer needed "passports" to enter Okinawa, and published materials from the mainland were no longer screened by military censors. However, as in Okinawa itself, the terms of the reversion agreement provoked anger and a sense of betrayal because U.S. bases remained virtually intact despite the Japanese government's constantly repeated promises to reduce the military presence in Okinawa to "mainland levels" (*hondo-nami*). As a result, the reversion agreement (*henkan-kyōtei*) came to be known sarcastically among Okinawans as the "discriminatory agreement" (*henken kyōtei*).

While the Hyōgo Okinawa Prefectural Association has continued to advocate for removal of the bases, including a petition drive in 2001, the Osaka League has been comparatively quiet on the issue. Residents of the community in Taishō Ward explained to me that one reason is that, since reversion, some community residents, including prominent league members, have been receiving substantially increased "rental" payments from the Japanese government for land seized from them by the U.S. government in the 1950s. In an effort to "stabilize" land use for bases after reversion, the Japanese Defense Facilities Agency immediately increased these payments to "military landowners" (*gun-jinushi*) by as much as six times the prereversion rates paid by the U.S. government.[66] During 2000 and 2001, I met four individuals receiving such payments, including one interviewee in Taishō Ward who showed me her contract from the Defense Facilities Agency that specified annual payments of twelve million yen, or about $100,000 in 2001. Her land in Oroku, seized originally to build barracks for U.S. Naha Air Base, is now a dependents' housing area for Japan's Air Self-Defense Forces, which took over the base after reversion.

The Japanese government's "hush money" strategy has not always worked, however, either in Okinawa, where "antiwar landowners" (*hansen jinushi*) have formed an active protest organization, or on the mainland. Another interviewee in Taishō Ward told me in February of 2000 that his family in Okinawa, whose land was confiscated in the 1950s to expand Kadena Air Base, contributes these payments to support the antibase movement while he personally devotes much of his time to organizing protests and speaking at rallies in greater Osaka. Meanwhile, in another example of diverse opinions on this issue, not all Okinawan residents of Hyōgo Prefecture agree with that association's opposition to military bases. One interviewee from the Hyōgo Okinawan community in Takarazuka City told me in April of 2001 that her father, who also receives "rent" for land seized in the 1950s, gets angry whenever he reads about another protest demonstration, insisting that, if the bases are to be removed, landowners should receive compensation for lost income.

Partly because of such diversity of views and circumstances among members, Osaka League leaders have sometimes been hesitant to "lead" on other issues as well, taking up the banner only after a clear membership consensus develops. Officials explain that their organization, descended from the second, less activist incarnation of the Kansai Okinawa Prefectural Association, has a more conservative membership and is necessarily less "political" than the Hyōgo association, founded in 1946 during a time of vigorous activism on issues such as reversion and military bases in Okinawa. League leaders in Osaka are still haunted by memories of the brutal government suppression during and after the 1926 strike at the Tōyō Cotton Industries' Sangenya factory, and they see their most pressing issue as maintaining their organization of an estimated seven thousand members, of whom an increasing proportion are elderly, first-generation migrants.[67] This trend is borne out by results from my survey that showed a 20 percent higher rate of prefectural association membership among respondents in their sixties and seventies (53.6 percent and 51.5 percent respectively) as compared with respondents in their forties and fifties (35.7 percent and 30.4 percent respectively).

Some league officials believe that elderly members would prefer not to be reminded of hardships they have suffered simply for being Okinawan or to attract too much attention. In the years before Okinawan culture became trendy in the early 1990s, one official discouraged a group of younger community residents in the mid-1970s from organizing performances of *eisa* dances and presenting this annual Okinawan festival in the neighborhood because he feared that for mainlanders to see these traditional dances in colorful costumes would "embarrass" the Okinawan community. Another league official in his late sixties has refused to acknowledge in interviews that there has been discrimination against Okinawans in Osaka. Such denials contradict league publications that fully document it[68] and interviews by me and others of league members who described discrimination they have personally encountered.[69]

Nowadays, amid the nationwide "Okinawa boom," all the prefectural associations in greater Osaka organize events to which the public is eagerly welcomed, where *eisa-odori* and other traditional dances and music are performed. The Osaka League now actively supports and promotes Okinawan culture in many ways, sponsoring concerts, offering space for training studios in the performing arts, and inviting speakers in various fields from Okinawa to lecture in the Osaka area. The most important functions of this organization today include providing space and organizational support for such social occasions as banquets to celebrate the New Year, honor elderly members, and commemorate such special occasions as the anniversary of the league's founding, events at which Okinawan music and dance are almost always performed. The Osaka League also organizes the annual September "sports festival" in which local Okinawa prefectural associations in greater Osaka and nearby prefectures compete in relay races and other events. In addition, the League sells tickets and rents buses for the semiannual pilgrimages to root for Okinawa's representative team in the National High School Baseball Tournament held at Kōshien Stadium in Nishinomiya, an Osaka suburb, where officials from the Osaka League and Hyōgo Association also distribute tickets, arrange bus transportation, help rooters find seats, and clean up discarded trash at the game's conclusion.

Over the years, the prefectural associations have not only provided for survival-support, advocated vigorously in the 1920s for labor reform and in the 1950s and 1960s for reversion, but have also contributed to postwar infrastructural and economic improvements in the community. Prefectural associations in greater Osaka were crucial for the community during the chaotic period immediately after World War II. They aided in the resettlement both of Okinawa residents who had evacuated to rural areas on the mainland but whose status changed to "refugees" after their prefecture was devastated by the battle and of Okinawan soldiers and civilians who chose to be repatriated to greater Osaka from Taiwan, Micronesia, the Philippines, and other areas formerly part of the Japanese empire because many of them had nothing left to go back to in Okinawa. Prefectural associations continue to assist new arrivals from Okinawa to settle in greater Osaka. The Osaka liaison office of the Okinawa Prefectural Government also helps people from Okinawa find jobs in greater Osaka, and to secure housing. In the years following reversion, this office recruited migrants to work mostly in factories, while in today's economy they are more likely to work as nurse trainees, cooks, or waitresses. Approximately 260 young people each year find jobs in greater Osaka through this office. Although some of these people settle in the area, often becoming managers of stores, restaurants, or small factories, virtually none choose to live in Okinawan communities, preferring, like many other Okinawans coming to the mainland today, to reside near the places where they work or study.[70] In contrast, many who migrated in the early 1970s before reversion in "group hirings" (*shūdan-shūshoku*) organized by commercial recruiters settled in Taishō Ward after their contract periods ended.

WHERE THINGS STAND: LINGERING PREJUDICE, A NEW PRIDE IN "ROOTS," AND MIXED BLESSINGS OF THE "OKINAWA BOOM"

From what were often troubled beginnings, life for most residents of the Okinawan communities in greater Osaka has improved over the years as many migrants saved their factory wages, started businesses, bought property, and sent their children to colleges or professional schools. And, while their economic resources have not reached the average level of Japanese "salarymen" in more upscale residential areas, many have enjoyed relative prosperity in recent years.[71] Mainlanders living in the more affluent areas of greater Osaka refer to these communities as "downtown" (*shita-machi*) or, in the case of Taishō Ward in southwestern Osaka, somewhat disparagingly as "the deep south." With the currently heightened interest in Okinawa throughout Japan, many mainland visitors have been attracted to the community where they shop in stores that sell Okinawan products, eat in restaurants serving Okinawan cuisine where Okinawan music is often performed, and learn to perform Okinawan dance and music themselves at the culture centers and studios. This influx has provided relief for some in the community from the economic doldrums that have been felt in Japan as a whole since the early 1990s.

In the year and a half between June 1999 and December 2000, a new store selling Okinawan products and four new restaurants, one with nightly performances of music and dance, opened in a four-block area near the Taishō train station. There were already three Okinawan restaurants, one offering live performances, making a current total of seven in this area which is still three miles from the Okinawan neighborhoods in Kobayashi, Hirao, and Okajima where such businesses can be found in virtually every block. Community residents often make fun of the *Yamatun-chu* tourists and sometimes express regret for what they see as growing dilution (or "mainlandization") of Okinawan arts and culture. But most proprietors eagerly welcome the large crowds of visitors who regularly pack local restaurants offering Okinawan cuisine and live music, especially on Saturday nights when even the local regulars (*jōren*) are turned away unless they have reservations.

Many Okinawans in greater Osaka today have themselves developed greater interest and pride in their "roots" (*rūtsu*), using the English word in describing this trend.[72] Today, second- and third-generation Okinawans, as well as mainlanders, are studying the traditional performing arts, design arts, and cuisine, along with learning some Okinawa dialect.

Their motivations are many and varied. Interviewees cited the influence of parents and grandparents, strong impressions from a visit to Okinawa, or the effects of a performance they had attended. A professional writer in her late thirties said in November 2000 that she had never felt pride in her family's origins, largely because she associated being Okinawan with being poor, until Shō High School became the first team from Okinawa to win the National High School Baseball Tournament in April 1999. She felt proud, she said, because Okinawans had "finally beaten the Yamatun-chu at something." She is now writing her first novel, which is based largely on her father's experience as a migrant from Okinawa living in Osaka. On the other hand, some second- and third-generation Okinawans in greater Osaka still seek to minimize their connections with Okinawa, emphasizing, for example, that "I'm Osakan, though my father came from there."[73]

Today, amid the "Okinawa boom" and a popular trend for exploring one's ethnic "roots," it is much too easy to look back with a smirk at people who never spoke their local dialect or ate Okinawan foods in public, only practiced *sanshin* secretly in closets, and changed their names. Yet it must be remembered that, during the years of malicious prejudice and blatant discrimination, for Okinawans living and working on the mainland, the issue was often physical and psychological survival. Though discrimination is now illegal, it has by no means disappeared (see the previously cited interviews). Today prejudices based on stereotypes persist on the mainland despite—and to some extent because of—the recent fascination in Japan with an exoticized and commercialized "Okinawa" that has made recordings of Okinawan pop music into best-sellers and singers from Okinawa into superstars. A woman in her mid-sixties who had migrated to greater Osaka in 1962 commented on her questionnaire that "I was shocked when I first came at how many people were ignorant about Okinawa, mostly because it wasn't mentioned in school curriculums. But nowadays everyone's trying to ride the wave of interest in it."[74] Since reversion, community residents are no longer asked whether people in Okinawa speak English at home or use knives and forks for daily meals, but they are still subjected to such double-edged praise of Okinawans as "so relaxed and carefree" (implying a certain indolence and lack of responsibility) or "so casual and easy-going" (implying a lack of courtesy and diligence). Koreans and Chinese are also subjected to such "praise" in Japan for being "clever" (implying wily or tricky). The president of a loan agency in Taishō Ward told me he never lends money to Okinawans because "they don't pay it back." And an executive of a manufacturing company in Osaka told me his firm decided not to locate a factory in Okinawa because "people there can't do quality work."

In official ways, too, there are still problems, as when the All-Japan High School Baseball Federation banned the wearing of *eisa* robes by second-generation Okinawan rooters from Amagasaki for the semiannual national baseball tournament at Kōshien Stadium in Nishinomiya, near Osaka. The federation explained that its regulations forbid the wearing of "strange" (*kii*) garments, though the Okinawan rooters pointed out that fans from Kōchi and Hiroshima Prefectures were allowed to wear their brightly colored local costumes. Fans have defied this ban recently by carrying their packaged *eisa* robes in through the stadium entrances, then changing clothes in the rest rooms. In recent years, teams from Okinawa have placed high in the tournament, regularly reaching the finals or semifinals. Then in the spring of 1999, when Okinawa Shō High School became the first team from Okinawa in the tournament's fifty-five-year history to win the championship, residents of Okinawan communities on the mainland, which always send busloads of rooters to their games, celebrated joyously. Savoring this victory of *Uchinaan-chu* over *Yamatun-chu*, Okinawans commented that "the postwar period is finally over for us." This is a mocking reference to the phrase used by Prime Minister Satō Eisaku who negotiated the Okinawa reversion agreement with U.S. president Richard Nixon in 1969, viewed by Okinawans as yet another mainland betrayal for failing to include promised reductions in the U.S. military presence.

In September 1995, the movement among community activists opposing American military bases in Okinawa shifted into high gear after the September 1995 rape of a twelve-year-old elementary school girl in Kin by two U.S. marines and one sailor.[75] Protest marches were organized in Osaka to coincide with the massive demonstration of an estimated eighty-five thousand in Ginowan City, Okinawa. Subsequent marches and rallies drew large numbers of participants in Osaka and Kyoto. In addition, regular information meetings (*gakushū-kai*) have been held in public auditoriums and university lecture halls with activists and scholars from Okinawa as featured speakers. Former Okinawa governor Ōta Masahide has given a number of well-attended lectures recently in Osaka auditoriums. In greater Osaka and elsewhere on the mainland, singers from Okinawa perform antiwar and antibase protest songs at regular concerts. Yet, while members of the greater Osaka Okinawan community often take the lead in organizing these events, the proportion of community residents who participate in political activism is comparatively small. Among respondents to survey questionnaires, only 6.8 percent of migrants and 4.5 of descendants indicated such participation. Though many Okinawans in greater Osaka joined protests against the military bases following the 1995 rape, most of the time one tends to notice the same core of activists from the community turning out for events, which usually draw larger numbers of mainlanders, and for organizational meetings.

The "Okinawa boom" has also made residents aware of the need to convey full and accurate information about the communities to outsiders, especially to the media which is now reporting on them frequently. To keep up with growing demands, the Kansai Okinawa Bunko (Culture Center) has assumed what has become an increasingly heavy burden, offering written materials, recordings, videotapes, lectures, and guided tours to the public at very low cost and with an extremely small, largely volunteer, staff. Groups of students and teachers from public and private schools in greater Osaka and nearby prefectures come regularly to the Bunko for "field work" seminars that include lectures and guided tours as well as performances of Okinawan music. Demands on the Bunko for information and interviews reached a fever pitch during the months leading up to the 2000 G-8 Summit Conference held in Okinawa. Scholars from the Taishō Ward community and from Okinawa have subsequently met there regularly to prepare fuller information and check existing materials for accuracy.

Though the influx of tourists and consumers has provided income for some, the greater Osaka communities, where small and medium industries depend heavily on subcontracts from larger companies, have been hit hard by economic doldrums afflicting Japan as a whole in the 1990s and 2000s. Residents have suffered in the continuing series of layoffs, euphemistically called "restructuring" (*risutora*), at the medium-size metalworking factories, and orders for extracted metal and molded metal parts have dwindled at the smaller workshops. Local merchants often complain that business has fallen off sharply since the "bubble burst" on Japan's economy in 1990–1991, and the incomes of construction workers have dropped sharply with local labor agencies offering fewer jobs. A growing number of homeless wander Osaka streets now, sleeping on sidewalks or in parks, as elsewhere in Japan's cities. And, as elsewhere, the economy is the issue community residents say is of the greatest concern to them.

Clearly, the "Okinawa boom" has brought mixed blessings to Okinawan communities in greater Osaka as well as to Okinawa itself. Nowadays visitors from the mainland sometimes comprise the majority in audiences at live performances there of Okinawan music and a high proportion of the participants in such antibase demonstrations as the recent "human chains" around Kadena Air Base. Okinawans themselves are divided over whether to welcome mainlanders to partake in the islands' culture and politics or to discourage their participation. At least one *eisa* performance group in Osaka bars mainlanders because, as the director explains, *eisa* has special religious significance for Okinawans. (This group does accept people with only partial Okinawan ancestry.) Okinawans inside and outside the prefecture are caught between a desire, on the one hand, to convey accurate information about their culture and political oppression to mainlanders and non-Japanese, and frustration, on the other, when these efforts result in a superficial fascination with "Okinawa" that encourages dilettantism, stereotyping, and commercial exploitation.

Interviewed in April 2000, a teacher at a local junior college in his early forties complained that, for too many mainlanders, "Okinawa" has become a "tasty morsel" to consume in the media and on forays to Okinawa or the greater Osaka community and that, for some academics, it has become a "hot topic" they can use to publish research which is too often based on one-dimensional portrayals of Okinawans and the issues confronting them. Perhaps the most important message conveyed in the interviews and questionnaires collected for this study is that Okinawans in greater Osaka have responded in a wide variety of ways to these challenges, and that their responses have frequently changed over time to adjust to new conditions. What is often presented as a dichotomy of "assimilation versus cultural preservation" is, more often today, a continuing series of choices made in daily life that depend on individual preferences rather than on decisions to take one side or the other. An eighteen-year-old musician interviewed in February 2001 explained that, although both her parents were from Okinawa, she had chosen to make her career performing mainland folk music from northeastern Japan (*tsugaru-jamisen*) because she was better able to express what she felt in its melodies and rhythms. At the same time, she preferred Okinawan food that her mother cooked at home.

Nowhere is diversity more evident than in the ways Okinawans in greater Osaka remember or conceptualize a "homeland" they might have left many years ago or where they never lived at all. Among interviewees, several women who came originally to work in textile factories before World War II said they had decided to remain in greater Osaka after their contract periods ended because Okinawa did not offer comparable economic prospects for them, their spouses, or their children. Other migrants from both the prewar and postwar period cited limited social and cultural horizons in the rural Okinawan villages where they grew up as reasons for remaining on the mainland. Descendants who had visited Okinawa only during the U.S. occupation period described a place of natural beauty, but with widespread poverty and an oppressive atmosphere under foreign military occupation. Other descendants associated Okinawa with poverty on the mainland as well as with discrimination their parents experienced there, and tried to minimize their connections with it. The magazine journalist quoted earlier, who came to appreciate her heritage after Shō High School won the national baseball tournament in 1999, had previously associated Okinawa with her family's poverty, employment discrimination her father had encountered, and teasing she had suffered in school for her parents' origins. On the other hand, many Okinawans in greater Osaka, migrants and descendants alike, have visited their "homeland" regularly and describe highly positive memories, associating Okinawa with a congenial natural and cultural environment, as well as a leisurely and healthy lifestyle, where people suffer less stress and live longer. A number of individuals over sixty expressed a desire to relocate to Okinawa when circumstances in their lives, such as family obligations, would permit. In the case of one couple in their seventies, the husband had in fact returned in 1999 to enjoy his retirement years living in the family's home on the seashore in a quiet village north of Nago while his wife remained to live with their son's family in Taishō Ward, where she preferred the urban lifestyle. Such diverse responses, shared by people in many places with memories of an ancestral "homeland," should remind us that, far from being static and monolithic, attitudes and choices vary widely among individuals in diaspora communities.

NOTES

1. "Ryukyu" never caught on as a place name during the U.S. occupation, either in Okinawa or on the mainland. This was partly because the word *Ryūkyū* evoked memories of derogatory references by mainland Japanese who identified people from Okinawa Prefecture with what had recently been a "foreign" kingdom. This implied that Okinawans were not fully Japanese and, thus, "inferior" to mainlanders.

In addition, Okinawans at home and on the mainland easily saw through the U.S. military's insistence on calling Okinawa "The Ryukyu Islands" and the people there "Ryukyuans" as part of a heavy-handed effort to separate them from Japan. The failed American attempt to re- "Ryukyuanize" Okinawans was undertaken in hopes of suppressing the reversion movement, which had gained support steadily since the early 1950s.

2. In a sense, I was one of those "occupiers," though my job as a U.S. Army draftee in the maintenance platoon at an ammunition depot in Henoko from July 1967 to June 1968 had nothing to do with administering the occupation.

3. Kaneshiro Munekazu, "Esunikku gurupu to shite no 'Okinawa-jin'" (Okinawans as an Ethnic Group), *Ningen Kagaku* 37 (1992): 29–57.

4. Fukuchi Hiroaki, ed., *Okinawa jokō aishi* (The Tragic History of Okinawa's Women Factory Workers) (Haibaru, Okinawa: Naha Shuppan-sha, 1985), 18, 37.

5. Higa Michiko, "Jokō" (Women Factory Workers), *Yōju* (Banyan) (April 1996): 3.

6. Meiō University historian Higa Michiko, interview, November 2000.

7. *Yūhi* (Launching Forth), a volume of essays and photographs commemorating the fortieth anniversary of the founding of the Osaka League of Okinawa Prefectural Associations (Osaka: Osaka Okinawa Kenjin Rengo-kai, 1987), 40, 47; *Yūhi*

(Launching Forth), a volume of essays and photographs commemorating the fiftieth anniversary of the founding of the Osaka League of Okinawa Prefectural Associations (Osaka: Osaka Okinawa Kenjin Rengo-kai, 1997), 50, 62.

8. Kaneshiro, "Esunikku gurupu to shite no 'Okinawa-jin,'" 1992.

9. *Yūhi,* 50, 61.

10. Interviews in Okinawa, June 2000. Officials at the Okinawa Prefectural Association of Hyōgo complained to me in June 2001 that commemorative publications of recent "Uchinan-chu Taikai," highly publicized gatherings of people from the Okinawa diaspora held periodically in Okinawa, devote many pages of text and color photographs to participants from Hawaii and North and South America, but they include barely two paragraphs on a back page for Okinawans in greater Osaka.

11. *Okinawa-ken heiwa kinen shiryō-kan: Sōgō annai* (Okinawa Prefectural Peace Memorial Museum Guidebook) (Okinawa: Itoman, 2001), 27.

12. Ryūkyū Shinpō-sha, ed., *Okinawa: Nijū seiki no kōbō* (Okinawa in the Twentieth Century) (Naha: Ryūkyū Shinpō-sha, 2000), 130–31.

13. *Okinawa-ken Heiwa Shiryō-kan,* 31.

14. *Shima o deta tami no sensō taiken-shū* (Collected War Experiences of People Who Left the Islands) (Kobe: Okinawa Kenjin-kai Hyōgo-ken Honbu, 1995), 276–79.

15. Ōta Jun'ichi, *Osaka no Uchinaan-chu* (The Okinawans of Osaka) (Osaka: Burein Sentaa, 1996), 88–89; more of this interview is translated in Chalmers Johnson, ed., *Okinawa: Cold War Island* (Cardiff, Calif.: Japan Policy Research Institute, 2000), 89.

16. Questionnaire, April 2001.

17. This currently estimated figure is cited in such official publications of the Okinawa Prefectural Government as "Heiwa no ishiji" (Cornerstone of Peace), 1995, and "Okinawa heiwa shiryō-kan sōgō annai" (Okinawa Peace Museum Guidebook), 2001.

18. Kaneshiro, "Esunikku gurupu to shite no 'Okinawa-jin,'" 1992.

19. They are concentrated mostly in its Hirao, Kobayashi, Kitamura, Kita Okajima, and Minami Okajima precincts, and they comprise about one-fourth of the ward's total population officially listed at 75,043 for 2000 (Taishō Ward Office, General Affairs Section, 2001). For the other communities in greater Osaka, unofficial and unpublished estimates are that 7,500 migrants and their descendants live in Osaka's Nishinari Ward, next to Taishō Ward, and approximately 10,000 live in or around the Tonouchi section of Amagasaki City, just across the Kanzaki River from Osaka City in Hyōgo Prefecture, where another 1,500 are estimated to live in the Takamatsu section of Takarazuka City and 900 in Itami City.

20. Mizuuchi Toshio, *Ōsaka Okinawa Ajia: Ōsaka Shiritsu Daigaku Zengaku Kyōtsu Kyōiku Sōgō Kyōiku Kamoku: Ajia no Chiiki to Bunka Enshū* (Osaka: Osakai Shiritsu Daigku Kyomubu, 1999), 46–47.

21. Ōta, *Osaka no Uchinaan-chu,* 89–90.

22. "Hochi sareru Okinawa suramu" (Okinawa Slum Long Neglected), *Asahi Shinbun,* 15 July 1968, 7.

23. Mizuuchi, *Osaka Okinawa Ajia,* 47–48.

24. Interviews for this study conducted in September 1999.

25. Ōta, *Osaka no Uchinaan-chu,* 91.
26. Ōta, *Osaka no Uchinaan-chu,* 119.
27. Mizuuchi, "Ōsaka-shi Taishō-ku ni okeru Okinawa shusshin-sha shūjū chiku no 'suramu' kuriaransu" ("Slum" Clearance in an Okinawan Residential Section of Taishō Ward, Ōsaka City), Kūkan, Shakai, *Chiri Shisō* 5 (2000): 37–61.
28. Mizuuchi, *Ōsaka Okinawa Ajia,* 52.
29. Ōta, *Osaka no Uchinaan-chu,* 98.
30. Arasaki Moriteru, *Okinawa no sugao* (The True Face of Okinawa) (Tokyo: Tekuno, 2000), 44.
31. Hokama Shuzen, *Okinawa no rekishi to bunka* (Okinawan History and Culture) (Tokyo: Chūkō Shinsho, 1989), 94–99.
32. Tomiyama Ichirō, *Kindai Nihon shakai to "Okinawa-jin"* (Modern Japanese Society and "Okinawans") (Tokyo: Nihon Keizai Hyōron-sha, 1990), 1.
33. Some Okinawans over fifty articulate the consonant *s* as "sh" in words like *sensei* (teacher), pronounced *"shenshei,"* or *sensō* (war), pronounced *shenshō.* Some of them also articulate the vowel sounds "o" and "e" as "u" and "i," respectively, in words like *"teiki"* (commuter pass), pronounced *"tiiki,"* and *"hako"* (box), pronounced *"haku."*
34. Written comment on questionnaire, April 2001.
35. Interview, April 2000.
36. Uda Shigeki, *Uwa-nu ukami-sama: Tokeshi Kōtoku no han-sei* (The Divine Pig: The Life of Tokeshi Kōtoku) (Nara: Uda Shuppan Kikaku, 1999), 173–96.
37. Written comment on questionnaire, December 2000.
38. Shinjō Eitoku, "Kansai ni okeru Uchinaanchu no ayumi" (The History of Okinawans in Kansai), *Jichi Okinawa* 353 (July 1996): 18.
39. Chinen Seishin's acutely satirical stage play "Jinruikan" (Human Pavilion, 1976) features a uniformed "trainer" brandishing a whip who barks commands at "male" and "female" specimens.
40. Yamanokuchi Baku, "Mr. Saitō of Heaven Building" (Tengoku-biru no Saitō-san) (originally published in 1938), in *Southern Exposure: Modern Japanese Literature from Okinawa,* ed. and trans. Rie Takaki in Michael Molasky and Steve Rabson (Honolulu: University of Hawaii Press, 2000).
41. Molasky and Rabson, *Southern Exposure,* 89.
42. Interviews, June and August 2000.
43. Oyakawa Takayoshi, *Ashiato: Oyakawa Takayoshi no kaisōroku* (Footprints: Recollections of Oyakawa Takayoshi) (Osaka: Matsuei Insatsu, 1995), 21–22.
44. Oyakawa, *Ashiato,* 26.
45. Fukuchi, *Okinawa jokō aishi,* 78–79.
46. Nakama Keiko, "1920, 1930 nendai ni okeru zai-Han Okinawa-jin no seikatsu ishiki" (Lifestyles among Okinawan Residents of Osaka in the 1920s and 1930s), *Osaka Jinken Hakubutsu-kan Kiyo* (Bulletin of the Osaka Human Rights Museum) 3 (1999): 61–74.
47. Tomiyama, *Kindai Nihon,* 130.
48. Tomiyama, *Kindai Nihon,* 111.
49. Higa Michiko, "Aware na ringu" (That Wretched Ring-Twisting), in *Karajishi* (Naha: Okinawa Taimusu-sha, 1989), 6.
50. Fukuchi, *Okinawa jokō aishi,* 120.

51. Kinjō Kaoru (20 March 1987), "Osaka to Okinawa" (Osaka and Okinawa), a month-long series of interviews in *Mainichi Shinbun*, from 9 March to 9 April 1987.

52. Ryūkyū, *Okinawa: Nijū seiki no kōbō*, 52, 56.

53. Molasky and Rabson, *Southern Exposure*, 82.

54. Though references to the former Ryūkyū Kingdom and its cultural legacy were usually free of negative connotations, calling someone "Ryūkyū" or "Ryūkyū-jin" was more problematic. As in examples quoted earlier, mainlanders used the term *Ryūkyū* or *Ryūkyū-jin* derisively when scolding factory workers returning late for curfew or when announcing on signs in front of factories and rooming houses "*Chōsen-jin, Ryūkyū-jin o-kotawari*" (Koreans and Ryūkyūans prohibited). Women from Okinawa who were displayed like circus animals in the notorious "Human Pavilion" at a 1903 international exposition in Osaka were called "Ryūkyū-jin." And Hirotsu Kazuo's 1926 novel, which he titled "*Samayoeru Ryūkyū-jin*" (The Vagabond Ryūkyūan), was widely criticized by Okinawans on the mainland for a protagonist caricatured through negative Okinawan stereotypes. Its author subsequently made a public apology and canceled scheduled reprintings.

Recently, however, the status of the word *Ryūkyū* seems to have improved among Okinawans and mainlanders alike, though some connotations remain problematic. Okinawans at home and in the diaspora express varying degrees of pride and nostalgia from historical memories of the formerly independent Ryūkyū Kingdom, in part because hopes have been unrealized for a significant reduction of the military presence and healthy economic development in Okinawa after reversion. Furthermore, there is currently a widespread fascination among mainlanders with cultural manifestations of an often exoticized "Ryūkyū," which has been exploited commercially. NHK television's 1993 serial historical drama, criticized by some Okinawans for stereotyped characterizations, was entitled, like the book it was based on, *Ryūkyū no kaze* (The Winds of Ryūkyū). The word *Ryūkyū* now occurs frequently in the titles for recordings of widely popular Okinawan folk and folk-rock music, such as the 1995 album *Ryukyu Magic* (Air-4001, Tokyo). Okinawans in the prefecture and on the mainland offer lessons in *Ryūkyū buy ō* (classical dance), *Ryūkyū ryōri* (cuisine), and *Ryūkyū min'yō* (folk music) to a growing clientele.

55. Oyakawa, *Ashiato*, 2–22.

56. Johnson, *Okinawa: Cold War*, 77.

57. Molasky and Rabson, *Southern Exposure*, 82.

58. Quoted in Ōta, *Osaka no Uchinaan-chu*, 97–98.

59. Quoted in Nakama, "1920, 1930 nendai," 99.

60. Quoted in Nakama, "1920, 1930 nendai," 99.

61. Tomiyama, *Kindai Nihon*, 164.

62. Interviewed in September 1999.

63. Miyawaki Yukio, "Kansai ni okeru Okinawa shusshin-sha dōkyō sōshiki no seiritsu to tenkai" (The Establishment and Development of Organizations of Okinawans in Kansai), *Ningen Kagaku Ronshū* 28 (1997): 91; Oyakawa, *Ashiato*, 293.

64. *Koko ni yōju ari* (The Banyan Tree Here), a volume of essays and photographs commemorating the thirty-fifth anniversary of the founding of the Hyōgo Okinawa Prefectural Association (Kobe: Okinawa Kenjin-kai Hyōgo honbu, 1982), 145–216.

65. *Koko ni yōju ari,* 94–95; Steve Rabson, *Okinawa: Two Postwar Novellas* (Berkeley: Institute of East Asian Studies, University of California, 1989; reprinted 1996), xi–xii and 22–23.

66. Arasaki, *Okinawa no sugao,* 71–72.

67. Interview, November 2000.

68. See *Yōhi,* 1987 and 1997.

69. See Ota Jun'ichi, *Osaka no Uchinaan-chu* (Osaka: Burein Sentā, 1996).

70. Interviews of Yamashiro Kenkō, Osaka Office of Okinawa Prefecture, September 2000.

71. Johnson, *Okinawa: Cold War,* 88.

72. Published interview of Kinjō Kaoru, codirector of the Kansai Okinawa Bunko (Culture Center), in *Yomiuri Shinbun,* 13 May 2001.

73. Comment from interview of descendant in his mid-thirties, February 2001.

74. Questionnaire, March 2001.

75. For analysis of this crime and its impact in Okinawa, see chapter 5 by Linda Angst in this volume.

5

The Rape of a Schoolgirl

Discourses of Power and Gendered National Identity in Okinawa

Linda Isako Angst

In September 1995, relations among the United States, Japan, and Okinawa were transformed when three U.S. servicemen brutally gang-raped a twelve-year-old schoolgirl. Okinawan feminists called public attention to the rape, but the media and political leaders quickly shifted their focus to concerns about Okinawa's colonial history and its postwar occupation by the United States. A crisis of sovereignty replaced the crisis for a particular girl as the agenda of feminist activists faded from view. This chapter asks why this particular crime, in a long list of crimes against Okinawans by U.S. personnel since 1945, has resonated so strongly both in Okinawa and in mainland Japan. Evaluating the rape in the context of the islands' contentious identity politics, it assesses how the crime evoked a powerful symbolic theme: Okinawa as sacrificed schoolgirl/daughter. The rape evoked prior narratives of Okinawan victimhood, most notably the Himeyuri girl students who were sacrificed to Japanese military ambitions in the Battle of Okinawa.

THE RAPE OF A SCHOOLGIRL

On the night of 4 September 1995, as she walked home after purchasing a notebook from a neighborhood store, a twelve-year-old Okinawan schoolgirl was abducted at knifepoint by three U.S. servicemen in a rented car in the town of Kin and gang-raped. This was the Labor Day holiday for U.S. forces in Okinawa, and the three men—two marines and one sailor—had been partying all day in the capital city of Naha, an hour south of Kin. According to a fourth marine who was with them earlier in the day, the three plotted to "get a girl" after failed attempts to meet women in Naha. Unwilling to join them should they follow through with their plan, he left the others but did nothing to prevent the impending crime.

The three then drove back to Kin, the location of their home base, Camp Hansen. The old bar and brothel area outside the main gates of Camp Hansen had thrived during the Vietnam War era. In 1995 and today, this area, which relies on the patronage of dwindling numbers of U.S. marines from the camp across the road, is filled with timeworn, seedy sex and entertainment establishments that appear to be on the verge of collapse. The town is a far cry from the lively, sophisticated entertainment district of Kokusai-dori (International Boulevard), the hub of tourist commerce in downtown Naha, where the men had been that day. But on weekends and on that particular American holiday night in 1995, Kin was thronged with bar hostesses, prostitutes, service workers, and young marines.

From the 1950s through the present, troops at Camp Hansen and other Okinawan bases have been deployed throughout the Pacific region and beyond, serving in the Korean, Vietnam, and Gulf Wars. Camp Hansen's primary purpose is to train recruits for artillery and other kinds of combat. For most of the young men, the tour of duty on Okinawa is their first time abroad—indeed, the first time many of them have ever been away from their hometowns. The military services hype such tours of duty as cross-cultural experiences, opportunities to "see the world." In fact, recruits often find that, for a variety of reasons, including lack of useful introduction to the local culture, unfamiliarity with the language, high costs of the local economy, and sometimes local resentment of their presence, their lives are confined to the narrow world (and worldview) of the base and the bars and brothels in its immediate periphery.

The marines in Kin are physically isolated from the general population, living and working within the barbed-wire fences of the camp and removed from the urban centers of life on the island. Since the salaries of recruits are notoriously low (and the value of the dollar since 1985 has remained low compared to the yen), many recruits rarely venture far from the base. Marines at Camp Hansen are also separated from others through the nature of their work as combat soldiers, labor that is physically and mentally focused on learning to fight. Through their work and their isolation, the attention of many is intensely fixated on their own physicality. As well as being outside the bounds of ordinary Okinawan life, they most profoundly experience their difference from local people in terms of their physical (including racial) difference. All of these factors contribute to producing a situation in which an occupation army of restless young, foreign men who have received little preparation for understanding Okinawan society constitute a clear and present danger to the local community, especially its women and girls.

On the night in question, the three U.S. soldiers returned from Naha to the familiar terrain of Kin. After cruising the neon-bright area outside the gates of Camp Hansen, they headed for the darker local neighborhood streets of Kin.

At 8 P.M., the world of a twelve-year-old schoolgirl was forever changed by her brutal encounter with the three servicemen. After pulling the girl from the street into the car, the soldiers silenced and immobilized her by taping her mouth and binding her arms and legs. They then took her to the remote beach that military officials label the Kin Blue Amphibious Training Area—a peninsula of jagged rocks jutting into the deep waters of a wild-looking, dark-blue sea. At night the area is pitch black, and locals steer clear. Discarded beer bottles reveal that marines frequent the spot late at night, sneaking past the military's "off-limits" sign once the lights from local houses and streets are out. At this lonely site, the three men repeatedly raped the girl, who was still bound, then discarded their bloodied undershorts in a trash bin before abandoning her limp form on the beach.

The girl managed to drag herself up to one of the houses beyond the stretch of mangrove trees on cliffs overlooking the beach. She gave a description of the car and the men, even remembering the rental number of the vehicle, according to one source, and the three rapists were apprehended within hours of the crime. Initially taken into U.S. military custody, as a result of public outrage over the rape, the men were eventually handed over to the local authorities. They were tried and convicted in Japanese courts of law in Okinawa, the first such trial and conviction in the half century since the start of the U.S. occupation. Navy Seaman Marcus Gill and Marine Private Rodrico Harp were convicted of abduction and rape and given seven-year sentences; Marine Private Kendric Ledet received a six-and-one-half-year term on a slightly lesser charge.[1]

SOVEREIGNTY, GENDER, AND POSTWAR IDENTITY POLITICS

The abduction and gang-rape of the schoolgirl prompted immediate powerful Okinawan responses. These included the demand by women's groups in Okinawa to publicize the crime and increase protection for women, particularly around U.S. bases, renewed protests by landowners forced for decades to lease lands to the U.S. military, and strengthened calls by then-governor Ōta Masahide to pressure Tokyo to reduce and ultimately rid the island of U.S. bases. Internationally, the most profound effect was to spark a debate over the nature and role of the U.S.–Japan Security Treaty, particularly the provisions of the Status of Forces Agreement (SOFA) regarding the treatment of U.S. military personnel accused of crimes, an agreement that had guaranteed servicemen, in effect, extraterritoriality—that is, trial by U.S. military courts rather than by Japanese courts.[2] Protest of the rape also forced postponement of President Bill Clinton's November 1995 Tokyo visit and triggered a premature end to Prime Minister Murayama's tenure as the first non–Liberal Democratic Party (LDP) postwar Japanese leader in decades.

The immediate response to this rape was conditioned by the long history of military violence in Okinawa and the political mobilizations that had sought to respond to the outrages. Quickly, however, media coverage shifted from the rape to "larger" political issues of lands leased for U.S. bases, base returns, and troop reduction, pointing out the long-standing victimization of Okinawans whose lives and livelihood had been transformed by the confiscation of their lands and the subordination of economy and society to the U.S. bases. Initial coverage of the rape carried by CNN, the *New York Times,* and the *Asahi Shinbun* among others showed images of women demonstrating in downtown Naha, with Naha City councilwoman Takazato Suzuyo playing a leading role,[3] and of eighty thousand people protesting the rape at Okinawa's Ginowan City Convention Center in the largest demonstration in Okinawan history.[4] These reports were soon replaced by editorials debating the base issue,[5] photos of antibase landowner and activist Chibana Shōichi[6] sitting in protest on his ancestral property in Yomitan Village[7] and of vast, virtually empty tracts of land comprising the Marine Corps Air Station (MCAS) at Futenma, cheek by jowl with the crowded urban sprawl of Ginowan City.[8] The rape itself gradually disappeared from the media.

Later media coverage of Okinawa spoke metaphorically of the rape in terms of the rapacious behavior of imperialist powers acting on a historically marginalized population. Commentators in the media and in the antibase movement shifted the public intellectual and ethical focus from the young female victim to the Okinawan body politic. While feminist groups protested the rape as the figuration and potential rape of all women in and around U.S. military installations in Asia, the Okinawan political establishment and international media moved from a particular sexual crime of violence against a young girl to a crisis of sovereignty. Okinawan prefectural officials and political activist leaders focused increasingly on the perpetrators' identity and agency, thus emphasizing the political/nationalist dimension of U.S. military domination over the personal and gendered dimensions of the act. For political leaders, women and the body of the schoolgirl became significant mainly because they pointed to the crisis of sovereignty. Most stories situated the rape not only among the many heinous crimes perpetrated by U.S. soldiers against local Okinawans in the fifty years since the war but also within a broader historical context that included colonial and neocolonial oppression of Okinawa by Japan and the United States. The *Okinawa Times*, for example, editorialized that it took the "sacrifice of a schoolgirl" to make progress in the movement to scale back the American military bases that occupy 20 percent of the land on this Japanese island.[9]

The female victim, a Kin schoolgirl, and the rape (*her* rape), were hidden from view as they were appropriated by all sides, including the prefectural government, various women's groups, landowners, and other activist groups throughout Japan and Okinawa. Her pain was transformed into a symbol of national subjugation with its own narrative: Okinawa, as the feminized body politic, remains a site of contestation between contending political powers, local and international.

Although both political leaders and feminists appropriated the image of the rape for their own agendas, for feminists and women's rights activists the rape itself continues to inform a larger feminist politics as a violent physical act against a female victim. But within the broader protest movement for Okinawan rights, the abstracted idea of the ravaged female body, victim of a grotesquely twisted sexual desire, has been juxtaposed with Okinawan soil as the object of the nationalist imagination. In short, the rape of a child is transformed into the rape of the body politic. In this reading, inflicting violence on a girl becomes a metonym for the perversion of U.S., or U.S. and Japanese, desire to maintain the bases in Okinawa. Both woman (or her representation) and soil are of course critical symbolic elements within (emergent) nationalist discourses.

When various groups appropriate the incident and the victim for larger political purposes, they are participating in the complex field of identity politics in Okinawa. By engaging feminist and other critical approaches, I wish to reframe and reposition questions of agency, determination, human rights, and victimization.[10] In explaining why this particular incident in the long history of abuses committed by U.S. servicemen against Okinawan people and property resonates so strongly throughout Okinawa and mainland Japan, I suggest that the answer has to do with more than the literal (political) on-the-ground conditions of the violation of a local child by soldiers of an occupying force at a particular moment in Okinawan history—though this cannot be minimized—and must include a figurative (poetic) reading of the rape as the defilement and victimization of the idea of a pure and innocent Okinawa. Clearly, the rape of the schoolgirl is enmeshed in these complex discursive realms.

I argue that a feminist politics can counteract the objectification of the twelve-year-old girl (and the rape event) and reclaim her subjectivity—indeed, her very humanity. We must return to the rape to understand it both concretely and symbolically as an act of violence between perpetrators and victim. It is also necessary to understand rhetorical strategies and agendas to politicize and thus transform the rape into a metaphor for contemporary Okinawa's condition of subjugation.

I problematize the idea of a unified voice of Okinawan identity politics as presented in the media explosion surrounding the rape and promoted especially in the rhetoric of the prefecture's elected leaders at the time, who quickly assumed the position of main spokesmen after the rape. While a unified voice may help to build momentum for social change, I question to what degree this unified voice acts hegemonically in Okinawa to subsume and defer other voices and agendas. In examining the antibase protest movement's response to the rape, I highlight certain internal Okinawan tensions—ideological, regional, classist, and gender based—that are welded together into local antibase demands. Here, too, I work from a feminist critique.

As Judith Butler and Joan Scott have shown, women's voices are often lost in a generalized voice of identity politics,[11] and as Cynthia Enloe has pointed out, feminist agendas are often subsumed under the rubric of the larger political good, their goals deferred, ostensibly for the short term but often indefinitely.[12] The presumably more pressing needs of the "good of the political whole"—repatriation of land, political sovereignty, and base and military force reduction, in the Okinawa case—replace the "private" importance of the rape and the suffering of the young female victim.

The focus on sovereignty displaced the issues of women's (and general human) rights, including the initial efforts of local women's groups to improve safety and work/living conditions for all Okinawan women.[13] The rape victim and the rape have been absorbed into existing political ideologies and discourses, local and international, including feminist discourses. The rhetoric used by each group explains the rape as something else: as a catalyst in local political leaders' long-standing negotiations with the Japanese government over rights to land and Okinawan sovereignty,[14] as a consequence of post–Cold War military alignments involving Japan and the United States, and as a stimulus to feminist campaigns to further women's rights. In each instance, groups draw upon and interpret particular aspects of the colonial and occupation eras to buttress their representations of the rape. Such conscious remembering of the past generates sometimes competing images of contemporary Okinawan identity, attesting to the heterogeneous and mutable character of a politics of identity and ethnic identity formation.

Not only has the rape been redeployed in a representational capacity, it has simultaneously been absorbed into and has redefined symbolic expressions of Okinawan victimhood. Particularly in nationalist discourse, as Carol Delaney tells us, "Women do not represent, they are what is represented. . . . This observation opens theoretical space to think about the differences between symbolization and representation, often held to be the same." In many countries, women symbolize the nation, but men represent it, and often the nation is referred to as female and represented as a female statue. Most fundamentally, "because of their symbolic association with land, women are, in a sense, the ground over which national identity is played out."[15]

As symbol, the 1995 rape and the rape victim can serve in many capacities to many Okinawans, and as such, the event made it possible, beyond the immediate exigencies of political protest, for a variety of groups with competing agendas to come together as a unified Okinawan voice of dissent. Identity politics is implicitly one of resistance—in this case, simultaneously against the Japanese state and the powerful myth of Japanese cultural homogeneity, and against U.S. military power with its repeated abuse of the Okinawan people whom it claims to defend. How, then, have Okinawan antiwar activists appropriated the rape as a symbol of Okinawan subjugation? This writing explores the nature and practice of hegemony within a politics of protest.

THE TROPE OF THE SACRIFICED/PROSTITUTED DAUGHTER

The fervor with which Okinawans protested the rape—and by implication the ongoing policies under the U.S.–Japan Security Treaty—cannot be explained solely by a literal reading of the rape as an act of violence by members of a foreign occupation force against a local girl. A fuller consideration of Okinawan politics requires understanding how the image of a victimized schoolgirl resonates over time as a symbol of both wartime and postwar Okinawa, and thus of Okinawa as a victim of both Japanese and American violence and hegemony. The unity of the antibase movement in Okinawa rests on a shared symbolic understanding of Okinawa and Okinawan history as a parable of the violated and sacrificed schoolgirl/daughter. Behind that unity, however, lies the "split" to which Ernesto Laclau and Chantal Mouffe refer—that is, the pluralistic and often competing nature of interest groups, with their "specific literal demands," within the totalized idea of Okinawan identity politics and the shared goals of greater autonomy and Okinawan rights to recover confiscated land.[16]

One possible way to focus attention on the actual experience of Okinawan women would be to highlight the direct experience of the raped girl herself. Yet direct attention to the personal experience of the victim of the 1995 rape is not possible. Her youth, as well as the crime itself, which traditionally stigmatizes its victims, require that she be protected through anonymity. It is precisely because she goes unnamed—and is thus anonymous—that the rape victim serves so well in a general symbolic capacity. Her youth also contributes to this symbolic power. As a child, she symbolizes innocence and purity; she does not yet know the world of work or women. Her position shifts from that of general female victim symbolizing (all) women to a more abstract, and therefore more generalizable, category of victimization: the symbol of an innocent, pure, and feminized Okinawa sacrificed to the interests of the dominant powers, the United States and Japan.

The potency of this image of violated innocence and purity has great power precisely because it is already part of an existing iconography of modern Okinawan victimhood. The Himeyuri, or Maiden Lily Student Nurse Corps, is a powerful symbol of Okinawan sacrifice. In 1945, 219 female students at the top two girls' higher schools in presurrender Okinawa accompanied Japanese soldiers into battle as student nurses. Most were killed, trapped between Japanese soldiers and U.S. troops. In the minds of many Japanese, the Himeyuri have come to embody an idea of Okinawa as sacrificial victim. To both Okinawans and mainland Japanese, the Himeyuri provide the canonical narrative of Okinawan identity in the postwar era, with an entire museum dedicated to telling their story.[17] (See chapter 3 by Gerald Figal in this volume for competing efforts to commemorate the Himeyuri.) Here the socially peripheral becomes the symbolically central.

There is a crucial difference, however, between the Himeyuri and the 1995 rape. The Himeyuri were victimized by being sent to the front by the Japanese military to face U.S. attack in a foredoomed defense that had nothing to do with protecting Okinawa and everything to do with slowing the U.S. advance against the main Japanese islands. In the case of the rape, the actual violence was perpetrated by American soldiers. Yet in each case, both countries are implicated: The Himeyuri, literally trapped between Japanese and American forces on the battlefield, were sent to their death by the Japanese military. The rape of a schoolgirl was perpetrated by three GIs, yet the structure of power that subordinates Okinawa today is one crafted through the U.S.–Japan alliance. With Okinawa caught between the political agendas of the two world powers (this time in alignment), the schoolgirl's pain highlights Okinawa's powerlessness. For Okinawans, the resonance with the story of the Himeyuri Student Nurse Corps is enormous.

Drawing direct parallels between the rape of women nationals and the invasion of land by foreigners has long been a staple of nationalist discourse.[18] Carol Delaney shows how Turks conceived of the modern nation-state as their mother who was raped and violated by the West when the victorious powers at the end of World War I sought to divide up the Ottoman Empire. This motivated Turks to protect their threatened soil. Takazato Suzuyo, a Naha City Council member and feminist activist who led the Okinawan delegation to the 1995 Women's Conference in Beijing, explicitly links the 1995 rape to an allegorized image of Okinawa as a daughter sold by Japan into prostitution: "Okinawa is the prostituted daughter of Japan. Japan used her daughter as a breakwater to keep the battlefields from spreading over the mainland until the end of World War II. After the war, she enjoyed economic prosperity by selling the daughter to the United States."[19]

As I show at greater length elsewhere,[20] oppositional discourse about Himeyuri (as symbol, not representation) actually reinscribes Okinawa and women's marginality and subordination. The few aging survivors of the Himeyuri now find that, rather than speaking their own story, the story of their wartime experiences "speaks" them. Transposable to any agenda and hence universally appealing, it is as symbol that the Himeyuri are contained (the passive voice is deliberate here) inescapably within competing discourses, just as they were inescapably engulfed by a presurrender nationalist ideology that compelled them to follow the orders of Japanese military commanders to their death. Once physically positioned between Japanese and American forces on the battlefield, today they find again that their quiescence positions them discursively between contending Okinawan and Japanese political agendas.

Similarly, referring to the 1995 rape victim as a sacrificed or prostituted daughter both enshrines and subordinates her within an existing nationalist patriarchal discourse that consistently tropes women as helpless victims. The language of sacrifice and/or victimization is used not only by male leaders of Okinawa's political movement but more disturbingly by some feminists, including Takazato. This language reinscribes Okinawa as a dependent of the patriarchal family state, even as Okinawans (especially feminists) adamantly reject that role as one imposed on them by coercive U.S. and Japanese policies.[21] Under the circumstances, Takazato seems aware of the need to strategize ways to best influence male leaders—and other Okinawans—to focus on women's issues within the protest movement. Consider, for example, this exchange between Takazato and a male peace activist:

> "A man pointed his finger at me as I entered—'You! You always only raise the violence against women issue. That's not political. That's not what the U.S.-Japanese Security Treaty is about!' I just pointed my finger back at him and said, 'You know only one-half of what security means if you don't think military violence against women is part of this issue!'"[22]

It nevertheless remains extremely difficult to disengage from the compelling trope of a national family, particularly given the powerful model of the Himeyuri as Okinawa's sacrificed daughters in wartime. It is also difficult because of the lack of general support by male activist leaders in the protest movement and because the trope holds emotional power for the general populace. The Himeyuri and the rape discourses both thrive on the relationship between the tropes of virginity and purity betrayed, on the one hand, and nationalism, on the other. Purity seems to be a critical component of nationalist symbols that are gendered female. In the Okinawan case, however, it is not the purity of selfless motherly love that was mobilized in Turkey. Rather, the virginity—read innocence and youth—of the Himeyuri maidens as well as of the schoolgirl rape victim is celebrated here. The danger is that, in doing so, patriarchal authority, as the foundation of the modern nation-state may also be celebrated, as in official Japanese appropriations of the Himeyuri story. The implication is not just that the rape victim is a daughter violated because her father failed to protect her but also that patriarchy should be restored. As many Okinawans told me over the course of my fieldwork, the Imperial Japanese soldiers in wartime failed to carry out their duty to protect Okinawans, which was ostensibly the reason they were stationed on the island. Despite the many sacrifices Okinawans endured, the soldiers and the state never seemed to believe that Okinawans were deserving of protection.[23] (See chapter 2 by Allen.) The schoolgirl raped in 1995 was also caught between American and Japanese political/military agendas; once again, the Japanese state failed to protect its Okinawan citizens. If the 1995 violation of the schoolgirl is understood to be a sacrifice, then the Japanese parent/nation is even more gravely implicated since mainland Japanese have lived a safer life under the U.S.–Japan Security Treaty because their leaders continue to sacrifice their Okinawan daughters by maintaining the lion's share of bases on Okinawa.[24]

Okinawans build their identity politics on a narrative of reconstructed Okinawan history. They look to a precolonial past marked by the flourishing of an independent and cosmopolitan Ryūkyū kingdom living in peace and assuring prosperity. In this narrative, there are discursive parallels between how the rape ended the schoolgirl's innocence and defiled her purity and how the colonization of the Ryūkyūs by Satsuma in the seventeenth century fundamentally changed—that is, politicized—Okinawa. Both violations brought about a transformation toward a new, critical self-consciousness: the end of innocence and the birth of a political consciousness.

The appropriation and virtual colonization of Ryūkyū by Satsuma represented a fundamental shift in political status (the loss of autonomy), while the rape of the schoolgirl shattered and reformulated her personal identity (through the loss of childhood innocence) and repoliticized Okinawa. Okinawans consciously claim a past as an inherently peace-loving people, despite the reality of precolonial internal struggles for territorial power. This creates a seamless whole, short-circuiting Okinawan history and creating a compelling narrative of mythic proportions. But to be compelling, the story has to be accessible—that is, simple. The 1995 rape, too, lends itself well to this purpose of creating a mythical past as the foundation for a unified Okinawan voice of protest. Thus, myth and symbol operate in the service of Okinawan identity politics.

Analysis of this strategy raises the question of whether gender is reinscribed in the international political relations between the powerful nation-states of Japan and the United States, on the one hand, and occupied Okinawa, on the other. This is an explicit area of difference among Okinawans. In one view, Okinawa is gendered as woman by virtue of a negation—the emasculation of Okinawan cultural and political autonomy. Other Okinawans, who purposely seek to distinguish themselves from traditionally warlike Japanese and who stress the continued integrity of Okinawan culture, however, read their cultural persona as "peace loving" rather than "emasculated."

TOWARD A FEMINIST UNDERSTANDING OF THE RAPE

Although the 1995 rape may be read as an allegory of long-standing Okinawan suffering, it should first be read on its own terms, prior to and independent of any appropriation as a symbol of Okinawan victimhood. Considered as an event with its own ontology, occurring at a specific place and point in time, the rape evokes outrage as a particular act of violence. Yet its facticity has been eclipsed by the power of its metaphorical, representational significance. Sharon Marcus, in "Fighting Bodies, Fighting Words," argues for a shift in focus, from the scene of the rape and its aftermath to "rape situations themselves and to rape *prevention*."[25] Women need to empower themselves by understanding rape as a process to be analyzed and prevented rather than as a fact that is accepted, opposed, tried, or avenged. This challenges the view of rape as endowed with a "terrifying facticity."

Attention to the event of the rape helps to unpack a variety of its possible meanings. First, the rape embodies a fundamental power differential defined in terms of an inherent gendered asymmetry: a girl overtaken by three men. The shift in media representation of the rape from violation of one girl's body to that of the Okinawan body politic signals an interpretive reorientation of the rape from the private/personal realm to the public/political realm. Strictly speaking, however, the political cannot be separated from the private in any instance of rape. As Marcus has argued, "A rapist chooses his target because he recognizes her to be a woman, but a rapist also strives to imprint the gender identity of 'feminine victim' on his target. A rape act thus imposes as well as presupposes misogynist inequalities; rape is not only scripted—it also scripts."[26]

Moreover, the affiliation of these men with the U.S. military—the very reason for their being on Okinawa—is a critically defining aspect of this basic political relationship. That is, we can locate the rape within the parameters of serious crimes committed by U.S. servicemen. According to the Base Measures Office of Okinawa Prefecture, of the 5,006 recorded crimes committed by U.S. servicemen between 1972 and 2000, 527 were heinous crimes such as murder and arson, and 949 were violent crimes involving injuries.[27] In this case, the girl's gender may be primarily what drew the men to her, but it is impossible to separate issues of gender, race, ethnicity, class, age, and national identity from the identity of the victim or the act of the rape. Indeed, the rape is simultaneously the rape of an *Okinawan* girl by *foreign*—U.S. military—men who are part of an occupying military force.[28] Furthermore, the men imprint "the gender identity of 'feminine victim' on [their] target,"[29] and, in this case, they also imprint the victim as "Okinawan." Finally, the sheer physical power of three men over one girl signifies the position of power that the United States exercises over Okinawa.

As feminist activists argue, the rape represents the potential endangerment of all women in Okinawa from the presence of twenty-six thousand U.S. servicemen, mostly young men from working-class backgrounds, including many blacks and Hispanics, who train on a regular basis to fight and kill enemy forces.[30] In this sense, the rape of a female Okinawan forces us to appreciate the daily reality of all women in Okinawa.

OKINAWAN IDENTITY POLITICS—OFFICIAL VOICES

Many interest groups with competing agendas shape Okinawan identity politics, but elected prefectural officials comprised the official representative voice of Okinawan protest after the rape, especially Governor Ōta. The power of the protest movement in the nineties was largely the result of Ōta's success as governor (1990–1998) in prioritizing base removal as a public issue. Many groups in Okinawa, including feminists seeking improved conditions for women, have identified with this cause.

Although most Okinawans say they are committed to the removal of the U.S. bases, and antibase forces have grown in strength over half a century, the antibase movement embraces diverse and sometimes conflicting interests.[31] The demands made by Okinawan groups within the antibase movement vary. They include demands for the return of or compensation for base lands, many of which have been contaminated by toxins; policies and programs to protect women; stronger environmental regulations against noise and other pollution generated by the U.S. military; and greater access to ancestral tombs located on bases. Yet at the prefectural level, many elected officials, including then Governor Ōta, called for eventual removal of bases, a goal that may be at odds with some of these demands. Even looking at landowners whose property is within fences surrounding U.S. bases, we find mixed sentiments. While some demand the return of their land, many now prefer the high rent paid them by the Japanese government as compensation for hosting the bases. At reversion in 1972, out of the 30,000 Okinawans leasing their land to the U.S. military, the Anti-War Landowners group numbered 2,850. But that number would plummet to seventy members by 1988 as a result of Japanese government payment of substantially higher rent. In 1982, the One Tsubo Anti-War Landowners Association formed to support the antibase landowners. The organization buys land from owners, then subdivides it and sells one-tsubo (3.3-square-meter) plots to individuals who oppose the bases in Okinawa and Japan.[32] In this way, the number of landlords hostile to the bases has grown, although many of them hold the land as a symbolic statement rather than because they or their families once lived on or farmed it. Yet with the Japanese and U.S. governments unified in supporting the bases, and with an LDP governor in power since 1998, the ability of antibase forces to shape policy remains limited.

The main tension within the movement is the internal pull between various groups promoting their own goals and the desire to present the overarching goal of a unified voice of protest. The shock of the rape initially bridged that tension. Okinawans felt both a deep compassion for the raped girl and rage toward the perpetrators, and they were profoundly affected by the girl's suffering. The crime galvanized long-standing anger about U.S. bases and the abuses inflicted by U.S. personnel against local people.

However, to the extent that Okinawans recall a history in which U.S. servicemen have committed repeated offenses against Okinawans—not just Okinawan women—in the years since 1945, the gender dimension of the crime at hand is overshadowed by the numerous human rights violations by soldiers of a foreign occupation force and felonious crimes against the local civic order. Ironically, the metaphorization of rape as the violation of the Okinawan body politic takes the focus off the specific experience of Okinawan women. The focus is placed explicitly on the imperialist relationship of U.S. military dominance over Okinawa, not on the sex-related crime at hand—and therefore not on women per se. These absences reveal how the rape—and its unwilling subject, a young girl—have been appropriated (and in effect erased) by all sides.

GENDER IN IDENTITY POLITICS

Referring to Homi Bhabha's interpretation of nations and nationalist discourse, Lydia Liu comments that by foregrounding marginal spaces and peoples of the "nation-space," the taken-for-granted boundaries of imagined national communities are clearly revealed. Distinctions between "us" and "others" provide the grounds on which resistance can take place. Okinawans raise the question of the "otherness of the people-as-one" by highlighting their distinctiveness from Yamato culture: Okinawan identity resists the model of a racially and culturally homogeneous Japan.[33] The potency of that politics today is reinforced by transformations inside and outside Japan in the decade since the end of the Cold War and the Shōwa emperor's death. In particular, this coincides with myriad demands from Asian peoples and governments that Japan compensate or make reparations to victims of colonial and wartime aggression, most prominently Asian "comfort women" who served as sex slaves to Japanese soldiers.[34]

The relationship between military aggression (including occupation) and sexual abuse of local women is systemic, as the work of Cynthia Enloe and Carol Delaney demonstrates. Enloe provides a comparative examination of the profane dimensions of the relationship among women, nationalism, and war—including how base economies embed and exploit women's work and the mechanisms of exploitation of prostitutes and comfort women—while Delaney focuses on the ways in which the relationship between woman and nation is elevated to the status of sacred symbol in nationalist discourses. In either case, they argue, woman is objectified, compromising her (political) human rights. Feminist activists have put together a long roster of crimes, including hundreds of sex crimes, committed by U.S. servicemen in Okinawa since 1945.[35] Enloe cites two particularly heinous pre-1995 cases, one in which six-year-old Yumiko was raped and murdered by an American serviceman in 1955; the other, a 1993 crime in which the assailant brought the victim on base, raped her, then dropped her off base and fled.[36] The assailant in the 1993 rape was eventually apprehended but never brought to trial because the girl was persuaded to drop charges when she realized the damage that a public trial would do to her "reputation."[37] This raises a critical problem with Okinawan identity discourse, which is precisely the problem suggested by Liu's critique of Bhabha: It fails to acknowledge the diversity of the groups that comprise that identity politics. Just as Bhabha makes the mistake of conflating distinct modes of oppression and lumping marginal groups into one category, thereby "level[ing it] down to homogeneous totality,"[38] Okinawan political leaders, who insist on a unified Okinawan voice, effectively silence the voices of groups, including Okinawan women activists, who seek to promote women's rights.

While Okinawan feminists participate in the broader politics of Okinawan rights, grappling with the dual hegemony of Japanese politics and culture and U.S. bases, they simultaneously engage in a universal movement for women's rights. Hegemony is associated with male dominance and patriarchal institutions, including those within Okinawa.[39] As indicated in the above quoted exchange between Takazato and another Okinawan activist, some feminists bridle at the expectation that they defer their own agendas "for now"[40] in the interest of showing Okinawan solidarity. In linking local social ills and the presence of U.S. bases, the prefectural government invariably advocates the development of valuable base-leased lands into profitable (generally tourist) businesses. In effect, the rape becomes an opportunity for business and political leaders to emphasize (and conflate) the volatile issue of U.S. occupation in ongoing discussions about the economy.

Before the rape, a member of the Okinawa Prefecture Policy Regulation Board at the Okinawa Peace Seminar '94,[41] welded issues of the environment, peace, safety/human rights, and economic development into a package. While it is imperative to foster a more independent Okinawan economy, for some the economic issues seem to override all others, including women's safety—which is co-opted to serve development agendas. The development plans of male prefectural leaders subordinate all so-called women's issues, such as the education of biracial children of absent American servicemen fathers by single Okinawan mothers, as tangential to their primary concerns with pursuing corporate agendas. For example, at a meeting with former Governor Ōta in Washington, D.C., in 1998, the governor and his delegation spent the bulk of their time discussing the removal of bases for environmental and development reasons. As an afterthought, the governor mentioned in the last two or three minutes of his two-hour presentation at the Woodrow Wilson Center the matter of U.S. funding for the bilingual education of abandoned biracial children and only then in response to my question about women's issues.

An interesting contrast is the rhetoric of "women-peace-environment" by feminists, not only in Okinawa but worldwide. At the Japan Foundation European Women's Study Tour on the Environment, entitled "Looking toward Tomorrow: Women, Environment, Peace," speakers addressed these issues in their presentations to an assembly of several thousand (mostly) women in Naha, in April 1994. The forum focused on changes at the grassroots level. One example of the kind of grassroots "development" they encouraged is the Churasa Soap Factory. Built and run by a woman farmer from Onna Village, the enterprise recycles cooking fat and oil donated by local women for her handmade soaps at a small, two-person factory, then sells the soap to earn a modest living. This stands in stark contrast to prefectural officials' plans to develop base lands for major resorts, an approach that has been dominated by mainland Japanese enterprises.

While bases continue to dominate the landscape, Okinawans today no longer rely as heavily on income associated with bases as they did before 1972, when the bulk of the labor force was employed directly or indirectly in a military service economy.[42] While some Okinawans continue to work in sex and entertainment trades, most sex workers near the bases are now Filipinas. This poses yet another challenge to Okinawan, Japanese, and international feminists: to speak out on behalf of the rights of Filipina women who are separated by language, citizenship, and experience from Okinawans and Japanese.

Figure 5.1. During a 1994 conference and tour of Okinawa, European feminists pose with Takazato Suzuyo and other Okinawan feminist leaders in the rainbow garden outside the Himeyuri Peace Memorial Museum. "While Okinawan feminists participate in the broader politics of Okinawan rights . . . they are engaged simultaneously in a universal protest movement for women's rights." (Watanabe, "Militarism, Colonialism, and the Trafficking of Women," 258. See note 34.)

Source: Photo by Linda Isako Angst

As both Carolyn Bowen Francis and Cynthia Enloe have shown,[43] Okinawan feminists have been actively engaged in establishing work cooperatives and other forms of grassroots aid for former Asian women sex workers in Okinawa, the Philippines, Vietnam, and South Korea, the locales of former and still-existing U.S. military bases. Many women are the sole supporters of their families, including their own (often biracial) children and extended family. The goal has been to enable women to provide for themselves independently by training them in traditional crafts. This activity has been especially intense since the 1995 Beijing Women's Conference, although Okinawan activists, especially Christian groups, were already setting up study tours and visits well before the Beijing conference.[44]

In the wake of the 1995 rape, some feminist activists expressed concern that the Ōta government took advantage of the groundswell of antibase sentiment following the rape to promote an economic development agenda that ignored women's concerns. Feminist activists worked hard to get a prefectural government contribution of 500,000 yen per year, or slightly less than $5,000 in 1995–1996, toward the funding of a Rape Intervention Crisis Center in Okinawa. This became a reality in October at the initiative of women's groups. However, the Ōta government refused to house the center in the new prefectural government building (the Kento), as Takazato and other feminists had proposed, although it did house the prefectural Women's Affairs section there. Since then, prefectural funds have been cut for this and other social services. Women active in the prefectural government were also upset that, although they were part of a delegation from Okinawa to Washington in 1998 to argue for base closures, they were merely visual props and were not given the opportunity to raise their concerns about women's safety.

The new government supports the development of a new base in Nago against the opposition of antibase peace, women's, and environmental movements and without attention to issues of women's safety. This indicates not only that the rape has receded from view but that the broader issue of women's safety has also been set aside.

THE RAPE IN METADISCOURSES OF IDENTITY POLITICS

The shifting of focus, from the rape to its political representation, and from feminist protest to identity politics, reveals the nature and direction of Okinawan politics. The discourse has been transformed from protests voiced largely by women concerning human rights, with feminist activist Takazato Suzuyo playing an important role, to protests by (male) landowners about rights to land, and hence to issues of national sovereignty, political identity, and development, led by former governor Ōta. At its most basic, we can say that feminists address the issue of individual rights as they inhere in female bodies, while male politicians generalize in order to address the identity and rights of the body politic.

I suggest that the problem of an overarching Okinawan voice that both subsumes feminist/women's agendas and interprets the rape of the schoolgirl metaphorically as the defilement of an image of a pure and chaste Okinawa is grounded in an inherently patriarchal political outlook.

The problem with the language that represents Okinawa as a sacrificed or prostituted daughter is its tacit acceptance of the nationalist trope of the family state. The chastity of the victim as daughter becomes the locus of concern and the condition for regarding the rape as sacrifice. While this language is not immediately in conflict with feminists' highlighting of the systematic violation of women's civil rights through violence, it fails to criticize a sexual double standard in which raped girls are "ruined," although it presents their loss as a blow to all. Indeed, the Japanese state, in readily agreeing to turn Okinawa into a U.S. military colony, and even after reversion in 1972, to keep 75 percent of U.S. bases there, in effect created a situation in which Okinawan women would suffer the majority of rapes and other crimes to lighten the burden on women in other Japanese prefectures.

Women working in Okinawa's base-related and (now) resort tourism-related sex and entertainment industry have long borne the brunt of their socially stigmatizing, physically debilitating, dangerous work. Protest leaders, who define an idea of collective cultural self through reference to a pristine, precolonial past, draw upon images of purity and chastity, such as the Himeyuri and the raped schoolgirl; in the process, the real prostituted daughters of Okinawa are excluded. Indeed, in many ways, bar and brothel women are lingering and unwanted images of prewar era Okinawa as low ethnic other, while Filipina women, the new sex workers, are largely absent from the discussion.[45]

Despite their many sacrifices, these women are coded as less deserving of public concern by many groups because they are not "pure." The lack of sensitivity to the fact that women with little education have few work opportunities other than bar and sex work melds with the focus on the twelve-year-old raped girl as the primary symbol of sacrifice and victimhood (just as the Himeyuri served in this capacity for wartime and postwar Okinawa). Yet the raped girl differs fundamentally from other women in Okinawa: Precisely because she is a girl, her chastity places her within the protection of the patriarchal family.

In the first decades after the war, the survival of many Okinawan families rested on the incomes of sex workers—sisters, mothers, and other female relatives. Now that most Okinawans have put the hardscrabble years behind them, the women who still bear the burden of such sacrifices—now mainly a few older Okinawan women and increasing numbers of Filipinas—have been forgotten or stigmatized.[46]

Ironically, the very women who have experienced the life of the prostituted daughter are excluded from public recognition as that particular symbol of Okinawan victimhood. That is, Okinawan women (and still more Filipinas) working in the sex trade, around bases and in the tourist industry, are ineligible for inclusion within the protective embrace of the collective family, despite having sacrificed their own reputations as "decent women" in the service of families. A major challenge facing the feminist movement in Okinawa is inclusion of these marginalized and forgotten women in contemporary human rights agendas.

The 1995 rape provoked a broad reexamination of policies that had long permitted the U.S. military to dominate Okinawa. Many have justifiably used the rape as leverage against Tokyo for the removal of U.S. bases and the return of Okinawan lands. Feminist groups have challenged the focus on an agenda of economic development spearheaded by Japanese corporate capital, as in the case of resort development, which fails to address the need to protect and improve women's lives. They interrogate the new development agenda: What efforts will be made to prevent the violent assaults on women by GIs and others? And to what degree would small businesses owned and run by women be protected and encouraged under a new development regime? Much Okinawan development has centered on large Japanese corporations, and there has been scant effort to promote the needs of small business owners, women like Keiko and Kaa-chan, who ran a snack shop and bar in Kin or the proprietress of the Churasa Soap Factory in Onna Village.

Indeed, the issue of how women will figure in the service economy of tourism is not addressed.[47] While women have been called on to support men in their political protests demanding Okinawan rights, they have been expected to defer their goals to the aims of Okinawan identity politics (read: economic development). Okinawan women with whom I have spoken fear that in this way, women will continue to be the base of a new tourist economy pyramid, mostly earning minimum wages and enjoying few if any employee benefits or protections.[48] An economically and socially marginalized existence will continue for these women, with more and more of them coming from the Philippines and other poorer regions of Asia, within the sexual economy of tourism.[49] The problem will remain invisible as long as officials insist on subordinating issues of women's human rights to the cause of Okinawan nationalism and ignoring the increasingly Filipina profile of entertainment workers.

In raising these issues, one of my goals has been to remind those of us who so readily appropriate the rape for our various purposes of the person at its core: the twelve-year-old Okinawan girl whose body was brutally violated and whose life was forever altered one night in 1995. Indeed, I began to write about this rape in order to understand and work through how to come to grips with this tragedy as a feminist scholar—that is, without losing sight of the girl herself. This is why it is necessary to revisit the rape. For it was initially from compassion for the victim that most of us became "involved" in our various ways with this rape. While the compassion may not have disappeared, many have shifted focus to the so-called larger political issues. A feminist politics calls on us to maintain and reaffirm the connection to the subjects of our study. In the end, we must remember that the victim is a child in an Okinawan family deprived of her youth and innocence. Whatever else we have had to say about the connection between her and Okinawa belongs to the political world of adults, a world into which she was violently and prematurely thrust.

NOTES

This chapter is a revised version of an essay published in *Critial Asian Studies* 33, no. 2 (June 2001) and is used with permission. Thanks to Tom Fenton, Gerald Figal, Carolyn Francis, Takashi Fujitani, Yoko Genka, David Howell, William Dean Kinzley, James Roberson, Nobue Suzuki, Takazato Suzuyo, and especially the editors, Laura Hein and Mark Selden, for comments and suggestions. An earlier version of this essay was presented in January 2000 as a reworking of a dissertation chapter at the Washington and Southeast Japan Seminar, held at George Washington University in Washington, D.C. The material for this chapter is drawn from my dissertation research on Okinawan women's wartime memories and experiences and the gendered nationalism and identity politics of wartime and postwar Okinawa.

1. Andrew Pollack, "3 U.S. Servicemen Convicted of Rape of Okinawa Girl," *New York Times*, 7 March 1996.

2. The clause that stipulated that U.S. soldiers accused of crimes while stationed abroad be tried by U.S. military courts was amended, in the case of Japan, as a result of this trial. Accused offenders in Japan may now be tried in local courts of law, though it is not clear whether this occurs in all cases. Other countries that host U.S. bases have also attempted to revise their SOFA agreements along these lines as a result of the legal outcome in Okinawa, including South Korea.

3. *New York Times*, 4 October 1995; *Asahi Shinbun*, 3 December 1995.

4. *New York Times*, 22 October 1995.

5. *Asahi Shinbun*, 22 November 1995.

6. Chibana Shōichi is the activist who burned the Japanese flag in protest of the visit of the then–crown prince to the 1987 national sports meet held that year in his village of Yomitan, which had been the site of one of the first "forced mass suicides" of Okinawans provoked by Japanese officers during the Battle of Okinawa.

See Norma Field, *In the Realm of a Dying Emperor: Japan at Century's End* (New York: Vintage, 1993), 33–106.

7. *Asahi Shinbun*, 11 November 1995 and 9 March 1996; *Japan Times*, 25 June 1996.

8. *New York Times*, 3 December 1995.

9. *New York Times*, 9 March 1996.

10. See Cynthia Enloe for a feminist assessment of the peace movement, in *Maneuvers: The International Politics of Militarizing Women's Lives* (Berkeley: University of California Press, 2000), 121–23.

11. Judith Butler and Joan Scott, eds., *Feminists Theorize the Political* (New York: Routledge, 1992).

12. Cynthia Enloe, *Bananas, Beaches, and Bases: Making Feminist Sense of International Politics* (Berkeley: University of California Press, 1989).

13. Admittedly, "solving" the problem of sovereignty—that is, ridding the island prefecture of U.S. bases—may seem on the surface to present the conditions women demand—namely, a safer living and work environment for Okinawans, especially Okinawan women, freed from twenty-six thousand mostly young, foreign, male troops. However, given the scant likelihood of the United States and Japan agreeing to major reduction or elimination of U.S. bases any time soon, the deferral of a feminist agenda is likely to be a long-term and therefore serious problem in local identity politics. An example of such deferral is the minimal coverage of the international women's summit (entitled "Redefining Security"), sponsored by the San Francisco–based East Asia–U.S. Women's Network Against Violence, held in Okinawa in June 2000, one month before the Group of 8 summit in July (personal communication from women's summit organizers, May 2000).

14. "Ōta Eyes Budget for Plebiscite on Future of Okinawa Bases," *Japan Times*, 21 May 1996.

15. Carol Delaney, "Father State, Motherland, and the Birth of Modern Turkey," in *Naturalizing Power: Essays in Feminist Cultural Analysis*, ed. Sylvia Yanagisako and Carol Delaney (New York: Routledge, 1995), 190, 191.

16. Ernesto Laclau and Chantal Mouffe, *Hegemony and Socialist Strategy: Towards a Radical Democratic Politics* (London: Verso, 1985), 11.

17. Linda Angst, "Gendered Nationalism: The Himeyuri Story and Okinawan Identity in Postwar Japan," in *PoLAR: Political and Legal Anthropology Review*, special edition, 20, no. 1 (May 1997): 100–13.

18. See Michael Molasky's discussion of the imagery of raped Japanese prostitutes as "an allegory of national crisis and shared victimhood," in *The American Occupation of Japan and Okinawa: Literature and Memory* (New York: Routledge, 1999). Molasky provides a provocative analysis of ways in which the Himeyuri image enjoys popular appeal in the mainland, in part through its sexualization. See also Lisa Yoneyama, who shows how maternal purity is evoked in nationalist discourse on the atomic bombing of Hiroshima. Lisa Yoneyama, *Hiroshima Traces: Time, Space, and the Dialectics of Memory* (Berkeley: University of California Press, 1999).

19. Takazato Suzuyo, "I Refuse," in "Fort Okinawa," *Bulletin of the Atomic Scientists*, special issue (July/August 1996).

20. Angst, "Gendered Nationalism" and "In a Dark Time: Community, Memory, and the Making of Ethnic Selves in Okinawan Women's Narratives," Ph.D. diss., Yale University, May 2001.

21. While I share the reading of many Okinawans—Okinawa was sacrificed by Japan both in wartime and after the war, leading to protracted U.S. military occupation, followed by a permanent base economy—the issue here is the adoption by feminists of the language of the national family in defining Okinawa's position. My point, elaborated later, is that feminist activists, who seek not merely to criticize but also to transform a patriarchal system, must disengage from the very language of that system. Transformation requires a language that posits feminists as active agents, not continuing victims, in order to work against an identity politics that defines us "by our violability." See Sharon Marcus, "Fighting Bodies, Fighting Words: A Theory and Politics of Rape Prevention," in *Feminists Theorize the Political*, ed. Judith Butler and Joan Scott (New York: Routledge, 1992). Rather than use the metaphor of the sacrificed daughter, feminists might, for example, discuss the Japan–Okinawa relationship in terms of a political economy of coercion and subordination.

22. Enloe, *Maneuvers*, 120.

23. Angst, "In a Dark Time."

24. This fact has implications for Japanese democracy as well: The most controversial aspect of the Himeyuri story is whether the girls sacrificed themselves willingly or were coerced into dying. This ambiguity speaks directly to the assessment of contemporary Japanese democracy. If Okinawa was abandoned by the nation, what does this say about Japan's leaders' claims to act in the best interest of all citizens?

25. Marcus, "Fighting Bodies, Fighting Words."

26. Marcus, "Fighting Bodies, Fighting Words," 387.

27. Figures cited in *Mainichi Shinbun*, 3 July 2001. Thanks to Sheila Johnson for providing this reference.

28. Not only are the assailants American servicemen, but they are also African Americans, which raises additional questions about power and hegemony in the U.S. military. Enloe (*Maneuvers*, 114–16) discusses the identities of the three rapists, African Americans from poor backgrounds, and considers issues of American social and military racism.

29. Marcus, "Fighting Bodies, Fighting Words," 391.

30. Gwen Kirk, Rachel Cornwell, and Margot Okazawa-Rey, "Women and the U.S. Military in East Asia," in *Foreign Policy in Focus*, Interhemispheric Resource Center and Institute for Policy Studies 4, no. 9 (1999): 2.

31. Tony Barrell and Rick Tanaka, *Okinawa Dreams OK* (Berlin: Gestalten Verlag, 1997), 120–21.

32. Carolyn Bowen Francis, "The One Tsubo Antiwar Landowners Association," in *Okinawa Voice*, Ginowan Seminar House Christian Center Newsletter (May 1992): 1–5.

33. Lydia Liu, "The Female Body and National Discourse: *The Field of Life and Death Revisited*," in *Scattered Hegemonies: Postmodernity and Transnational Feminist Practices*, ed. Inderpal Grewal and Caren Kaplan (Minneapolis: University of Minnesota Press, 1994), 40.

34. See Kazuko Watanabe, "Militarism, Colonialism, and the Trafficking of Women: 'Comfort Women' Forced into Sexual Labor for Japanese Soldiers," in *Bulletin of Concerned Asian Scholars* 26, no. 4 (1994): 3–16; and Laura Hein, "Savage Irony: The Imaginative Power of the 'Military Comfort Women' in the 1990s," *Gender and History* 11, no. 2 (July 1999).

35. Angst, "In a Dark Time."

36. Enloe, *Maneuvers.*

37. Angst, "In a Dark Time."

38. Liu, "The Female Body and National Discourse," 41.

39. See Sara Ruddick's discussion of an "antimilitarist feminism in which feminist and antimilitarist commitments are interwoven from the start." In this scenario, any man or woman becomes simultaneously feminist and antimilitarist by linking war making with masculine domination. My argument here questions the authenticity of—or at least the degree of commitment to—such claims by male and other nonfeminist leaders of Okinawa's antibase movement. Sara Ruddick, "Notes toward a Feminist Peace Politics," in *Gendering War Talk,* ed. Miriam Cooke and Angela Woollacott (Princeton, N.J.: Princeton University Press, 1993), 109–27.

40. Enloe notes that this is a common problem (*Bananas, Beaches, and Bases,* 19–41).

41. Okinawa Prefectural Government pamphlet, "Okinawa no Beigun Kichi" (U.S. Military Bases on Okinawa), 30 July 1994.

42. Several sources estimate that in 1969, when there were eighty thousand U.S. personnel on Okinawa at the height of the Vietnam War, U.S. spending on the island amounted to $260 million per year, or 40 percent of Okinawa's gross national product. The per capita income of Okinawans was then $580 per year. James Billiard, "Okinawa: The Island without a Country," in *National Geographic* 136, no. 3 (1969): 423–88. See also Kyan Shinichi, ed., *Okinawa no Rōdō Keizai* (Okinawa's Labor Economics) (Naha: Okinawa Labor Economics Office, 1989).

43. Carolyn Bowen Francis, "Women and Military Violence," in *Okinawa: Cold War Island,* ed. Chalmers Johnson (Cardiff, Calif.: Japanese Policy Research Institute), 189–204; Enloe, *Maneuvers,* 119.

44. Personal interviews and discussions with Francis and Takazato, 1993–1995; see Francis, "Women and Military Violence."

45. Angst, "Gendered Nationalism" and "In a Dark Time."

46. Angst, "In a Dark Time."

47. Suzuki Noriyuki and Tamashiro Satoko, "Okinawa no Fuiripinjin: Teijūsha to shite, mata gaikokujin rōdōsha to shite" (Okinawa's Filipinos: As Permanent Residents and as Foreign Laborers), in *Ryūdai Hōgaku* (University of the Ryukyus School of Law Publishing) 58 (1997): 1–23.

48. Takazato, "Testimony," 21–22.

49. See Enloe, *Bananas, Beaches, and Bases,* and Lenore Manderson and Margaret Jolly, eds., *Sites of Desire, Economies of Pleasure: Sexualities in Asia and the Pacific* (Chicago: University of Chicago Press, 1997).

II

CONTEMPORARY CULTURE, IDENTITY, RESISTANCE

6

Medoruma Shun

The Writer as Public Intellectual in Okinawa Today

Michael Molasky

SITUATING OKINAWAN LITERATURE

What is "Okinawan literature"? Is it best understood as a subset of Japanese literature—for example, as either a Japanese "minority literature" or "regional literature"? Or should it be seen as constituting a separate literary tradition altogether? These questions echo a fundamental question posed, implicitly or explicitly, throughout the present volume—namely, how to understand Okinawa's relationship to "mainland Japan."[1] This complex, emotionally charged issue has informed nearly all political and cultural struggles in Okinawa during the past century and continues to frame its most contentious debates today.

Medoruma Shun (1960–) has emerged as one of Okinawa's most influential, insightful, and iconoclastic voices in these debates while at the same time forging a reputation in Japanese literary circles as an unusual and promising writer of fiction. He moves fluidly between the roles of reclusive writer and public intellectual. He has created a fictional world deeply enmeshed in Okinawan life yet has managed to render this world accessible to readers far removed from his homeland.

Before considering Medoruma's writing, I wish to reflect on several of the categories widely used to discuss contemporary Okinawan literature. I begin with minority literature, followed by regional literature and conclude with a proposal for a nuanced understanding of the category

Okinawan literature. Given that all classification entails some form of bias but that classification is nonetheless inescapable ("literature" itself being a contentious category with its own histories), we have a responsibility to reflect on the particular bias that a particular form of classification introduces. Specifically, I view the following inquiry into literary categories as a way to better grasp two basic issues that lie at the heart of the present volume: (1) how Okinawans have represented themselves and (2) how they have been represented by others, especially by Americans and mainland Japanese, who have (alternately or together) exerted hegemony over Okinawa for more than a century.

It is tempting for readers from ethnically diverse societies, such as the United States, to view literature written by Okinawans as a "Japanese minority literature." This rubric links Okinawan literature with that written in Japanese by authors of Korean descent (*Zainichi bungaku*), by the outcaste *burakumin* and, some would say, with literature by the Ainu.[2] Certainly, many writers from all these groups feel as if they have been relegated to the margins of Japanese society, and this awareness informs a good deal of their literature. The category "minority literature" highlights shared thematic concerns and historical experiences that are assumed to bind these groups to one another and to minority writers in other societies (African American, Irish, etc.). It therefore reveals commonalities between Okinawan literature and that of other subordinated populations. Yet minority literature remains a problematic concept in Japan for two reasons. First, the ideology of ethnic homogeneity that has dominated much of Japan's postwar history inhibits real recognition of internal minority groups. Second, those who would seem to qualify as "minorities" in Japan are often reluctant to view themselves as such. If, for example, few Okinawans refer to themselves as a "minority group," is it meaningful to nonetheless impose on them this label?[3] We Americans must be especially cautious about doing so since our government repeatedly emphasized, during its twenty-seven-year occupation of the islands, Okinawans' "minority status" as part of a propaganda campaign to weaken the movement calling for reversion to Japan.[4]

The concept "minority literature" not only ignores a people's right to self-definition (i.e., "You people are a minority whether you acknowledge it or not"). It also lumps together the literature produced by populations whose historical relations with Japan, despite superficial similarities, differ significantly. It tends to represent these peoples as lacking agency—or, to use a term frequently employed by Okinawan critics, including Medoruma Shun—as lacking "subjectivity" (*shutaisei*). Furthermore, the category "minority literature" serves to delimit the scope and value of a given body of writing, implying that it is produced at the nation's margins and holds little appeal for those in the mainstream. In this regard it resembles the category "regional literature" discussed later and also the patronizing and patriarchal category "*joryū bungaku*" ("women's literature"), frequently decried by feminist critics.[5] Arguably, these categories beg more questions than they answer: Does one have to be an Okinawan (Ainu, *burakumin*, or *zainichi*) writer for the label to be applicable? What about mainland Japanese writers, such as Shimao Toshio and Ikezawa Natsuki, who settled in the Ryūkyūs and wrote about its culture and people? Do they become "honorary minority writers" as a result of their prolonged residence and intense, sympathetic engagement with local cultural issues?[6] Conversely, how are we to view those Okinawans, ethnic Koreans, Ainu, and *burakumin* whose work has no discernable basis in a "minority experience"? Are they to be understood as minority writers who betray their people, as minority writers whose work nonetheless fails to qualify as "minority literature"? Finally, what about those writers from a "minority" background, such as Nakagami Kenji, who eventually emerge as leading Japanese writers? At what point do they cease to be minority writers and simply become "Japanese writers"? The latter question may well apply to Medoruma Shun as his reputation continues to grow in Japanese literary circles.[7]

The label "regional literature" similarly presents problems with respect to Okinawa. As the present volume demonstrates, Okinawa is far more than just one among many prefectures or regions in Japan. At issue is not whether other regions have distinctive characteristics that enable its residents to claim a coherent identity but rather the degree to which, and the ways in which, those people differentiate themselves from—and are differentiated by—the rest of the nation. As noted earlier, Okinawans often refer to themselves as *Uchinanchū*, a term in local dialect that literally means "Okinawan person" and most closely approximates the standard Japanese term "*Okinawajin*." The very use of local dialect in such a context underscores a sense of difference, a difference that is constructed at least partly in opposition to the Japanese nation-state. (*Uchinanchū* is most often used in binary opposition to *Yamatunchū*, or "Japanese person.") Assertions of regional identity by citizens of other prefectures—from Aomori in the north to Kagoshima in southern Kyushu—rarely entail defining oneself in opposition to "Japanese people."[8]

Because Japanese national subjectivity does not yet admit the possibility of hyphenated identities such as "Okinawan-Japanese," Okinawans have often found themselves having to choose between one end of the hyphen or the other. This poses far more of a dilemma for Okinawans than for residents of other regions. First, Okinawa features countless qualities, both tangible (i.e., topography, architecture, cuisine) and less tangible (i.e., music, language, religious beliefs), which sharply distinguish it from the rest of Japan. Yet at least as crucial in shaping Okinawa's sense of difference is its distinct historical experience. Okinawans remember being treated as inferior by Japan's prewar colonial policies, by the nation's wartime military policy and the actions of its soldiers on the Okinawan battlefields, by Japan's secret postwar negotiations with the United States that left Okinawa under American military occupation while the rest of Japan was "liberated," and, of course, by today's massive U.S. military presence, which derives in part not only from American governmental pressure but also from Japanese official complicity.

Okinawa's sense of difference is readily apparent in much of the region's contemporary literature, which retains a strong focus on local life. Most of Okinawa's leading fiction writers today continue to live in the prefecture and write stories deeply rooted in the surrounding social and physical landscape.[9] This holds true not only for Medoruma but for other writers born after the war, such as Matayoshi Eiki (1949–) and Sakiyama Tami (1954–), as well as for the preceding generation of fiction writers, including Ōshiro Tatsuhiro (1925–) and Nagadō Eikichi (1932–).[10] In this regard, they have much in common with regional writers elsewhere in Japan. But the term "regional literature," like "minority literature," often implies that the given body of writing has had little impact on the literary mainstream, and it, too, relegates Okinawan writing to the margins, assuming that this literature will have limited appeal among readers outside the marginalized population. I wish to suggest that Medoruma Shun and his contemporaries are best viewed as neither minority writers nor simply regional writers but specifically as *Okinawan* writers. At the same time, I believe they must be recognized as full-fledged *Japanese* writers—because they regularly publish for and engage a national readership, and because the critical recognition they have received makes clear that they are extending the boundaries of what constitutes Japanese literature today.

In other words, I am calling for a redeployment of the categories "Okinawan" and "Japanese" in a way that most closely approximates the use of these terms by Okinawans as both overlapping and antithetical categories. Understanding "Okinawan literature" in these dialectical terms enables us to see how Medoruma and others are expanding the category of Japanese literature while keeping their feet firmly planted in Okinawan soil.

In several ways their relationship to Japan's literary mainstream resembles that of an earlier generation of American writers from the Deep South: Like postwar Okinawan writers, many southern writers represent their homeland as geographically and culturally removed from the nation's center, as a region where modernity has yet to fully unravel the social fabric, where religious beliefs continue to shape everyday life, where regional pride battles with humiliation and shame, where the spirits of the dead lurk amid the dense vines and branches of ancient trees, and where memories of a distant war still linger in the air. William Faulkner and other "southern writers" are viewed as a coherent group not only because they were born in the same remote region but because their fictional worlds hewed so closely to the life and landscape of the Deep South. Yet at the same time, their work gained recognition as an integral and vital part of America's literary tradition.

Of course, Okinawa is not the Deep South and has yet to produce a writer whose stature within Japan rivals that of Faulkner in the United States.[11] The two regions and their respective literary traditions differ in several obvious ways. For example, Okinawans, in contrast to American southerners, share not only geography and historical memories but a sense of ethnic difference from those to the north. This is partly manifested in the Ryūkyūan dialects (discussed later), which remain virtually incomprehensible to mainland Japanese, although many if not most Okinawans today have limited command of their local dialect.[12] Perhaps the most salient difference between Okinawa and the Deep South is the extent to which slavery and its legacies defined and continue to define "the South," unifying southerners vis-à-vis northerners even as it divides their people along racial lines.[13]

Literary categories shape our understanding of a body of writing by constituting that same writing as a coherent body. The circularity of this relationship can be dizzying, and the categories themselves always seem deficient in some way, yet we cannot seem to manage without them. Categories not only shape our understanding of a particular body of literature but define the reader's relationship to it (i.e., majority/minority, national/regional, mainstream/ethnic). Fortunately, regardless of the categories imposed on their work, writers themselves, however reflective, continue to go about their business of writing stories. In the case of Medoruma Shun and other accomplished Okinawan writers of fiction, this entails providing readers both inside and outside the prefecture with a glimpse of Okinawan life in its full complexity. By doing so, these writers (including those who pride themselves on being "apolitical") inevitably take part in a discursive struggle in which their work serves to offset the facile, fragmented, and stereotypical views of Okinawa that dominate the public sphere. Medoruma clearly situates his writing within this struggle, although he continues to experiment with structure, style, and tone, in both his fictional stories and his nonfictional essays.

SITUATING MEDORUMA SHUN

Medoruma Shun is generally regarded as Okinawa's most adventurous and promising writer of fiction today. He has won numerous literary prizes—regional and national—and has earned the respect of Japanese authors such as Ōe Kenzaburo, Kōno Taeko, Hino Keizō, and Ikezawa Natsuki. Although he has been publishing fiction since the early 1980s, Medoruma first gained national recognition in 1997 when his story "*Suiteki*" (Droplets) was awarded the Akutagawa Prize for literature.[14] This work, discussed later, explores the issue of Okinawan war memory through the figure of Tokusho, an unremarkable seventy-year-old man suddenly incapacitated by a remarkable malady. "Droplets" was praised for its imaginative amalgam of realist and surrealist narrative technique as well as for its probing examination of Okinawans' struggle with their war memories. Here was a new author, born fifteen years after the war ended, who managed to produce one of the most haunting Japanese fictional accounts of wartime battle (and its postwar legacies) published in decades.

While working full-time in Okinawa as a high school teacher of Japanese language, Medoruma has continued to write short stories and to garner critical acclaim. In 1998, he published a story entitled "*Mabuigumi*," for which he received both the Kawabata Yasunari Prize and the Kiyama Shōhei Literary Prize. "*Mabuigumi*" became the title work for Medoruma's second collection of stories, published in 1999 by Asahi Shinbunsha, the publishing arm of Japan's most prestigious national newspaper. His third and most recent collection, *Gunchō no ki*, appeared in April 2001, also from Asahi Shinbunsha. It consists of four stories originally published from the winter 1998 to the summer 2000 editions of *Shōsetsu torippaa* (Fictional Traveler), a quarterly literary magazine issued by the popular Japanese weekly, *Shūkan Asahi*. Medoruma is quickly making a name for himself as a fiction writer of national repute.

Although his reputation is growing rapidly among Japanese writers and literary critics, Medoruma remains deeply tied to his homeland. This is evident in his life as well as in his writing. He was raised in Nakijin, a rural village in the northwestern part of the island of Okinawa, and grew up in an extended family. He seems to have had an especially close relationship with his grandmother, who related to him many memories that serve as source material for his stories. Unlike most Okinawans his age, Medoruma spoke dialect both at home and school until graduating from high school.[15] He then attended the University of the Ryukyus, where he majored in Japanese literature under Professor Okamoto Keitoku, a leading scholar of modern Okinawan literature and an important Okinawan intellectual. After graduating from the university, Medoruma worked as a security guard and taught at a *juku* (cram school) before becoming a high school teacher, mainly at vocational schools in the prefecture. "Droplets" was published while he was teaching on the island of Miyako. Life on Miyako provided Medoruma with firsthand experience of Okinawa's cultural diversity. He seems to have taken special interest in local religious practices, and several of his recent stories explore the role of religion (especially shamanism) in Okinawan daily life.[16] Miyako also seemed to offer greater privacy and a change of pace from life on the main island. For several years, Medoruma had pursued a life of isolation to concentrate on his fiction writing. He discussed this desire for isolation with author Ikezawa Natsuki in the September 1997 edition of the literary journal *Bungakukai*:

> Starting about ten years ago, I cut myself off from all personal and professional relationships having to do with literature. I was asked to participate in literary circles, to attend publication parties, etc., but I turned down every invitation. During the past few years, I have even tried to avoid conversations about literature as much as possible. I felt that in Okinawa, going out on the town and drinking, etc., would interfere with my writing. So sometimes I'd leave and go to the Japanese mainland to earn money, or I'd teach in a local cram school and spend the rest of the time secluded in my apartment. I created that kind of isolation for myself, then immersed myself in reading and writing fiction. Stated differently, I think it was probably the frustration stemming from this lifestyle that enabled me to write "Droplets." Without a degree of severity [*kibishisa*] in your daily life, I don't think you can effectively portray the Battle of Okinawa or the U.S. bases. Your writing would lose its edge, become too soft.[17]

Medoruma has long kept his personal life from public scrutiny. He insists that only his pen name, "Medoruma Shun," be mentioned in publications; he refused all television interviews after receiving the Akutagawa Prize; and he dons sunglasses whenever being photographed—less out of pretension than a desire for privacy. Yet Medoruma eventually left behind his self-imposed "exile" in Miyako to accept a teaching job in Nago. A small, sleepy city in the northeastern part of the main island of Okinawa, Nago was emerging as the center of political controversy by the late 1990s, and Medoruma was by this time clearly ready to plunge into the political fray. The Japanese government, together with the U.S. military, proposed moving Futenma Air Base to a site offshore the town of Henoko, adjacent to Camp Schwab. Nago and the residents of nearby Henoko faced an all too common Okinawan dilemma: whether to accept a financial stimulus package from Tokyo in exchange for an expanded U.S. military presence. In other words, they were asked to tolerate an inevitable increase in crime, military accidents, and environmental depredation in exchange for money and jobs. Not long after the Japanese government proposed the stimulus package, it upped the ante by announcing that Nago had been selected as the site of the G-8 summit. (See Julia Yonetani's chapter 9 in this volume.)

Although he has continued writing fiction after moving to Nago and has kept his personal life from the public eye, Medoruma was developing into a more public intellectual. He began speaking in public forums and has since become a familiar figure at gatherings of local activist organizations while remaining aloof from their social functions. He has written countless essays opposing the relocation of Futenma and decrying the shameless attempt of the Japanese government to use the G-8 summit as bait. Finally, true to his ascetic demeanor and uncompromising notion of personal integrity, he has written biting critiques of Okinawans' complicity and cowardice in the face of political pressure from Tokyo and Washington.

Today Medoruma divides his writing between fiction and criticism. In his recent fiction (and to a lesser extent in his criticism), he regularly incorporates local dialect into his texts—sometimes even using dialect in a story's title—which further distinguishes his work from most contemporary Japanese literature. There have been, of course, other critically acclaimed postwar writers whose work is comparably rooted in the soil and society of remote locales (e.g., Shimao Toshio in Amami Ōshima and Fukazawa Shichirō in the Tōhoku region), but they remain rare, and most such writers have spent considerable time in either the Tokyo or Kansai metropolitan area.

Medoruma is not alone among local writers who continue to live in the prefecture while writing stories set almost exclusively in Okinawa. Among those of roughly the same generation, Matayoshi Eiki and Sakiyama Tami are respected by Okinawa critics and regularly publish in national literary magazines. Matayoshi, in particular, is a prolific writer of fiction who has also received his share of critical acclaim, including having won the Akutagawa Prize the year before Medoruma for his novel *Buta no mukui* (Pig's Revenge). What, then, distinguishes Medoruma from his Okinawan contemporaries?[18] Some would point to his literary style, which fuses earthiness with refinement, and brooding intensity with a gentle humor. Others would emphasize his ongoing experimentation with narrative form and technique, especially his interest in Latin American magical realism as a way of excavating the sublimated layers of Okinawa's cultural and historical memory. Yet perhaps what most separates him from his Okinawan contemporaries is his willingness—even eagerness—to assume the dual role of fiction writer and public intellectual delving into some of the most contentious issues in Okinawan politics.

SOCIAL CRITICISM

Shortly after being awarded the Akutagawa Prize, Medoruma began to establish his credentials as a public intellectual by publishing incisive social criticism in local newspapers. He soon began writing for national publications as well and by the late 1990s was regularly speaking about local politics and culture at gatherings of Okinawan activist groups. In assuming the dual role of writer and critic, Medoruma resembles intellectually ambitious, politically engaged Japanese authors of previous generations, especially Ōe Kenzaburo (1935–) and Nakagami Kenji (1946–1992), each of whom developed a distinctive literary style, wrote imaginative and original works of fiction, and at the same time published influential critical commentary on political events of the day. Among his Okinawan predecessors, Medoruma most resembles poet, critic, and journalist Arakawa Akira (1931–). Both men wield a combative, take-no-prisoners prose style as they explore the cultural and political ramifications of contemporary events affecting Okinawa.[19] Often, they find their fellow Okinawans to be complicit in the region's present-day plight, and both insist that a willingness to sacrifice comfort and security is essential if Okinawa is to overcome its problems.

In his commitment to political engagement, Medoruma stands out from other Okinawan writers of his generation who seek to avoid political commentary.[20] He insists that there is no contradiction between writing fiction and social criticism, between the private artist and public intellectual. Consider, for example, the following dialogue between Medoruma and Sakiyama Tami, published in *Keeshi kajii*, a small Okinawan journal of cultural criticism:[21]

> *Sakiyama:* I'm someone who has consciously avoided making public political statements, and I've confined my writing to works of literature, but you've written a lot of critical articles in the newspapers. It seems to me that this must play a significant role in your writing, your thought process, your work as an author. As a writer of fiction myself, I want to better understand the author Medoruma Shun, and yet I can't help but think about how much energy you must expend on your criticism. I'm a little worried about the impact your critical writing style might have on your literary work, if you keep this up. I realize that the shabby state of journalism today might make you feel compelled to write criticism, but I'd like to hear your thoughts on the issue.
>
> *Medoruma:* My guess is that the journalists who ask me to write articles for their newspapers simply want to have one person with a critical perspective who can say what they themselves are not permitted to write. . . .
>
> *Sakiyama:* So, it's safe to assume that what you were being asked to write was consistent with what you wanted to say in the first place?

Medoruma: When I write, I write what I want, regardless of what anyone else expects. I simply use the forum presented me to express my own views. . . . If writing criticism is all it takes to interfere with my fiction writing, then I should probably give up literature altogether.

Sakiyama: What I mean is that when I read your critical essays, they seem as if they could have been written under the name of any newspaper journalist. . . .

Medoruma: I don't recall ever having been that disparaging about journalists. For example, Garcia Marquez wrote not only *One Hundred Years of Solitude,* but also countless newspaper articles and investigative reports; he even interviewed Castro. How this journalistic work affected his ability to write *One Hundred Years of Solitude* . . . the very question seems like the kind that Japanese authors always feel compelled to ask. I think it's fine to have authors who can write in only one style and who want to devote all of their energy to writing fiction. I wouldn't ask anything else from them. But I also think it's good to have writers who don't fit the mold, who do all sorts of weird things. If I reach the point where journalistic writing occupied most of my energy and feel that I should stop writing fiction, then I'll stop writing fiction.

This dialogue between two relatively young Okinawan writers harks back to an old Japanese (and international) debate about the relationship between art and politics, one that preoccupied not only Marxist theorists and their liberal humanist detractors but Medoruma's predecessors, most notably Ōe and Arakawa. Yet for all his willingness to assume the role of public intellectual, Medoruma also seems careful to ensure that these two facets of his writing remain in separate "compartments." This is readily apparent, as Sakiyama intimates, from the written style he employs in his essays versus that of his stories. The early essays, in particular, often resemble newspaper editorials, albeit more indignant and sardonic in tone than what one normally encounters in such writing. They rarely reveal the fertile imagination, restrained lyricism, gentle irony, or empathy for common folk that has earned Medoruma's fiction praise. The difference between these two bodies of work can appear so stark, in fact, that admirers of Medoruma's fiction have remarked, after reading his critical essays, that the stories and essays "seem to have been written by two completely different people."[22]

Medoruma regularly began publishing critical pieces in local newspapers shortly after receiving the Akutagawa Prize, and Sakiyama's assertion about his generic critical style during these early years is well founded. But he has clearly grown bolder in his critical writing during the past few years, adopting a style that is far from innocuous or generic. Consider, for example, the opening passage from an essay Medoruma published in the Japanese national weekly magazine *Shūkan Asahi,* in October 2000. The second in a series of seven essays, it is representative of his style and tone throughout the series.

> The *Yamatunchū* (Japanese) have their favorite images of the *Uchinanchū* (Okinawans).
>
> There's the simple but good-hearted middle-aged man, his skin dark from the sun, an Orion beer in his hand; the sturdy, hard-working, cheerful old woman who suddenly grows sad when talking about the Battle of Okinawa, but then laughs away her suffering; the young man, who at first looks a little scary but turns out to be just a shy, simple islander; the young woman, always bright and cheerful. When told that these are the only kind of people in Okinawa, even those who normally read the newspaper and grumble about the *Yanayamatu* (rotten Japanese) end up feeling as if they must live up to the expectation and suddenly transform themselves into a "good *Uchinanchū*." A visitor arrives from the Japanese mainland, so they hold a beach party and break out the Orion beer (even though they always drink Kirin or Sapporo because Orion isn't really that good); they talk about Koza (present-day "Okinawa City") before reversion; they bring along one of the local *Obaa* so that the old woman can complain about how the young people these days don't appreciate the horrors of war; and finally, the guest will say, "In Okinawa, you can't end a party without dancing the *kachaashi*, right?" so they oblige and stumble their way through the unfamiliar movements.[23]

This opening passage to the essay is relatively restrained. The bile begins to flow as Medoruma turns to Okinawa's "finely honed tradition of toadyism and animal loyalty," after which the essay culminates in the full-fledged diatribe here:

> And then, as if this weren't enough, the members of the opposition movement drag out their tired clichés, such as "Life is a treasure," and are praised to the gills for their polite behavior (based on "nonviolence" and other relics of postwar democracy) while people here are being raped and murdered, and if this happened in another country violent protests would break out, yet the most they can manage here is to call a meeting—not a real protest—where they let off steam without doing a thing to paralyze the U.S. bases, and although they think they've put pressure on the government, in fact they've played right into the government's hands and end up strengthening the SACO agreement, the guidelines, and the bases, after which they're rewarded with a speech given by the American president, who stands in front of the Cornerstone of Peace and proclaims, using their very own words, that "Life is a treasure"—right there at the memorial on which are inscribed the names, coexisting blissfully, of Japanese soldiers and the Okinawan civilians they slaughtered, of Japanese military commanders and Okinawan babies strangled in the caves—and in spite of it all, the members of the opposition groups, having successfully formed a "human chain" around an American military base, are under the delusion that they've publicized their anti-base

> movement to the world, although they have failed to even press the issue with the Japanese (who don't give a damn about Okinawa's base problems anyway), and they once again end up performing that familiar role, so beloved by *Yamatunchū*, of the peaceloving Okinawan.

I have translated this passage a bit loosely in hope of conveying the seething, sardonic tone that permeates the essay. On the other hand, I have tried to retain the rhythm of the passage (at the risk of sacrificing readability) by translating it into a single English sentence, as it appears in the original text. This seems crucial, given Sakiyama's earlier claim that Medoruma's style in his essays is interchangeable with that of a journalist. In fact, one would be hard-pressed to find a journalist who could get away with such prolix sentences. Although the style is less carefully crafted than that found in Medoruma's fiction, it is emphatically not an example of generic journalistic prose. I wish to suggest, then, that while Medoruma clearly strives to compartmentalize his writing of fiction and nonfiction, in recent years, at least, his criticism is not always as prosaic as Sakiyama claims. On the contrary, the writing style in his critical essays seems more imaginative, more "literary" than it once was. Rather than worrying about how Medoruma's critical essays (politics) threaten his fiction (art), it might be more productive to ask how his work as a fiction writer informs and invigorates his criticism. As we will see, many of the issues addressed in his critical writing have been central concerns in his fictional works for many years.

FICTION

Contrary to the widespread perception that Medoruma's fiction and essays have little in common, both reveal the author's insistence on intellectual honesty and ethical integrity, his disdain for all forms of social discrimination, and his ongoing concern with the intersection of private and public memory. These concerns, as well as key elements distinguishing his literary style, are evident from his earliest stories, such as "*Gyogunki*" (Taiwan Woman, 1983).[24]

"*Gyogunki*" is a retrospective first-person narrative about an adolescent boy in a remote Okinawan village shortly before reversion. The retrospective quality of the narrative is announced in the opening line: "Even now I clearly recall that feeling on my fingertip."[25] He goes on to describe "the tight, transparent membrane" of the eye of a tilapia during his days "hunting" them in the local river with other village boys. The boys used a bow and homemade arrow with an attached sewing needle for the tip, and they would try to pierce the fish through the eye. In this opening passage, the eye is described in strikingly sensuous language, and as the fish's life seeps away, its eye undergoes "a brilliant change in color from blue to indigo, and then to black." Tactile impressions (the sensation of the membrane on his fingertip) give way to the visual (as he observes the dying fish), resulting in an erotically tinged reverie on death. Later in the story, the erotic undertones emerge more clearly when the image of the fish eye is overlaid in the boy's mind with the eye of a "Taiwan Woman" ("*Taiwan onna*"). The woman is one of several female migrant workers in the local pineapple cannery who are viewed with disdain by the local Okinawans. "'Taiwan women.' That's what we called them. The words echoed with a feeling of contempt and indecency. We picked up on these nuances from the adult conversations we overheard, and we began using the expression ourselves with no compunction whatsoever" (62). Yet, only a few paragraphs later, the narrator observes, "Unlike Okinawan women, these factory workers had beautiful skin, so white as to seem translucent. Seeing this, for the first time I felt the desire to touch a woman's skin" (62). Disdain mixes with desire not only in this boy's fantasies but also among the local men who sleep with these foreign women. In an ending that recalls the novels of Nakagami Kenji and William Faulkner, the boy discovers that both his brother (who works at the cannery) and his father have been sleeping with the very woman he has pursued in his fantasies.[26]

"*Gyogunki*" is the first of many works by Medoruma that reveals his concern with social discrimination in its myriad manifestations, although this is by no means the narrative's main focus.[27] Whereas this story exposes local discrimination against Taiwanese in Okinawa, subsequent stories and essays examine discrimination in other forms, including Japan's social and institutional discrimination against Okinawa throughout the twentieth century; America's discriminatory policies toward Okinawa during the occupation and today; discrimination within Okinawa by the political and cultural "center" (e.g., Naha and Okinawa City) toward the periphery (e.g., Nago, Henoko and the outlying islands); Okinawan as well as Japanese segregation of citizens with Hansen's Disease (leprosy); and, in one of his most recent stories, "*Gunchō no ki*," Okinawans' treatment of wartime "comfort women."[28]

Medoruma has always written fiction that reveals his strong social conscience, but his work ranges widely in the degree to which he allows "political issues" to dominate the surface of his narrative. "*Gyogunki*" occupies one end of the spectrum, where the author's concern with social discrimination is evident yet never allowed to overshadow either the fictional story line or the lyrical style. At the other end are his 1989 story "*Ichigatsu nanoka*" ("January 7") and "*Machi-monogatari Koza—Kibō*" ("Hope"), published in 1999. Although critics (and, one suspects, most readers) have found these adamantly "political" stories to be less satisfying than his other fiction, these works nonetheless shed light on both Medoruma's literary ambitions and his social criticism.

"Ichigatsu nanoka" concerns a young Okinawan man's troubled response to the announcement of Emperor Hirohito's death in 1989.[29] Both the protagonist and the narrative itself quickly spin out of control with his involvement in two egregious acts of violence. Despite its weaknesses, this story offers among the earliest fictional examples of Medoruma's sardonic humor. In fact, the most memorable point in this story is not the histrionic rampage that is intended to serve as the story's violent climax but rather an incongruously humorous scene early in the narrative, when it finally dawns on the main character (who is a bit of a dullard) that the public cry for "self-restraint" following the emperor's death promises to impinge on his favorite leisure activities:

> Even so, he couldn't understand why the pachinko parlor should be closed for the day just because His Majesty the Emperor had died. But he resigned himself to the fact and decided to try another place nearby, only to find it shut down as well, with the same notice posted on the door. Gradually overcome by doubt, he mulled things over for a while until reaching the conclusion that His Majesty the Emperor must surely be the Honorary Chairman of the Japan Pachinko Parlor Association. So, he gave up on pachinko and headed for a porno theater in Sakurazaka that was showing a triple feature.

This passage offers a taste of the piquant, sometimes blasphemous, humor that Medoruma would later incorporate into many of his critical essays, including the *Shūkan Asahi* series quoted earlier. Other than this humorous passage, *"Ichigatsu nanoka"* offers few pleasures, but it is among the first indications of Medoruma's interest in violence as a possible Okinawan response to the problem of the U.S. bases.

Medoruma explores the idea of violence more explicitly a decade later in the terrorist fantasy *"Machi-monogatari Koza—Kibō,"* which was published in the evening edition of the national daily, *Asahi shinbun*, and later translated into English as "Hope."[30] Set in the late 1990s, several years after the 1995 rape incident and ensuing protests (see Linda Isako Angst's chapter 5 in this volume), this story is narrated from the perspective of a young Okinawan man who kidnaps and murders the child of an American serviceman. The narrative could be described as a political idea masquerading as a work of fiction. Certainly, sentences such as the following will leave some readers confused as to whether "Hope" should be read as a short story or manifesto: "What Okinawa needs now is not demonstrations by thousands of people or rallies by tens of thousands, but the death of one American child."[31] The demonstrations clearly refer to those in the wake of the 1995 rape, the same demonstrations that Medoruma mocks in his *Shûkan Asahi* essay quoted earlier.

Whether one chooses to read "Hope" as a work of fiction or as an essay, it serves as a rhetorical warning that Okinawans' pent-up frustration with the U.S. military bases could explode into acts of violence against the American forces. Medoruma's own views on violence as a form of resistance remain unclear in this work, although the story does attest to his interest in violent protest as a possible alternative to those peaceful gatherings that he disparages in essays he published around that time.[32] Readers might find themselves puzzled about Medoruma's decision to write this story in the first place. Does writing such a work constitute a courageous gesture, as the *Zainichi* novelist, Suh Kyung-sik, asserts?[33] Or does the cloak of fiction, however flimsy, provide Medoruma with safe cover to explore an idea that would be even more disturbing if proposed in one of his essays? Perhaps it is an attempt to exorcise dangerous social (and personal?) fantasies through fiction, thereby forestalling the eruption of homicidal anger by fellow Okinawans while drawing wider attention to the urgency of the prefecture's problems.

Obfuscating Medoruma's position on the issue of violent resistance, and particularly of terrorist violence in "Hope," is his cryptic use of the word *kibō* in the story's title. Should the title be construed as signifying the "hope" that violence will succeed (presumably where peaceful protest has failed) in forcing the U.S. military to withdraw from Okinawa? Or does it refer to the very absence of hope—a profound hopelessness—that can lead to such desperate actions? The latter interpretation would seem to accord most closely with Medoruma's own views at the time, if one accepts his comments below from an interview with the *Okinawa Times,* published one month after "Hope":

> *Medoruma:* These days in Okinawa, people discussing the [U.S. military] base problem often use the words "realistic option" or the "best" or "better" choice. Yet no one is discussing the worst option. That's what I wanted to consider [in "Hope"]. It may be the type of action that comes from hopelessness and is unavoidable, but I wanted to imagine such a possibility as one of the available options. It's the most heinous terrorist act, but it isn't inconceivable if someone really wanted to carry it out, so it does remain as one of the worst options.
>
> Okinawa Times: This work conveys a sense of anger, pessimism, and humiliation, which seems to reflect a feeling of hopelessness with the current situation.
>
> *Medoruma:* I do have such feelings. Maybe it stems from Okinawans' weakness or fragility.
>
> Okinawa Times: Doesn't this contradict the idea of nonviolence (*hibu no shisō*)?

Medoruma: "Nonviolence" (*hibu*) and "pacifism" (*heiwa shugi*) are illusory ideals advocated by former Governor Ōta and other representatives of the so-called era of postwar democracy. The reason we have no terrorism in Okinawa today is that we don't feel desperate at the moment, thanks to the generosity of the Economic Giant, Japan. But if we reach the point where people are starving and must struggle just to make ends meet, we'll no doubt see acts of terrorism.[34]

Although there is no indication that Medoruma himself advocates terrorism, "Hope" and passages such as the one quoted earlier suggest that he was becoming fed up with what he viewed as the ineffectual efforts of both the Okinawan government and their opponents to peacefully resolve "the base problem." In his first essay (8 September 2000) for the *Shūkan kin'yōbi* series mentioned earlier, Medoruma again publicly contemplated the option of antibase violence:

> However many thousands or tens of thousands gather to call for peace or a removal of the U.S. bases, as long as their protests are conducted peacefully and in a nonviolent spirit, the U.S. and Japanese governments just seem to look down their noses at them and brush them aside. Could it be that the bases will never be removed from Okinawa unless the American military is physically threatened or unless the situation escalates to the point where people get killed?

Unlike the vast majority of Medoruma's fictional works, "Hope" seems to generate fewer questions about the story itself than about the author's intentions and motivations for writing it. This might be a sign that as a work of fiction, "Hope" fails to engage its readers. However one chooses to view Medoruma's motivations for writing this story, in the aftermath of the 11 September 2001, hijackings and attacks on the World Trade Center and the Pentagon, one cannot help but wonder what Medoruma thinks about "Hope" today.[35] Would he have written the same story? If so, would the *Asahi* have published it?

On 11 October 2001, exactly one month after the attacks in the United States, Medoruma published an op-ed piece in the *Okinawa Times* addressing terrorism in relation to the war in Afghanistan and within the broader context of American and Japanese foreign policy. The article does provide a clearer articulation of Medoruma's thoughts on terrorism than is available from his earlier essays and interviews. His main argument is that by engaging in military action in Afghanistan, the United States has "fallen into the trap" set for them, since it is destined to encourage even more young Islamic men to join their "Holy War" and will only lead to an increase in anti-American sentiment worldwide. "Before singing the praises of 'freedom and prosperity,'" he writes, "in countries such as the United States and Japan we must first consider how much 'oppression, war, and poverty' exists in the world." He criticizes Japan's support of the U.S. military response and insists on the need to "break the vicious cycle of 'terrorism' and 'war'" by confronting its root causes. Such views constitute an unambiguous rejection of violence as an acceptable form of conflict resolution, a position that is not articulated in his earlier essays. Medoruma is most original and provocative when discussing Okinawa's role in the "war on terrorism":

> Since September 11, the U.S. bases in Okinawa have been on a state of high alert. The number of tourists has dropped drastically, and we've had to face the undeniable fact that Okinawa is an "island of military bases," integrally linked to wars throughout the world. Even so, one can't help but wonder about those Japanese tourists from "the mainland" ("*hondo*") who have cancelled their travel plans to Okinawa due to the danger. Have they given any thought to how dangerous it is for the citizens of Okinawa Prefecture (*Okinawa kenmin*) who actually live here?
>
> Japan is a nation that has had comparatively little historical contact with the Arab states and Islamic peoples, and it should establish a dialogue that focuses on combating poverty and providing economic assistance. And Okinawans, as a people with first-hand experience of wartime battle on their homeland, and as a population surrounded by military bases and who live in a constant state of anxiety, should be more assertive in urging all of Japan to seek a peaceful resolution to these problems.

Notwithstanding his stated desire for a peaceful resolution of the conflict in Afghanistan, Medoruma's other writings—from "*Ichigatsu Nanoka*" to "Hope" to his subsequent essays and interviews—bespeak a deep-seated ambivalence about how best to rid Okinawa of the U.S. bases and of the prefecture's excessive dependence (both economic and psychological) on Japan's government in Tokyo. When confronted with real acts of terrorism, he condemns war and violence and advocates peaceful solutions, yet, as we have seen, he has often mocked such efforts in the past and has clearly felt disenchanted with the results of peaceful protest in Okinawa.

NEW DIRECTIONS IN FICTION: "DROPLETS"

The 1996 story "Droplets" helped launch Medoruma's career while forging a new approach to fiction that has constituted the mainstream of his subsequent work. "Droplets" is often described as a work of magical realism, in that certain events—such as men walking through walls and insects vanishing before one's eyes—challenge our notion of reality, and because it moves seamlessly between different temporal and experiential realms. For many readers, it brings to mind the literature of Gabriel García Marquez, whom Medoruma often cites as a source of inspiration. But in a published dialogue with Ōe Kenzaburo in July 2000, Medoruma expressed reservations about the term *magical realism,* at least as it applies to Marquez and to his own work:

> I think that Marquez's fictional world is seen as "magical" only through the gaze of the West. For the people who live in that world, it is truly *real*. . . . There is a method used when trying to represent a type of phenomenon that cannot be seen or perceived by the Western gaze: you construct an imaginary place and then accept all of the events that occur there as being real. It is from this point that literary expression begins. I imagine that Marquez's new approach to literature was born when he made this discovery. In Okinawa, too, one can take the reality before one's eyes, transform it through fiction, convince oneself that all of the events are truly possible, and then allow oneself to enter into that world. The idea for "Droplets" began with this conscious approach to the material.[36]

Medoruma's views on magical realism accord with much that has been published in English by literary scholars during the past decade. Franco Moretti, for example, reminds us that "the expression 'magical realism' appears for the first time in a book by [Cuban novelist] Alejo Carpentier, *The Kingdom of This World*." After quoting the relevant passage, he points out that the term Carpentier used was

> not magical *realism*, as it has unfortunately been translated (and as it will inevitably continue to be called), but marvelous *reality*. Not a poetics—a state of affairs. In Haiti, Carpentier writes, surrealism is in the things themselves. It is an everyday, collective fact, which restores reality to modernist techniques: which takes the avant garde, and sets its feet back on the ground.[37] (emphasis in the original)

The editors of a volume of critical studies on magical realism elaborate:

> For the characters who inhabit the fictional world, and for the author who creates it, magic may be real, reality magical; there is no need to label them as such. . . . Texts labeled magical realist draw upon cultural systems that are no less "real" than those upon which traditional literary realism draws—often non-Western cultural systems that privilege mystery over empiricism, empathy over technology, tradition over innovation.[38]

They further note that magical realism often enables writers to revitalize fading cultural practices in (and perhaps even through) fiction. As I argue later, Medoruma is himself quite conscious of this possibility, and he has pursued it most clearly through his deployment of local dialect in "Droplets" and in subsequent works of fiction. His fictional method, understood in these terms, not only allows for a representation of Okinawan life in its full complexity but also attempts to intervene against those forces that threaten it. As we have seen, Medoruma is no rosy-eyed idealist merely intent on "celebrating" Okinawa's distinctiveness, nor is he a naïve captive of nostalgia who wishes to return to the imaginary purity and peacefulness of rural life from an earlier era. On the contrary, he is above all committed to interrogating and revealing the underpinnings of Okinawa's present-day condition, a condition that is inextricably linked to Japanese colonial rule, the Asia–Pacific War, the American occupation, and the postreversion hegemony of Japan and the United States. In his critical essays and in a few of his stories, such as "*Ichigatsu nanoka*" and "Hope," Medoruma's exploration of these issues is often brutally direct and his tone heavily ironic. In most of his fictional work, however, the irony is tempered and suffused into a satisfyingly subtle and empathetic representation of everyday life. Among these stories, "Droplets" is arguably the first that does justice to Medoruma's critical ambitions by fully exploiting the unique possibilities of fiction.

"Droplets" is set in a small farming village in northern Okinawa around 1995, fifty years after the Battle of Okinawa. One morning the protagonist, a seventy-year-old man named Tokushō, wakes up to find himself seemingly paralyzed. He is aware of what is happening around him but can neither move nor speak. His right leg has swollen up and turned green, and it so closely resembles a gourd melon (which is roughly the shape and size of a watermelon) that his wife at first mistakes the leg for a melon. At one point his wife, Ushi, slaps the leg, causing his big toe to split open. Water spews out of the toe but quickly slows to a trickle. Ushi places a bucket under his foot to catch the flow of water, which now drips steadily. The droplets of the story's title refer, in part, to the water that rolls down the bottom of his foot and falls, drop by drop, into the bucket. This passage appears early in the story:

> The following morning rumors about Tokushō's leg spread through the village. Curiosity seekers feigning concern formed a line outside the house, and by noon it was nearly fifty meters long. There hadn't been such a long line in the village since the American troops started passing out food rations after the war, and even those with little interest in the ruckus felt compelled to queue up. At first Ushi served tea and sweets to the visitors, thanking them for their concern, but she finally lost her temper when an ice cream peddler showed up at the scene.
>
> "What do you think this is? Some kind of freak show?" she shouted. Then she went to the shed, grabbed a machete and began waving it around as she admonished the crowd. "Bunch of lazy good-for-nothin's!" The villagers

knew how much Ushi relied on Tokushō; anyone who dared talk back risked serious injury, so they quickly dispersed.

After Ushi disappeared into the house, the crowd began to regroup in shady spots throughout the village—beneath the *gajimaru* tree in front of the farmers' co-op, under the eaves of the community center, on the benches shaded by the long branches of the *kuwadisaa* tree near the Japanese croquet field. Those who had actually seen Tokushō's leg dominated the conversations, describing its shape and smell, its luster and consistency, the disfiguration of the toenails. Some villagers recounted earlier examples of swollen extremities and speculated about whether this was a good or bad omen; others began placing bets on when the swelling would subside.

By the time they started to debate the impact of Tokushō's leg on the village economy, evening had rolled around and the liquor was flowing freely. Before long they were singing and playing the *sanshin*. Then the dancing and karate performances began, prompting a candidate in the upcoming village council election to go out and slaughter a goat, which he offered as the evening's feast. Meanwhile, the man rumored to be his likely opponent sent his son off to buy liquor for the occasion. Unsold mangos and pineapples were peeled, their sweet fragrance mixing with the smell of canned mackerel and dried squid. Women surrounded the pot of goat stew, their faces glowing from the heat; children set off firecrackers; the young adults drifted down to the beach, where their bodies were soon merging together and moving in unison with the waves; dogs ran wild through the village with pig bones clutched between their jaws.

"Damn fools! Just don't appreciate a person's worries." Ushi stood at the window and shook her fist at the revelers in the distance. She then returned to Tokushō's bedside to change the ice on his leg.[39]

Medoruma's lyricism tinges this passage with nostalgia for the vitality and intimacy of Okinawan village life. Although this scene ostensibly takes place in the mid-1990s, readers familiar with the social and economic changes in Okinawa during the past few decades will recognize the village as a site relegated to the past, for nearly everything described is rapidly disappearing under the relentless assault of Japan's metropolitan culture and the leveling forces of capitalism. The farmers' co-op is losing its role as a center of the village economy, the young people are leaving for jobs in the cities or on the Japanese mainland, the local dialect is rarely heard except in elderly voices, and spontaneous celebrations of the sort described here are destined to vanish from everyday life and reappear only as local legends. The passage is reminiscent of Ōe Kenzaburo's early works set in rural Shikoku, in its admiring yet critical view of the contradictions of village life. Despite their evident fondness for the pleasures of life in the village, both authors refuse to simply wallow in nostalgia; they also expose the insensitivity and occasional cruelty of the villagers toward one another.

Medoruma further reveals, through his use of dialect when describing the local landscape, a desire to resist those outside forces that threaten to absorb the village into an undifferentiated national culture. In the earlier passage, for example, the names of local trees are written in dialect and are left unglossed in the original text, thereby underscoring the uniqueness and incommensurability of Okinawa's local landscape. His 1998 story "*Mabuigumi*" goes even further by employing dialect in the title itself, leaving the mainland Japanese reader uncertain as to its meaning.[40] At one level, it is this very semantic inaccessibility that serves the author's purpose: Precisely because the meaning will be unclear to most Japanese readers, it places them face-to-face with Okinawa's cultural difference, a difference deployed in his work not as a site of exotic fantasy but as a challenge to the linguistic hegemony of standard Japanese.

In a 1998 interview with the Okinawan cultural journal *Edge*, Medoruma discussed his thoughts on the use of local dialect in texts, emphasizing that "even when the meaning of the dialect is unclear to the reader, it jumps off the page as something alien (*ibutsu toshite tachiagatte kuru*), and this is what I'm trying to accomplish with words, to see how far I can take this process."[41] At another point in the interview, he referred to his predecessors in Japanese literature who struggled with the dialect problem:

> The problem of using dialect [in literary texts] isn't limited to Okinawans, you know. I'm particularly conscious of the standard set by Miyazawa Kenji way back in the 1930s, when he began wrestling with the question of how to make a local language accessible to readers throughout the nation. Right now in Japan you've got writers—part of the linguistic realm centered on Tokyo—who feel no resistance to writing in standard Japanese. But then there are those for whom a local dialect is their native language. For these authors, writing entails friction between these two languages. These two types of writers are scattered throughout the country, forming concentric circles, and among them are Okinawan writers such as myself.
>
> As for what we can do about this situation, I think we are being challenged to create something, based on our own social environment, that is capable of shaking up the power structure of the Japanese language. I view Okinawan dialect as a weapon that can be used in this effort. (35–36)

Medoruma goes on to discuss the many choices facing writers who incorporate dialect into their texts. One option, he notes, is based in standard Japanese but absorbs certain words or expressions from dialect; another reverses the ratio; and, of course, there are infinite variations in between. He notes that in "Droplets," he confined dialect largely to dialogue and that he varies its use in accordance with the age and occupation of the given character. A careful look at this text reveals that the least educated of the older characters in the story, such as Ushi, speak solely in dialect (or in a modified form of it). In contrast, Tokushō's young Okinawan physician, Dr. Ōshiro, does not use dialect at all, nor does Ishimine, the close friend from school whom Tokushō abandoned on the battlefield fifty years earlier. Ishimine returns to Tokushō as a ghost from the past, frozen in time, still a student at the Teacher's Higher School, where he was forced to eschew Okinawan dialect for standard Japanese. He is thus a reminder of Japan's colonial policy in Okinawa from the prewar era as well as the embodiment of Tokushō's most disturbing war memories.

"Droplets" is above all concerned with memory. The story jumps back and forth through time, gradually revealing a man who has repressed his painful memories of the war and of those people he abandoned to die on the battlefield—only to have them return to haunt him after a half century as he lay paralyzed in bed. Tokushō is visited every night by wounded soldiers who appear through the walls and line up in front of his bed, waiting to drink the water dripping from his toe. He eventually recognizes them as the men from a cave where, as a student serving in the Blood and Iron Imperial Workers Corps, he transported munitions and delivered water. Many of the soldiers were suffering from thirst and were on the brink of death; Tokushō failed to bring them water as promised, and their nightly reappearance fifty years later is testimony to his lingering guilt and to their ongoing presence in his world.

Medoruma's adoption of a magical realist approach in this and many subsequent stories provides him with a powerful way of representing the ongoing salience of the past—particularly the war and postwar occupation—in Okinawan life today. It is especially suited to exploring the complex workings of memory, not as merely a filter for viewing, preserving, and repressing the past, but as an unsettling, unpredictable, and irrepressible part of the present. As Zamora and Faris note, "Magical realism often facilitates the fusion, or coexistence, of possible worlds, spaces, systems that would be irreconcilable in other modes of fiction."[42] Medoruma seems to choose this mode of representation in part because it enables him to articulate a conflicted, multilayered experience of the world that more closely approximates Tokushō's private reality. The scenes in "Droplets" depicting the soldiers' nocturnal appearance is therefore perhaps best understood not as mere "flashbacks" or "nightmares" but as real eruptions of the past, eruptions that continue to live on in Tokushō, shaping his most mundane activities as well as his most intimate relationships during the ensuing decades. In "Droplets" and in most of his subsequent stories to date, Medoruma employs this fictional approach to reconfigure the boundaries separating life from death, past from present, war from peace, and socially sanctioned public memory from the individual, private memories that partially constitute it.

"Droplets" has been praised not only for its subtle inquiry into war memory but for its haunting evocation of the battlefield experience itself. Few Japanese authors without direct experience of war have attempted to write about it, and fewer still have done so convincingly. The next quoted passage from "Droplets" takes place at a cave during the brutal fighting on Okinawa in June 1945. This is the same cave where Tokushō, together with his closest friend, Ishimine, was entrusted with carrying water to the wounded soldiers. In the following scene, Tokushō is sitting inside the cave's opening with Ishimine, who had been hit by shrapnel and "was moaning and gripping his stomach. Between his fingers oozed something that looked like the guts of a slaughtered pig or goat" (37; 277):

> The cave, formed by Ryūkyū limestone, was located midway up a small, forested mountain. The pouring rain fell on the tree leaves, where it turned into a fine mist and then seeped into Tokushō's and Ishimine's skin as they hid behind a stone wall near the cave's entrance.
>
> Two sentries took their rifles and quickly moved down the hill through the forest. The redeployment had begun. One after another, dark lumps would appear from the shadows and slowly assume a human form before descending the slope. Tokushō held Ishimine in his arms and pressed against the wall, hardly daring to breathe as he watched the soldiers go. Few of the men could walk normally, so they supported themselves on each other's shoulders or with canes. As they slid down the slope, they became entangled and cursed each other, then exchanged muted cries of "Shut up!" The girls from the Student Nurse Corps passed by carrying one of their wounded on a stretcher, then a shadow approached from the group. It was Miyagi Setsu. After learning that Tokushō and Ishimine were from her own group of villages, she had always stopped by to say hello. "How is Ishimine-san?" she asked. Ishimine leaned against the stone wall, letting out shallow breaths. He looked as if he would fall to pieces if not supported. Tokushō shook his head at Setsu, who asked nothing more. Coarse fingers gripped Tokushō's wrist, squeezing hard. A canteen and paper bag were forced into his palm. Tokushō tried to refuse, pushing her hand away, but Setsu brought her face close and said, "We're heading for the surgery shelter in Itoman, so be sure to follow us!" She spoke forcefully, grabbing his shoulder. Then she reached out, gently touched Ishimine's face and said goodbye. Tokushō watched as her pigtailed figure slid down the hill and disappeared into the forest shadows.
>
> Tokushō wasn't sure how long he had been sitting there. The shapes of the men passing before him had grown flattened and twisted. Soldiers leaning on canes were now replaced by those crawling on all fours or dragging themselves along on their stomachs, shadowy figures squirming forward on arms and legs like half-submerged amphibians. Mixing with the sounds of men

> wriggling through mud were the curses, cries, and pleadings of those left behind. Tokushō listened vacantly to the moaning of those soldiers who had slid off the cliff and couldn't climb back up. (38–39; 277–78)

In addition to its vivid representation of life and death on the battlefield, "Droplets" offers a subtle critique of contemporary Okinawa's facile use of war memory. The critique is articulated primarily through irony, and the story's central irony is that Tokushō—who has done everything in his power to repress his painful war memories—emerges as something of a local celebrity for his skill at recounting his wartime experiences to the village's schoolchildren. Every year at the official commemorations of the end of the Battle of Okinawa around 23 June, Tokushō is asked by the local schools to talk about the war so that future generations are mindful of its horrors. (See chapter 2 by Matthew Allen on this practice on Kume Island today.) Tokushō becomes remarkably adept at doing so, often bringing his audience to tears while carefully avoiding his most potent memories, such as those involving Ishimine. He also receives a nice honorarium for each talk. In the process, he serves as a reminder of the difficulties that often confront oral history projects, which were especially popular throughout Japan during the mid-1990s as the nation prepared for the fiftieth anniversary of the war's end. While oral histories can restore perspectives occluded by more conventional sources, they can also end up, as in Tokushō's case, sanctioning misleading and self-serving personal narratives. Precisely because public memory in Okinawa is valued for challenging the hegemony of Japan's national war narrative, it is easy to overlook how Okinawans have constructed their own public memory in part through dubious individual testimonies. "Droplets" thus offers a critique of Okinawans' desire for a relatively painless public memory of the war, the type of memory that permits cathartic tears without recurring nightmares.

The story also serves as a sharp indictment of those who attempt to benefit from the suffering of others. Tokushō's wife, Ushi, is unaware of the ghosts that haunt her husband, but she serves as the voice of conscience when she warns him, "You'll get your comeuppance for trying to profit off people's suffering in the war." Ushi issues this warning twice in the story, and Medoruma clearly wants his readers to reflect on this issue, one that he frequently raises in his critical essays as well. It is an urgent question about the commodification of social memory in Okinawa today, but it is also a more general question about how any society can do justice to its past. Medoruma offers no easy answers in this story. Yet, through the very act of storytelling, he reminds us that the power of words, coupled with a fertile imagination, can lead us into those cavernous spaces where we are confronted with our most disturbing yet potentially valuable memories.

CONCLUSION

In "Droplets" and in many subsequent works of fiction, Medoruma brings his readers face-to-face with the "marvelous reality" of Okinawan life today. He writes about Okinawa's farming villages as well as its cities, about young and old, women and men, the living, the dead, and those in between. His narratives unfold against a social and physical landscape where the past remains an ineluctable part of the present, where brilliant flora suffused with sunlight give way to dark caves that shelter long-kept secrets. In his fiction, Medoruma presents us with extraordinary moments that animate ordinary lives.

The critical essays, too, often sparkle with imagination, insight, and rhetorical brilliance, making them worthy literary pieces in their own right. The two bodies of writing clearly have much in common: Both his fiction and criticism reveal Medoruma's acute perspective on contemporary society, and both demonstrate his willingness to experiment with different voices, written styles, and approaches to storytelling. In recent years, especially, Medoruma has drawn on his skill as a fiction writer to enliven his nonfiction. The critical essays, in turn, afford Medoruma the chance to shape public opinion about contemporary political debates to an extent rarely possible through fiction, while helping him overcome the temptation to solely write stories such as "*Ichigatsu nanoka*" and "Hope." The essays allow him, in other words, to channel his didactic impulses into what admirers of his fiction seem to view as a more suitable genre.

Thus, while critics have claimed that Medoruma preserves a rigid division of labor between his fiction and nonfiction writing, the relationship between the two is better understood as being dynamic and dialectical. He has increasingly imbued his essays with the wit and rhetorical flourish of his fiction while taking advantage of the comparatively direct and casual format of the essay to address social problems, some of which he later explores (albeit in a more subtle and subdued manner) through his fiction.

As a writer who continues to experiment with both fiction and nonfiction, Medoruma is well attuned to the possibilities and contradictions of each. He knows that certain "realities" are most effectively represented through ostensibly "antirealist" methods and that no single person (fictional or otherwise) can truly embody an entire population. At the same time, he repeatedly demonstrates to his readers that those willing to plunge into the lives of imaginary individuals often emerge with a greater understanding of the broader society that their real-life counterparts inhabit. Permeating all of Medoruma's writing—from the most vituperative essays to the most lyrical fiction to the violent fantasies that fall somewhere in between—is the author's deep affection for Okinawa and his fierce commitment to its future. Medoruma pursues this commitment as both a writer of fiction and as a public intellectual, as both an Okinawan writer who views his homeland in opposition to Japan, and as a full-fledged Japanese writer determined to expand that rubric beyond its self-imposed cultural and linguistic limitations. He is aware that forging a meaningful future entails preserving part of the past. He knows that excavating long-buried memories entails a leap of imagination, that remembering is also an act of creation. Through his writing, Medoruma Shun strives to keep the past alive and to illuminate its value, not as a nostalgic refuge from the present but rather as a foundation for building a better future.

NOTES

All translations in this chapter are my own, except those of Medoruma's story *"Machi-monogatari Koza—Kibō," Asahi Shinbun* (26 June 1999), translated by Steve Rabson as "Hope," *JPRI Critique* 6, no. 12 (December 1999): 1. Translated passages of "Droplets" are from my complete translation of the story in Michael Molasky and Steve Rabson, eds., *Southern Exposure: Modern Japanese Literature from Okinawa* (Honolulu: University of Hawai'i Press, 2000), 255–85.

1. All terms for referring to "Okinawa" in relation to "Japan" are unsatisfactory for one reason or another, and in this chapter I have reluctantly settled on "Okinawa" and "mainland Japan" or "Japan's main islands." *Ryūkyū* is commonly preferred to *Okinawa* when signifying geographic or cultural phenomena that preceded the Meiji state's forced annexation of the islands in the 1870s. Unlike *Okinawa,* which is the name of the main island and center of power, the term *Ryūkyū* is less ambiguous in signifying the entire cultural and geographical realm, including those islands stretching from Yoron (just north of Okinawa Island) to Amami Ōshima, all of which were incorporated into Kyūshū's Kagoshima Prefecture in December 1953. But because *Ryūkyū* is preferred by Okinawan nationalists and was also the term used by the American occupation administration, many Okinawans today seem uncomfortable using it to refer to their homeland. When referring to themselves, Okinawans (including Medoruma Shun) sometimes use *Uchinanchū*, the dialect term for "Okinawan(s)." Yet perhaps because it is an expression from local dialect, this term tends to be inflected with a sense of exclusivity that makes it difficult for non-Okinawans such as myself to adopt, especially when writing in English. In referring to themselves, Okinawans variously use the terms *Okinawajin* (Okinawans), *Okinawa kenmin*

(citizens of Okinawa prefecture), *Ryūkyūjin* (Ryūkyūans), and *Uchinanchū* (Okinawajin in local dialect).

On the question of how to best refer to "Japan," Okinawans must constantly grapple with whether one should use *Nihon* (Japan), which seems to distinguish Okinawa from the Japanese nation-state, or *hondo* (the mainland), which relegates Okinawa to the periphery but still locates it within the nation-state. Many Okinawan intellectuals prefer the term *Yamato,* which harks back to the tribal conflicts of early history and rejects nationalism (and perhaps modernity) as the proper source of Okinawan subjectivity.

As Arakawa Akira and others have remarked, the choice of terms depends on where you stand. Medoruma, like many thoughtful Okinawans today, employs different terms, depending on the context and intended audience. Lately he seems to favor *Nihon* and *Yamato* for Japan and *Uchinanchū* (sometimes glossed in *kanji* as *Okinawajin*) when referring to his fellow Okinawans. I have discussed these rhetorical choices briefly in Michael Molasky, *The American Occupation of Japan and Okinawa: Literature and Memory* (New York: Routledge, 2001), 3–4. Also see my discussion of the "rhetoric of reversion" in my chapter on Arakawa Akira in Glenn Hook and Richard Siddle, eds., *Japan and Okinawa: Structure and Subjectivity* (London: Routledge Curzon, forthcoming).

2. While the Ainu have a rich tradition of orally transmitted tales and songs, they have produced comparatively little modern or contemporary fiction (*shōsetsu*).

3. The Japanese term *shōsū minzoku* is roughly comparable to "minority group."

4. See Miyagi Etsujirō, *Senryōsha no me: Amerikajin wa "Okinawa" o dō mita ka* (Naha: Naha shuppansha, 1982), especially chap. 1. Also, Nakano Yoshio and Arasaki Moriteru, *Okinawa sengoshi* (Tokyo: Iwanami shinsho, 1990 [1976 first ed.]).

5. On the problematic category *"joryū bungaku,"* see Ueno Chizuko, Ogura Chikako, and Tomioka Taeko, eds., *Danryō bungakuron* (Tokyo: Chikuma shobō, 1992); Joan E. Ericson, "The Origins of the Concept of 'Women's Literature,'" in *The Woman's Hand: Gender and Theory in Japanese Women's Writing,* ed. Paul Gordon Schalow and Janet A. Walker (Stanford, Calif.: Stanford University Press), 74–105. In contrast to the category "minority literature," the rubric "women's literature" remains deeply ensconced in Japan's literary world.

6. Shimao settled in Amami Oshima (an island under the jurisdiction of Kagoshima Prefecture but arguably part of the Okinawan geographic and cultural sphere) and built his literary reputation in part on his many stories and essays about life on Amami. Ikezawa Natsuki had already established his literary reputation before moving to the island of Okinawa in the early 1990s and has claimed that he intends to remain there. Like Shimao, he has been intensively involved in local cultural life. Significantly, he has also played a role, through his service on the selection committee for literary prizes, in bringing Medoruma and other Okinawan writers to the attention of a broader readership in mainland Japan. On Shimao, see Philip Gabriel, *Mad Wives and Island Dreams: Shimao Toshio and the Margins of Japanese Literature* (Honolulu: University of Hawai'i Press, 1999).

7. The difficulties involving the category "Okinawan literature" have been discussed by Okamoto Keitoku and Shinjō Ikuo. See the interview with Okamoto, *"Kono hito ni kiku," Okinawa Times,* 12 April 2000, 17; and Shinjō's article, *"Tadayō*

Okinawa bungaku no tame ni (1)," *Okinawa Times*, 2 July 2001, 17. Asked in a published interview "whether the category 'Okinawan literature' even exists," Medoruma apparently sidestepped the question. See "*Ima wa kataru*," *Okinawa Times*, 30 August 1999, 11.

8. Needless to say, I am offering generalizations here, and the degree to which one identifies oneself as "Japanese" varies with the individual and social context. Clearly, many Ainu and "resident Koreans" define themselves in opposition to the modern Japanese nation-state, but they do so not so much as members of a particular region of Japan but as an ethnic group.

9. There are exceptions. Several authors, including Ōshiro Tatsuhiro, have written about Okinawans living abroad or on Japan's main islands, and others (including Medoruma) have occasionally written about imaginary or generic spaces, but the generalization holds.

10. I use "fiction writers" instead of "novelists" because most postwar Okinawan writers of fiction primarily write short stories. In fact, Medoruma has yet to publish a full-length novel (nor has Sakiyama Tami). See Molasky and Rabson, "Introduction," in Molasky and Rabson, eds., *Southern Exposure*, especially 4–5.

11. Medoruma has given careful thought to how Faulkner's literature provides hints for forging a viable regional yet national literature in Okinawa. In particular, he has cited Faulkner's work as one model for thinking about how to incorporate local dialect into literary texts. See "*Kotoba o 'ibutsu' no yō ni*" in the Okinawan quarterly *Edge* (Winter 1998): 36.

12. Young Okinawans, in particular, have limited (if any) facility in their local dialect. Language should be understood as a common, but not necessary, marker of ethnic identity. See John Edwards, *Language, Society and Identity* (New York: Blackwell, 1985).

13. Rather than comparing Okinawa to the American South, Komesu Okifumi, an Okinawan scholar of English literature, has argued that his homeland's historical and cultural relationship with mainland Japan most closely resembles Ireland's relationship with Great Britain. This comparison underscores Okinawa's ethnic, cultural, and linguistic difference from Japan's main islands while illuminating its history of subordination and its citizens' attendant ambivalence toward full-scale assimilation into the nation-state. Pointing to Irish writers such as John Keats and James Joyce, Komesu's comparison further enables us to view modern Okinawan literature as both an integral part of Japan's literary tradition and as a distinctive literature in its own right, written in Japanese but informed by a sensibility forged by separate historical and cultural experience. Komesu Okifumi, *Piromera no uta: Jōhōka jidai ni okeru Okinawa no aidentitii* (Naha: Okinawa taimususha, 1991).

14. The story was first published in the April 1996 issue of *Bungakukai* and was republished in the September 1997 issue of *Bungei shunjū* as the recipient of the Akutagawa Prize and again in Medoruma Shun, *Suiteki* (Tokyo: Bungei shunjū, 1997). My translation of the story was first published in *Southwest Review* 83, no. 4 (Winter 1998). A revised version was included in Molasky and Rabson, eds., *Southern Exposure*.

15. Medoruma is generally very protective of his personal life, but he does speak freely about his upbringing in Nakajin and its impact on his writing in a

published dialogue with Ōe Kenzaburo: Ōe Kenzaburo and Medoruma Shun, "*Okinawa ga kenpō o tekishi suru toki*," *Ronza* (July 2000): 176–77.

16. I once traveled to Miyako to meet with Medoruma, and he showed me around the island. He was especially interested in one sacred site, a cave hidden away yet right in the middle of town, where islanders (mainly older women) visit and commune with spirits of the dead.

17. Medoruma Shun and Ikezawa Natsuki, "'*Zetsubō' kara hajimeru*," *Bungakukai* (September 1997): 179. This dialogue took place within weeks of Medoruma's receipt of the Akutagawa Prize. Ikezawa, who was a member of the Akutagawa Prize Selection Committee, had been living in Okinawa for over three years at the time of this publication, and they engage in a wide-ranging and substantive discussion of Okinawan literature, culture, and politics.

18. Although Matayoshi is eleven years older than Medoruma, both were born after the war. It seems justifiable to distinguish writers such as Ōshiro Tatsuhiro and Nagadō Eiichi, who have clear memories of wartime, from those born after 1945.

19. Medoruma's nonfictional style is more accessible than Arakawa's, which tends toward the abstruse, and Medoruma's fiction is far more critically acclaimed than Arakawa's poetry ever was. Arakawa is a major figure in postwar Okinawan thought and journalism. In addition to being a formidable critic, he served as a catalyst for the development of Okinawan literature, especially during the 1950s through the 1970s; was at one time editor of the leading literary and critical journal *Shin Okinawa bungaku* (New Okinawan Literature); and eventually rose to the position of president of the *Okinawa Times* newspaper. See my chapter on Arakawa in Hook and Siddle, eds., *Japan and Okinawa,* and Molasky, *The American Occupation of Japan and Okinawa*, 93–102; see also chapter 9, this volume.

20. This is not to suggest that his contemporaries are all apolitical writers. Matayoshi, for example, has confronted occupation rule, environmental degradation, and gender politics in many of his stories, but he confines these concerns to his fictional world, rarely writing social criticism or political commentary.

21. The expression "*Keeshi kajii*" is dialect for "*kaeshi kaze*," which might be rendered "returning wind." For the entire published dialogue between Medoruma and Sakiyama, see "'*Shōsetsu' no genjō kara*," *Keeshi kajii* (n.d.): 22–33. The passage cited appears on 22–23.

22. Japanese literature scholar Yonaha Keiko, who is from Okinawa, made this remark at a workshop in Tokyo where she was discussing Medoruma's literature. Others have commented on the disparity in tone between Medoruma's literary and critical writings. For example, Ōno Takayuki, of Okinawa International University, wrote in December 2000, "Medoruma Shun has claimed that this year is an historic turning point, and he has repeated radical political assertions that appear somewhat doctrinaire. Yet this has not compromised his literary expression one bit. He is a most unusual writer." Ōno Takayuki, "*Shosetsu: Shusshoku no dekibae*," *Okinawa Times*, 25 December 2000, morning edition, 17. And Ikezawa Natsuki remarked when comparing "Droplets" to one of Medoruma's essays that "the two works seem as if they were written in two different rooms." Medoruma Shun and Ikezawa Natsuki, "'*Zetsubō' kara hajimeru*," *Bungakukai* (September 1997): 179.

23. Medoruma Shun, "*Umi nari no shima kara (2)*" in *Shūkan kin'yōbi,* 13 October 2000, 58–59. All expressions in italics are from Okinawan dialect and appear in the original text written in *katakana*. Any parenthetical gloss in my translation is also glossed for the benefit of Japanese readers in Medoruma's text.

24. I have used the following text for passages cited in this chapter: Medoruma Shun, "*Gyogunki,*" in *Okinawa bungaku zenshū: Vol. 9,* ed. Okinawa bungaku zenshū henshū iinkai (Tokyo: Kokusho kankōkai, 1990), 58–73. Some sources list the original publication date as 1984, but it is listed as 1983 at the back of Medoruma's book *Suiteki.*

25. This passage is oddly reminiscent (given the sharp differences between the two writers) of the opening scene of Kawabata Yasunari's *Snow Country:*

> In his boredom, Shimamura stared at his left hand as the forefinger bent and unbent. Only this hand seemed to have a vital and immediate memory of the woman he was going to see. The more he tried to call up a clear picture of her, the more his memory failed him, the farther she faded away, leaving him nothing to catch and hold. In the midst of this uncertainty only the one hand, and in particular the forefinger, even now seemed damp from her touch, seemed to be pulling him back to her from afar.

Kawabata Yasunari, *Snow Country,* trans. Edward Seidensticker (New York: Perigree, 1981), 6–7.

26. Above all, the story recalls Ōe's "Prize Stock" ("*Shiiku,*" 1958; also translated as "The Catch")—in its lyricism, its retrospective and somewhat nostalgic narrative voice, and its focus on a boy whose life in a rural village is suddenly disrupted by his encounter with a highly sexualized outsider. In a scene particularly evocative of "Prize Stock," the narrator of Medoruma's story recounts how he and his friends forced one boy to pretend he was copulating with a goat—as does the black soldier in Ōe's story.

27. For an analysis of the story that focuses on the role of the Taiwanese woman, see Shū Keisoku, "*Medoruma Shun: Gyogunki e no shiten,*" *Okinawa Times,* 5–7 June 2001. For a different reading, see Okudaira Erika, "*Gyogunki,*" *Edge* 5 (Autumn 1997): 30–31.

28. See the following two essays for examples of Medoruma's comments on discrimination: "*Gisei to sabetsu no rensa o tachikire,*" *Buraku kaihō* 470 (June 2000): 75–85; "*Shichō 2000: Mattari toshita nichijō,*" *Okinawa Times,* 7 December 2000, 13.

29. For a brief critical treatment of this story, see Shinjō Ikuo, "*Medoruma Shun shiron: 'Suiteki' o jiku toshite,*" *Okinawa bungei nenkan* [1997 ed.] (Naha: Okinawa Taimususha, 1997): 185. Shinjō, a professor of Japanese literature at the University of the Ryukyus, is writing a book-length study of Medoruma. The story itself can be found in: Medoruma Shun, "*Ichigatsu nanoka,*" *Shin-Okinawa bungaku* (Winter 1989): 90–99.

30. Medoruma Shun, "*Machi-monogatari Koza—Kibō,*" *Asahi Shinbun,* 26 June 1999. Steve Rabson, trans., "Hope," *JPRI Critique* 6, no. 12 (December 1999): 1. An approximate translation of the full title would be "Hope—A Tale of Koza City."

31. The interview appears in "*Ima wa kataru,*" *Okinawa Times,* 30 August 1999, 11. The quoted passage appears in Rabson, trans., "Hope," 1. Even the interviewer seems confused about the status of this work, referring to it as "an essay."

32. For one example, see his essay "*Sentaku no omomi,*" *Ryūkyū shinpō,* 4 December 1999, 12.

33. Suh's comments are contained in his essay "'*Kibō" ni tsuite,*" in *Eureka* (August 2001): 144–47. The August 2001 issue of the monthly journal is devoted to Okinawa.

34. Interview with Medoruma, "*Ima wa kataru,*" 11.

35. Although he does not directly discuss this story, Medoruma has also addressed the topic of terrorism in an essay published exactly one month after the 11 September attacks. See Medoruma Shun, "*Okinawa no sentaku—Bei dōji tero o koete,*" *Okinawa Times,* 11 October 2001, 19.

36. Ōe Kenzaburo and Medoruma Shun, "*Okinawa ga kenpō o tekishi suru toki,*" *Ronza* (July 2000): 178–79.

37. Franco Moretti, *Modern Epic: The World System from Goethe to García Marquez* (New York: Verso, 1996), 234.

38. Lois Parkinson Zamora and Wendy B. Faris, eds., *Magical Realism: Theory, History, Community* (Durham, N.C.: Duke University Press, 1995), 3–4. Although I find the introduction and selected chapters in this volume useful, I believe that it attempts to include an excessively wide range of writing (both culturally and historically) under the rubric "magical realism," thereby compromising the overall value of the book.

39. Medoruma Shun, *Suiteki* (Tokyo: Bungei shunjū, 1997), 9–10. Where I have given page numbers parenthetically, the first refers to this Japanese text, and the second (following a semicolon) refers to my translation in Molasky and Rabson, eds., *Southern Exposure.*

40. The story "*Mabuigumi*" first appeared in 1998 but was reprinted in 1999 by Asahi Shinbunsha in a book of the same title.

41. Published interview with Medoruma, "*Kotoba o 'ibutsu no yo ni,' Edge* (Winter 1998): 37. Medoruma began using dialect with "*Gyogunki,*" but a careful examination of his deployment of dialect in these early texts suggests that he was writing with Okinawan readers in mind and offered fewer glosses than he later would to accommodate mainland Japanese readers. This is not surprising, since he was publishing primarily in small circulation local forums. Thus, even though he used dialect in these early works, I would argue that their salience as "something alien" is diminished because it is less alien to Okinawan readers. On the other hand, I do not wish to suggest that by using dialect in the title, "*Mabuigumi,*" he has left his mainland Japanese readership completely at bay, for it does appear in *kanji,* with the dialect pronunciation appearing in an adjacent gloss. Nonetheless, the precise meaning of the word, which refers to an Okinawan shamanistic practice of calling back a spirit that has separated from a dead person and is floating through the world waiting to be reclaimed, remains unintelligible to most Japanese until they read the story.

42. Zamora and Faris, *Magical Realism,* 6.

7

Uchinā Pop

Place and Identity in Contemporary Okinawan Popular Music

James E. Roberson

Since the early 1990s, Uchinā (Okinawan) pop music has become popular in mainland Japan and abroad. Okinawan groups such as Kina Shoukichi and Champloose, the Rinken Band, and the Nenes have been perceived as Japan's contribution to world music. Certainly part of the appeal of such new Okinawan music lies in innovative and enjoyable hybrid syntheses of traditional Okinawan folk music with Western musical styles and instruments. However, there are other levels of cultural and political significance reflected and constructed within the music that are silenced by writing and audiences that focus only on its colorful "ethnic" appeal. This chapter examines the cultural politics of the images of Okinawa—as both place and space—that are constructed within Uchinā pop music. I argue that these images construct "Okinawa" as internally hybrid and, thereby, as marked by differences from mainland Japan, including linguistic and cultural distinctiveness, a(n endangered) purity of heart, closeness to nature, and a proud and sometimes overtly political defense of Okinawan identity. I suggest that such musically constructed images of Okinawan hybridity and difference must be understood within a set of national and international political-economic dynamics that render any simple listening to Uchinā pop problematic.

OKINAWA BOOM AND WORLD MUSIC

Since the early 1990s, there has been an ongoing boom in Okinawan music, especially in what is called Okinawan pop or Uchinā pop—a combination of traditional Okinawan and Western popular musical elements. This music is popular in Okinawa, mainland Japan, and, to varying degrees, around the world. Although there were various precursors such as Kina Shoukichi's mid-1970s hit "Haisai Ojisan," China Sadao's 1978 album *Akabana*, and the experimentation with Okinawan sounds and songs in the 1970s and 1980s by various mainland musicians (discussed later), the Okinawa boom is usually considered to have begun with the 1990 and 1991 mainland releases of compact discs by Kina Shoukichi and Champloose, the Rinken Band (figure 7.1), and the Nenes. New CDs continue to appear by these big three and by an increasing number of other artists. Some people, such as China Sadao, the creative force behind the Nenes, speak of Okinawan music as having entered its third golden age.[1]

The (re)appearance of these and other Okinawan groups initially coincided with the ethnic boom among younger Japanese in Third World and (Southeast) Asian foods, designs, culture, and travel. With the global rise of the market for world music, Uchinā pop music often has been consumed and interpreted as Japan's contribution to ethnic or world music.[2] Such interpretations are not limited to Japan. In the "Ethnic Pop" section of his book *Nipponpop*, Steve McClure, for example, writes:

> Some Japanese musicians . . . make an effort to use homegrown rhythms and instruments to give their music an ethnic flavor. . . . But only a handful of Japanese groups have managed to update traditional musical forms and put them in a more contemporary context without sounding gimmicky or bogus.
> Foremost among them is Champloose, led by Shoukichi Kina.[3]

Ogawa interprets the interest in Okinawan music among mainland Japanese musicians as the search for ethnic musical resources and among fans as the search for roots, for a "homeland of the heart" (*kokoro no furusato*) of nature and culture not found in the Tokyo-dominated mainland. Through Okinawan music, he suggests, Japanese mainlanders are beginning to face and connect with Asia, not the West, and to question Japan's westernized, economistic culture.[4] Ogawa's observations and comments have a degree of political significance and truth that must be recognized. However, Ogawa and many other commentators interpret the Okinawan music boom from the point of view of the Japanese mainland, putting aside Okinawan experience itself.

While there are exceptions, this kind of discourse in Japan also replicates a long-running mainland "discourse of the vanishing" on Okinawa

Figure 7.1. ***Banji*** **(Rinken Band). The song "Yu-Yu-Yu/You-You-You" appears on this compact disc.**
Source: Photo by Gerald Figal.

(and other peripheral sites). Here, a culturally pure, "authentic and unchanging Japan"[5] is nostalgically imagined as still existing at the margins of Japanese society, in faraway places and in premodern practices. Yanagi Sōetsu, the prewar leader of the *mingei* folk arts movement, for example, saw Okinawa as potentially redemptive for Japan. As M. William Steele writes, "Yanagi saw modern industrial institutions and values as a sort of creeping disease. Japan was already inflicted, especially at its centre, but the periphery was still capable of salvation. Okinawa, with its unspoiled beauty, offered a key to the salvation of Japan."[6]

This view resonates with current discourses as well. Moreover, Murai notes more broadly in his analysis of "*Nantō* [Southern Islands] Ideology" that Japanese interest in Okinawa as the deep structural origin of Japanese culture worked before and now still works to hide the political and historical realities of Okinawa and of Japanese colonialism. Celebration of Okinawa as a resort island has the same effect.[7]

Mainland Japanese and indeed world interest in Okinawan music is important and worthy of attention for many reasons, but that topic is beyond the scope of this chapter.[8] Here, it is important to note that popular interests and interpretations (of the music itself and of the interest in the music) are all too often fixated on the exotic appeal of the musical and performative manifestations of a colorful and commercial ethnic Okinawan Otherness.

In this chapter, I use this observation as a critical point of departure in order to explore dimensions of the cultural and political significance of Uchinā pop music that are silenced by a focus only on its ethnic or world music consumer appeal.[9] I argue that Uchinā pop is also a set of musical sites (both sounds and sights) through which contemporary Okinawan cultural identities are constructed, reflected, and set in contrast to—and sometimes in resistance against—powerful national and international forces. Uchinā pop is one kind of cultural practice that is involved in the creation of local Okinawan identities of place, within broader cultural and political contexts.

MUSIC, IDENTITY, AND PLACE

Music is an important way of articulating identity, as has been emphasized in many recent discussions. Two poles of debate have been staked out. At one end, Stokes suggests that "music is socially meaningful not entirely but largely because it provides means by which people recognize identities and places, and the boundaries which separate them." At the other pole, Negus notes that "as the stability and coherence of social identities [have] been called into question, so the idea that there may be any fixed link between a social group and particular musical sounds has also become an issue of contention."[10] I stand between these positions, arguing that music is a symbolic resource and that musical production and consumption are important practices in the ongoing, creative use of music to construct identities.[11]

Music connects identity to place through a sense of belonging somewhere, as Taylor notes in his discussion of Sheila Chandra and Apache

Indian, two Anglo-Asian musicians.[12] Lipsitz likewise writes of the importance of the poetics and politics of place in music:

> A poetics of place permeates popular music, shaping significantly its contexts of production, distribution, and reception. . . . Through music we learn about place and about displacement. Laments for lost places and narratives of exile and return often inform, inspire, and incite the production of popular music. Songs build engagement among audiences at least in part through references that tap memories and hopes about particular places. Intentionally and unintentionally, musicians use lyrics, musical forms, and specific styles of performance that evoke attachment to or alienation from particular places.[13]

Music, then, is one of the "range of discursive and nondiscursive modes of expression through which everyday and poetically heightened senses of place are locally articulated."[14] Negus makes a useful distinction between a "place" and a "sense of space," noting that "a place as the particular, concrete site of specific social activities does not always coincide with a 'sense of space,'" the more abstract way in which people locate themselves in the world.[15] People use their "sense of place" to feel connected to the past, anchored in their social community, rooted in their culture, and at home in their selfhood.[16] Or, as Casey has put it, "Places not only *are*, they *happen*."[17]

Music operates symbolically like place. Moreover, music does not simply *reflect* a place, sense of space, or local identity but also creates (and is used to create) these. In a discussion of the political uses of popular music, Pratt notes that music involves both "purposive" (explicitly intentional) and "effective" (influential whether intended or not) dimensions.[18] The creative work of music in constructing and connecting to senses of place and identity may likewise be seen as operating on these two levels.

Okinawan music, to paraphrase Frith, is not Okinawan just because it reflects or authentically articulates some sort of Okinawan taste or experience but because it creates our understandings of what "Okinawa(n)" is.[19] Music is a primary means through which images of and connections to Okinawa as a particular kind of place, senses of emotional and social-cultural Okinawan space, and both cultural and political identity claims are sung, played, performed, and otherwise brought onto the public stage. The significance of Uchinā pop lies thus in part in the identities of place and space it creates. Understanding these practices, processes, and interrelations requires listening and seeing with politically sensitive ears and eyes.

Music(s) in Okinawa

Discussions about the relations between music and identity often tend toward essentialism, associating one musical style with one particular social/cultural group or identity. Things have never really been so simple. Indeed, "many so-called indigenous or traditional musical cultures, which are often revered for their purity or authenticity, are actually 'hybrid' forms," as Negus notes.[20] Hybridity, furthermore, is not just a matter of cultural creolization; it has often been the product of (sometimes very violent) political economic histories of colonialism and imperialism.[21]

This is certainly the case in Okinawa, where no one kind of Okinawan music naturally expresses a singular Okinawan identity. While the focus of this chapter is on Uchinā pop, Okinawa enjoys a very interesting mix of musics, a music *champuru* (literally, "mix").[22] There are at least three schools of classical Okinawan music, derived from the court music of the Ryūkyūan Kingdom (1429–1879). There are also active Okinawan folk musics (*min'yō* or *shima-uta*), with subregional variations and both classical (*koten*) and modern repertories. An important basis of Uchinā pop, Okinawan folk music remains an integral and active part of daily (and nightly) life in Okinawa. In addition to folk song contests and performances at festivals, weddings, and many other events, Okinawa is the only prefecture in Japan with *min'yō sakaba* (folk song bars) where semi-professional singers perform. Even "in the karaoke industry, local folk songs are indispensable to Okinawan users."[23]

During the 1970s, Okinawan popular music was also known for hard rock bands such as Murasaki, Condition Green, and Mari with Medusa. These grew out of the live club scene patronized by American soldiers.[24] Other Okinawan musicians include acoustic bluesman Chinen Ryōkichi; Okinawa folk guitarist and singer-songwriter Sadoyama Yutaka; the trio Begin, which has enjoyed nationwide success for its harmonic, light acoustic rock; the Diamantes, a band led by third-generation Peruvian-Okinawan Alberto Shiroma that plays Latin-based music; pop/rock singer and songwriter Cocco; and the female duo Kiroro, whose soft, piano-based ballads brought them much attention during 1998 and 1999. There is also an active hip-hop and punk rock "indies" scene in Okinawa featuring bands such as Mongol 800. However, the nationally most popular and widely known Okinawan performers since the mid-1990s have been the techno/dance pop singer Amuro Namie, two singing/dancing female groups called SPEED and MAX, and the male vocal/dance group Da Pump.[25]

The presence and importance (at least in terms of sales and recognition) of these musicians and their music(s)—as also with the Uchinā pop music(ians) to be discussed below—suggest that questions of musical "authenticity"[26] are at stake here: What is "Okinawan" music? Who are "Okinawan" musicians?

I agree with Stokes that

> [a]uthenticity is definitely not a[n inherent, essentialized] property of music, musicians and their relations to an audience. . . . [Instead,] "authenticity" is a discursive trope of great persuasive [and political] power. It focuses a way

> of talking about music, a way of saying to outsiders and insiders alike "this is what is really significant about this music," "this is the music that makes us different from other people."[27]

In other words, contemporary music is not only not a pure expression of the Japanese past; it is also not a pure expression of the Okinawan past either. However, even here, Stokes is in danger of essentializing, seeming to suggest that there is only one truly authentic style per ethnic group or music. In fact, Middleton suggests that "really authentic music is appropriated music, that is, it is integrated into subjectively motivated social practice";[28] and as this is rarely uniform or unchanging, there is always likely to be an (ongoing) internal cultural debate regarding "authenticity" with claims and counterclaims of great discursive and political significance.

This issue of who makes "real" Okinawan music is further complicated because mainland Japanese musicians such as Kubota Makoto, Hosono Haruomi, Sakamoto Ryūichi, the Southern All Stars, Soul Flower Mononoke Summit, and the Boom have all recorded songs of Okinawan origin or that employ Okinawan musical elements.[29] Although actually from the Yokosuka area, the band Shang Shang Typhoon is sometimes assumed by mainlanders to be an Okinawan band because the banjo played by band leader Kōryū often sounds like an Okinawan sanshin.[30] The 1992 hit "Shima-Uta," by the mainland band the Boom, has given rise to some debate within Okinawa itself regarding the "Okinawan-ness" of the song. However, "Shima-Uta" has also been remade and recorded by Okinawa folk-song/Uchinā pop singer Ganeko Yoriko, included in volume 11 of the *Ryūkyū Folk-Song Song Book,* and used as accompaniment for Eisā drum group performances.[31]

Not everyone is receptive to updating revisions, creative remakes, or reimaginings of Okinawan music, whether done by mainland or by Okinawan musicians. Many Uchinā pop musicians—from Kina Shoukichi at the time of his early hit "Haisai Ojisan," to Daiku Tetsuhiro and Ara Yukito Parsha Club—have been accused of not making "real" Okinawan music and of failing to preserve tradition. Some of the critics are Okinawan traditionalists, but others are not. Uechi Masaaki notes that Ara Yukito Parsha Club encountered more criticism from mainland Japanese "Okinawa freaks" for combining Okinawan music and Black music than they did from local Okinawan audiences. As Taylor observes, "It is worth wondering who is asked to be authentic and whose music is labeled as hybridized." And, as Ota suggests, it is important also to wonder *who* is doing the asking (and, perhaps, the wondering).[32]

Like musicians in many other parts of the world who experiment with combinations of traditional and new (often but not necessarily Western) influences, many Uchinā pop musicians stress the mutual importance of change and of tradition in the champuru music that they are creating.[33] Daiku Tetsuhiro, for example, while recognizing the wonderfulness (*subarashisa*) of traditional songs, also says he wants to break down the fixation with "the form called tradition." "Tradition," he says, "is in your heart and whatever instruments you play, if your spirit is Okinawan (*Uchinanchū*), it [tradition] won't collapse."[34] While defining an Okinawan spirit might be considered problematic, in some ways Daiku's attempt to remobilize the terms of the debate with his argument that pride in Okinawan language and culture does not necessarily mean a denial of change is important. Conversely, change does not necessarily mean a rejection of tradition.

The music of Ara Yukito Parsha Club must be listened to in this way. This band's first full-length CD was composed almost solely of traditional folk songs from the southern Yaeyama region, from which Ara comes. These include "Hanjo-bushi/Sakida-bushi," "Tsuki nu Kaisha," and the very often recorded "Asadoya-Yunta." However, as suggested (in English) on the jacket to the band's 1995 short CD *Parsha*, this is "Okinawan New Generation Music" that features both sanshin and a very cool, funky, bass-heavy feel. This music updates and re-creates tradition, but it is also (and thereby) culturally meaningful in Okinawa to both Okinawan musicians and audiences. Ara explains: "I would definitely never say that I'm carrying on the traditional arts. I'm not doing things with that intention at all. It's just that I can only do things the way I like, the way I feel."[35] While some musicians and music fans in Okinawa simply ignore "traditional" music in favor of one or another form of "modern" (Western) music, it is significant on a number of levels that young Okinawan musicians like Ara retain some inclusive relationship to traditional music forms, if not to tradition as such, as part of the way they feel.

My intent here is neither to enter into nor to analyze the debates about Okinawan cultural authenticity as such. Instead, I want to more firmly situate and so deessentialize Uchinā pop within the various kinds of musics and musicians, and the discourses surrounding them, in Okinawa. The variety represented by these musicians is culturally and politically important, in considering both what is (claimed to be) authentically Okinawan music and in discussing the broader issues of the relationships among music, politics, and cultural identity.[36] This musical diversity also points to the importance of musical (and other) performance in Okinawa as an important dimension of contemporary Okinawan cultural hybridity. As Hall notes of other marginal peoples' self-representation, in a comment that foregrounds the politicality of such artistic practice,

> [t]hey had to locate themselves somewhere but they wanted to address problems which could no longer be contained within a narrow version of ethnicity.

> They did not want to go back and defend something which was ancient, which had stood still, which had refused the opening to new things. They wanted to speak right across those boundaries, and across those frontiers.[37]

Okinawan Music: Place and Identity

I now want to explore a bit more fully the ways in which Uchinā pop is imbricated within a specific cultural politics of local identity construction and may also be understood as a means of struggle and resistance against extralocal forces.[38] Many of the songs recorded and performed by Uchinā pop musicians imagine, construct, and localize various senses of place and space. In other songs, Okinawa is delocalized and constructed as a transnational, diasporic space of identity/identification. Still others sing of the need to preserve Okinawan cultural identity or give voice to more overtly political anger and protest.

LOCAL MIX AND DIFFERENCE

Okinawa is constructed within much Uchinā pop music and performance as a local cultural place marked by both its internal champuru hybridity and its differences from dominant mainland Japanese culture and society. While not as easily separable as the following discussion may suggest, these two kinds of markers of Okinawa and Okinawan identity—as internally mixed and therefore different from Japan and Japanese identity—are nonetheless usefully distinguished. In both, the primary point of reference is local Okinawan identity and experience.

The significance of Okinawan champuru hybridity and difference, and their ultimate interrelatedness, derives in part from constructions of Japaneseness. Evidence of this appears in the exoticizing gaze of Japanese ethnologists and enthusiasts who have looked to Okinawa to discover what is felt to be vanishing from Japan. The significance of musical and other constructions of Okinawa as marked by a creole, champuru culture as one important difference from Japan lies also in the popularity and political influence of a hegemonic ideology that imagines Japan to be highly homogeneous. As Ivy notes, "The hybrid realities of Japan today . . . are contained within dominant discourses on cultural purity and nondifference, and in nostalgic appeals to premodernity."[39] In its construction and celebration of Okinawa as a place marked by a champuru cultural identity, Uchinā pop sings not just of Okinawa but also of—and, more significantly, against—Japan.

Ota has pointed out that "popular culture forms—theater and music, in particular—have been important sources for articulating Okinawan identity as mixing (chanpurū)."[40] Ota's primary focus is on the theatrical group Shōchiku Kagekidan, but the construction of a local champuru identity is also a prominent part of Uchinā pop music and performance (and, the discourse surrounding it). As noted earlier, Uchinā pop is generally taken to refer to music that combines traditional Okinawa musical elements (scales, songs, language) and instruments (most importantly and symbolically, the sanshin, but also Okinawan taiko drums, sanba castanets, paranku hand-drums, koto, and kokyū [erhu]) together with Western, popular-music-based instruments (electric guitars, keyboards, synthesizers, etc.) and musical elements (rock, reggae, and sometimes jazz beats and scales). Such musical creolization marks Uchinā pop as distinct from both traditional folk and classical musics in Okinawa, giving rise to the debates about authenticity and tradition noted above. At the same time, such hybridity, with its clearly Okinawan notes, marks Uchinā pop as distinct from other rock and pop musics, even as performed by Okinawan musicians.

How these various elements are combined and used differs from one Uchinā pop band or musician to another. Ara Yukito Parsha Club's funk-based music, Hirayasu Takashi's blues/rock and Hawaiian influenced songs, Hidekatsu's Asian stylings, and the more pop- and ballad-based harmonies of the Nenes, for example, are all different and distinctive.[41] Yet, at the same time, all these Okinawan musicians share a creative hybridity and see both the hybridity and the creativity as valuable aspects of who they are as Okinawan musicians. Uechi Masaaki, former Rinken Band member and current musical leader of Ara Yukito Parsha Club, says in an interview in which he criticized Teruya Rinken's musical creativity as overly conscious of the image of Okinawa held by mainland tourists and "Okinawa freaks": "But, for me, as someone actually living in Okinawa, I want to try to make music from the perspective of the Okinawa that I myself feel." And, "even someone like me born in Naha and soaked in Western music . . . already from the time I first became aware of what was going on, folk music [*min'yō*] was all around me like air."[42]

Teruya Rinken himself actually holds similar views. He, too, criticizes the overly powerful influence of the United States on mainland Japanese music(ians), and says that, in contrast, "our music is our music."[43] Both these musicians are making claims about the connection of music, place as local culture, and identity. In their view, the creolized combination of both Western and local Okinawan influences more or less naturally means "from the perspective of Okinawa." And, while indicating some of the contradictions of commercial appeal, these statements of the musical hybridization being created in Okinawa may also be heard as direct or indirect claims to difference from (and as critiques of) mainland Japanese musicians who lack the same kind of cultural groundedness—even when the mainlanders include mixes of influences into "their" music.

Okinawa is also imagined as a creole place/space in songs whose lyrical points of reference are located inside the spatial boundaries of Okinawa. One example is the song "America Dōri" (American Avenue) performed by the Nenes. Here, a happy hybrid mixing is constructed as something happening within Okinawa, as a variety of peoples, languages, and cultures is celebrated:[44]

Languages of many countries
Are spilling out into the town
In the twilight between day and night
The liveliness of the pawn shop
The neon of the audio shop
The East Indian's clothing store
Like a town of a foreign country
The horizontal letters are dancing
American Avenue twilight
Rock, shima-uta, rap, reggae
Our home, this Koza town
Mixed up, mixed together
Mixed up, mixed together
American Avenue
Jet exhaust clouds, like lines being pulled
Painting pictures in the sky
In the twilight between day and night
White-skinned women
Dark-skinned men
Brown-skinned island people
In the store-front windows
Lovers are reflected
[*repeat refrain*]
Stores like a movie set
Brighten up the town
In the twilight between day and night
Smiles of GIs
Blond hair flowing with the wind
The odd English of merchants
The town's like a box of toys
With dreams and romance spilling out
[*repeat refrain*]

"America Dōri" valorizes a vision of a dreamlike champuru Okinawa that does not really exist but, perhaps, could. Here, there are no confusions, no conflicts. The music, which prominently features sanshin in a light pop frame, is also used to construct an upbeat hybridity, while background English interjections provide an added "hip" feel. Koza, the reference town, is a fantasy town of beautiful people and colorful sights and sounds, where U.S. military jets don't make noise or crash into elementary schools, where children of mixed parentage don't encounter discrimination, and where GIs don't fight or rape twelve-year-old girls. The musical construction of imaginary sites inside Okinawa such as "America Dōri," with its blond American GIs and East Indian merchants, simultaneously indexes the evolving set of real and imagined external relationships between Okinawa and other outside forces, places, and peoples.

The champuru mixing celebrated in "America Dōri" also creatively constructs Okinawa as distinct and different from homogeneous mainland Japan. While not without the danger of self-exoticization—valorizing mainland Japanese "world music" fans as they "look toward the former margins for anything real," primal, and authentic[45]—such self-differentiation appears in language use, costuming, the indexing and incorporation of traditional cultural practices, and the construction of images of Okinawa as a natural place.

Together with more strictly musical elements such as the use of the sanshin, the predominant use of Okinawan-language lyrics and words (within otherwise Japanese language songs) is one of the most immediately recognizable and distinctive characteristics of Uchinā pop and folk musics. Although there are also regional and subregional dialects that complicate things even more, the Ryūkyūan language has been described as being as distinct from Japanese as English is from German.[46] On CDs that include liner notes, most songs with Okinawan-language lyrics are accompanied by Japanese language translations, summaries, or other explanations.

The continuing use of Okinawan-language lyrics is significant for a number of cultural and political reasons. Use of the Okinawan language has come under Japanese government and proassimilationist proscription at various points in history—as was also the case with the Ainu language. Many Okinawans can recall *hōgen-fuda* (dialect labels) employed to punish students who spoke the Okinawan dialect at schools. That attitude has not completely disappeared. According to singer Teruya Rinken, mainland Japanese recording companies were initially reluctant to release Okinawan-language recordings and pressed him to perform in Japanese.[47] Moreover, as is also common throughout Japan, the willingness and ability of younger Okinawans to use local dialects has declined, regardless of conscious policies of assimilation.

Yet, it also seems undeniable that the decline in older patterns of language use in everyday life makes the use of Okinawan-language lyrics both more culturally and more politically significant. Depending on the song and the musicians, lyrics may also be written and sung in Japanese. Words or phrases from other languages such as Portuguese or English are also used occasionally. Even in Japanese-language songs, however, Okinawan words or phrases are commonly used. Especially important within the context of this chapter, are distinctive local place names. These names, as Basso notes elsewhere, acquire "the stamp of human events, of consequential happenings, of memorable times in the life of a people."[48]

The creative mixing of Okinawan and Japanese (and English) languages, known as *Uchinā-Yamato-guchi,* has been analyzed by Ota, who importantly contends that this new language champuru should itself be considered as a newly emergent and authentic Okinawan language creation.[49] The use of Okinawan lyrics within the otherwise dominantly Japanese-language social-political context makes language particularly distinctive as a marker of Okinawan ethnic "other"ness and, conversely, of Okinawan "self"-identity. Teruya Rinken explains his use of Okinawan thus: "You can only best express yourself in the language that is truly yours. You can't change that, or get rid of it, or you'll lose the essence of what you are doing."[50]

Another significant characteristic of many Uchinā pop songs is lyrical references to and performative uses of various aspects of Okinawan culture. Many groups, for example, record and perform songs from the repertory of Eisā dances, which are performed during the Okinawan Obon season, welcoming and sending off ancestral spirits. The Rinken Band has also, for instance, recorded a song "Nenjūkuduchi" (Song of Yearly Events) that describes the progression of a yearly cycle of traditional cultural events.[51]

Costuming as a visual marker of a culturally distinct Okinawan-ness has been most fully employed by the Rinken Band—vocalist Uehara Tomoko wears traditional hairstyles and bingata-dyed Okinawan kimonos and the men in the band wear Eisā-style costumes (see the *Banji* CD jacket photo in figure 7.1). The four women of the Nenes change costumes several times during a night's performance, appearing in Okinawan bingata and folk kimonos, original but "ethnically marked" costumes, and sometimes in jeans. Kina Shoukichi and Champloose have been more chameleon-like over the years, but they wear costumes that seem to complement Kina's more universalistic sense of "ethnic" difference and identity. Other performers, however, choose not to wear "Okinawan" costumes. Members of Ara Yukito Parsha Club, for example, wear clothes that match the cool, funky music of the bass- and sanshin-heavy band. Within that champuru of styles, the use of Okinawan dialects, costuming, and cultural "traditions" reflects a pride in the language and culture of Okinawa and also makes claims as to their local importance and their difference from (if yet within) Japan. Those expressions of linguistic and cultural pride and difference must be seen within historical assimilationist pressures.

Okinawan difference is also often constructed by musical, lyrical, and visual imagery that pictures Okinawa as a place of natural beauty. The attraction to Okinawan culture and nature among mainland Japanese, noted at the beginning of this chapter, is thus not without reason or roots in Okinawan self-representation. CD jackets and liner notes commonly picture musicians and singers surrounded by lush, tropical greenery or posing beside beaches fronting blue seas and blue skies. Others show culturally distinctive and historically important sites, such as houses with traditional Okinawan tile roofs or Shuri Castle, to create a unique Okinawan image and identity (see the CD jacket covers in figures 7.1 and 7.2).[52]

Lyrical and audio references abound to Okinawa's blue ocean and skies, waves, wind, and flowers (especially akabana [hibiscus] and deigo). A "natural" Okinawa also emerges in songs that describe men and women who, through work, religious practice, or character are close to nature themselves. In the Rinken Band's song "Sabani," for example, the ocean and the strength of the local fisherfolk are lyrically celebrated.[53] Sounds of the ocean are mixed into the sound track, and in live performances of the song, members of the band enact the parts of fishers, paddling their single-hulled sabani boats, reeling in their nets, and whistling and calling to each other. The Okinawa constructed here is one in which people and nature exist together, timelessly, naturally. In songs describing or invoking nature, as in other musical constructions of Okinawa as place and space, Okinawa is celebrated both for what it is (imagined to be) and for what Japan (as Tokyo) is not.[54]

OKINAWA IN THE FLOW OF TIME

From the late fourteenth to the late nineteenth centuries, Okinawa, then the independent Ryūkyūan Kingdom, maintained tributary relations with China.[55] In 1609, the Ryūkyūs were invaded by the Satsuma feudal domain of southern Japan. While maintaining internal sovereignty and relations with China, the Ryūkyūs entered a 270-year period of subordination to Satsuma, and thence to the Tokugawa Bakufu in Edo (Tokyo). In 1879, Okinawa was brought under direct Japanese control when it was forcefully incorporated into the modern (Meiji) Japanese nation-state. From the end of the Battle of Okinawa in 1945, through the end of the Allied Occupation of mainland Japan in 1952, the Ryūkyūs remained under U.S. control until reversion to Japan in 1972. Since 1972, Okinawa has (again) been under Japanese control. Okinawa (especially the main island) is also dominated by the continuing presence of U.S. military bases and personnel. Close to 20 percent of the main island is occupied by U.S. military bases on which 28,531 American soldiers and military personnel were stationed in 1995, accompanied by some 23,757 family members.[56]

A number of Okinawan songs directly comment on this history and construct Okinawa as a place/space that is betwixt and between and as a place in which, with all of the changes and accompanying confusions to which Okinawa has been subject, there is a need to maintain an optimistic sense of Okinawan self-identity. Perhaps the best-known song in this genre is "Jidai no Nagare" (The Flow of Time), a folk song first recorded by Kadekaru Rinsho in the early 1960s, when Okinawa was still under U.S. control. In a comical and critical way the song reflects on post–World War II changes in Okinawa. Recently rerecorded by Rinsho's son Rinji and by Hirayasu Takashi, it begins:

From the Chinese era to the Japanese era
From the Japanese era to the American era
This Okinawa sure does change a lot.

The song then goes on to comment on changes in money, transportation, and women's fashions. On the one hand, these lyrics reflect, comment on, and playfully (re)construct the historical realities of Okinawa. On the other hand, the song locates Okinawans as witnesses to and on the receiving end of, if not quite as the victims of, changes in the wider world. "Jidai no Nagare" thus contains important themes of the location of Okinawa(ns) in interrelation with powerful outside "others" and of the cultural changes in Okinawa resulting from this location. Ota has noted:

> "From the world [*yu*] of China to that of Japan, and then to the world of America, and finally back to the world of Japan," is a common expression heard these days. Many Okinawans recall their history in terms of the politically dominant with whom they have been negotiating their lives, and because of whom a highly creolized culture of contact zone has emerged.[57]

Kina Shoukichi's song "Akisamiyo!" similarly comments on and constructs an Okinawan cultural space in reference to Okinawa's relations with China, Japan, and America. Kina, however, simultaneously conveys a comic sense of confusion and maintains a critical, local, Okinawan reference. Recorded in 1980, eight years after Okinawa's reversion to Japan, Kina sings:

"Akisamiyo!" (Oh, No! Kina Shoukichi and Champloose)[58]
Hey, Nabi,
Is Okinawa part of Japan?
In the past grandpa used to say

Okinawa, Japan,
Ryūkyū was part of China
Oh, No! Oh, No!
Japan, China, America
They're all mixed up
and I just don't understand at all
Hey, Tara,
Where is Japan?
In the past grandma used to say
It's somewhere way over the mountains
[*repeat refrain*]
Hey, Nabi,
Which do you like, Japan or America?
In the past grandpa used to say
Japan is poor and America is rich
[*repeat refrain*]
Hey, Tara,
Where are our ancestors from?
In the past grandma used to say
Not Japan or America
but China
[*repeat refrain*]
Oh, No! Oh, No! What should we do?
This small little Okinawa
Why is it always being forced to go
Here and there?
[*repeat refrain*]

These themes are also repeated and playfully yet critically extended in the Rinken Band's "Yu-Yu-Yu/You-You-You." There is a fair amount of word play in this song, linguistically reflecting and constructing Okinawa's betwixt and between location and internal creolized mix, or champuru. What I want to draw attention to here, in addition to these themes, is the song's call not to "forget your gentle kindness," despite the changes in the world. These appeals for optimism are put into dramatic relief in Teruya's movie *Tink, Tink, Tink.*[59] An energetic live performance of the song is framed, first, by a long, slow, silent drive down Okinawan streets dominated by the weathered English-language signs of stores, bars, and clubs that (once) cater(ed) to American soldiers. The live performance is also framed, afterwards, by an airborne shot of the Mabuni coast—the scene of the last organized resistance by the Japanese army during the 1945 Battle of Okinawa and now the site of the Okinawa Peace Memorial.[60]

"Yu-Yu-Yu/You-You-You" (Rinken Band)[61]
Yu-Yu-Yu/You-You-You [*throughout*]
We had the American era
We had the Japanese era
We had the Okinawan era
We had the Chinese era
Even if the world changes
Even if everything changes
Don't forget your gentle kindness
Yu-You, days of import
Yu-You, troubled times
Yu-You, in the middle of the night
Yu-You, I love you
Yesterday, today, tomorrow,
the day after Tomorrow
This Time/era is all of ours
Last year, this year, next year
Even if the times
and young hearts are shaken
Time goes by, we're all the same
Don't forget your gentle kindness
Yu-You, oh, you liar
Yu-You, only you
Yu-You, clever people
Yu-You, hard workers
At the gates to people's hearts
let's place a lantern
and let it shine
Yu-You, this is your world
Yu-You, world, era, time
Even if reborn, in whatever age
Don't forget your gentle kindness
Yu-You, the wide world
Yu-You, is spinning round
Yu-You, busily
Yu-You, slowly
Yu-You, ah, Okinawa
Yu-You, eternally
Yu-You, Japanese era
Yu-You, whatever era
Yu-You, whatever place's era
Yu-You, whoever's era
Yu-You, your world

Yu-You, a happy world
Yu-You, celebration world
Yu-You, carefree

Teruya is himself from Koza (now Okinawa City), home of many other Uchinā pop musicians and as well as of the huge Kadena Air Base and related facilities. In a chapter also entitled "Yu-Yu-Yu/You-You-You" in his book *Nankuru-gurashi* (Laid-back Living), Teruya briefly portrays life in Koza in the late 1960s and early 1970s toward the end of the American Occupation. While noting that some American soldiers behaved well and some Okinawans were attracted to the United States, Teruya describes the U.S. military as colonialistic (*shokuminchiteki*), ignoring the human rights of Okinawans. "When I was a teenager in the Koza of the 'American Era,'" he writes, "it was as though every day, day and night, there was some accident or incident involving American soldiers once every two minutes."[62] It seemed, he says, not so much as though the U.S. military were inside Okinawa but as though Okinawa were alone, trapped inside the metal fences of the U.S. military. It is this context of Okinawan experience that gives songs like "Yu-Yu-Yu/You-You-You" their cultural *and* political significance. In a statement that must be read within these overlapping layers of experience and meaning and that suggests the importance of Pratt's distinction between purposive and effective politicality in popular music,[63] Teruya explains:

> Our music is not overtly political. We don't use lyrics as a means to directly convey political messages. We don't sing antiwar songs, for example. We sing about how wonderful it is being alive here and now. It's the celebration of life like this which negates war and other acts that involve violence and killing. Our message is also in the sound. We try to give an uplifting and positive sound to our songs.[64]

DIASPORIC CONNECTIONS

When Okinawa was incorporated into the Meiji state, it became, and indeed remains, Japan's poorest prefecture. In March of 1999, when the mainland Japanese unemployment rate was 4.4 percent, in Okinawa it was 7.7 percent (19.3 percent among youth aged between fifteen and twenty-four).[65] Beginning just before the turn of the twentieth century, such poverty led many Okinawans to emigrate—to mainland Japan (to which migration is still common), to Japanese imperial possessions and occupied territories overseas (in Micronesia, the Philippines, etc.), to Hawai'i, and to South America (notably, Brazil, Argentina, and Peru).

Some three hundred thousand Okinawans and their descendants now live overseas, with an equal number living in mainland Japan. Taira—himself a member of the Okinawan diaspora in North America—contends that they "are fiercely proud of their Okinawan roots."[66] Miyasaki notes that "music is perhaps the most popular and widely practiced of Okinawan cultural activities today in Hawaii."[67]

It is not my intention here to discuss the place of music among the members of the Okinawan diaspora. Instead, my interest is in how music in the home culture of Okinawa that describes the experiences of migration also reflexively constructs images of Okinawa. While the songs discussed earlier portray Okinawa in reference to external processes of change and mixing (be they derived or imposed), another set of songs recalls the destinations outside to which Okinawan people have migrated, from which they have returned, and to which Okinawan identity is thereby extended. There are, for example, a number of Okinawan folk songs that describe setting out for Hawai'i and other parts of the world, including "Hawai'i Bushi," "Imin [Emigration] Ko-uta," and "Nanyō [South Seas] Ko-uta." The Uchinā pop song "Ikawū" (I'll Be Going), performed by the Nenes, follows in this tradition.[68]

I'll be going, on my journey
to South America, to Argentina
Choose an auspicious day,
aim for a new heaven
I'm a man and so I set sail
into the wide world
My life's journey now begins
I'll be going, now we must part
Our hands still holding tight
I'll be going, my dear friends,
my loving brothers and sisters
Stay well, my dear father and mother
Take good care of each other
Please take care of your health
I'll be going, on my journey
to South America, to Argentina
I'll be going, now we must part
Our hands still holding tight

I'll be going, now we must part
Our hands still holding tight
Stay well, take care of your health
I won't forget the language of this island

I'll work hard, get rich, and return home
However far apart, this island is my home
I'll be going, now we must part
Our hands still holding tight
I'll be going, on my journey
to South America, to Argentina
I'll be going, now we must part
Our hands still holding tight

In this song, we hear of the sadness of leaving Okinawa, departing from family and friends, we hear of the emotional ties to Okinawa as home "however far apart," and we hear of the importance of language. These themes are repeated in other songs as well. Songs such as "Nmarijima" (Island of My Birth), recorded by the Rinken Band (and written by Teruya Rinken's father, Teruya Rinsuke, one of the major figures in postwar Okinawan popular music),[69] describe the longing to return *home* to Okinawa among those living in faraway sites in mainland Japan, especially near major industrial cities such as Tokyo, Kawasaki, Nagoya, and Osaka.[70]

Far from the island of my birth
Living in the city
On occasion returning home
There is nothing happier
Maybe I'll return today
Home to the island of my birth

In whatever city I am
There is none better than home
Maybe I'll return today
Home to the island of my birth
Meet my friends, that pleasant time
In the language of our island
Maybe I'll return today
Home to the island of my birth

While Okinawans may go afar, Okinawa—as a place where home, family, lovers, and friends are—is also kept near, in the heart.

In his introduction to *Global Diasporas,* Robin Cohen discusses several types of diasporic experience—victim, labor, trade, imperial, and cultural—that generally share a number of traits including "a collective memory and myth about the homeland . . . an idealization of the supposed ancestral home . . . [and] a return movement."[71] In the case of Uchinā pop, the memories, myths, and idealizations of home are also constructed in part by songs that celebrate returning by, now third- and fourth-generation, emigrant Okinawans. The musical creativity and the musical construction of these returnees is perhaps best represented by third-generation Okinawan-Peruvian Alberto Shiroma and his Latin music band, the Diamantes. Among this group's songs are those (sung in Spanish and Japanese) with titles such as "Okinawa mi amor," "Okinawa Latina," and "Con el sanshin en la mano."[72]

A female trio called TonTonMi, whose members are returnee Okinawan-Brazilians and who primarily play rearrangements of Okinawan folk songs, has also recently released a CD called *Saudade de Uchinā* (Homesick for Okinawa). The title track, written by China Sadao, sings of returnee diasporic experience and identity in terms of a longing to return to Okinawa, the homeland of their grandparents. It elides economic motives for emigrating while emphasizing the emotions associated with a home place. While the Latin American destination in "Ikawū" was musically indicated by the use of a plaintive nylon-string guitar, the dual points of reference in "Saudade de Uchinaa," abroad and back home in Okinawa, seem reinforced by the prominent, alternating use of steel-string acoustic slide guitar, keyboards, and the sanshin.[73]

I was born and raised in São Paolo
In the land of the Amazon, in South America
My language and lifestyle
Are Portuguese, those of a foreign country
I'm third-generation Okinawan!
I've gotta go to the island
of my grandparents' birth
Homesick for Okinawa

Sanshin, Shima-Uta
were my mother's lullabies
They remain painfully in my heart
Nostalgic longing, for my Okinawa
I've gotta go to the island
of my grandparents' birth
Homesick for Okinawa
I've gotta go to the island
of my grandparents' birth
Homesick for Okinawa

Rey Chow notes that diaspora embodies a "question of borders," which "is not so much about the transient eventually giving way to the permanent as it is about an existential condition of which 'permanence' itself is an ongoing fabrication."[74] "Ikawū," "Nmarijima," and "Saudade de Uchinaa" are part of the local Uchinā pop repertory and reflexive (self-) representation of Okinawa. Like other songs that describe the emotions of the Okinawan diaspora, they also construct Okinawa in reference to places beyond Okinawa, which then itself becomes much more an unbounded, transnational cultural space.

Singing Resistance

"Colonized and exploited communities," George Lipsitz writes, "have a long history of cultural expression that uses the protective cover offered by seemingly innocent play . . . to address and redress their traditional grievances."[75] This disguised politicality may be heard in Okinawan music, for example, in traditional songs such as "Mayagwa" (Little Cat), a Yaeyama folk song that satirizes a central government official from the Ryūkyūan Court at Shuri and, perhaps reconceived, with Tokyo replacing Shuri, in recent remakes by groups such as Kotobuki.[76] A number of songs narrate and mourn—and may be heard as protests against—Okinawan experiences during and after the Battle of Okinawa.[77] Contemporary forms of cultural resistance may, as well, be evident in the musical, linguistic, and visual elements of Okinawan difference (discussed above) that mark Uchinā pop (and much folk) music. There are also more directly articulated calls to resist change and maintain an Okinawan identity as well as songs protesting the violence perpetrated against Okinawan life and land by Japanese and U.S. political and military forces.

KEEPING PURE HEARTS

Messages calling for Okinawan audiences to remember their Okinawan identities, language, and culture are present in several Uchinā pop songs. The song "Namikaji" (Sea Breeze), written by China Sadao and recorded by the Nenes, combines references to changes in the political winds blowing from Japan and America with an appeal not to forget the heart or spirit (*kokoro*) of Okinawan music (*shima-uta*).[78] The song "Kogane no Hana" (Flowers of Gold), also performed by the Nenes, contains a more generalized appeal, in lyrics directed to someone working away from his family and home, not to lose one's pure (and presumably Okinawan) heart for the sake of money. Here, perhaps, Okinawans echo the mainland Japanese idealization of Okinawan beauty and purity discussed at the beginning of this chapter. However, while the phrases are similar, the position of the singer/writer and so the meanings of the words are different—reframing the songs as cultural resistance rather than Tokyo-centric discourses of the vanishing. The refrain to "Kogane no Hana" includes these lines:[79]

Simple and pure-hearted people
. . .
Don't throw away
Your hearts for money
Flowers of gold will fall sometime

Another example of a song calling for the protection of local Okinawan identity is Kina Shoukichi's early "Shimagwa Song" (Island-Child Song). He recorded two versions of this song: one using a simple garage-band-like but powerful arrangement in which an electric guitar is used much like a sanshin; the other featuring sanshin instead of guitar. In both versions, Kina is almost literally crying out for his listeners not to forget their island spirit, and, in the second verse, not to forget the Okinawan language:[80]

Don't forget
Never forget
The spirit of the Islands
Don't throw away your heart
Don't throw away your love
We are the children of these Islands
Don't throw away
the spirit of the Islands
Don't forget
the spirit of the Islands

Don't throw away
Never throw away
The spirit of the Islands
Don't throw away your heart
Don't forget our Okinawan language
We are the spirit of these Islands

Grab hold
Never let go
The spirit of the Islands
Don't throw away your heart
Don't throw away your love
We are the children of these Islands
Grab hold of the spirit of
the Islands

Never forget the spirit of
the Islands

Songs such as this, which simultaneously construct an imagined or endangered Okinawan identity or heart and call for the preservation of that Okinawan identity, must also be heard as songs of political and cultural resistance against all those external and internal forces that erode distinctly Okinawan identities.

PROTEST MUSIC

While some musicians such as Teruya Rinken disavow overt political messages and action, other Okinawan performers are more directly political in both their actions and songs. Perhaps more consistently than any other Okinawan artist, Kina Shoukichi has included political and environmental themes in his music, lyrics, and performances—although he also tends toward the mystical. Kina has participated in various activities related to his vision of Okinawan cultural and ethnic identity, minority rights, and environmental ethics. Much to the ire of more conservative Okinawans, for example, Kina joined Chibana Shōichi to play the sanshin and sing when, in May 1996, the latter won permission to visit his plot of land within the U.S. Navy's Sobe Communications Station (also called Camp Hansen and, popularly, the "elephant cage," *zō no ori*).[81]

During the first twenty-three years after Okinawa's reversion to Japanese control, some 4,790 reported crimes were committed by U.S. military personnel or their family members. Although most were petty thefts, there were also 255 robberies, 111 reported cases of violence (including rape) against women, and 12 murders.[82] In September 1995, a twelve-year-old Okinawan girl was kidnapped and raped by three U.S. Marines.[83] This rape occurred at a time of already heightened criticism of the continuing presence of U.S. military bases in Okinawa. In response to the rape, Kina Shoukichi composed a song called "Shōjo no Namida ni Niji ga Kakaru Made" (Until There Is a Rainbow around the Young Girl's Tears):[84]

Walking, walking, looking for Something
I've climbed up to here, but still
In my heart, the flowers
That had been blooming
One by one have all withered
Tears flow out, without stop
I want to give my heart to you
Until there is a rainbow

Around the young girl's tears,
Let's sing

Flowing, flowing, looking for an Answer
I've traced my steps to here, but still
In my heart, the birds
That had been flying
One by one have all disappeared
Tears flow out, without stop
I want to give my heart to you
Until there is a rainbow
Around the young girl's tears,
Let's dance

The skies opened and your face,
Somehow, I could see it laughing
Blown by the wind, flowing
Tears and clouds, melted together
Flowers too, surely
Birds too, surely
Wrapped in the rainbow's light
Until there is a rainbow
Around the young girl's tears
Let's sing, let's dance, until it reaches Her

Bringing her a beautiful aura

While not directly explained in the song lyrics, the meaning of "young girl" and the reason for her tears are obvious within the Okinawan context, making the song lyrical but still strongly political.[85] Performed as a slow, acoustic-guitar-based ballad, this song is sung in Japanese, making the audience effectively all of Japan.

Although previously rarely political, the Nenes (under the guidance of China Sadao) released a CD in 1997 that included a number of songs with peace as their theme.[86] One of these songs is called "Nasake Shirazuya" (translated as "You Are Inhumane"). Set to a light electric guitar pop tune, this song excoriates Japanese politicians and America for being so uncaring about the lives of Okinawans, even fifty years after the end of World War II. While lamenting the coldness of outside dominant Others toward the continuing suffering of Okinawa(ns), the immediate context for "Nasake Shirazuya"—as also for "Okinawa o Kaese," cited later—includes both the 1995 rape and the renewed struggle to regain control of land occupied by U.S. military bases (figure 7.2). During the 1990s, the is-

Figure 7.2. The "movement" song "Okinawa o Kaese" (Return Okinawa), by Daiku Tetsuhiro, appears on this compact disc. This version of the song calls for the return of Okinawan land to Okinawans.

Source: Photo by Gerald Figal.

sue of forced rental of Okinawan land for U.S. military bases became heated, especially after then-governor Ōta Masahide refused to sign documents allowing continued American use of the land.[87]

Another politically active Okinawan musician, Daiku Tetsuhiro, has gained much positive and negative attention for his rerecordings of the song "Okinawa o Kaese" (Return Okinawa).[88] This song was originally composed in the mid-1950s in Kyūshū as a "movement" song calling for the return of Okinawa to Japanese control. Daiku has recorded this song twice, once on his *Okinawa Jinta* CD of 1994, and again on a 1997 collaboration album entitled *Chibariyō Uchinā* (Fight! Okinawa). These two recordings, as is often noted, are significantly different.[89] The first recording is the thirteenth of fifteen songs and is an up-tempo, brass and saxophone-dominated remake.

The second recording is the opening song of the CD *Chibariyō Uchinā* (which concludes with the song "Ganbarō" [Let's Fight for It!], originally also a union theme song from the strident unionization struggles in mainland Japan in the 1950s). Daiku's second rerecording of "Okinawa o Kaese," further, begins with a simple sanshin and taiko introduction, marking this version of the song as more fully *Okinawan*. Daiku sings with anger in his voice. He also made a very important change in the lyrics of the refrain, from "*Okinawa* o *Kaese*" to include the line "*Okinawa* e *Kaese*," changing the meaning of the line from "Return Okinawa [to Japan]!" to "Return [it—the land] to Okinawa."

On 21 October 1995, Daiku performed "*Okinawa o Kaese*" at the people's rally in Ginowan, Okinawa, where an estimated eighty-five thousand people gathered to protest the September 1995 rape of the schoolgirl and to call for reduction and return of U.S. military bases in Okinawa.[90] Making a claim for Okinawan land for Okinawans, against both Japanese and U.S. domination, the lyrics of the song, simple, direct, and powerfully performed, are as follows:[91]

Breaking down the enemy land
Island burning with a people's anger
Oh, Okinawa
We and our ancestors
With blood and sweat
Protected and raised in this Okinawa
We will shout—Okinawa!
This is ours—Okinawa!
Return Okinawa!
Return it to Okinawa!

Connections

While much recent social theory on globalization has usefully problematized our notions of bounded place and has emphasized the transnational connections of "modernity at large," it also recognizes the importance of local places of practice and everyday experience.[92] Uchinā pop music is, likewise, a set of local cultural practices that help construct various kinds of meanings and identities. Not least is the claim that Okinawa is a hybrid culture mixing traditional Okinawan elements with those derived from the West (mainly the United States) and Japan. The active, creative character of music as cultural practice—both production and performance—is especially important since, as Jonathan Friedman points out in his critique of "creolization as confused essentialism": "Cultures don't flow together and mix with each other. Rather, certain actors, often strategically positioned actors, identify the world in such terms as part of their own self-identification. Cultural mixture is the effect of the practice of mixed origins."[93]

In other words, cultural mixing is a specific choice of people who seek to combine seemingly separate traditions in their lives. The champuru "multiple consciousness"[94] reflexively employed and constructed in Uchinā pop is simultaneously used to meld and maintain distinctions between senses of Okinawan and non-Okinawan identities. The points of reference include Okinawa, Japan, the United States, and intra- (Japanese) and transnational destinations. Uchinā pop music and musicians thus mediate "contested relations between difference, identity and place."[95]

Stuart Hall, meanwhile, has recently discussed the cultural and political significance of the "coming into representation" of peoples on "the margins." He also notes the importance for political and cultural protest and resistance by marginalized peoples of the rediscovery and reimagination of local place: "The moment of rediscovery of a place, a past, of one's roots, of one's context . . . [is] . . . a necessary moment of enunciation. . . . [T]he margins could [not] speak up without first grounding themselves somewhere."[96]

Writing and singing about Okinawa—as a place that is distinct and different, betwixt and between, beautiful, and home—then, potentially makes other political protest easier to imagine and execute. Uchinā pop music must be understood not simply as fashionably consumable ethnic or world music but as an important means through which Okinawans can situate themselves in relation to local, national, and transnational contexts. Mainland Japanese and American subordination of Okinawa—whether manifest as geopolitical policy, social ideology, or cultural practice—makes these local musical representations of Okinawan place and identity especially significant. Uchinā pop music may be marketed as fun, colorful, and different—which it often is—but to view Okinawa(n music) only as an exotic landscape, reproducing mainland Japanese (American and world) desires and discourses, endangers blindness (and deafness) to the fact that Uchinā pop is also an important site in the contemporary Okinawan cultural politics of place, pride, and protest.

> From the Chinese era to the Japanese era to the American era . . . champon, champuru . . . don't forget the spirit of the islands . . . Return [it to] Okinawa!

NOTES

I would like to thank Linda Angst and Laura Hein, especially, as well as Chris Yano, Hosokawa Shuhei, Terada Yoshitaka, Laura Miller, Nagafuchi Yasuyuki, Kumada Susumu, Gerald Figal, and Wesley Ueunten for their encouragement and comments. Versions of this chapter were presented at the annual meeting of the Association for Asian Studies, San Diego, 10 March 2000, and at the Washington and Southeast Region Japan Seminar, George Washington University, Washington, D.C., 29 January 2000. Attendance at the Association for Asian Studies meeting in San Diego, March 2000, was supported by a faculty travel grant kindly provided by the Reves Center for International Studies at the College of William and Mary, while I was a visiting assistant professor of anthropology, 1999–2000.

I would also like to thank all the musicians and publishers for their permissions to use the English translations of song lyrics and images included here and in the version of this chapter previously published in *Critical Asian Studies* (33, no. 2 [2001]: 211–42).

1. *Uchinaa* is an Okinawan-language version of *Okinawa*. I henceforth use "Uchinā pop" to indicate the hybrid music highlighted here in contrast to "Okinawan pop." CDs cited here are Kina Shoukichi and Champloose, *Kina Shoukichi and Champloose* (Japan Records, 25JC-357, 1989 [1977]); China Sadao, *Akabana* (Pony Canyon, PCCA-00581, 1978); Kina Shoukichi and Champloose, *Nirai Kanai Paradise* (Toshiba EMI, TOCP 6270, 1990); Nenes, *Ikawū* (Akabana, APCD 1001, 1994); Rinken Band, *Arigatou* (Wave, EVA 2016, 1990 [1987]). Other relevant musicians include Ara Yukito Parsha Club, Daiku Tetsuhiro, Hidekatsu, Oshima Yasukatsu, Kadekaru Rinji, Hirayasu Takashi, Ganeko Yoriko, Tamaki Kazumi, Iha Chieko, Yano Kenji, and Shima Sachiko.

The boom in interest in Okinawan music is also reflected in the publication of, for example, Aoki Makoto, *Okinawa uta no tabi* (Okinawa Song Journey) (Tokyo: PHP, 1995); Fujita Tadashi, ed., *Uchinā no uta: Meikyoku 101-sen & CD gaido* (Okinawan Songs: 101 Selected Famous Songs and CD Guide) (Tokyo: Ongaku-No-Tomo-Sha, 1998); Isoda Kenichirō and Kurokawa Shūji, eds., *Okinawan Music Guide for Beginners* [in Japanese] (Tokyo: Tōa Ongaku-sha, 1995); Kaneshiro Atsumi, *Yamatonchu no tame no Okinawa ongaku nyūmon* (Introduction to Okinawan Music, for Mainland Japanese) (Tokyo: Ongaku-No-Tomo-Sha, 1997); Nakasone Kouichi, *"Shima-uta" nagare* ("Shima-uta" Stream) (Naha: Bōda-Inku, 1995); Nakazato Isao, *Okinawan Beat* [in Japanese] (Naha: Bōda-Inku, 1992); Radio Okinawa, *Okinawa no uta 100-sen* (Okinawa Music Best 100) (Naha: Radio Okinawa, 1994); Tenku Kikaku, eds., *Uchinā Pop: Okinawa Culture Book* [in Japanese] (Tokyo: Tokyo Shoseki, 1992); Teruya Rinken, Naka Bokunen, and Murakami Akiyoshi, *Okinawa no ima gaido bukku* (Okinawa Now Guidebook) (Tokyo: Iwanami Shoten, 1995).

Books by or about Uchinā pop musicians include Fujisaki Yasuo, *Kina Shoukichi: Inori* (Kina Shoukichi: Prayer) (Tokyo: Shichiken Shuppan, 1994); Kina Shoukichi, *Subete no buki o gakki ni* (All Weapons to Musical Instruments) (Tokyo: Bōkensha, 1997); Kina Shoukichi and Champloose, *Subete no hito no kokoro ni hana wo: Kina Shoukichi no kosumorojii* (A Flower for Your Heart: Cosmology of Shoukichi Kina) (Naha: Okinawa Times, 1996); Okano Makino, *Ryūkyū shinpi: Rinken Band de shiru Ryūkyū* (Ryūkyū Mystery: Knowing the Ryūkyūs through the Rinken Band) (Tokyo: Yomiuri Shimbun-sha, 1993); Teruya Rinken, *Nankuru gurashi* (Laid-back Living) (Tokyo: Chikuma Shobō, 1995).

For commentary on the "third golden age," see DeMusik International, ed., *Oto no chikara—Okinawa: Koza futtō* (The Power of Music—Okinawa: Koza Boiling) (Tokyo: Impact Shuppansha, 1998), 126ff.; Fujita, *Uchinā no uta*, 10–12.

2. See Timothy Taylor, *Global Pop: World Music, World Markets* (London: Routledge, 1997). For Okinawa, see John Clewly, "Enka, Okinawa and the Masters of Clone," in *World Music: The Rough Guide*, ed. Simon Broughton, Mark Ellington, David Muddyman, and Richard Trillo (London: Rough Guides/Penguin, 1994); Steve McClure, *Nipponpop* (Tokyo: Tuttle, 1998); Osuga Takeshi (and Asian Beats Club), ed., *Asian pop music no genzai* (Contemporary Asian Pop Music) (Tokyo: Shinjuku Shobō, 1993); Philip Sweeney, *The Virgin Directory of World Music* (New York: Holt, 1991), 160–61; Tony Barrell and Rick Tanaka, *Okinawa Dreams OK* (Berlin: Gestalten Verlag, 1997), 53.

3. McClure, *Nipponpop*, 47.

4. Ogawa Hiroshi, "Nippon no popular ongaku ni awareta Okinawa" (The Appearance of Okinawa in the Popular Music of Japan), in *Orient-gensō no naka no Okinawa* (Okinawa within the Orientalist Fantasy), ed. Fukuzawa Tōru (Osaka: Kaifūsha, 1995), 159ff. and 170.

5. H. D. Harootunian, "Figuring the Folk: History, Poetics, and Representation," in *Mirror of Modernity: Invented Traditions of Modern Japan*, ed. Stephen Vlastos (Berkeley: University of California Press, 1998), 156. See also Marilyn Ivy, *Discourses of the Vanishing: Modernity, Phantasm, Japan* (Chicago: University of Chicago, 1995); Ota Yoshinobu, *Toransupojishon no shisō: Bunkajinruigaku no saisōzō* (Transpositional Thought: Reimagining Cultural Anthropology) (Tokyo: Sekai Shisō Sha, 1998); Hashimoto Mitsuru, "*Chihō*: Yanagita Kunio's 'Japan,'" in Vlastos, ed., *Mirror of Modernity*. For exceptions, see DeMusik International, ed., *Oto no chikara—Okinawa: Koza futtō*; DeMusik International, ed., *Oto no chikara—Okinawa: Amami/Yaeyama/Gyaku-ryū* (The Power of Music—Okinawa: Amami/Yaeyama/counter-current) (Tokyo: Impact Shuppansha, 1998).

6. M. William Steele, "Nationalism and Cultural Pluralism in Modern Japan: Sōetsu Yanagi and the Mingei Movement," in *Diversity in Japanese Culture and Language*, ed. John C. Maher and Gaynor Macdonald (London: Kegan Paul, 1995), 43.

7. Murai Osamu, *Nantō Ideology no Hassei: Yanagita Kunio to Shokuminchishugi* (The Rise of Southern Island Ideology: Yanagita Kunio and Colonialism) (Tokyo: Ota-shuppan, 1995).

8. Kina's band, for example, was invited to represent Asia at the cultural events associated with the 1996 Atlanta Olympics. For Kina's own critical reflections on this, see Kina, *Subete no buki o gakki ni*. It must also be recognized, however, that compared to African and Middle Eastern musics, Western (European and American) interest in East Asian music remains limited, since "most western listeners find [it] the most foreign, *despite the spate of press coverage of such albums as the Okinawan Shoukichi Kina's* Peppermint Tea House" (emphasis added; Taylor, *Global Pop*, 9).

9. This chapter is, in part, also a critique of and an attempt to go beyond my own original interests in Okinawan music, which were related mainly with the fun of the music and its "ethnomusicological exoticism." See Richard Middleton, *Studying Popular Music* (Milton Keynes: Open University Press, 1990).

10. Martin Stokes, "Introduction: Ethnicity, Identity and Music," in *Ethnicity, Identity and Music: The Musical Construction of Place*, ed. Martin Stokes (Providence, R.I.: Berg, 1994), 5; Keith Negus, *Popular Music in Theory: An Introduction* (Cambridge: Polity, 1996), 100.

11. Peter Manuel, *Popular Musics of the Non-Western World* (New York: Oxford University Press, 1988); Middleton, *Studying Popular Music*; Taylor, *Global Pop*.

12. Taylor, *Global Pop*, 147.

13. George Lipsitz, *Dangerous Crossroads: Popular Music, Postmodernism and the Poetics of Place* (London: Verso, 1994), 3, 4.

14. "Introduction," in *Senses of Place*, ed. Steven Feld and Keith H. Basso (Santa Fe, N.M.: School of American Research Press, 1996), 8.

15. Negus, *Popular Music in Theory*, 184.

16. Keith H. Basso, "Wisdom Sits in Places: Notes on a Western Apache Landscape," in Feld and Basso, eds., *Senses of Place*, 85.

17. Edward S. Casey, "How to Get from Space to Place in a Fairly Short Stretch of Time: Phenomenological Prolegomena," in Feld and Basso, eds., *Senses of Place*, 27.

18. Ray Pratt, *Rhythm and Resistance: Explorations in the Political Uses of Popular Music* (New York: Praeger, 1990), 4.

19. Simon Frith, "Music and Identity," in *Questions of Cultural Identity*, ed. Stuart Hall and Paul Du Gay (London: Sage, 1996), 121.

20. Negus, *Popular Music in Theory*, 175; see also Karin Barber and Christopher Waterman, "Traversing the Global and the Local: Fuji Music and Praise Poetry in the Production of Contemporary Yoruba Popular Culture," in *Worlds Apart: Modernity through the Prism of the Local*, ed. Daniel Miller (London: Routledge, 1995).

21. Sanjay Sharma, John Hutnyk, and Ashwani Sharma, *Dis-Orienting Rhythms: The Politics of New Asian Dance* (London: Zed, 1996); Lipsitz, *Dangerous Crossroads*; Manuel, *Popular Musics of the Non-Western World*.

22. For general overviews, see: Akabane Yukiko, "Ryūkyū ongaku no miryoku o sakaru" (Investigating the Appeal of Ryūkyūan Music), in *Okinawa kara mita nippon* (Japan as Seen from Okinawa), ed. Meiji University, Human Sciences Research Center (Tokyo: Kazama Shobō, 1994); Aoki, *Okinawa uta no tabi*; Higa Etsuko, "Okinawa minzoku ongaku e no sasoi: Kamiuta kara Okinawa pops made" (An Invitation to Okinawan Folk Music: From Sacred Chants to Okinawan Pops), in *Nantō bunka e no sasoi* (Invitation to the Culture of the South Islands), ed. Okinawa Kokusai Daigaku Kōkaikōza Iinkai (Naha: Naha Shuppansha, 1998); Kaneshiro, *Yamatonchu no tame no Okinawa ongaku nyūmon*.

23. Otake Akiko and Hosokawa Shūhei, "Karaoke in East Asia: Modernization, Japanization, or Asianization?" in *Karaoke around the World: Global Technology, Local Singing*, ed. Mitsui Tōru and Hosokawa Shūhei (London: Routledge, 1998), 189.

24. See Okinawa City, *Rock 'n' Koza*, rev. ed. (in Japanese) (Naha: Naha Shuppan, 1998). While these hard-rock bands and their members have variously disbanded and rebanded, the recent formation of an "Okinawan Rock Society" among rock musicians in Okinawa suggests that (these musicians, at least, feel that) this is a "tradition" in decline and in need of active protection. See "Okinawa rokku no pawā futatabi" (Okinawan Rock Power Once More), *Asahi Shinbun*, 19 October 1998, evening edition.

25. One could also include here Chinen Rina. The national popularity of Okinawan performers of pop music was also symbolized by the selection of Kiroro, Da Pump, SPEED, MAX, and Amuro Namie as performers in the NHK 1998–1999 New Year's Eve "*Kōhaku Uta Gassen*" (Red-White Song Contest).

26. See Ota Yoshinobu, "Appropriating Media, Resisting Power: Representations of Hybrid Identities in Okinawan Popular Culture," in *Between Resistance and Revo-*

lution: Cultural Politics and Social Protest, ed. Richard G. Fox and Orin Starn (New Brunswick, N.J.: Rutgers University Press, 1997); Simon Frith, "Music and Identity;" Paul Gilroy, "Sounds Authentic: Black Music, Ethnicity, and the Challenge of a Changing Same," in *Black Music Research Journal* 11, no. 2 (1991): 111–37; Middleton, *Studying Popular Music*; Negus, *Popular Music in Theory*; Taylor, *Global Pop*.

27. Stokes, "Introduction: Ethnicity, Identity and Music," 6–7. Lipsitz makes a similar point in *Dangerous Crossroads*, 126–27.

28. Middleton, *Studying Popular Music*, 139.

29. See Kitanaka Tadakazu, "Yamatonchu ga fukikonda Uchinā no uta" (Okinawan Songs Recorded by Japanese), in Fujita Tadashi, *Uchinā no Uta*, 104; Ogawa, "Nippon no popular ongaku ni awareta Okinawa." Sakamoto has recorded at least two CDs that include Okinawan elements, *Neo Geo*, released in 1987, and *Beauty*, released in 1990. Currid suggests that on *Beauty*, the juxtapositioning of Senegalese singer Youssou N'Dour's vocal improvisations with call-and-response verses featuring Sakamoto and "a 'backup' trio of three Okinawan women" acts as a "supplement to a Japanese coherence . . . which depends on the erasure of present and historical difference . . . [where] Okinawan voices stand in . . . unproblematically for 'Japanese.'" See Brian Currid, "'Finally, I Reach to Africa': Ryuichi Sakamoto and Sounding Japan(ese)," in *Contemporary Japan and Popular Culture*, ed. John Whittier Treat (Honolulu: University of Hawai'i Press, 1996), 94. Unfortunately, Currid participates in the erasure of Okinawan identity by failing to recognize "Chinsagu No Hana" as, in fact, a "traditional" (if here very rearranged) Okinawan folk song and by suggesting that it is possible to hear the Okinawan voices as "unproblematically . . . Japanese." He also fails to give names to the "three Okinawan women," who are, in fact, each recognized performers whose careers predate—and postdate—their work with Sakamoto: Koja Misako, especially well known for her subsequent years as central member of the Nenes; Ganeko Yoriko, also well known as a folk (*min'yō*) singer, but who has performed with Miyazawa Kazushi of the Boom and released at least two CDs; and Tamaki Kazumi, a lesser-known but still veteran performer who has recently also released a very interesting CD. For brief discussions of all three, with positive notes about their work with Sakamoto, see Oshiro Manabu, *Okinawa shin-min'yō no keifu* (New Okinawan Folk Music Genealogy) (Naha: Hirugi-sha, 1996).

30. Sometimes mistakenly referred to as "jabisen" by mainland Japanese (the "ja" coming from a reading of the Chinese character for *snake*, for the snakeskin with which its body is covered), the sanshin was modified from Chinese instruments brought to Okinawa in the fourteenth and fifteenth centuries and is the predecessor of the Japanese shamisen. For a discussion, see Kaneshiro, *Yamatonchu no tame no Okinawa ongaku nyūmon*.

31. On the Boom's "*Shima-Uta*," see Teruya, Naka, and Murakami, *Okinawa no ima gaido bukku*, 40; Takihara Yasumori, *Ryūkyū min'yō kun-kun-shi 11-kan* (Ryūkyū Folk-song Song Book, vol. 11) (Naha: Okinawa Geinō Shuppan, 1998); Ganeko's rerecording is on Ganeko Yoriko, *Kui nu hana* (VAP, Inc., VPCC-81075, 1995).

32. See Isoda and Kurokawa, *Okinawan Music Guide for Beginners*, 62–70; Taylor, *Global Pop*, 201; Ota, *Toransupojishon no shisō*.

33. See interviews in Fujita, *Uchinā no uta*; Teruya, Naka, and Murakami, *Okinawa no ima gaido bukku*; Teruya, *Nankuru gurashi*. For general discussions, see Simon

Frith, ed., *World Music, Politics and Social Change* (Manchester: Manchester University Press, 1989); Lipsitz, *Dangerous Crossroads*; Deanna Campbell Robinson, Elizabeth B. Buck, and Marlene Cuthbert, *Music at the Margins: Popular Music and Global Cultural Diversity* (Newbury Park, Calif.: Sage, 1991); Stokes, *Ethnicity, Identity and Music;* and Taylor, *Global Pop*.

34. In Fujita, *Uchinā no uta*, 14.

35. The two CDs referred to here are Ara Yukito Parsha Club, *Ara Yukito Parsha Club* (Yuratic Music, PYP-001, 1994) and Ara Yukito Parsha Club, *Parsha* (Toshiba-EMI, TOCT-9248, 1995). The quote by Ara is from Osuga, *Asian pop music no genzai*, 189. See also Isoda and Kurokawa, *Okinawan Music Guide for Beginners*; Tenku Kikaku, *Uchinā Pop*.

36. See: Ota, "Appropriating Media, Resisting Power"; Ota, "Okinawa to iu pojishon: Nijū ishiki no kanōsei" (The Position of Okinawa: The Possibilities of Double Consciousness), *Impaction* 103 (1997): 22–27; Ota, *Toransupojishon no shisō*.

37. Stuart Hall, "The Local and the Global: Globalization and Ethnicity," in *Culture, Globalization and the World System: Contemporary Conditions for the Representation of Identity*, ed. Anthony D. King (Minneapolis: University of Minnesota Press, 1997), 38.

38. See Ota, "Appropriating Media, Resisting Power," 165. Wesley Ueunten (personal communication) warns, however, that music in Okinawa can also be a site of co-optation, both further complicating the field and suggesting the importance of recognizing moments of resistance.

39. Ivy, *Discourses of the Vanishing*, 9.

40. See Ota, "Appropriating Media, Resisting Power," 165.

41. See Ara Yukito Parsha Club, *Ara Yukito Parsha Club*; Hirayasu Takashi, *Karayushi no Tsuki* (Respect Record, RES-25, 1998); Takashi Hirayasu and Bob Brozman, *Nankuru Naisa* (Riverboat Records, TUGCD1023, 2001); Hidekatsu, *Tsukiakari* (Studio Hibiki, STH-001, 2001); Nenes, *Ikawū*; Nenes, *Koza dabasa* (Ki/oon Sony Records, KSC2 83, 1994).

42. In Isoda and Kurokawa, *Okinawan Music Guide for Beginners*, 68–69.

43. Teruya, Naka, and Murakami, *Okinawa no ima gaido bukku*, 30.

44. Nenes, *Koza dabasa* (lyrics by Bise Katsu, music by China Sadao; Soytzer Music Inc.). Translations of song lyrics throughout the chapter are my own—but note that I have translated Japanese lyrics and Japanese translations of Okinawan lyrics. In the latter case of double translation, there is likely to be more distance between the English and the original.

45. Taylor, *Global Pop*, 21–26. On the self-exoticism in Uchinā pop, see Kumada Susumu, "90 nendai Okinawa poppu ni okeru minzokusei hyōgen no shosō" (Aspects of the Expression of Ethnicity in 1990s Okinawan Pop), in *Okinawa kara geijutsu o kangaeru* (Contemplating the Arts from Okinawa), ed. Okinawa Prefectural Arts University, Department of Art Culture (Ginowan: Yuju Shorin, 1998), 134–62; "Okinawa ekizochishizumu no genzai" (Current Okinawan Exoticism), *Kokusai Kōryū* (2000): 31–35.

46. Arasaki Moriteru, *Okinawa o shiru: Nippon o shiru* (Know Okinawa; Know Japan) (Osaka: Kaihō Shuppansha, 1997), 16.

47. On the Ainu, see Tessa Morris-Suzuki, *Re-Inventing Japan: Time, Space, Nation* (Armonk, N.Y.: Sharpe, 1998), 23–28. On Okinawan *hōgen-fuda*, see Teruya,

Naka, and Murakami, *Okinawa no ima gaido bukku*; William P. Lebra, *Okinawan Religion: Belief, Ritual, and Social Structure* (Honolulu: University of Hawai'i Press, 1966), 132. The complicity of Okinawan educators in this is discussed in Oguma Eiji, *"Nipponjin" no Kyōkai* (The Boundaries of the Japanese) (Tokyo: Shinyōsha, 1998). For Teruya Rinken's experiences, see Teruya, *Nankuru gurashi*, 198ff.; and Barrell and Tanaka, *Okinawa Dreams OK*, 115.

48. Basso, "Wisdom Sits in Places," 66.

49. Ota, "Appropriating Media, Resisting Power."

50. Quoted in Barrell and Tanaka, *Okinawa Dreams OK*, 115; see also: Teruya, Naka, and Murakami, *Okinawa no ima gaido bukku*.

51. Rinken Band, *Arigatou*. Gerald Figal (personal communication) also interestingly suggests that given the cultural context of eisā, the use of eisā riffs to structure much of the music seems particularly potent in terms of place (the site of spirits of the dead) *and* time (generations of ancestors).

52. Exceptions most notably include photographs taken in Koza (Okinawa City) and the jacket of Ara Yukito Parsha Club's first CD, where the band, with their typical urban cool, are pictured at night outside a shuttered building, which one assumes to be in Naha, the band's base, not Koza.

53. This is an especially interesting image given Ota's contention that fishers historically were looked down upon in Okinawan society (Ota, *Toransupojishon no shisō*).

54. See Ogawa, "Nippon no popular ongaku ni awareta Okinawa"; Kumada, "90 nendai Okinawa poppu ni okeru minzokusei hyōgen no shosō"; "Okinawa ekizochishizumu no genzai."

55. On Okinawan history in English, see George Kerr, *Okinawa: The History of an Island People* (Rutland, Vt.: Tuttle, 1958); Koji Taira, "Troubled National Identity: The Ryūkyūans/Okinawans," in *Japan's Minorities: The Illusion of Homogeneity*, ed. Michael Weiner (London: Routledge, 1997).

56. See Nagamoto Tomohiro, "Okinawa—kichimondai no rekishi to genzai" (The History and Contemporary Status of the Base Problem in Okinawa), in *Kore ga Okinawa no beigun da: Kichi no shima ni ikiru hitobito* (This Is Okinawa's American Military: People Living in the Island of Bases), ed. Ishikawa Mao, Kuniyoshi Kazuo, and Nagamoto Tomohiro (Tokyo: Kōbunken, 1997), 205.

57. Ota, "Appropriating Media, Resisting Power," 152.

58. "Akisamiyo!" is an exclamatory phrase that means something like "Oh, no!" or (more colloquially) "Oh, shit!" Kina Shoukichi and Champloose, *Blood Line* (Polydor K.K., H25P 20307, 1989 [1980]; lyrics and music by Kina Shoukichi; Nichion, Inc.).

59. *Yu* means "world" or "era" and is the Okinawan pronunciation of *yo* in Japanese. Teruya Rinken, *Tink-Tink-Tink* (Tokyo: Sony Records, SRVM 463, 1994).

60. See Arasaki Moriteru, *Gendai Okinawa-shi* (Contemporary Okinawan History) (Tokyo: Iwanami Shoten, 1996), 200–202; and Gerald Figal, "Historical Sense and Commemorative Sensibility at Okinawa's Cornerstone of Peace," *positions: east asia cultures critique* 5, no. 3 (1997): 745–78.

61. Rinken Band, *Banji* (SR WAVE SRCL-2728, 1993; lyrics and music by Teruya Rinken; Sony Music Artists, Inc.)

62. Teruya, *Nankuru gurashi*, 122.

63. Pratt, *Rhythm and Resistance*.

64. Barrell and Tanaka, *Okinawa Dreams OK*, 114.

65. See Kerr, *Okinawa;* Taira, "Troubled National Identity"; Tamamori Terunobu and John C. James, *A Minute Guide to Okinawa: Society and Economy* (Naha: Bank of the Ryūkyūs International Foundation, 1995); *Asahi Shimbun,* "Shima o deru hi" (Day of Leaving the Islands) (20 March 1999).

66. Taira, "Troubled National Identity," 167.

67. Gail Miyasaki, "Okinawans and Culture in Hawaii," in *Uchinanchu: A History of Okinawans in Hawaii,* Ethnic Studies Oral History Project (Honolulu: Ethnic Studies Program, University of Hawai'i at Manoa, 1981), 167. See also Chika Shirota, "Dancing beyond the U.S. Military: Okinawan *Eisā* as Identity and Diaspora," *Theatre InSight* 10 (Spring 1999): 4–13; R. Anderson Sutton, "Okinawan Music Overseas: A Hawaiian Home," *Asian Music* 15, no. 1 (1983): 54–80.

68. Nenes, *Ikawū* (lyrics and music by Tamae Masaaki; Soytzer Music, Inc.).

69. See Chikushi Tetsuya and Teruya Rinsuke, *Okinawa ga subete* (Okinawa Is Everything) (Tokyo: Kawade Shobōshinsha, 1997); Tenku Kikaku, Inc., *Uchinā Pop;* Teruya Rinsuke, *Terurin jiden* (TeruRin Autobiography) (Tokyo: Misuzu Shobō, 1998).

70. Rinken Band, *Arigatou* (lyrics by Teruya Rinsuke, music by Teruya Rinken). Note, however, that "*shima*" in the Okinawan dialect can also mean "town" or "village," and so the song may also, simultaneously, be heard with an intraprefectural reference. "Nmarijima" has also been recorded by Rinken Band lead vocalist Uehara Tomoko on her solo CD *Zan* (1997, Sony Records, SRCL 3992). The Okinawan-Hawaiian band Nami Kaji recorded a Hawaiian language version, "Home Aina," on their debut CD (1995, Ajima Records AR 95001), further extending the Okinawan diasporic connections of "Nmarijima."

71. Robin Cohen, *Global Diasporas: An Introduction* (Seattle: University of Washington Press, 1997), 180.

72. Diamantes, *Lo Mejor de Diamantes (1993–1997)* (Mercury Music Entertainment, PHCL-5083, 1997). Alberto Shiroma, leader of the Diamantes, writes many of his songs in his native (Peruvian) Spanish. Because this band otherwise rarely uses distinctively "Okinawan" elements in their music and performances, I am somewhat reluctant to treat them as an Uchinā pop group. Their presence in the Okinawan music scene is, however, important. The song "Con el sanshin en la mano" was chosen as the theme song for the Third Worldwide Uchinanchu Festival, held in Okinawa (Ginowan), 1–4 November 2001.

73. Ton Ton Mi, *Saudade de Uchinā* (Fukuhara Records, FCD-104, 1998; lyrics and music by China Sadao; Soytzer Music, Inc.).

74. Rey Chow, *Writing Diaspora: Tactics of Intervention in Contemporary Cultural Studies* (Bloomington: Indiana University Press, 1993), 15.

75. Lipsitz, *Dangerous Crossroads,* 71.

76. Included on the CD: Daiku Tetsuhiro, *Chibariyō Uchinā* (Ongaku Center, CCD760, 1997).

77. Included would be songs such as "Nuchi Du Takara" (Life Is a Treasure) and "Himeyuri no Uta" (Song of the Himeyuri); see also the collection *Champuru Shingurusu,* vol. 2: *Heiwa no Negai (Sensō to Imin)* (Champuru Singles: Prayer for Peace [War and Migration]) (Toshiba EMI TOCT-9552, 1996).

78. Nenes, *Ikawū.*

79. Nenes, *Koza Dabasa* (lyrics by Okamoto Osami, music by China Sadao; Nichion, Inc.).

80. Kina Shoukichi and Champloose, *Kina Shoukichi and Champloose* (lyrics and music by Kina Shoukichi; Shinko Music Publishing). In comments regarding the English translation given here, Kina notes that *Shimagwa* means "a child of the island," a reference to "the people who were born and raised in Okinawa." The term also represents "Okinawans' spirits themselves." Furthermore, it should be noted that Kina intends here, as elsewhere, to extend his thinking to "the universal spirits of living as human beings." I thank Kina for his comments.

81. For Kina, see Fujisaki, *Kina Shoukichi*; Kina Shoukichi and Champloose, *Subete no Hito no Kokoro ni Hana wo*; Kina, *Subete no buki o gakki ni*. For Chibana, see Chibana Shoichi, *Burning the Rising Sun: From Yomitan Village, Okinawa, Islands of U.S. Bases* (Kyoto: South Wind, 1992); Barrell and Tanaka, *Okinawa Dreams OK*.

82. Arasaki, *Gendai Okinawa-shi*, 204.

83. See Taira, "Troubled National Identity"; Chalmers Johnson, ed., *Okinawa: Cold War Island* (Cardiff, Calif.: Japan Policy Research Institute, 1999).

84. Kina Shoukichi and Champloose, *Subete no Buki o Gakki ni* (Columbia, COCA-14509, 1997; lyrics by Kina Shoukichi, music by Riruru Mareran; Columbia Music Publishing).

85. For Kina's own critical comments on the surrounding political contexts and controversies, see Kina, *Subete no buki o gakki ni*.

86. Nenes, *Akemodoro* (Antinos Records, CDORBD 096, 1997).

87. See Arasaki, *Gendai Okinawa-shi*; Taira, "Troubled National Identity."

88. See interview in DeMusik International, ed., *Oto no Chikara—Okinawa: Amami/Yaeyama/Gyaku-ryū*.

89. Daiku Tetsuhiro, *Okinawa Jinta* (Off Note, ON-1, 1994); Daiku, *Chibariyō Uchinaa*. For reviews, see Fujita, *Uchinā no uta*, 37; Kanehira Shigenori, "1995 Nen no 'Okinawa o kaese'" ("Return Okinawa" of 1995), CD liner notes to Daiku Tetsuhiro, *Chibariyō Uchinā* (Tokyo: Ongaku Center, 1997); Tomiyama Ichirō, "Okuni wa?" (Your Country Is?), in *Oto no chikara—Okinawa: Koza futtō* (The Power of Music—Okinawa: Koza Boiling), ed. DeMusik International (Tokyo: Impact Shuppansha, 1998).

90. See Tomiyama Ichirō, "Okuni wa?"

91. Daiku, *Chibariyō Uchinā*.

92. See Arjun Appadurai, *Modernity at Large: Cultural Dimensions of Globalization* (Minneapolis: University of Minnesota Press, 1996); Jonathan Friedman, *Cultural Identity and Global Process* (London: Sage, 1994); Ulf Hannerz, *Transnational Connections: Culture, People, Places* (London: Routledge, 1996); Kirsten Hastrup and Karen Fog Olwig, "Introduction," in *Siting Culture: The Shifting Anthropological Object*, ed. Karen Fog Olwig and Kirsten Hastrup (London: Routledge, 1997).

93. Friedman, *Cultural Identity and Global Process*, 210.

94. Here I expand on Ota, "Okinawa to iu pojishon"; Paul Gilroy, *The Black Atlantic: Modernity and Double Consciousness* (Cambridge, Mass.: Harvard University Press, 1993).

95. Gupta and Ferguson, "Culture, Power, Place: Ethnography at the End of an Era," in *Culture, Power, Place: Explorations in Critical Anthropology*, ed. Akhil Gupta and James Ferguson (Durham, N.C.: Duke University Press, 1997), 3.

96. Hall, "The Local and the Global: Globalization and Ethnicity," 36.

8

Okinawan Identity and Resistance to Militarization and Maldevelopment

Asato Eiko

Okinawa was the only Japanese territory on which a ground battle was fought between American and Japanese forces during the Pacific War. That battle, the fiercest of the war, lasted from 26 March to 23 June 1945, and it took the lives of more than one-quarter of Okinawa's population. The damage inflicted on both the environment and people was so massive that it deprived virtually the entire surviving population of all means of livelihood: homes, property, tools, even food. Nearly all of the survivors, whether military or civilian, were captured and detained in camps, many for up to two years.

When they were finally released and returned to their native villages and towns, they found their communities and land devastated. Residents of Yomitan Village, one of the first groups released from the camps, described the scene as follows:

> As far as we could see, there were American military facilities, and there was no longer a trace of the village that we knew before the war. Trees were cut down; stone walls and hedges had been taken away; pampas grass and weeds were growing everywhere; wild birds from the mountains were nesting and mongooses were roaming in the midst of what used to be our village; it was sheer desolation. We could even see the bones of goats, horses, and cows lying on the ground.[1]

The members of one family, who came from Tobaru in the northern town of Motobu-cho, recorded their return home:

> Though permitted to go home from the Oura Camp in Kushi Village [now a part of Nago City], we could not go straight back to our home village, so we stayed in a place called Furijima for several days. From there looking at our village, everything looked white like snow. We discovered that the village had been turned into an airfield. Every house had been burned down, and the fertile farms were buried under the runway.[2]

The Battle of Okinawa and its aftermath thus thoroughly destroyed the village, community, and agrarian foundations on which Okinawan society had historically rested.

Destruction of the Okinawan environment was not limited to war. In the postwar period, the United States turned the islands into a military colony and built military facilities there, compounding the onslaught. Seventy-five percent of the American military bases in Japan today are concentrated on the islands of Okinawa, which is home to less than 1 percent of the Japanese population; 10.5 percent of its total land and more than 20 percent of the land on the main island are occupied by bases. As a result of U.S. confiscation of such large areas, many villagers were deprived of their land and forced to relocate. "In the village of Kamiseidobaru," for example, "farms, houses, and trees were all leveled to build barracks for American servicemen; the dozen houses that had managed to survive the war were torn down by the U.S. military."[3]

The village structure, the center of Okinawan life, was also damaged by the war and then by the construction of the military bases. Local people were forced to relocate en masse to areas designated by the U.S. military without concern for either agriculture and fishing or the integrity of the community. The U.S. military forced many to leave the main island, particularly its southern half where the bases were concentrated, and move to outer islands of Okinawa or emigrate to mainland Japan or abroad.[4]

In 1972, when the United States finally ended direct military rule of Okinawa and the islands "reverted" to Japan, the U.S. military presence and the bases remained intact. The Japanese government subsequently established an agency for the development of the islands and also enacted the Okinawa Promotion and Development Plan, pumping in financial aid to redress the economic gap between Okinawa, Japan's poorest prefecture, and the rest of the nation. However, Japanese-style development in subsequent decades not only further destroyed the natural environment but also had a devastating impact on the social and spiritual life of the people. For example, Okinawans had long adhered to a strong taboo against cutting down village forests (considered sacred places). Under developmental pressure, not only were forests clear-cut, but communal lands also became subject to commercial transactions, which transformed village social and spiritual life. The following sections document these processes.

MILITARY BASES AND THE DESTRUCTION OF VILLAGE COMMUNITIES

Base Construction and Relocation of Villages: The Case of Yomitan

On 1 April 1945, U.S. forces landed on the main island of Okinawa at the village of Yomitan, near the center of the island. The U.S. Navy immediately set up the first military government in Yomitan and issued the so-called Nimitz Proclamation that initiated the military occupation and set in motion a process whereby local residents were detained in POW camps. Twelve such internment camps were established throughout the main island of Okinawa. These were surrounded by barbed wire, as though the entire population were the enemy. At the same time, they were styled by the occupation forces as "cities," with a "mayor" appointed in each. In most of the histories of postwar Okinawa, the word *city* is used uncritically, which tends to conceal the true nature of life under the U.S. military occupation. Approximately three hundred thousand people, the great majority of surviving Okinawans, were forced to live in these camps, ranging in size from ten thousand to fifty-five thousand people. It is unusual, to say the least, to treat civilians this way, especially in peacetime. The same strategy was widely criticized in both Japan and the United States when the U.S. government forced some South Vietnamese civilians to live in "strategic hamlets" twenty-five years later. In Okinawa, however, this policy involved virtually the entire population.[5]

In Yomitan, the first group of detainees was finally permitted to return to their village on 20 November 1946, more than a year and a half after internment. A second group returned on 21 April 1947; a third on 27 June, and a fourth on 9 November after more than two years in detention. They found, however, that 90 percent of Yomitan had been requisitioned by the U.S. military. For some time, villagers were allowed to build and live in makeshift houses on their own property and even grow crops on land that was standing idle within the base area. However, after the Korean War began in June 1950, U.S. commanders rigorously asserted control over all bases, and villagers were ordered to relocate. In Yomitan, the residents of eight hamlets were forced to resettle elsewhere. Sobe and Toguchi hamlets became one U.S. facility, Torii Communication Station; Uza and Gima were turned into the Bolo-Point Firing Range; and Hijabashi, Kina, and Nagatamakihara were designated the Kadena Ammunition Storage Area.

Similar resettlement took place all across Okinawa, including Kadena, Chatan, Ginowan, Urasoe, and Naha, all of which had to accommodate U.S. bases within their boundaries. Much of Kadena Town, which included the small hamlets of Noguni, Nozato, Kuninao, Higashi, as well as parts of Kaneku, Mizugama, Kadena, and Kudoku, was requisitioned for construction of the Kadena Air Base. Kadena Town formerly had been part of Chatan Town, but it became a separate village in December 1948 as the air base cut into these two locales. Forced relocation of residents also occurred in Chatan Town, where lands were seized for military facilities from such communities as Chatan (Hamby Airfield), Dendo (Camp Zukeran), Tamayose (ditto), Tamaue (Rycom), Kuwae (Camp Kuwae), Irei (ditto), Henzan (Kadena Air Base), Kamisedo (ditto), and Shimosedo (ditto). In the area where the present city of Ginowan is located, eight out of twenty-two villages were similarly forced to move.

These villages were leveled for the construction of runways or for other purposes. All eventually disappeared from the map, destroyed as a result of the construction of bases.

Land Confiscation and Resettlement

Military Government Ordinance 29 set up guidelines for the forcible resettlement of people, including entire villages. In Yomitan, nine military facilities were established where eight hamlets had once existed. The U.S. military relocated these communities elsewhere. This was the beginning of the Land Allotment System.

One Yomitan hamlet, Uza, was entirely requisitioned by the United States for the construction of the Bolo-Point Firing Range. The 1974 issue of the village magazine, *Uza: Home at Zampa*, recalls, "Most of the community was destroyed during and after the war and the entire hamlet became an airfield. Cape Zampa too became the site of military maneuvers, where they fired live ammunition from aircraft." In Uza, 138 people were killed during the war, and the survivors were not allowed to return to their homes. In 1947, the former residents were forced to resettle in an adjoining area where they eventually built a community center and attempted to begin new lives.

The Breakup of Village Communities

Uza was a village community located on a peninsula, subsisting mainly by farming and fishing. From the magazine cited earlier, one can discern the quality of people's lives before the war:

> Uza was located at the northern tip of the peninsula. To the west of the village, the ocean was abundant with fish, and one could command an exquisite view of the pine trees of Cape Zampa. About 2 kilometers to the east was the port of Nagahama, which flourished due to trade with Southeast Asia.

> Uza also developed, backed by this bustling port. In the northeast part of the village, rich springs supplied water to the community. At the beach, thick shrubs of pandanus [screw pine] grew, and local women collected the leaves of the plants, which they then knit into slippers and rugs. Dense forests surrounded the village shrine, pine trees were reflected in the sea, and fish were naturally drawn into the area.

As the village depended on the neighboring rich coral sea, detailed rules governed its use. "From long ago, Uza had organized a group called '*Umikai*,' or 'marine guild.'[6] The guild members would select a leader, *Umigashira*, who had overall responsibility for the activity of the group. In addition, they assigned such roles as boat guards and handymen."

Today the life of Uza has been fundamentally transformed; pandanus and pine trees have vanished, as has the sand on the beach, due to the construction of military facilities. No trace of the former landscape remains; when the entire area of Uza became a site for a U.S. base, even the natural environment was destroyed.

The Transformation of Ritual Practice

Prewar Okinawan villages historically had a host of events and rituals in every month of the year. For instance, in Uza Village, on New Year's Day of the lunar calendar, "the first pure water of the year" would be drawn from a village well (*Ubuga*), which was imbued with a special meaning associated with the birth of the village, and villagers would use the water to cleanse their hands.[7] Formerly Uza residents had thirteen shrines devoted to their local deities, of which five were wells dedicated to water gods. However, after these shrines and wells were enclosed in bases, the customs associated with them withered away. On 3 March, the time of the *Seimei* festival honoring the ancestors, people used to visit the graves of their ancestors.[8] On the day before this festival, villagers would catch fish together, which were then distributed to each household to prepare offerings at the graves. This practice has also declined since the war, while many other practices that had a spiritual association with land or sea disappeared altogether. Thus, the structure of village communities disintegrated, not only in terms of the main economic activities, farming and fishing, but also in terms of ceremonies and rituals rooted in rural life.

Military Destruction: Effects on Local Residents

Beginning with the Battle of Okinawa and continuing with the construction and maintenance of the military bases, war and preparation for war by the U.S. military have devastated village life. Indeed, they have destroyed nature itself, both the land and coral reefs in the surrounding ocean. At present, U.S. forces conduct live ammunition exercises in eight different areas of Okinawa at the Torishima Firing Range, Idesuna Firing Range, Kumejima Firing Range, Ukibaru Training Area, Tsukenjima Training Area, Kobisho Firing Range, Sekibisho Firing Range, and Okidaito Firing Range.

Idesuna is now an uninhabited island, located four kilometers off the island of Tonaki. Tonaki, with a population of 483, is renowned for its natural beauty. Recently, one of its villages won official recognition "for the preservation of traditional architecture" and for its exquisite landscaping of traditional-style houses and surrounding trees, thus assuring that it would be preserved. By contrast, since 1955, firing drills have been conducted on Idesuna from 6 A.M. to 11 P.M., Monday through Saturday.

It is possible to watch military exercises from Tonaki, parts of which are also designated as danger zones by the U.S. military. Each time low-flying military aircraft fire live ammunition, there is a blast and white fumes rise in the air. Under this continued assault, the topography of the island has been transformed, leaving no trace of its prewar features. The areas of Tonaki designated by the U.S. military as danger zones are close to villages, and over the years many houses have been damaged by falling flares and debris.

Torishima is another now unpopulated island that is exclusively used as a firing range. In 1995, soldiers there inadvertently used depleted uranium bullets. The American government delayed notification of the accident to the Japanese government for a full year after it occurred, and neither the Okinawan prefectural government officials nor the general Okinawan public were informed by the Japanese government until one month after that. This reveals how marginalized Okinawa is by both the U.S. and Japanese governments.

The Status of Forces Agreement prioritizes military matters, while such matters of human concern as the health effects of depleted uranium bullets on the people of Okinawa are ignored. This is one example of the physical and psychological damage caused by military exercises that have continued for more than fifty years.

Before the war, the people of Idesuna cultivated watermelons and mulberry trees and raised cattle. The island was surrounded by coral reefs and was known as a good area to catch prawns, luminous turban shells, and octopi and to gather sea weed. Nowadays, fishermen go to sea near there only on Sundays, when no military exercises are scheduled.

Ancient rituals are still occasionally conducted on some of the islands. The ceremonies are attended exclusively by women acting as *kaminchu*, or priests who preside over rituals. Idesuna was long worshipped by local people as sacred ground, and important rituals and prayers were held on the island. Now Okinawans can only pray toward the blasted island from afar.

POSTREVERSION DEVELOPMENT AND ENVIRONMENTAL DESTRUCTION

The Okinawa Development Agency and the "Okinawa Promotion and Development Plan"

In 1971, an extraordinary session of the Japanese Diet deliberated on Okinawan reversion. The debate was disheartening to Okinawans, for it revealed Japan–U.S. collusion to continue indefinitely the full complement of American military bases. The legislation was passed by the assembly amid protest by members of the Okinawa Youth League, who set off firecrackers to protest both the bills that left the U.S. military position intact and their own exclusion from political decision making. When Okinawa reverted to Japan on 15 May 1972, seven new laws were written to administer the islands; one of them was the "Law Concerning Special Measures for Promotion and Development of the Islands of Okinawa."

The Promotion and Development Plan was drafted to redress the inequality that existed in social and economic infrastructure between Okinawa and mainland Japan. However, the plan was based on the industry- and development-oriented thinking that dominated Japan in the 1960s. In 1973, the mayor of Nago City issued a report that criticized the Tokyo government's development plan and the thinking behind it. It stated in part:

> Human beings have become enslaved to productionism, which results in the destruction of the basis of our existence. Rather, we citizens of Nago should take as our goal the creation of the most favorable life environment. We need to strive to make our city proud and comfortable, not to pursue short-term profit. Okinawa, which has long been isolated due to the American occupation, has looked at the superpowers with a sense of longing. However, we have nothing to learn from this development law designed only to close the economic gap with Japan.

This statement was remarkable for its time. However, Nago was the scene of a very similar debate twenty-five years later in 1997. This time the spirit expressed by the 1973 mayor suffered a severe setback when the new mayor announced his support for the construction of a new heliport for the U.S. military in Nago (a plan that was sweetened by offers of yet more development aid from Tokyo), even though local citizens had just overwhelmingly rejected the plan in a nonbinding referendum. The struggle over this issue continues in Nago at the time of this writing.

Japanese government spending in Okinawa has grown dramatically since the 1972 reversion under the auspices of the Promotion and Development Plan. Okinawa, with only 0.6 percent of Japan's land area and 1.0 percent of its population, has received 1.1 to 1.6 percent of Japan's public investment since reversion. This has resulted in accelerated economic growth and, not surprisingly, in remarkable environmental destruction.

Use and Development of Returned Land

Following the 1972 reversion to Japan, the United States returned some of the land it had requisitioned. The Bolo-Point Firing Range was divided into sections and given back to Japan in seven increments. In 1977, more than 80 percent of it was returned, and the facility retained by the United States was renamed the Senaha Communication Station. A number of former villagers came back to the returned land and rebuilt their houses there. They could, however, restore neither the agrarian and fishing foundations nor the religious and community practices that had been the essence of earlier village life.

Both public works and private initiatives transformed the landscape. In at least one case, Okinawans have reclaimed a culturally important site, but many other efforts failed. Although the Zakimi Castle, an important heritage of the old Ryūkyū Kingdom era, was once encompassed by U.S. Nike and Hawk bases, the castle area became a designated development zone in 1970, and the site was subsequently reestablished as a popular sightseeing place. Zakimi Castle, constructed in the fifteenth century, is uniquely Okinawan. A large quantity of Chinese porcelain has been excavated on the site, indicating substantial direct trade with China. This long history of independent foreign trade is a source of pride for Okinawans, as is the restoration of the castle, which contributes to the recovery of their regional identity.

When the so-called Resort Act was enacted in Japan in 1987, Yomitan actively promoted the construction of resorts in the returned regions. The Zampa Royal Resort Hotel and Hotel Nikko Alivila were built at the former site of the Bolo-Point Firing Range. The Hotel Nikko, which towers over a 2.7-kilometer-long coast, now monopolizes the entire local beach.

Yomitan's coast extends over three village sections; the region abounds with coral reefs and was long regarded as the best fishing spot near the village. After the war, when the base was constructed, the sand beach along the coast was dug up and hauled away, leaving the rock base exposed, but after the base was returned, the villagers still valued the shoreline as a place of repose. Tourist development did not preserve the sea coast for the local people; when the resort hotels were constructed, the seaside was again fenced off and villagers barred from access.

The beach facing the rich coral ocean was also a place where the ancients of Okinawa had placed their domiciles. Along the coast, seven ruins of varying ages were discovered, including a shell mound from seven thousand years ago, one of the earliest-dated sites anywhere in Okinawa. In addition, a number of old graves were relocated prior to the building of hotels. For Okinawans, the tomb has represented the encounter between death and life, so forced relocation of their tombs almost certainly disturbed their sense of the spiritual world.

The destruction of the natural and social environment in the area, which began with the devastation of war, was followed by the degradation of the environment through military base construction followed by industrial and tourism development. Yomitan's ocean, which had long supported the life of villagers, was encircled after the war first by military bases and, following the return of part of the land, by resort facilities; in this way, local people lost touch with their bountiful sea and beaches. This assault on nature was at the same time a continuing assault on Okinawan cultural practices.

Environmental Destruction and Its Impact on Local Communities Following the Okinawa Marine Exposition

The Okinawa Marine Exposition of 1973 celebrated the return of Okinawa to the mainland. Total investment in the project is said to have been two hundred to three hundred billion yen; the figures rise if related infrastructural construction of highways and an airport are included. This project, too, brought destruction rather than regeneration to the local community. For example, the old coastal road leading to the exposition site had been beautifully curved. However, highway construction destroyed the coast or buried it under concrete and also divided communities in two, geographically and socially. The main issues surrounding the Marine Exposition may be summarized as follows.

Parts of four villages on the main island were selected for the exposition site: Ishikawa, Bise, Yamakawa, and Hamamoto. In Ishikawa, nearly 20 percent of the land was expropriated for the site, and a further 22 percent was bought up by private companies from outside the village. Thus, Ishikawa lost 45 percent of its land due to the exposition.[9]

Until then, people of Ishikawa had lived by farming. They brought their crops to the market five kilometers from their village. This small-scale production, as well as the transportation and marketing, was carried out by women. Though they could not expect big profits, they did not face poverty. However, when they lost their land, more and more went to work as cooks and service personnel at the exposition. Men worked as assistant construction laborers at building sites or as nighttime security guards. Though restaurants, hotels, and souvenir shops were built in anticipation of the exposition, many went bankrupt. Moreover, all these jobs disappeared when the exposition ended.

Land Speculation

The Marine Expo temporarily stimulated business not only in the host town of Motobucho but throughout Okinawa, including remote islands such as Miyako and Yaeyama, where airports were constructed.

Land prices soared, and companies from mainland Japan aggressively bought up land, touching off a land speculation boom. Nevertheless, while some areas were developed, much of the land was actually left idle.[10] The land bought up by speculators included farmland. However, since it was no longer zoned for agricultural use, even the land that was not developed and was abandoned remained idle, while the agrarian foundations of local society were destroyed.

Crisis of Loss of Okinawa

In 1973, an organization dedicated to the preservation of Okinawan environment and culture was formed: the Ten-Person Committee to Protect the Culture and Nature of Okinawa. In the preface of the group's 1976 book *The Crisis of Loss of Okinawa*, the authors assess the effects of industrial development in postreversion Okinawa:

> In a mere one or two years since Reversion, large companies from the mainland established themselves in Okinawa, bought up local land, and went on a building spree of leisure facilities, vacation cottage complexes, and golf courses; coastal land was reclaimed for manufacturers, and a host of other environmentally destructive public projects were carried out for the Marine Exposition. These development projects all came in a rush; in a short span of time, there was a crisis of destruction of Okinawa, that is, the destruction of its culture and nature, which was clearly evident to all.

The group warned, moreover, of the crisis of identity contingent on the loss of nature: "The loss of the natural environment will lead to the loss of Okinawan thought."

THE OKINAWAN VIEW OF NATURE AND ITS EVOLUTION

Throughout Okinawa, despite the massive environmental destruction caused by war, military bases, and large-scale public works projects, Okinawans still retain profound elements of their historic culture and worldview. Indeed, historical memory and identity form a powerful basis for the critique both of militarization and Japanese-style modernization.

It is worth recalling that Okinawa consists of a number of small islands, which has made it possible to retain some of its distinctive values and identity even as militarization and maldevelopment have proceeded apace, especially in the main island. Ironically, the fact that modernization was brought in slowly during the Meiji era due to the discriminatory treatment given Okinawa by the Tokyo government contributes to this. Indeed, it appears that the islands continue to retain two opposite and antagonistic faces: "the Islands of Bases" and "the Islands of Prayer." Here I introduce some of the core elements of Okinawan spiritual values that continue to provide alternatives to powerful forces associated both with the U.S. military, on the one hand, and Tokyo-centered maldevelopment, on the other.

The Idea of the Forest

In Okinawa, sacred forests are called *utaki*. At these *utaki*, spirits of ancestors are worshipped. The green forests in Okinawa today, even if these now are found for the most part amid humdrum topographical features surrounded by thoroughly modern structures, still function as *utaki*.

Okinawan villages historically face south, with the *utaki* forest at their back. People used to describe such a natural landscape as "a child in its mother's arms." The forest is the mother, and the village expanding from its protective embrace is the child. As the village faces south, the forest protects it against the cold winter wind, while the mild southern wind cools the village in summer. There is always a spring near *utaki*, where the god of water is believed to live.

Okinawan rituals are presided over by women. Only women are allowed to set foot in the sacred forest. It is believed that when a woman dies, her spirit goes back to the forest or *utaki*, and the spirit of ancestors (that of grandmother) is transferred to another woman (granddaughter) through a ritual, thus achieving a reincarnation. This women's ritual of reincarnation across the generations symbolizes the eternal recurrence of all lives. Hence, the forest is deemed to be the point of contact between this life and afterlife.

It is forbidden to enter the forest where important rituals take place except for good reason, including collecting grasses and timber. Because of this taboo surrounding *utaki*, the forest was richly endowed with flora and fauna. To destroy *utaki* means to annihilate a forest that is a treasure house of life as well as to lose the fountainhead of the Okinawan view of life.

Common Lands, Communal Traditions, and Okinawan Identity

In Okinawa, private land ownership was legalized in 1903 following a Japanese government land survey.[11] Before then, all land was collectively owned, managed, and used by village communities. This system was called *jiwarisei*. A piece of land was cultivated by a certain person (generally a household head) for two to thirty years, and then, because the quality of the land differs from place to place, the land was rotated to another person to maintain equality. Nowadays, the common property of a village is restricted mainly to the forest of *utaki* and communal wells where these continue to exist.

One island that has maintained its communal traditions, however, is Kudaka. All land on the small island remains collectively owned. Kudaka's circumference is five miles, and its population is less than three hundred. The preservation of Kudaka's common land has been associated with women. In 1905, "men on the island held a meeting and decided to distribute and privatize the land. But the women got together and forced the men to repeal the decision, saying that it was wrong to change a system that had lasted from ancient times, and that the land had been originally and traditionally managed by women."[12] To be sure, this is not the only reason why Kudaka's common land ownership has been preserved to this day. Nonetheless, women's public role was unusually strong. In those days, most men on the island engaged in fishing, and were at sea almost six months out of the year; hence, it was women who managed the land, and village rituals and governance were also mainly administered by women.

The most fundamental reason for the preservation of common land long after its disappearance elsewhere is the people's commitment to it. In 1926, they submitted a petition for a land tax exemption, and the land was recognized as the common property of a fifteen-person group. This form existed until 1968, when the land was again titled to the ownership of the island community. This shows that the system has been preserved by the will of the people.

After reversion, however, land problems arose due to the emergence of wealthier families and the construction of restaurants. In 1987, Kudaka, too, was targeted for resort development. Furthermore, the government's land improvement program forced the people to face again the question of land rights and to plan for the future.

The islanders' response was to enact the Kudaka Island Land Charter. Its purpose was to keep the land ownership system while making it compatible with contemporary laws. The charter was written by a group of islanders, some living on the island and some living away from it, and was approved at a general assembly of the islanders. It is composed of a preamble and ten articles that spell out land rights. The charter reaffirmed the islanders' commitment to common land ownership. Its preamble reads:

> The Kudaka Island Land Charter hereby confirms and declares the following. The land of the island of Kudaka, with a few exceptions such as land owned by the national government, has traditionally been owned in common, and the village people have hitherto shared the right to the use and benefit of the land which has been handed down from their ancestors. Therefore the village shall fundamentally maintain this practice, aiming at both the preservation of a good natural environment as well as village priorities and the fair and appropriate use of the land.

The charter is administered by the Land Management Committee, which consists of thirteen representatives from the village. When a villager wishes to use new land to build a house, farm, or construct a family tomb, he or she must apply to the committee and obtain permission to use the land for private purposes. Moreover, individual purchase or sale of land is tightly controlled by the community. The charter contains language that admits of more than one interpretation, and so it is the source of a great deal of lively debate. But it is clear in its intention that the fate of Kudaka's land be decided by the will of the community, not by anonymous market forces.

Conclusion

The instance of common land ownership in Kudaka Island is provided here as food for thought for the future and as a model of self-government and cooperative utilization of land by communities. The charter demonstrates that a tradition, when it is creatively reassessed in the framework of contemporary circumstances, may, like Kudaka's traditional land ownership system, prove to be relevant to contemporary needs.

Historically, nature was managed by local residents, and communities—not individuals—were the repositories of ownership. Management and usage in this context were historically linked to treasuring and conserving nature.

However, this does not mean that Kudaka is without its problems. The island has a depopulation problem due to the lack of a high school and of jobs. To deal with such problems, the residents have established the Association for Kudaka Island Development. The fact that land conservation and economic development are not always compatible is reflected in the fact that many older women on Kudaka who have never left the island prefer development to a certain degree, while many younger people between their twenties and fifties tend to look at development from the viewpoint of nature conservation.

Despite its pressing problems, the experience of Kudaka Island can provide insight and inspiration to Okinawans, many of whom have lost their land and seen their communities disintegrate, as they search for alternatives to Japanese-style developmentalism and a base-centered economy, alternatives compatible with both their cultural heritage and the preservation of nature's bounty.

NOTES

This chapter is a revised version of an essay published in *Critical Asian Studies* 33, no. 2 (June 2001) and is used with permission.

1. *Yomitanson heiwa no honō—Daijūgo* (Yomitan Village—Flame of Peace), no. 10, Yomitan Village office, undated.

2. From the author's interviews, 1997.

3. *Kichi to Chatanchō* (Military Bases and Chatan Town) (Chatan: Chatan Village Office, 2001).

4. In 1954, the United States Civil Administration Ryukyu Islands (USCAR) published the "Yaeyama Development Plan" to send sixteen thousand Okinawans overseas. Around that time, USCAR also stepped up its forcible acquisition of lands. "Okinawa o shiru jiten," henshū Iinkai, *Okinawa o shiru jiten* (Encyclopedia of Okinawa), 62 (Tokyo: Nichigai Asoshietsu: Hatsubaimoto Kinokunia, Shoten, 2000).

5. On 15 August 1945, representatives of local residents were summoned from each camp to form the Okinawa Advisory Committee; this was the first step toward self-government of the islands. In September of the same year, according to the regulations drafted by the Advisory Committee, a "mayor" and "city/town council members" were elected. Furthermore, women were given the right to vote, the first such instance in Japan. Nichigai Asoshietsu, *Okinawa o shiru jiten*.

6. In 1961, the issue of compensation for lost fishing grounds came to the fore, and the *Umikai* reformed as the Uza Fishermen's and Friends' Association and became a subordinate body to the Yomitan Fishermen's Association. Members of the *Umikai* included not only those who were engaged in fishing but also the heads of households in the village. This arrangement is based on the idea that the sea is the common property of everyone.

7. Uzaku Kōminkan, *Zanpa no sato: Uzashi* (A Village in Zanpa: Uza) (Uza: Uza Community Center, 1974).

8. In many parts of Okinawa, on the early morning of New Year's Day (lunar calendar), the first pure water of the year is drawn from a well, which is used to

make tea to be offered to the ancestors' spirits and the god of fire. It is said that the tea made from the first water has rejuvenating power.

9. Miyamoto Ken'ichi, "Kankyō o hakaisuru kōkyō jigyō" (Environmently Destructive Public Works Projects), in *Sōgō shakai eikyō jizen hyōka seidō no juritsu o* (Calling for the Establishment of a System of General Social Impact Studies) (n.p.: 1997), 272; and Kuruma Yasuo, "Okinawa Kaiyōhaku niyureta ichikanson—Motobucho Ishikawachiku" (The Case of a Lonely Village Shaken by the Okinawa Marine Exposition: Ishikawa, Motobu-cho), in *Okinawa no nōgyō to nōson* (Okinawa Farms and Farming) (Okinawa: Okinawa Cooperative Farmers Association, Central Committee, 1976).

10. Asato Eiko, *Yureru seiiki, rizōto kaihatsu to shima no kurashi* (Confused Sanctuary: Resort Development and the Life of the Islands) (Naha: Okinawa Times Publishing, 1991).

11. Between 1899 and 1903, land reform carried out by the Japanese government in Okinawa acknowledged private land ownership and determined the proprietor as taxpayer.

12. "Kudakajima no Chisō Menzei Chinjōsho" (Land Tax Exemption Charter for Kudaka Island), in *Chinenson shi* (History of Chinen Village), undated.

9

Future "Assets," but at What Price? The Okinawa Initiative Debate

Julia Yonetani

In May 2000, as the rainy season drew to an early end, preparations for the G-8 Summit, which would be held in the northern Okinawa city of Nago that July, began in earnest across the island. Along the edge of Highway 58, the primary roadway running across Okinawa from the main city of Naha to Nago, groups of workers began planting a variety of tropical flowers. Police from mainland Japan (approximately twenty-two thousand officers from around Japan were mobilized for the event[1]) could be seen riding their bicycles on the highway's footpath alongside the U.S. Kadena Air Base, sweltering in full patrol uniform. Meanwhile, Okinawa's two main local newspapers featured summit precursors of a different kind, as intellectuals and political activists, many of them old school friends and longtime acquaintances, lashed out at one another in a dispute over Okinawa's role—past and present—on this global stage. At stake were issues of historical memory and the future of the economy, of the natural environs and public works projects, of autonomy and dependence, and of the U.S. military bases. In the hot months leading up to July, the war of words intensified in what became known as the "Okinawa Initiative Debate" (*Okinawa inishiatibu ronsō*).

Four years earlier, in April 1996, U.S. president William Clinton and Japanese prime minister Hashimoto Ryūtarō reconfirmed U.S.–Japan security relations in the post–Cold War order. On 18 April, during his visit to Japan, Clinton told the Japanese Diet that while the Soviet Union had collapsed and Russia was far less of a military threat, this development did not mean that U.S. forces should be withdrawn from Japan. Increased globalization and technological and information revolutions had created a world where, the president enthused, "ideas flash across our planet in the stroke of a computer key, bringing with them extraordinary opportunities to create wealth, to protect the environment, to prevent and contain disease, to foster greater understanding among people of diverse cultures." Yet, Clinton added, "greater openness and faster change also mean that problems that start beyond our borders can quickly penetrate our borders." The opportunities for expanding capital and markets in short coincided with new threats which required a strengthened "global partnership" between the United States and Japan.[2] The subsequent joint declaration issued by the two leaders reconfirmed the importance of the U.S.–Japan Security Treaty and called for increased bilateral military cooperation and the formulation of guidelines for joint operations in a "time of crisis."

Yet events on the small archipelago of Okinawa posed a direct challenge to this global agenda. Simmering resentment over the U.S. military presence on Okinawa had already reached the boiling point following the rape and abduction of a schoolgirl by three U.S. servicemen in September 1995, and in the same month, Okinawa's governor, Ōta Masahide, announced his refusal to acquiesce in the signing of leases of land used by the U.S. military.[3] Ōta opposed the maintenance and possible expansion of the U.S. military presence on Okinawa as laid down in the Pentagon's "Nye Report" of February 1995.[4] His stance, and the upsurge of Okinawan antibase sentiment, challenged the role imposed on Okinawa to support postwar U.S.–Japan security relations. Ōta also advocated political, historical, and cultural autonomy for Okinawa, calling into question many of the tenets of postwar Japan's historical canon and its claims to homogeneity.

Official discourse in Japan has never found an obvious place for Okinawa.[5] The modern history of Okinawa itself attests to the contested nature of nation-building, and discontinuities within national collective memory.[6] Following the Ryūkyū Kingdom's disposition and forced incorporation into Japan during the early Meiji period (1872–1879), Okinawans were gradually mobilized for service throughout Japan's expanding empire. Since then, the contradictions and ambivalence embedded within assimilationist policy—stressing the necessity for Okinawans to become Japanese while already being Japanese—have never been fully resolved.[7]

After the war, multiple and contradictory meanings of "Okinawa" and "Japan" have been fought over and negotiated within, and against, U.S. military power. Okinawa has simultaneously stood at the geographic and ideological margins of Japan, while it has been at the center of the

U.S.–Japan strategic relationship as the "keystone of the Pacific" in U.S. military strategy. Under the circumstances, claims to Okinawan identity, place, and past have inevitably been highly politicized and contested. One of the consequences of that history, as Laura Hein points out, "is that all expressions of culture are 'always already' politicized and all claims of Okinawa distinctiveness become part of this larger debate over contemporary political identity."[8] Within this politics of identity, the reverse also appears highly pertinent; that is, not only are claims to an Okinawan culture and history "always already" politicized, but struggles over Okinawa's position in relation to Japan and against U.S. military control have necessarily been cultural and historical struggles, too.

In his testimony to the High Court in March 1996, Ōta argued that the highly disproportionate burden of U.S. bases in Okinawa was unfair and illegal. He also challenged official Japanese historical narratives that presumed cultural homogeneity, arguing instead for a distinctive sense of Okinawan appreciation of the islands' history and culture. In explaining his call for a reduction and ultimate withdrawal of the bases, he appealed to the Ryūkyū Kingdom's peaceful heritage, contrasting it to the "warrior culture" of mainland Japan; recalled the tragedy of the Battle of Okinawa, which took the lives of close to a third of the local population; and stressed Okinawans' desire for peace and autonomy. More than any previous Okinawan governor, Ōta drew connections between the base issue—or what he has repeatedly termed the "Okinawan problem"—and struggles over identity, autonomy, and cultural diversity. He envisaged a future that would "enable Okinawa to stand on its own, or to put it more simply, to enable Okinawa to determine its own destiny."[9]

Ōta's antibase, proautonomy stance was widely endorsed in Okinawa. In a public opinion poll jointly conducted by *Asahi* newspaper and the *Okinawa Times* in May 1997, for instance, support for Ōta's antibase position stood at over 90 percent (46 percent strongly support, 45 percent support). Only 10 percent of Okinawans agreed that the U.S. bases should be maintained at the present level, with over 85 percent calling for either gradual reduction or immediate withdrawal. Only a minority (37 percent agreed in contrast to 49 percent disagreed) of Okinawans thought that maintenance of the U.S. military presence in East Asia was necessary at all.[10]

Despite broad support for his stance on the bases, however, after three tumultuous years of conflict and attempted negotiation with the Japanese government, Ōta was defeated in the gubernatorial elections of 1998.[11] His successor was Inamine Keiichi, the Liberal Democratic Party–backed candidate and former president of Okinawa's largest petroleum company, Ryūseki. During the hotly contested election campaign, Inamine focused primarily on Okinawa's weak economy and tried to avoid association with the national government's support for the U.S. bases. Following his victory, however, the Japanese government stepped up plans to build a new U.S. Marine base in the northern Okinawan city of Nago to replace one situated in densely populated Ginowan City, in central Okinawa.[12] In an effort to woo Inamine's and local Okinawans' support, central government officials immediately announced a supplementary economic stimulus package of ten billion yen, and later a hundred billion yen stimulus plan for northern Okinawa. The G-8 Summit was the "trump card" of these tactics—Prime Minister Obuchi disclosed his surprise decision to select Nago as the joint winning site for the event in early 1999. In November of the same year, Inamine bowed to government pressure and officially declared his conditional consent to the Nago base. Leading up to the Summit in July 2000, the Okinawa Prefectural Government (OPG) worked in conjunction with the Japanese government to create an environment in Okinawa more supportive of the U.S. bases and Japanese national security goals.

Although the contemporary controversy is over U.S. military bases and the Japanese government's development strategy, issues of Okinawan historical consciousness, war memory, and collective identity underlie political debate.[13] The "Okinawa Initiative" (OI) constituted an attempt to articulate an Okinawan historical and political position more in concert with the aims of the U.S.–Japan security partnership and Japanese government policy. The OI was outlined first in two key policy-oriented papers, formulated and sponsored by separate Tokyo-based think tanks and announced, respectively, in March and April 2000. The origins of both papers can be traced to the highest echelons within the Inamine administration and the national government. They were integrally linked to Japanese government compensation strategies toward Okinawa, as well as comprehensive domestic and foreign policy goals for Japan in "the new millennium."

The OI papers implicitly acknowledged Ōta's position that Okinawans had a different history from that of other Japanese. They sought to disavow the importance of, rather than rewrite, Okinawa's history and thereby avoid a debate over history per se. They also sought to portray compliance with Japanese and U.S. security policies as Okinawan autonomy. This inflamed many intellectuals and antibase supporters and activists in Okinawa. In the months leading up to the summit, prominent writers, journalists, academics, and artists throughout the islands published numerous articles and essays disputing or defending the OI's claims and analyses.[14]

In this chapter, I assess the political context of the OI's inception and the arguments put forth by both the advocates of the OI and its dissenters. In doing so, I trace the pervasive connections between the Japanese government's compensation policies toward Okinawa, the OPG's accommodation of these policies, and contests over Okinawa's place—both past and present—in Japan, Asia, and the world. The debate reveals the important ways in which political and economic issues complexly intertwine with contests over identity, culture, and historical memory within contemporary Okinawa. As intimately interconnected, the outcome of these struggles holds vital implications both for how the past is perceived, and for the future.

COMPENSATION POLICIES AND "COGNITIVE STRATEGIES"

The first OI paper was entitled "Toward an 'Okinawa Initiative': A Possible Role for Okinawa in the Asia-Pacific,"[15] and it was presented by three Ryukyu University professors, Takara Kurayoshi, Ōshiro Tsuneo, and Maeshiro Morisada, at the Asia Pacific Agenda Project (APAP) conference, held on 23–25 March in Naha, Okinawa. All three authors were core figures in the Inamine administration's "brain trust." The APAP meeting was attended by researchers and policymakers from the Asia–Pacific region, journalists, and then–Japanese prime minister Obuchi Keizō, in Okinawa to observe the progress of the G-8 Summit preparations.[16] The content of the APAP Okinawa Initiative paper was reported nationally at the end of March on the front page of the right-wing *Sankei* newspaper, which praised the document for "rejecting the empty political ideology of anti-base arguments" and for its "sharp observations of reality."[17]

As well as being joint author of the APAP "Initiative" paper, Takara Kurayoshi had been the sole member from Okinawa in the "Prime Minister's Commission of Japan's Goals in the 21st Century," established by the late Obuchi Keizō to chart the "future direction of Japan which the next generation of Japanese can aspire to in the new century."[18] The Prime Minister's Commission and the APAP "Okinawa Initiative" paper were integrally connected at the highest of levels.[19]

The APAP conference was closed to the public, yet it received attention in both the national and local Okinawan press and became the focus of the OI debate. A second, less well-known but more detailed version of the Okinawa Initiative, entitled "Okinawa Initiative: A Proposal on Okinawa, Japan, and the World," reveals more of the concept and its origins. This proposal was drawn up by Takara, Okinawa Prefectural Planning Adjustment Departmental head Uehara Akira, journalist Shima Nobuhiko, and Keio University professor Shimada Haruo, and it was sponsored by the Japan Productivity Center for Socio-Economic Development (JPC-SED).[20]

The JPC-SED, formed in 1994, was designed to prepare Japan to be economically competitive in a new global environment.[21] The JPC-SED's "Okinawa Initiative" lays out the group's ideas on how to incorporate

Okinawa into that larger goal. While similar to the APAP Initiative, the JPC-SED Initiative's tone is in parts very different. For example, the APAP Initiative asserts the need for Okinawa "to display an independent governance . . . in contrast to an extremely Tokyo-centered form of governance," but that concern for autonomy is missing in the JPC-SED-sponsored paper (herein referred to as the "Shimada Okinawa Initiative," after workshop leader Shimada Haruo).[22]

In his chapter in the Shimada Okinawa Initiative, Takara advocates a "pragmatic" solution to the Futenma relocation issue, one that is not dominated by "historical issues" such as the fact that the land within the base was originally appropriated by force during the Cold War. Uehara calls for a new airport and special infrastructure in the northern and more "backward" region of Okinawa. Both propositions mirror Inamine administration and central government attempts to secure Nago, in the northern area of Okinawa, as the site for the new base, now under the concept of "Joint Civilian and Military Airport." The Shimada Initiative endeavors to reaffirm the political, economic, and ideological "foundations" necessary to secure this site, as well as U.S. and Japanese strategic interest in Okinawa on a broader level. A focal point of this policy, and the Initiative proposal, is the holding of the G-8 Summit in Nago. "Just at this time, in July of this year," Shimada notes in the introduction, "the G-8 Head of States meeting will be held in Okinawa." "Utilizing this Okinawa Summit as an opportunity," he continues:

> Okinawa is being asked to redefine its own potential, and, as an Okinawan initiative, to conceive of and advance a plan as active player. . . . For the first time ever, Okinawa possesses in its hands the opportunity to pragmatically and rationally improve the U.S. military base issue through its own judgement, and furthermore use this as a chance to autonomously develop the Okinawan economy.[23]

Shimada, a mainland Japanese with intimate ties to the national government, has played a key role in the effort to diffuse the antibase movement in Okinawa. He was also director of late chief cabinet secretary Kajiyama Seiroku's Informal Council on Okinawa Municipalities Hosting U.S. Bases. This council is also often referred to as Shimada's Group, or Shimada-kon, in direct reference to Shimada's leading role. It was established in August 1996 as an advisory body to then–prime minister Hashimoto's cabinet. Under the Shimada-kon proposal, suggestions from municipalities on desired economic "projects" were made to the Shimada Group's Principal Council (*yūshokusha kondankai*), composed of five members from Okinawa and six from Tokyo, including Shimada. This council advised the cabinet on which projects to implement. All projects were funded directly by the central government, with a budget of one hundred billion yen over a seven-year period.[24] The Shimada-kon argued, "Taking account of the fact that the burden [of U.S. bases] is concentrated in Okinawa and in particular in those municipalities which host bases, special consideration should be given by the government in these areas."[25]

"Improvement" of the base problem and Okinawa's unique opportunity for "autonomous" economic development in this context clearly meant a cash-for-base deal. Financial aid has been employed in Okinawa as a means to placate opposition to U.S. military policy and the forced expropriation of private land for military use since the era of the U.S. occupation. In other regions within Japan, too, compensation politics has long been a government strategy for inducing specific communities to accept large-scale public works projects with potentially deleterious and undesirable consequences.[26] Yet Shimada-kon was unprecedented in at least two ways. First, it brought together the prime minister's cabinet, key members of Okinawa's business community, and the heads of local municipalities that host U.S. military bases within Okinawa under one informal umbrella organization. Second, although informal and thus politically unaccountable, Shimada-kon had the power to approve large-scale public projects financed directly and in full by national government funding.

Shimada himself recounts that, following the rape incident in Okinawa in September 1995, the Japanese government responded to the Okinawa base issue (1) on the bilateral front through the establishment of SACO, the joint U.S. and Japanese Government's Special Actions Committee on Okinawa; (2) on the national domestic front through the establishment of the Okinawa Policy Council, made up of key members within the OPG and central government agencies; and (3) on the local front through the Shimada-kon. The Shimada-kon was the government's attempt to "ease" (*kanwa*) the sentiment of residents at the most local level.[27] It deepened the connection between the U.S. military presence and economic stimulus packages, presented as Japanese government compensation to Okinawa. By strengthening links between local politicians, local business interests, and national government funding, the Japanese government sought to undermine the Ōta administration's strong stance against the bases from below. The present governor, Inamine Keiichi, was the deputy director of the Shimada-kon council, and Inamine's deputy, who was then acting auditor of the Bank of the Ryukyus, was also a member. The Inamine administration, then, is a direct beneficiary of the central government's compensation policies toward Okinawa.[28] The Shimada-kon linked the promise of funds to bases effectively enough to be a major factor in securing Inamine's defeat over Ōta in 1998.[29]

If Shimada-kon was the economic "carrot" through which the Japanese government sought to implement policy, the Shimada Okinawa Initiative was its more elusive "ideological" form. The Okinawa Initiative sought to disarm the antibase movement by building the ideological foundations of a probase, pro–Japanese government stance for Okinawa.

Inamine and the Japanese government were able to exploit weaknesses in the Okinawan economy, prolonged economic recession, and pervasive divisions within progressive parties to weaken Ōta's support base. The alliance linking local business (including influential construction lobby groups), the LDP, and the Kōmei Party ally has proven particularly effective in securing election victories for Okinawa's conservative coalition in recent years—in the Nago mayoral election of February 1998, the gubernatorial election in November of the same year, and the Naha mayoral election of November 2000. After Ōta officially announced his rejection of the relocation of Futenma base within Okinawa in February 1998, the Japanese government refused open dialogue with his administration, effectively paralyzing prefectural finances. Voters were aware that the national government controlled key resources against Ōta's behest, and Inamine took advantage of the situation. One poster in his gubernatorial election campaign featured a hand reaching toward a tap. The message was clear: Inamine could draw a direct pipeline with Tokyo to secure monetary flows.

Yet these election victories do not necessarily represent a turnaround in antibase sentiment. Events in Nago in 1997–1998 exposed the seemingly paradoxical sentiment of local residents pulled between promises of massive financial compensation and opposition to the bases. Although the LDP-backed candidate secured victory in the February 1998 mayoral election, less than three months before, in spite of direct pressure from Japanese government agencies,[30] a majority of Nago's residents expressed their opposition to a new base within their municipality in a local plebiscite. In another joint *Asahi/Okinawa Times* opinion poll taken in December 1999, a large majority (59 percent against, 23 percent for) of residents remained opposed to the relocation of Futenma Air Base to Nago.[31]

The OI was thus aimed at undermining Okinawan political mobilization against their allotted role as host of the majority of U.S. bases in Japan. In a presentation to Obuchi's Prime Ministerial Commission in July 1999, Takara made the point that "Okinawa's unstable local sentiment and a perception of being historically victimized has the tendency to obstruct future debate on the U.S.–Japan security system."[32] In other words, Okinawa's sense of identity and long-standing unequal treatment holds the potential to conflict with—or, for the Inamine administration and the Japanese government, "obstruct"—future attempts to secure U.S. and Japanese government interests in Okinawa. Takara warned that unless a way was found to "incorporate" and "absorb" Okinawan local sentiment within national policymaking processes, the "stability" of Okinawa could not be ensured. Takara's commission paper, the APAP Okinawa Initiative, and the Shimada Okinawa Initiative may be seen as an attempt to find this "way."

At least on the level of rhetoric, Inamine's brain trust was more inclined to support Okinawan "autonomy" than was the Japanese government or Shimada. Takara and his colleagues, Maeshiro and Ōshiro, presented the "OI" as an Okinawan-based proposal aimed to empower Okinawans. They called for Okinawa to display an "independent" role beyond the framework of Japan within the Asia–Pacific region. Yet at the same time, the three Okinawan professors acquiesced in national policy—above all, by accepting the bases, including the construction of the new base in Nago—in return for the Japanese government's financial benevolence. In coordination with the Shimada Initiative, the APAP paper is integrally connected to the type of compensation policies epitomized by Shimada-kon. As Takara suggested, the Initiative itself was part of a "cognitive strategy" endorsed by the Japanese government to, while indulging in an etiolated form of multiculturalism, "absorb" Okinawans' sense of identity and desire for political autonomy.[33]

FROM "HISTORY PROBLEM" TO "SOFT POWER" SOLUTION: TAKING THE "INITIATIVE"

Takara, Maeshiro, and Ōshiro called for a shift from an "emotional" position on the U.S. military bases to a more "logical" one.[34] They argued that Okinawans, who had been unable to devise an effective policy to resolve the base issue, should accept their role as host to the bases as the only economically viable option. Takara particularly criticized what he saw as the tendency for Okinawans to see themselves as historically victimized. In an interview with the *Asahi* newspaper in May 2000, he singled out Ōta as exemplary of this victim consciousness. Takara's stance was first and foremost a rejection of Ōta and his legacies. In the interview, Takara elaborated:

> The former governor Ōta Masahide's argument puts an excessive emphasis on the relevance of the past in the present context. In other words, he utilizes history—as in his assertions as to why Okinawans love peace, etc. He is not necessarily wrong. But there are other issues. How do we view the issue of the bases or security, problems that we should responsibly consider? It is not enough to leave these issues in the air, and merely explain the cause of your actions through past experiences. At the same time

that we face up to history, we must also face up to the problems we meet today.[35]

Before running for governor in 1990, Ōta had been an academic at the same university department as Takara. He has written over sixty books on Okinawa, all of which in some way emphasize the significance of Okinawan history, identity, and culture. Many of them focus on the Battle of Okinawa.[36] Ōta himself was a survivor of the Okinawa Normal School's "Imperial Blood and Iron Student Corps" and had been conscripted by the Japanese military command on 31 March 1945, the day before U.S. troops landed on Okinawa's main island (226 out of 386 of these students died in the ensuing battle). His academic concerns grew out of that personal experience. Ōta has repeatedly noted that during the battle, the Imperial Headquarters and Japanese command showed a blatant lack of concern for the fate of the Okinawan civilians. Japanese troops forced Okinawan civilians to commit suicide, stole their food, drove them out of caves where they sheltered, and even tortured and massacred them.[37] There is no doubt that both within Ōta's work and in Okinawa generally, historical memory of these atrocities and a consciousness of past discriminations has helped forge antimilitaristic, antibase sentiment.[38]

Figure 9.1. Okinawan Governor Inamine Keiichi (with his back to the camera) pays his repects to the dead in front of a Rising Sun (*hi no maru*) flower motif at the Ceremony in Memory of the Battle of Okinawa War Dead, held on the Day to Console the Spirits (*Irei no hi*), 23 June 2000.

Source: Photo by Julia Yonetani.

These historical issues flared up in 1999, when the Inamine administration attempted to alter exhibit content within the new prefectural museum. As discussed in chapter 3 by Gerald Figal, one point of contention was a diorama depicting a Japanese soldier pointing his rifle at an Okinawan mother and her baby (see figure 3.9).[39] Under instructions from Inamine and his two deputies, and without informing the museum planning committee, officials within the prefectural administration ordered the exhibit construction workers to remove the soldier's gun from the diorama.[40] In the same way, Takara's argument against "victimization" sought to counter criticisms against the Japanese military and the atrocities they committed in Okinawa during the war, as well as diffuse criticisms of the contemporary national and prefectural governments.

Yet Takara's strategy in the OI was more subtle and employed a distinctly different tactic to the Inamine administration's earlier and more blatant attempts to "change" history. Takara included in his analysis many of the historical factors that have become tenets of Okinawa's antiwar movement. The OI group even recognized that the Japanese military had carried out "barbarous" actions toward Okinawan civilians during battle. It discussed modern Japan's rejection of "its own Asian-ness" in the pursuit of a Western model of industrialization and referred to Okinawa's disproportionate burden of the bases.

However, this historical analysis was the prelude to a call for a "break" with history.

> The important thing is the question of how we face our "history" and our future, not remaining controlled by history, but assuming our responsibility and subjectivity as people living in the present. It is precisely we, in the present, who possess the capacity to take on our history in its entirety, and the "regional assets" supplied by history to the future are also only realized through us, living in the present, as its heirs.[41]

In short, while Takara and his colleagues acknowledged a distinctive Okinawan identity, they rejected many of the conclusions that follow from an assessment of that history.

Takara, Ōshiro, and Maeshiro employed a similar tactic in their observations on Okinawa's historical relation to mainland Japan. The three professors emphasized the hardships that Okinawa has experienced: the lingering wounds of war, U.S. occupation, and the unfair base burden.[42] While rhetorically affirming Okinawa's historical uniqueness, however, the OI emphasized the need for Okinawa's integration within Japan, arguing that Okinawans had always desired that integration.

The authors assert that Okinawa possesses a unique culture different from that of mainland Japan, yet they qualified Okinawa's uniqueness by stressing that this culture is "not 'totally foreign' (*kanzen na gaikoku*) to Japanese culture" and that its "roots are the same."[43] Analyzing the Okinawan reversion movement under U.S. occupation, Takara and his colleagues stress that "for the people of Okinawa, Japan was culturally their closest presence." The Initiative paper concluded that the people of Okinawa "chose Japan as the country to which they should belong."[44] In the analysis of both Okinawan culture and the reversion movement, the authors maintain this conflation of distinctiveness and Japaneseness by separating "origins" from "history": "If origins are emphasized, both Okinawa and Japan maintain a close affinity, but if one emphasizes historical outcomes, they are comparatively separate."[45]

Assuming an irreconcilable rupture between both "origins" and "history" and also between "history" and the "present," the Okinawa Initiative posits Okinawa's unique history and then subsumes it into national narratives, postmodern-style. As well-known Okinawan journalist and intellectual Arakawa Akira pointed out, the authors obscure the continuities between the past, present, and future by presenting them as separate entities. In doing so, they ignore the ways in which the present is related to both the past and the future. They also obfuscate any responsibility, collective or individual, for actions taken in the past.[46] In this sense, the OI employed a logic not dissimilar to mainland Japanese neonationalist "revisionist" scholars such as Fujioka Nobukatsu.[47] Fujioka criticizes what he refers to as a "masochistic" view of history: The Okinawa Initiative group rejects what they term a "victimized" historical perception. Both seek to discredit evidence of Japanese aggression during the war. While Fujioka claims that such historical amnesia would reinstall a sense of "pride" in national militaristic history, the Initiative claimed that by disregarding their own past Okinawans were choosing their destiny by accepting the bases—depicted in materialist terms as the "assets" of their future.

The OI also emphasized that the Okinawan reversion movement from 1952 to 1972 was fueled by an Okinawan desire to reunite with Japan, thereby downplaying the fact that reversion failed to bring about base reduction or withdrawal. This positive assessment of reversion directly contrasted with the stance of Ōta and many other Okinawan intellectuals. In his testimony to the Supreme Court in 1996, Ōta stressed that the fundamental aims of the reversion movement—to gain local autonomy, democratic rights, and the reduction and withdrawal of the bases—were not fulfilled. He argued, "[E]ven a quarter of a century after the reversion of Okinawa to Japan, conditions in Okinawa have hardly changed."[48]

The Initiative group acknowledged that Okinawa carried the burden of hosting approximately 75 percent of all U.S. bases in Japan and even recognized that antibase sentiment was "deep rooted" in Okinawa. Yet the OI also attempted to separate the reasons Okinawans did not want the bases—the legacy of the Battle of Okinawa, the forceful expropriation of base land from Okinawan landowners in the 1950s, and the ongoing damage the base inflicted on local communities—from the contribution the bases made to Japanese national security. In an implicit attack on Article 9 of the Japanese Constitution, the OI group rejected what they referred to as "absolute pacifist" ideals, and affirmed the importance of military intervention to ensure security. "The present issue of the U.S. bases is not an issue of the propriety of the bases," the group concluded, "but an issue of how their effective operation and the security of local residents may be reconciled."[49] The OI praised Okinawa for making the "greatest contribution" to Japan's security of any region of Japan.

The OI sought to diffuse Okinawa's history of discrimination and strong pacifist sentiment by conceiving of them in "universal terms" (*fuhen teki na kotoba*). As both an academic and governor, Ōta had repeatedly stressed the universal potential of Okinawa's pacifist sentiments and peaceful heritage as a transnational call to peace.[50] The OI offered a competing definition of universalism premised on the importance of a homogenous national identity. The Initiative paper stated, "In the present, when the foundations of the nation-state have begun to crumble, it is vital not to side with this trend, but rather for Okinawa to conduct a new self-definition that helps construct Japan's emerging national image."[51] The OI argued that Okinawans' concern for their own history was a "problem" that must be "overcome" for Okinawa to "become a joint partner in the process of constructing a new national image in the twenty-first century." History was a tool for state building: "We in the present are the ones who define history, and for this very reason, our responsibility and awareness in possessing 'universal terms' will be scrutinized by history."[52]

Those "universal terms," the OI argued, required Okinawans to reaffirm their commitment to Japan's national project. In return, the Japanese government promised greater financial compensation to Okinawa. The OI authors used the logic of the capitalist market to support their reasoning. Takara observed, "Economic factors, as expressed in the term market economy, are in this day and age the determinate factors which govern the world and our lives. I believe that a realistic debate is one which holds a comprehensive perception, knowledge, and stance."[53] Ōshiro spelled out, "The Japanese government will not recognize it officially, but the reality is that, in order to maintain the stability of the bases, the cornerstone of the US–Japan security alliance, a form of economic management has been employed that links the bases with the economic stimulus of Okinawa."[54] The OI's prioritization of nation and economy over local sentiment and history in the name of "universalism" was an implicit call to recognize and accept this "reality."

The OI suggested that Okinawa's place in the new millennium may be "discovered" at the intersecting point of two inscriptions, which read, "Here Japan Ends and Asia Begins" and "Here Asia Ends and Japan Begins." Reaffirming the very construction of Japan as not Asia that they earlier had criticized as the dilemma of Japan's modernity, the Initiative treated Okinawa as both part of and not part of Japan or Asia. It claimed that Okinawa can be the "nexus of a problem-solving solution" (*chi teki na kaiketsu sochi*) linking Japan with the Asian region. Ultimately, this entailed not only the negation of Okinawans' own cultural and historical experience but the separation of Japan from "Asia."[55]

The OI group hoped to use Okinawan difference to pave the way for better Japanese relations with other Asian nations. In the APAP paper, Takara, Oshiro, and Maeshiro concluded that the OI concept entailed "our self-awareness and sense of responsibility in seeking a solution to various 'historical problems' within the Asia–Pacific region, using the 'soft power' of Okinawa as a key."[56] Maeshiro defined "soft power" as the ability "to hold pride in our culture, to utilize the suffering felt as a minority, to hold a strong will in the love for peace and hatred of war, and furthermore, to speak in universal terms of the fact that Okinawa is a region which desires to convey such experiences to the people of the world."[57] Yet the OI evaded, rather than provided a solution to, the most pervasive historical issue concerning Japan and the rest of Asia: the legacy of Japanese military aggression. It sought to play down the significance of historical responsibility and emphasize the importance of national paradigms.

The OI also avoided any discussion on the perceived role of the U.S. bases in Okinawa—either as a deterrent against North Korea and/or China or as a means to ensure Japan's incorporation within U.S. strategy. While setting up Okinawa as the cultural and historical stepping stone to Asia, the Initiative reconfirmed Okinawa's paramount role as Japan's most vital military strategic link to the United States, within a framework that both expanded Japan's military role and maintained its subordination to U.S. global military power. The OI was itself intimately connected to Japanese government policy tools set in place in an effort to ensure Okinawan deference to this designated role. Critics of the OI pointed out that its calls to "soft power" were in fact premised on, and complicit with, the "hard power" of the U.S. military and U.S.–Japan security relations.

DISSENT: ALTERNATIVE CLAIMS TO OKINAWAN PEACE, PLACE, AND PAST

The claims of the Initiative paper were significant precisely because of the politicized context in which they were made and because they represented a stance intrinsic to Inamine's new administration. While some Okinawan economists and business entrepreneurs had long supported the bases for economic reasons, the OI questioned the very importance of Okinawa's history. The majority of Okinawa's prominent postwar historians, including Takara himself in earlier years, were critical of Japan's assimilationist policies and homogenizing forces.[58] The OI countered the historical perception and political position of Ōta and his supporters, and it bore the imprimatur both of the national and prefectural governments. Moreover, it was applauded by the right-wing *Sankei* newspaper as leaving a "deep impression" on its audience. The "brain trust" of the new prefectural administration not only supported the bases and actively collaborated with central government policies, but also articulated a new ideology for Okinawa that many progressive Okinawan intellectuals saw as in cadence with strong nationalistic trends in Japanese public discourse.

Following publication of the full text of the APAP presentation, Arakawa Akira severely criticized the OI paper as displaying a "sycophantic mentality" (*dorei shisō*).[59] Takara's subsequent defense and counterattack was followed by a flood of responses, almost all critical of the Initiative. These criticisms focused on four interrelated issues: military security, Japan and Okinawa's role in Asia, the historical significance of Okinawa reversion to Japan, and the Initiative's "assimilationist" and "collaborationist" stance toward the central government.

Many respondents reiterated that the key lesson of the Battle of Okinawa was that the military protected the interests of the Japanese state at the expense of Okinawan civilians. In an interview in the *Asahi* newspaper, Ōta claimed that the Initiative "could only be made by those who do not know war, or the sufferings of the people." He connected the lessons of 1945 to the debate on security strategy today. "If Okinawa," he asserted, "is said to contain some potential, it is precisely in the cherishing of peace. For what purpose, and to protect whom, was the Battle of Okinawa fought? Does the military really protect the safety of the people? How can one merely affirm that security is gained by the use of military force while brushing these issues aside, as is the current trend?"[60]

Others criticized the OI for not differentiating between limited military intervention based on international cooperation and the military role of the U.S. bases in Okinawa. Shimabukuro Jun, University of the Ryukyus associate professor and central organizer of the prefectural plebiscite on the base issue held in September 1996, acknowledged that limited military intervention may be a legitimate means to resolve international conflicts in cases where diplomatic measures fail. Yet he criticized the Initiative's security analysis for failing to state the site, circumstances, or form by which military action would or should be carried out. He called for a coherent Japanese foreign policy which strictly confined the U.S.–Japan military alliance to defense, restricted use of military force to instances in accordance with United Nations procedures and international law, and prioritized "above all else the building of relations of mutual trust with neighboring countries," rather than one in which Japan sought to exercise military force on a global level with the United States as joint hegemonic power.[61]

Central to Japan's security and the bilateral alliance with the United States is the unresolved issue of Japan's relationship to the rest of Asia. Pacifists and progressives in Japan have long seen Japan's postwar system of international relations premised on the U.S.–Japan Security Treaty as a major reason why Japan could evade responsibility for its wartime aggression in Asia. From this angle, they see the remilitarization of Japan, particularly Japan's projected expanded regional strategic role under the auspices of the U.S.–Japan security framework, as oil on the flames, rather than the solution to increased tensions throughout Asia. Ōta, for instance, rejected outright the notion that Okinawa contributes to Asia by hosting the U.S. military bases. In a direct reference to World War II, he asserted rather that such militarization holds "the potential to once again inflict suffering on the region."[62] Okinawan poet and former journalist Kawamitsu Shinichi went even further, suggesting that Japan's "initiative" toward Asia backed by the U.S.–Japan Security Treaty is dangerously close to the aims and rhetoric of the "Greater East Asia Co-prosperity Sphere," Japan's World War II ideology of domination.[63] Journalist and editor Nakazato Susumu concluded that the increase in information flow and cultural exchange through globalization provided opportunities to open up new transnational networks across Asia, and it should not be met by a reaffirmation of national ideals and further militarization. In short, the Initiative's critics opposed both the U.S. military bases in Okinawa and the increased militarization of Japan. They saw both this military presence and the OI's rhetorical moves to depict Japan as not Asia as only further reinforcing Japan's separation from, and increasing tensions within, the region.

Critics of the OI rejected the Initiative's analysis of Okinawa's historical relations with Japan. In particular, they did not see the Okinawa reversion movement as solely premised on a sense of common nationhood. Both Shimabukuro Jun and academic and activist Arasaki Moriteru emphasized that Okinawans' aspirations to realize democratic and civil rights were the core aim of the movement to return to Japan. The reversion movement was, from this perspective, primarily a call to uphold the pacifist and democratic ideals of the Japanese constitution. Arasaki quoted the reversion efforts to struggle against both the U.S. military control of Okinawa and the militarization of Japan. He also linked the Okinawan reversion movement to support for the antiwar clause of the constitution and to peace movements on the mainland. Okinawans desired to return to Japan not out of simple nationalism but on the basis of a perceived ideal of how Japan could or should be—as part of a demilitarized and democratic nation. They had hoped that the reduction or complete withdrawal of the U.S. bases would accompany reversion. But, Arasaki noted, reversion to Japan actually strengthened the U.S.–Japan alliance and preserved intact the inequitable base structure. In other words, "they asked for bread, and were given stone."[64]

All critics rejected the Initiative's claims that reversion was accomplished according to the terms and wishes of Okinawans. However, they did not all agree among themselves as to how to evaluate the reversion movement. Those disagreements highlighted the diversity of positions among the Initiative's most vocal critics. In a rebuttal of Arasaki Moriteru's analysis, Arakawa Akira in particular saw the Okinawa reversion movement as misguided.[65] Reminiscent of his antireversion stance in the early 1970s, Arakawa argued in the OI debate that even if the reversion movement had been premised on an ideal of Japan's potential as opposed to how it actually was, by working within Japan's national framework, it still played into the hands of Japanese conservative nationalists.[66] He pointed out that, as predicted, reversion did not result in demilitarization but in the concentration of U.S. bases in Okinawa, now under the joint framework of both the U.S. and Japanese governments. He argued that the only way to resist oppression by Japanese nationalism and U.S. imperialism was to subvert both the Japanese state and the U.S. military structure.[67]

Arakawa also questioned the nationalist reversion-era slogans such as the call for Okinawa to "catch up" (*kakusa zesei*) and "become the same" (*Hondo nami*) as mainland Japan. Arakawa saw such slogans as inherently assimilationist and accepting of the system of public works–centered development in Okinawa today.[68] Arakawa explicitly criticized economic stimulus and development policies that he saw as increasing Okinawa's economic dependency and environmental degradation. He challenged the idea that "prosperity" (*yutakasa*) should be the goal for Okinawans, and he argued that satisfaction lay not in reinforcing the modern system of nation-states but through what he termed "spiritual prosperity" (*seishin no yutakasa*) and the "indigenous" (*dochaku*). He concluded that all of us in the contemporary world need to discover a set of values to fight against the new "wave" of nationalist "assimilation" symbolized by the Okinawa Initiative in order to live in the twenty-first century. "The intellectual struggle necessary to critique and overcome the new form of 'assimilationist' ideology propounded by Takara et al.," Arakawa concluded, "is certainly not only an Okinawan problem."[69]

The most detailed criticism of the Japanese government's "economic stimulus" compensation policies and their corrupting effect on both local politics and democratic procedures was made by Miyagi Yasuhiro, Nago city councilor and former representative of the citizen group that had fiercely called for a referendum on the building of the new base off the coast of Nago in 1997. In Nago, in the northern region of Okinawa—in economic and development terms the periphery of Japan's periphery—the links between economic stimulus and the base issue are the most pervasive, as are the damaging effects on the environment of the proposed base expansion and public works–centered development. Miyagi pointed out that, in an obvious bid to buy local support for the base, Nago city was the beneficiary of seven out of twenty-three of the projects advanced by Shimada-kon, the highest of any municipality. Japanese government funds related to the bases have jumped from comprising 6.5 percent of the Nago municipal budget in 1996 to 21.3 percent in 2000. The overall budget increased by approximately 25 percent over the same period. Shimada-kon projects already implemented within Nago include the construction of a "Multimedia Center" that provides free space and facilities to private multimedia companies.

Miyagi argued that such projects mark the breakdown (and privatization) of the public sphere at the local level, as taxpayers' funds are used to directly fund the activities of private corporations. He predicted that the massive influx of money will result in an environmentally destructive development without solving the "drain effect" of base-related compensation—that is, the injection of large amounts of public funding into costly construction projects that only increase local government debt and economic dependence. Miyagi noted that the area marked for the air base runway will destroy one of the few remaining living coral reefs on the main island, as well as a feeding area for what are thought to be the last remaining dugongs (a marine mammal) in Japan. In an effort to bolster support for the project, the Inamine administration introduced a plan to combine the military air base facility with a civilian airport. This plan calls for a much larger runway than originally envisaged and so threatens to cause even more environmental damage.[70] Miyagi concluded, "I can only view the role played by Shimada-kon as that of an opiate set to destroy Okinawa from within."[71] Fiercely opposing these developments, Miyagi and his colleagues seek to transform the base issue in Nago into an opportunity to recommit to preservation of the natural environs of the region, and they search for an ecologically friendly alternative to uncontrolled developmentalism. In this light, he has sought to build a nationwide coalition between peace and environmental groups.

The Initiative's critics were debating over fundamental issues concerning the raison d'être of social movements and intellectual criticism in Okinawa. Are Okinawa's discontents focused only toward the U.S. military bases per se, or are they also directed at the larger development agenda of the Japanese state, including the structure of economic compensation and public works projects as a whole, integrally connected to the Japanese government's strategy of maintaining the bases? To what extent is this movement influenced, or limited by, mainland Japanese ideologies of peace and the upholding of Japan's so-called Peace Constitution? How do these ideologies negate, or reinforce, Japanese nationalism, and what is Okinawa's position in relation to Japan?

Integral also to these issues is the dilemma of political action. Are Okinawa's struggles best fought within the Japanese political system, or do they require a rejection of these structures? If the latter, does such a "rejection" logically translate into a call for independence? Or does it entail the broader yet extremely difficult task of challenging both the modern system of nation-states and the conceptualization of progress as economic development? At the heart of these dilemmas lies the pervasive question of Okinawa's position—past, present, and future—in, and against, Japanese politics, economics, and culture and within U.S.–Japan military strategies.

Whatever their differences, the OI's opponents were all highly critical of the Initiative group's "neoassimilationism" (*shin-dōkashugi*) and their strategy to integrate Okinawa into centrally conceived notions of the "national interest." In 1999, the Obuchi cabinet passed extensive legislation to strengthen the state's power to discipline its citizens, including laws designating a national flag and anthem, expanding state power during a time of military crisis (*yūji*) within "the area surrounding Japan" (*shūhen*), and enlarging police authority to conduct surveillance on the Japanese population. In the same year, the Inamine administration in Okinawa agreed to the relocation of the Futenma base within the prefecture, and it also attempted to change the exhibit content at the Prefectural Peace Memorial Museum. Many of the OI critics saw those acts as part of an attempt to reaffirm state power and promote centralization and homogenization. That project required a "redefinition" of both the nation and of Okinawa's identity, culture, and history that they fiercely resisted.

More than anything, the OI's critics shared a deep dissatisfaction with the present U.S. base situation in Okinawa and a sense that regardless of any trimmings, the "Okinawa Initiative" was one more instrument designed to force Okinawans to accept their accorded role within the U.S.–Japan security framework.[72] In an interview almost a year after the

G-8 Summit, antibase activist and local councilor Chibana Shōichi succinctly summed up this sentiment when he observed:

> The logic of the Okinawa Initiative is that no matter how much Okinawa has resisted the bases they remain, so therefore we should accept them and utilize their presence for our own gain. But the argument is premised on the notion that Okinawa cannot choose its own destiny. If this is accepted as "reality" the future necessarily will be that simply nothing changes.[73]

CONCLUSION: THE DRUG OF DEPENDENCE AND IDENTITY POLITICS

Okinawa Initiative member Ōshiro denounced the Initiative's critics for the "poverty" of their conceptualization of the future and the "obstinacy" of their intellect.[74] On the contrary, I would suggest the debate both encouraged and proved the existence of a critical intellectual community in Okinawa and, through the local media, a widely accessible forum within which important and open discussion could take place. Many of the issues raised pertain to the most controversial and contradictory aspects of Japan's postwar system of relations.

Certainly no consensus was reached in the OI debate, either on Okinawa's past and its significance or on the road that Okinawa should take in the future. The debate revealed important differences among the OI critics, as well as those between the two sides. The arguments put forth in the Okinawa Initiative, the context in which it was formulated, and the intense debate that ensued also show the deep linkages among compensation policies, Okinawa's structure of economic dependence, and fierce contests over Okinawan history and identity.

The Japanese government seems willing at least for the present to provide financial subsidies to ensure Okinawa plays its designated role within U.S.–Japan security strategy. While the authors of the APAP Okinawa Initiative presented their argument in the name of Okinawan autonomy, the Okinawa Initiative was itself designed to enmesh Okinawa more tightly within this system of compensation. As a result, the functioning of democracy at the grassroots level is compromised and Okinawa's economic dependence on Tokyo increased. As Miyagi Yasuhiro expressed it, the Japanese government is creating and deepening "morally hazardous" links among private enterprise, national government funds, and local politics. The Inamine administration has also thrown its support behind massive civilian as well as military public works projects. Two of the most controversial examples are an airport at Shiraho, Ishigaki Island, next to an internationally renowned reef containing rare species of blue coral, and the reclamation of Okinawa Island's largest tidal flat, in Awase, Okinawa City, now a breeding ground to hundreds of sea creatures and bird life.[75]

On an ideological level, the Okinawa Initiative articulated a new justification for the U.S. military presence and for the further incorporation of Okinawa into official national historical canons and centralized structures of authority. Just as the OI was connected to Japanese government-coordinated compensation strategies, it was also integral to centrally directed endeavors to formulate a new set of national goals for Japan in the twenty-first century. Okinawa may enjoy large compensatory economic stimulus packages. Yet this is at the price of accepting a version of Okinawan identity that firmly ties Okinawa to Japanese cultural politics of homogeneity and loyalty to the wartime and postwar state, to a strengthened U.S.–Japanese military alliance, and to hosting the U.S. bases. Reaffirmation of the U.S.–Japan Security Treaty and Okinawa's "contribution" as host to most of the U.S. bases in Japan came hand in hand with a renewed reneging of historical responsibility for Japan's historic colonial ambitions and military aggression and the distancing of Japan from Asia. This expansion of national ideology has also been accompanied by the increased militarization of Japan under the auspices of the U.S.–Japan Security Treaty. The (re)writing of security policy and the fortification of ideological paradigms of nation are interrelated.[76] The concurrently complicit and tense relation between U.S. military strategy and conservative nationalist forces in Japan is nowhere more manifest than in Okinawa.[77]

As illustrated by the case of Okinawa, the fall of the Soviet Union and the continued advance of capital on a global scale have not led either to a significant U.S. military withdrawal or to the decline of nationalist ideological rhetoric. This supports the thesis of Kang Sang-jung and Yoshimi Shunya that globalization and nationalism are often mutually reinforcing rather than opposing phenomena. As the dictates of the free market and increased competition threaten the foundations of Japan's developmentalist state structure, the ruling government coalition has sought to expand the state's symbolic-ideological resources in order to ensure its own legitimacy.[78]

Yet the economic and ideological incorporation of Okinawa within this process has also been fiercely contested. The OI's critics presented a strong argument against this vision of nationalism, the OI's assumptions on security, and the negation of Okinawan history. The memory of wartime suffering at the hands of the Japanese is still powerful in Okinawa. While the OI attempted to play down the importance of history, the "history question" was a vital and highly contested issue within the OI debate. History, far from ending or fading in significance, remains connected to the present in multiple ways, and the many ghosts from Okinawa's turbulent past will continue to haunt its volatile political landscape. Neither compensation strategies nor the Okinawa Initiative have been fully successful in assuaging antibase sentiment. On the eve of the G-8 Summit, a succession of environmental, peace, and women's groups held numerous forums in Okinawa. (See figure 9.2.) On 20 July 2000, a day before then–U.S. president Clinton's arrival in Okinawa, approximately twenty-seven thousand protesters formed a human chain around the seventeen-kilometer perimeter of Kadena U.S. Air Force Base. Those protests have led to longer-term international links, including those with anti–U.S. base activists in Puerto Rico.

The antibase sentiment has forced the OPG, the Japanese government, and the U.S. military command in Okinawa to develop what Okinawan academic Gabe Masaaki has termed "crisis management" on the base issue.[79] Each time the U.S. military commissioner in Okinawa refers to Inamine and his cohort as "wimps" or a U.S. marine molests an Okinawan schoolgirl or is involved in arson attacks, the scenario is familiar: Local municipalities and the prefectural government express indignation, and the U.S. military command proffers sincere apologies and then promises to tighten regulations and give greater consideration to local sentiment.

Figure 9.2. Newly elected Tōmon Mitsuko of the Social Democratic Party speaks at the Ginowan demonstration, 15 July 2000. Tōmon Mitsuko was the first woman to be elected from Okinawa as a National Diet represenitive. To the far right on the stage sits former Governor Ōta Masahide. The image in the background is the Cornerstone of Peace.
Source: Photo by Julia Yonetani.

The observation that "the U.S.–Japan Security Treaty is only as strong as its weakest link, and its weakest link is Okinawa" remained as legitimate after the G-8 summit as it was before.[80] In the context of the war on terrorism, these issues have been exacerbated by increased U.S. military activity, greater secrecy on military movements, an increasingly assertive and nationalist Japanese security policy, and a sharp decline in tourism in Okinawa.

At the same time, Arakawa Akira's observations on the political situation in Okinawa made just after the G-8 Summit also remain valid. No broad-based antibase movement that encompasses local municipalities in Okinawa and that could mobilize effective resistance against compensation strategies as typified by Shimada-kon has yet emerged. By upping the ante of pork barrel politics, Japan's groups have thus far assured electoral victories for Okinawa's LDP coalition. They have also contributed to disillusion and the increasing alienation of civil society and citizen-based groups from the political process.

Okinawa's system of economic dependence underlies the general atmosphere of political apathy and disaffection that exists across the prefecture. The manufacturing industry makes up only 6 percent of Okinawa's total gross product, compared to a national average of 22 percent. The construction industry, by contrast, makes up over 15 percent of all economic output. Local construction companies are highly dependent on national government funds for public works projects, and unemployment in Okinawa has constantly been the most severe in the nation.[81] Neither the progressive political parties nor the peace movement as a whole have been able to break this cycle of economic dependence, resulting in the further entrenchment of pork barrel politics and public works–centered development. As Gavan McCormack observes of Okinawa's predicament, "As with the drugs of dependence so with the economy of dependence: the more the subject is hooked, the more difficult it becomes to break free of the addiction, which in turn requires higher and higher doses to maintain."[82]

Yet opposition to this system and its political, social, environmental, and economic effects has also intensified, polarizing public opinion and resulting in deep divisions within communities, particularly in Nago. Soon after the G-8 Summit, Okinawan novelist and Nago resident Medoruma Shun lashed out at politicians at all levels: "Prefectural leaders and local heads in the northern Okinawan district, to say nothing of the Japanese government, are so sunk in debauchery they are not even ashamed at openly confessing to the link between the relocation of Futenma base 'within Okinawa' and the northern district economic stimulus policies."[83]

Takara Kuroyoshi's prediction, that the G-8 Summit would prove an "opportunity" for Okinawa to "learn" about the essence of "global power," proved only too true.[84] Both the Initiative debate and the G-8 Summit revealed the complex interweaving of the base issue with contests over identity and the connection of both these issues to Okinawa's structure of political and economic dependence. They also exposed the way in which the reinforcing of dominant historical knowledge, security discourse, and hegemonic political, economic, and military structures are inherently interrelated processes. The precise blueprint of the U.S.–Japan "global partnership for the twenty-first century," diplomatic relations with the East Asia region, the effect and extent of the remilitarization of Japan, and the future of the U.S. military presence in Okinawa are still open questions. Yet it is certain that, as Arakawa Akira observes, the nature and outcome of these multiple and interconnected struggles, as they are fought out locally and within an increasingly globalized world, is an issue of vital significance both for Okinawa and far beyond its ocean shores.[85]

NOTES

1. *Okinawa Times*, 20 July 2000, 4.

2. "Clinton Emphasizes Dual Leadership in Address before Diet," *Japan Times*, 19 April 1996.

3. Refusing to act as proxy in the signing of leases of land used by the United States military in Okinawa, Ōta became the first prefectural governor in Japan's history to be the subject of a lawsuit by the prime minister. He made his case both in the Supreme Court of Japan and within the corridors of the Pentagon on highly publicized visits to Washington. No other confrontation between local and national government in postwar Japan over functions carried out by local authorities on behalf of the national government, observes law professor Nakachi Hiroshi, placed the government in such a compromised position over a fundamental aspect of policy. Nakachi Hiroshi, "Kenpō, Okinawa, Nihonjin" (The Consitution, Okinawa, and the Japanese), *Gunshuku mondai shiryō* (February 1996): 38–43.

4. Officially entitled "U.S. Security Strategy for the East Asia–Pacific Region" or EASR, the report was released by the U.S. Department of Defense in February 1995. See, for example, "Pentagon Affirms Asia Commitment," *Japan Times*, 28 February 1995, 1.

5. For an insightful discussion of these discourses and their exclusionary practices, see Carol Gluck, "The Past in the Present," in *Postwar Japan as History*, ed. Andrew Gordon (Berkeley: University of California Press, 1993), especially 88–89.

6. Kang Sang-jung and Yoshimi Shunya "Sazameku aratana kōteki kūkan: Okinawa no toi" (Murmurs of a New Civil Sphere: Okinawa's Challenge), *Sekai* (May 2000): 161; reprinted in *Gurōbaruka no enkinhō: Atarashii kōkyōkūkan o motomete* (The Two Poles of Globalization: Toward a New Civil Sphere) (Tokyo: Iwanami Shoten, 2001), chapter 6.

7. For analysis of this period, see Julia Yonetani, "Ambiguous Traces and the Politics of Sameness: Placing Okinawa in Meiji Japan," *Japanese Studies* 20, no. 1 (May 2000): 15–31, and Alan Christy, "The Making of Modern Subjects in Okinawa," in *Formations of Colonial Modernity in East Asia,* ed. Tani E. Barlow (Durham, N.C.: Duke University Press, 1999), 141–70.

8. Laura Hein, "Introduction: The Territory of Identity and Remembrance in Okinawa," *Critical Asian Studies* 33, no. 1 (2001): 31–36.

9. "*Okinawa kenchiji shōgen: Kichi no nai heiwa na shima e*" (Tokyo: Nirai sha, 1996), 16. Ōta's testimony in the Supreme Court in July of the same year is reprinted in Ōta Masahide, *Okinawa: Heiwa no Ishiji* (Tokyo: Iwanami shoten, 1996), 168–81. David Tobaru Obermiller provides insights into the connection between the "Okinawa problem" and contested identities in "The Okinawan Struggle over Identity, Historical Memory, and Cultural Representation," *Japan Foundation Newsletter* 27, nos. 3–4: 12–16.

10. *Asahi Shinbun,* 12 May 1997, 15.

11. For insights on the reasons for Ōta's defeat, see Chalmers Johnson, "Okinawa between the United States and Japan," in *Ryukyu in World History,* ed. Josef Kreiner (Bonn: Bier'sche Verlagsanstalt, 2001), 365–94.

12. Prime Minister Hashimoto and U.S. ambassador Walter Mondale announced the commitment to return the Futenma Marine Air Station in Ginowan City on the eve of Clinton's visit in 1995. It later became clear that this agreement was contingent on securing an alternative site within Okinawa. For a detailed analysis of this issue, see Julia Yonetani, "Playing Base Politics in a Global Strategic Theatre: Futenma Relocation, the G-8 Summit, and Okinawa," *Critical Asian Studies* 233, no. 1 (2001): 70–96; Aurelia George Mulgan, "Managing the US Base Issue in Okinawa: A Test for Japanese Democracy," *Japanese Studies* 20, no. 2 (September 2000): 159–77; Sheila A. Smith, "Challenging National Authority: Okinawa Prefecture and the US Military Bases," in *Local Voices, National Issues: The Impact of Local Initiative in Japanese Policy-Making,* ed. Sheila A. Smith (Ann Arbor: University of Michigan Press, 2000); Chalmers Johnson, "The Heliport, Nago, and the End of the Ōta Era," in *Okinawa: Cold War Island,* ed. Chalmers Johnson (Cardiff, Calif.: Japan Policy Research Institute, 1999), 215–35.

13. See also Julia Yonetani, "On the Battlefield of Mabuni: Struggles over Peace and the Past in Contemporary Okinawa," *East Asian History* 20 (December 2000): 145–69.

14. While a minority, several mainland Japanese intellectuals and journalists also contributed to the debate. The vast majority of all published contributions were critical of the Okinawa Initiative paper. A comprehensive list of these articles is provided in Takara Kuroyoshi, Maeshiro Morisada, and Oshiro Tsuneo, eds., *Okinawa Inishiatibu: Okinawa hatsu chiteki senryaku* (Okinawa Initiative: A Strategy of Knowledge from Okinawa) (Naha: Okinawa Bunkō, 2000), 168–75.

15. The title of the English translation presented at the forum is "Toward an 'Okinawa Initiative': A Possible Role for Okinawa in Asia Pacific." All citations are my own translation from the Japanese original.

16. See the explanation included in the Japanese Center for International Exchange's website at www.jcie.or.jp/thinknet/apap/.

17. See "'Anpo' ni saidai kōken no chiiki ajia de sekinin aru yakuwari e" (The Region Which Contributes Most to the "U.S.–Japan Security Treaty": Toward Playing a Responsible Role in Asia), *Sankei Shinbun,* 29 March 2000, 1, and 30 March 2000, 1.

18. Summary and full text available at www.kantei.go.jp/jp/21century/990716summary.html.

19. The coordinator of this commission was Yamamoto Tadashi, president of the Japan Center for International Exchange, which was also the sponsor of the APAP Forum where the OI paper had been presented. In fact, Takara Kuroyoshi later explained that it was Yamamoto who first suggested to Takara that he and his colleagues present a paper at the APAP Naha Forum (*Okinawa Inishiatibu,* 20–21). A workshop, also attended by Prime Minister Obuchi, for the "exchange of opinions" between the participants of APAP and the members of the Prime Minister's Commission was held in Naha on the eve of the APAP Forum. The journalist Chino Keiko, who publicly endorsed the OI on the front page of *Sankei* the day after the APAP conference, was also a member of the same subcommittee of the Prime Minister's Commission as Takara (noted by Yakabi Osamu in his criticism of the OI in "Hoshii teige no haikei, kaisetsu" (I Want More Analysis and Explanation of the Proposal's Background), *Okinawa Taimusu,* 1 May 2000.

20. While the content of both the APAP and the JPC-SED Initiative is very similar, the JPC-SED paper is lengthier and includes more detailed policy formulations, according to workshop leader and coordinator of the JPC-SED Okinawa Initiative.

21. See www.jpc-sed.or.jp/eng/eng01.htm.

22. As well as lead the workshop, Shimada authored the entire first section of the final paper. In the second section, Takara outlined Okinawa's desirable role as a "potential player," Shima looked at the G-8 Summit, and Uehara proposed steps to promote the economic autonomy of Okinawa. Summary and full text available at www2jpc-sed.or.jp/fil. See also summary and analysis by Egami Takayoshi, "'Shinhoshu no ronri' tenkai 3kyōju to seisansei honbu no teigen" (Unfolding of the "New Conservatism": The Proposal of the Three University of the Ryukyus Professors and JPC-SED), *Ryukyu Shimpo,* 5 June 2000.

23. Summary and full text available at www2jpc-sed.or.jp/.

24. For various testimonies on the making of Shimada-kon, see Ōta Masahide, *Okinawa no ketsudan* (Okinawa's Decision) (Tokyo: Asahi Shinbunsha, 2000). See also Shimada Haruo, "Okinawa: Kusa no ne no koe o kike" (Okinawa: Listen to the Voices at the Grassroots), *Chūō Kōron* (May 1997): 60–69. From 1997 to 2000, eleven of the thirty-five proposed Shimada-kon projects were completed. The peak for the implementation and completion of further projects was predicted to be from 2000 to 2001 (*Okinawa Times*, 1 June 2000, 1).

25. Summary and full text available at kantei.go.jp/jp//singi/okinawa/okinawa-1127.html.

26. Mulgan, "Managing the US Base Issue in Okinawa," 166–67.

27. Shimada himself uses this expression; see his testimony in Ōta, *Okinawa no ketsudan*, 249, and Shimada, "Okinawa," 64–65.

28. I outlined these issues in Yonetani, "Playing Base Politics in a Global Strategic Theatre," especially 73–79.

29. Arakawa Akira most specifically cites Shimada-kon as an important factor, *Okinawa: tōgō to hangyaku* (Okinawa: Incorporation and Betrayal) (Tokyo: Tsukuma Shobō), 248–59.

30. In one of the most controversial examples, employees of Japan's Defense Facilities Administration Agency conducted extensive door knocking around the Nago district prior to the plebiscite.

31. Cited in editorial, *Okinawa Times*, 22 June 2000, 5.

32. Notes from the workshop available at www.kantei.go.jp/jp/21century/990810bunka1-7.html.

33. Miyagi Kimiko explores these issues in "'Shinwa' e no shiten" (A Perspective on "Myths"), *Uramaneshia*, no. 2 (February 2001): 11.

34. Aspects of the OI argument were anticipated in two previous books: Takara's *"Okinawa" hihan josetsu* ("Okinawa" Critique: An Introduction) (Naha: Okinawa Bunkō, 1997), and *Okinawa no jiko kenshō* (Verifying the Okinawan Self) (Naha: Okinawa Bunkō, 1998), coauthored with Maeshiro and Makino Hirotaka, then a leading executive at Okinawa's largest bank. Ōta Masakuni points out common threads between these works in "Misugosenai tosaku no rongi: Haijo dekinu chiiki kunō" (Not to Overlook the Warped Logic: The Regional Suffering Which Cannot Be Excluded), *Okinawa Times*, 6 May 2000.

35. *Asahi Shinbun*, 15 May 2000.

36. A selection of Ōta's works on the Battle of Okinawa include *This Was the Battle of Okinawa* (Naha: Naha Shuppankai, 1981); *Okinawa-sen: Senō to heiwa* (Okinawa: War and Peace) (Tokyo: Shakai Shinsho, 1981); *Sōshi Okinawa-sen* (A Comprehensive History of the Battle of Okinawa) (Tokyo: Iwanami Shoten, 1982); and *Okinawa-sen to wa nanika?* (What Was the Battle of Okinawa?) (Tokyo: Kumeshoten, 1985).

37. Ōta also fiercely opposed the Japanese Education Ministry's attempts to water down mention of these atrocities in Japanese high school history textbooks in the early eighties ("Remember Battle of Okinawa and Textbook Issue: Government Has Tradition of Misrepresenting—or Even Omitting—Facts on Ryukyus" [*sic*], *Japan Times*, 6 February 1983, 4). In 1988, he testified for Ienaga Suburô's counsel in the third Ienaga lawsuit against the Japanese government on the school textbook screening process; this testimony is reprinted in Kyōkasho Kentei Soshō o shien suru Zenkoku Renrakukai, eds., *Ienaga-kyōkasho saiban 5: Okinawa-sen no jissō* (Tokyo: Rongu Shuppan, 1990). On the textbook issue, see also Nozaki Yoshiko and Inoguchi Hiromatsu, "Japanese Education, Nationalism, and Ienaga Saburō's Textbook Lawsuits," in *Censoring History: Citizenship and Memory in Japan, Germany, and the United States*, ed. Mark Selden and Laura Hein (Armonk, N.Y.: Sharpe, 2000).

38. See also Matthew Allen's chapter 2 in this volume.

39. See also Yonetani, "On the Battlefield of Mabuni."

40. In the final permanent exhibit, the Japanese diorama is holding a gun, but away from the Okinawan family.

41. Takara et al., eds., *Okinawa Inishiatibu*, 47.

42. The entire text of the APAP paper is reproduced in Takara et al., eds., *Okinawa Inishiatibu*, 38–55.

43. Takara et al., eds., *Okinawa Inishiatibu*, 42.
44. Takara et al., eds., *Okinawa Inishiatibu*, 45.
45. Takara et al., eds., *Okinawa Inishiatibu*, 42.
46. Arakawa Akira, *Okinawa Taimusu*, 15–16 May 2000.
47. For an analysis of Fujioka, see Gavan McCormack, "The Japanese Movement to 'Correct' History," in *Censoring History*, ed. Hein and Selden, 53–73.
48. Ōta, *Okinawa*, 169–82.
49. Takara et al., eds., *Okinawa Inishiatibu*, 49–51.
50. See, for example, Ōta, *Okinawa*,, 36; *Okinawa: Sensō to heiwa* (Okinawa: War and Peace) (Tokyo: Asahi Bunko, 1983), especially 212–13.
51. Takara et al., eds., *Okinawa Inishiatibu*, 52–55.
52. Takara et al., eds., *Okinawa Inishiatibu*, 48.
53. Takara et al., eds., *Okinawa Inishiatibu*, 24.
54. Takara et al., eds., *Okinawa Inishiatibu*, 24–25.
55. Laura Hein and Ellen H. Hammond provide insightful observations on Japan's ambivalent and economically drawn efforts to "home" in on Asia in the context of the early 1990s: "Homing In on Asia: Identity in Contemporary Japan," *Bulletin of Concerned Asian Scholars* 27, no. 3 (July–September 1995): 3–16.
56. Takara et al., eds., *Okinawa Inishiatibu*, 55.
57. Takara et al., eds., *Okinawa Inishiatibu*, 129.
58. Historian and longtime university colleague of Takara's, Hiyane Teruo, greeted Takara's claims with a mixture of disdain and disbelief. "This is the sharp-witted historical researcher Takara," Hiyane commented, "who was a severe critic of assimilationism, who censured the ideology of the Emperor system, and who has problematized the arbitrary nature of the disposition of the Ryukyu Kingdom." Hiyane continued: "The more Takara preaches of 'the problem of history,' in loud remonstrations of the 'structure of "victimized" historical consciousness of Okinawa,' the more he is ill-fated to continual merciless betrayal of his own voluminous work and past utterances. Here is the cruel reality of the self-conversion (*jiko tenkai*) of a post-war Okinawan intellectual." Hiyane Teruo, "Sengo rekishigaku no seika hōki: Towareru hasshinsha no seijisei" (The Disposal of the Work of a Postwar Historian: Questioning the Speaker's Political Positionality), *Okinawa Taimusu*, 26 June 2000.
59. Arakawa Akira, "'Tōgō' ni koō suru gensetsu: Gunji yōnin no 'kokka shugi'" (A Discourse That Cheers "Unification": A "Nationalism" That Consents to the Military), *Okinawa Times*, 15 May 2000; and Arakawa Akira, "Kōsō naku 'doreishisō' arawasu: Kenryoku e shisōsha toyshite no chishiki jin" (Display of the Unstructured Ideology of a Sycophant), *Okinawa Times*, 17 May 2000.
60. "Sensō shiranu kokka shugi teki shuchō" (The Nationalist Claims of Those Who Do Not Know of War), interview with Ōta Masahide, *Asahi Shimbun*, 16 May 2000. A similar view is expressed by Ishihara Masaie, "'Hibōryoku shugi' e no chōsen: Wasureta shōmin no manazashi" (Toward an Ideology of Nonviolence: The Forgotten View of the People), *Okinawa Times*, 10 May 2000.
61. Shimabukuro Jun, "Chiiki kibō no dōmei ka: Kinrin shokoku to shinrai kōchiku mo kaku" (A Global Alliance? Lack of Trust Building with Neighboring Countries), *Ryukyu Shimpo*, 13 May 2000.

62. Interview with Ōta, *Asahi Shimbun*.

63. Kawamitsu Shinichi, "'Ajia' gainen ni gimon: Kokka shugi wa rekishiteki tanraku" (Doubts about the Concept of "Asia": Nationalism Is the Severing of History), *Okinawa Taimusu*, 13 June 2000. See also Tanaka Yasuhiro, "Chūshin shikō to ani na sutansu: Ajia to Nihon o kibetsu suru ishi" (Centralism and the Easy Position: The Will to Separate Japan and Asia), *Okinawa Times*, 25 May 2000.

64. Arasaki Moriteru quoting Nakano Yoshio: "Genjō tsuinin ronja no kotoba asobi: Fukki wa beigun shihai kara no dakkyaku" (The Word Play of Advocates of the Status Quo: Reversion Was the Escape from U.S. Military Control), *Okinawa Times*, 29 May 2000. For a similar view, see also Kuruma Yasuo "'Genjitsu taiōton' to 'Okinawa inishiatibu'" (The "Pragmatist Argument" and the "Okinawa Initiative"), *Okinawa Times*, 29–31 May 2000 (three-part series).

65. Arakawa Akira, "Kokka o sōtai taki ni toraeyo" (Call for the Relativized Depiction of the State), *Shūkan kinyōbi*, 6 June 2000.

66. Arakawa Akira laid out his antireversionist stance in *Hankokka no kyōku* (Tokyo: Gendai hyōronsha, 1973). See also Oguma Eiji's analysis of Arakawa in "'Nihonjin' no kyōkai" (The Boundaries of the "Japanese") (Tokyo: Shinyakusha, 1998).

67. On the eve of the G-8 Summit, Arakawa and others founded a new journal, *Urumanesia*, to promote "extensive, penetrating, and lively debate" in the endeavor toward the "self-government, autonomy, and independence" of the "Ryukyu Islands" (*Ryūkyū-ko*); *Urumaneshia: Ryukyu-ko no jiritsu, dokuritsu ronsō zasshi* (Urumanesia: The Magazine for Dialogue on Independence and Autonomy for the Ryukyu Islands), 1 (July 2000) and 2 (February 2001).

68. For an analysis of the impact of these policies see Gavan McCormack, "Okinawa Dilemmas: Coral Islands or Concrete Islands?" in *Okinawa*, ed. Johnson, 261–83.

69. Arakawa Akira, *Okinawa: Tōgō to hangyaku* (Okinawa: Unification and Betrayal) (Tokyo: Tsukuma Shobō, 2000), 248–59.

70. According to plans under negotiation, the runway will be up to 2,600 meters long and cost up to an estimated one trillion yen to construct.

71. Miyagi, "Tankō no kanaria no utagoe," 36. Gavan McCormack observes, "As with the drugs of dependence so with the economy of dependence: the more the subject is hooked, the more difficult it becomes to break free of the addiction, which in turn requires higher and higher doses to maintain"; Gavan McCormack, "Okinawa and the Structure of Dependence," in *Structure and Subjectivity in Okinawa*, ed. Glenn Hook and Richard Siddle (New York: Routledge, 2002).

72. Matsushima Yasukatsu, "Seisaku naku kichi yōnin ni shūshi: Ajia e no misumesseeji" (Merely Consenting to the Bases without a Policy: Sending the Wrong Message to Asia), *Okinawa Taimusu*, 20 May 2000.

73. Interview with Chibana Shoichi, 3 July 2000.

74. Takara et al., eds., *Okinawa Inishiatibu*, 80.

75. On the environmental impact of the Ishigaki Airport plans, see, for example, Amanda Suutari, "Concern over Threat to Blue Coral Reefs," *Japan Times*, 20 December 2001. According to a recent *Asahi Shimbun/Okinawa Times* opinion poll, 57 percent of local Okinawa City residents are against the reclamation of Awase (27 percent are for). At the time of this writing, however, local, prefectural, and

national governments were still pushing for the project to go ahead, in opposition to a local plebiscite on the issue (*Okinawa Taimusu*, 20 November 2001, 1).

76. David Campbell, *Writing Security: United States Foreign Policy and the Politics of Identity* (Manchester: Manchester University Press, 1992).

77. One consequence of this connection is a pervasive ambivalence toward the United States within Japanese nationalist discourse.

78. Kang and Yoshimi, *Gurobarizumu no enkinhō*, 83.

79. Gabe Masaaki, presentation at Daiwa House, London, 29 March 2001.

80. Gavan McCormack, presentation at Daiwa House, London, 29 March 2001.

81. See Miyamoto Kenichi and Sasaki Masayuki, eds., *Okinawa: 21 seiki no chōsen* (Okinawa: Challenges of the Twenty-first Century) (Tokyo: Iwanami Shoten, 2000).

82. McCormack, "Okinawa and the Structure of Dependence."

83. Medoruma Shun, "Uminari no shima kara: Henoko o migoroshi ni suru na" (From the Island Where the Oceans Roar: Do Not Leave Henoko to Die), *Shūkan Kinyōbi* 333 (8 September 2000): 24.

84. Takara Kuroyoshi, "Kichi no sonzai: Sekkyoku hyōka" (Positive Evaluation of the Bases), *Asahi Shimbun* (interview), 15 May 2000.

85. Arakawa Akira, *Okinawa: Tōgō to hangyaku*, 259.

10

From the National Gaze to Multiple Gazes

Representations of Okinawa in Recent Japanese Cinema

Aaron Gerow

The 1995 Japanese film *Goodbye Japan!* (*Sayonara Nippon!* directed by Tsutsumi Yukihiko),[1] begins with a quote that would bring to mind the story of Okinawa to anyone even slightly familiar with its historical plight:

> A long time ago, people of this island were independent and proud. Their wealth lay in nature: the beautiful sea and coral reefs. But with time, the nature they loved and worshiped was ruined by the evil hand of development. Their long history of being ruled by foreigners is a history stained with humiliation.

The film visualizes the plight of this island, a part of Okinawa Prefecture, from the very start. Far not only from mainland Japan but also from the Okinawan main island—and subordinate to both—it suffers severe hurricane damage but is ignored by the government and the media, and it receives neither help from national agencies nor even a consolation visit from the Okinawan governor. After years of such neglect and insensitivity (symbolized by a developer's ill-considered attempt to build a resort on sacred land), the mayor and many of the islanders decide to declare independence from both Okinawa and Japan, a bid that, despite the threat of Self-Defense Force air strikes, succeeds at the last minute after the wily mayor tricks the American military into supporting their effort.

The fact that this fictional movie about secession from Japan was made by commercial mainland capital and released throughout the Japanese archipelago may prompt surprise and make one wonder about its political stance. Critics might point out that, given that the island featured in *Goodbye Japan!* is a make-believe atoll, Akaonekoshima, the film obfuscates the reality of Okinawan suffering and grievance by transferring that history onto a fictional island which, through its comic antics, degrades the true pain of memory. Yet one can certainly also imagine alternative appropriations, perhaps by Okinawan spectators themselves, particularly those from smaller islands, that take derisive pleasure in an imaginary secession from the mainland.

Placing *Goodbye Japan!* among several other recent films that depict Okinawa, I would like to weave my way through such interpretations to ask why mainland filmmakers and producers create a film about the plight of Okinawans—that is, a film about Japan's other? What textual strategies articulate and differentiate Okinawa and Japan? How are audiences being addressed? What valences—political, cultural, and economic—do such cinematic representations of Okinawa and Japan evince? The last decade has seen a significant number of films involving Okinawa, including movies shot there, or featuring Okinawan characters, or invoking the prefecture. The reasons behind this increase include the boom in things Okinawan in the 1990s, particularly the rising popularity in mainland Japan of music from Okinawa (see the chapters by Steve Rabson and James Roberson in this volume), as well as the media focus on political issues such as the conflict over American bases, rapes of Okinawan women by GIs, and the performance of mainland concern for Okinawa in the G-8 summit (see the chapters by Linda Angst and Julia Yonetani).

It is my contention that Okinawa figures so prominently in contemporary Japanese cinema above all because it functions as a productive space for negotiating identities that have come into crisis in the postbubble, post–Aum Shinrikyo era. This can be seen by inserting these texts into the larger representational topography of both recent cinema and present-day Japanese culture, in which depictions of the marginal and the non-Japanese have proliferated. The films discussed here engage in such depictions out of a perception of anxious discontent in a time of economic and social crisis, but many end by validating Japanese identity, even when appearing to criticize some of its aspects. This is evident as far back as *The Tower of Lilies* (*Himeyuri no tō*, 1953, dir. Imai Tadashi) and Imamura Shōhei's *The Profound Desire of the Gods* (*Kamigami no fukaki yokubō*, 1968), which, despite their leftist politics, still function within a hegemonic nationalist imaginary, identifying both sameness and difference in Okinawa in order to confirm the self-sameness of Japan. Today, even an ostensibly nonpolitical film like *Goodbye Japan!* works off such feelings of discontent, making Japan the enemy and Okinawa the hero, yet it does so through a mode of representation that uses an "Okinawan" example to regenerate Japanese national identity. Similarly, *Free and Easy 11* (*Tsuri baka nisshi irebun*, 1999, dir. Motoki Katsuhide) and *The Legacy of the Sea, Sky, and Reef* (*Umi sora sango no iitsutae*, 1991, dir. Shiina Makoto) play off the touristic dissatisfaction with home to present a pleasurable spectacle of difference, but one that reincorporates the Okinawan other into the Japanese self through a consumable narrative of renewal. *The Legacy of the Sea, Sky, and Reef* and *Goodbye Japan!* both offer spectators a vicarious identification with marginals victimized by Japanese elites, yet only in a fashion that excuses them from association with these Japanese; the films' identification with Okinawans becomes a means of imagining a rejuvenated Japan. In these works, Okinawa often shifts back and forth between being Japan and being other, between being an object of identification (sometimes *because* it is different) and being too different to identify with. Ultimately, however, these representational processes work to reconfirm Japan's centrality and Okinawa's marginality.

These same crises in Japanese identity, however, have also empowered select Japanese films to criticize the national myth of homogeneity, recognize heterogeneity, and develop forms of cinema that respect the otherness of others. A number of filmmakers have produced significant films focusing on ethnic minorities in Japan or social marginals who do not fit the dominant national image, including Okinawans. Two directors discussed here, Sai Yōichi and Kitano Takeshi, make similar but still-diverging cinematic choices that permit them to approach Okinawa either to problematize the national myth of homogeneity or to reveal its ultimate emptiness.

Representing Okinawa in film is thus itself a site of struggle between conflicting forces. Combining textual analysis with an examination of the discourses with which texts are imbricated, it is my purpose to map the geography of this representational battlefield, eliciting the political, cultural, and economic valences of images of Okinawa, but always within a larger intertextuality that encompasses many other mainland films. In many works, Okinawa becomes the object of articulations of consumer desire and Japanese national identity on the level not simply of what is represented but also of cinematic structure. In these movies, filmic form renders otherness readable, understandable, and part of the familiar world of conventional distinctions between self and other. In contrast, and in conscious opposition, filmmakers like Kitano and Sai utilize a variety of cinematic styles to articulate Okinawa in its otherness and opacity, as part of a project to undermine the Japanese "self." Theirs is a struggle not merely of information about Okinawa but also over cinematic forms of expression.[2] Kitano tries to counter nationalist essentialism with nothingness and Sai with specificity, but both with a style that implies a form of detachment from their characters and stories. Looking at Okinawa from, as it were, afar, they respect the Okinawan other as other, and as opaque. However, their approach retains the danger of rendering Okinawa unarticulated and thus meaningless.

I will end by focusing on Takamine Go, whose recent work *Tsuru-Henry* (*Mugen Ryūkyū: Tsuru Henri*, 1999) offers a possible solution through strategic use of a collage of media and perspectives that avoids both the force of nationalist modes of knowing and the nihilism of detachment. Neither declaring what Okinawa is nor refusing to articulate it, the multiple positions in *Tsuru-Henry* not only bring the issue of representation to the foreground but wander through a deft mixture of fictional and real, past and present, Okinawan and non-Okinawan that deconstructs Japanese homogeneity, celebrates heterogeneity, reworks memory, and posits an Okinawan politics of collage.[3]

FROM ETHNOGRAPHER TO TOURIST: THE "ORIGINAL" OKINAWA

Okinawa has been a site for Japanese cinema since the 1930s. *The Vindictive Snake* (*Shūnen no dokuhebi*, 1931, dir. Yoshino Jirō) was made by Okinawans in Okinawa, and Toyoda Shiro's *Oyake Akahachi* (1937) was probably the first film made in the prefecture by a Tokyo studio.[4] In the years since, two dominant Japanese patterns of representing Okinawa cinematically have been the nationalistic and the touristic. *The Tower of Lilies* directed by Imai Tadashi in 1953 and Imamura Shōhei's *The Profound Desire of the Gods* represent Okinawa within a national imaginary. Interestingly, both are works of political protest (Imai's against war, Imamura's against Japanese capitalist modernity), but both also efface Okinawan differences in the process of constructing a unified oppositional (i.e., antiwar or anticapitalist), but still Japanese, identity. *The Tower of Lilies* tells the famous story of the elite school girls who committed group suicide rather than surrender to Americans soldiers toward the end of the Battle of Okinawa. Imai's 1953 hit film, the most famous of the four movie versions, helped immortalize the girls, but to some critics the film portrayed mainland conceptions of the war rather than Okinawan ones. Matsuda Masao has argued that in *The Tower of Lilies*, as well as in other war films set in Okinawa, "Okinawa was only manipulated as the perfect place for declaring the tragedy of war; in a word, Okinawans wandering about the Okinawan landscape amidst the ravages of war were . . . just given the role of objects [of that tragedy]."[5] The film was powerfully antiwar, but Imai, by obfuscating the differences between Japanese and Okinawans, not only hides the history of Okinawan suffering at the hands of Japanese but also uses the war to unify the postwar Japanese nation through images of a people sharing the same suffering.

Imamura Shōhei's *The Profound Desire of the Gods* similarly offered a critique of Japan, this time of its pursuit of high economic growth, yet treated Okinawa as the primitive object of an ethnographic gaze. Imamura's work throughout the 1960s, including *The Insect Woman* (*Nihon konchūki*, 1963) and *The Pornographers* (*Jinruigaku nyūmon*, 1966), valorized the preternatural desires that he saw as seething underneath, thus exposing the hollowness of postwar Japanese capitalism. *The Profound Desire of the Gods* used an Okinawan island as the site for a tale of an incestuous brother and sister ostracized from the closed community who are eventually killed for attempting to escape its confines; their nearly animal-like existence provides a contrast to the modernity that reasserts itself at the end of the film. Yet Imamura's ethnographic perspective on Okinawa, by equating its primitiveness with his "insect women" of Japan, is reminiscent of that of prewar ethnologists like Yanagita Kunio and Origuchi Shinobu who located Okinawa at the beginning of a narrative of Japanese origins.[6] This cultural nostalgia always posed the danger of rendering Okinawa in a Japanese version of an Orientalist palette, and in Imamura's case, the Okinawan self is rendered more natural, more original than the Japan of the high-economic growth era, often in order to imagine a Japanese self in opposition to Western modernity. The filmmaker Takamine Go, who was raised on Miyako Island, where the film was shot, reacted strongly to the movie, commenting, "The film doesn't try to see Okinawa as anything other than an ethnological object, and just endeavors to copy that Okinawa."[7]

Go's anger toward the film spurred not only his decision to begin filmmaking but also his critique of the ethnological perspective in his first feature work, *Paradise View* (*Paradaisu byū*, 1985). One of that film's characters is a Japanese ethnographer visiting Okinawa, who is rendered not only linguistically isolated (he is the only one using standard Japanese in the film) but also hopelessly antiquarian. As he seeks to preserve lost rituals and teach islanders Heian poetry (perhaps seeing in them the living remnants of the Yamato past), the ethnographer, while hoping to join the "natives" through marriage, seems unable to deal with their interest in modernization and their different articulations of desire. (Takamine's most recent work, *Tsuru-Henry*, continues his critique of nationalist perspectives.)

In recent years, many Japanese directors have retained that nationalistic pattern of representing Okinawa cinematically and joined it to a touristic vision. The two patterns are intricately intertwined, though not always without tension. The former, evident in *The Tower of Lilies* and *The*

Profound Desire of the Gods, utilizes Okinawa as a mirror to create and confirm articulations of Japanese national identity. Unlike those older films, the latter acknowledges that the national imaginary of homogeneity cannot satisfy all desire and portrays Okinawa as a consumable spectacle of difference. The first thus revolves more around sameness and the second around difference, but both operate within a dynamic of the sameness and difference of Okinawans and Japanese—usually with Japanese the intended audience. On one side, the sameness of even this "southern land" (*nankoku*) is affirmed in a process that reinforces the homogeneity and unity of the imagined Japanese national community. On the other side, Okinawa's difference is stressed in order to reflect on the Japanese self, becoming an idealized image functioning either to confirm cultural superiority or to fashion an alternative (as in counterculture appropriations of the islands). Either way, the structure is one of binary oppositions. These are often two sides of the same coin, and they operate in most films as a complex play of desire and envy, creating otherness, but only as a function of the same.

Quite a number of recent films, such as *Shakking the Movie: The Okinawa Scam* (*Shakkingu the Movie: Okinawa daisakusen*, 1999, part of a series directed by Izumi Seiji about large-scale debtors who scam even bigger baddies in order to pay off their debts), readily reduce the island to an exchangeable sign of the pleasurably exotic, commodified for consumption by the eye. Since they could have used any other location, Okinawa becomes simply another exotic locale exhibiting no significant difference from other locales, except for its pristine beaches and bright blue skies. Some films, however, present Okinawa as a touristic commodity significant in its difference, but never to the point of upsetting the logic of the nationalist imaginary. Two examples from the 1990s are *Free and Easy 11* and *The Legacy of the Sea, Sky, and Reef*.

The former is an episode in the popular "Free and Easy" film series based on a "salaryman manga" by Yamasaki Juzō and Kitami Ken'ichi centered on the character Hamazaki Densuke (affectionately known as Hama-chan), a rather inept but lovable employee of a construction firm who is such a fishing fanatic that he devotes more energy to the rod and reel than to work. The fantasy constructed in the stories, and one possible reason for the manga's and film series' success is that Hama-chan's skill with the rod enables him to become the fishing "teacher" to his own company's president, Suzuki Ichinosuke (known to Hama-chan as "Su-san"), thus offering spectators a vicarious reversal of the corporate power structure. The film focuses on Hama-chan's comedic adventures, but it also offers viewers the spectacle of travel. Most episodes feature a trip to some picturesque fishing spot in Japan, with Okinawa the destination of film number eleven.[8] Films that use locales are usually supported by local tourism boards and incorporate recognizable touristic images into the visuals. The alliance between tourism and film production appeared as early as the late 1950s in works like Nikkatsu's "Rider on the Plains" ("Wataridori") films, but it is epitomized by the extremely popular "Tora-san" ("Otoko wa tsurai yo") series produced by Shochiku, in which a bumbling but lovable itinerant peddler, Kurama Torajirō, travels back and forth between his birthplace of Shibamata, Tokyo, and various beautiful spots in Japan. (Tora visited Okinawa in the twenty-fifth episode.) "Free and Easy" is closely related to that series, since it is produced by Shochiku, scripted by Yamada Yōji (the director/creator of Tora-san), and was first released in double features with Tora-san films.

The Okinawa that Hama-chan visits in *Free and Easy 11* is an exchangeable commodity: just another attractive destination for the tourist fisherman and the audience to visually consume (as in Aichi's Irago Point in the first film, or Iwate's Kamaishi in number six). The logic of tourism, combining attractive authenticity, renewal, and inevitable return home, is played out in this use of Okinawa. Clearly the intended audience is mainland Japanese. After a company colleague, Usami, transfers to the Okinawa branch and buys an old Okinawan fishing boat (*sabani*), Hama-chan's envy spurs a desire to go to Okinawa even if it is, as he jokes, over his wife's dead body. Su-san's business trip there gives Hama-chan this opportunity, and Okinawa proves heavenly. However, the old engine of Usami's *sabani* fails, leaving him and Hama-chan stranded on a deserted island with only one palm tree. Okinawa now turns into a sunny hell, one humorously spiced with Hama-chan's homosocial delusions that Usami is his wife. His only wish now is to return home.

Okinawa thus promises the fulfillment of a fantasy that mainland Japan is unable to fulfill, one tied to a nostalgic past (the *sabani*'s engine is hand cranked), which invites the tourist to leave home and country. The experience of exotic otherness and authenticity is only meant to be temporary: At best, it reminds one of home, reaffirming the authenticity there; at worst, it reconfirms that the other is not the self (the *sabani* is too old and conks out in the rain, Okinawa is too hot, etc.). Okinawa's difference thus functions primarily as a space of renewal that ultimately demands a return to the mainland. This narrative of renewal is given specific form in the film in the case of Su-san. He has left Tokyo troubled: An American business consultant has recommended that the company undergo restructuring, a step that would necessitate firing many employees, especially someone as lazy as Hama-chan. However, the president's encounter in Okinawa with a fortyish woman taxi driver, who has inherited her small taxi company after her husband's death, offers him a reencounter with the Japanese corporate ideal of company as family. She actually cleans and cooks for her drivers, doing the best she can to keep the company together. Su-san's faith in Japanese business practices—dying out in Tokyo but still alive in Okinawa—is restored and he returns to Tokyo to snub the American and reconfirm his parental care for his employees, including Hama-chan. Against a background of real-life company restructuring, increased unemployment, corporate and government corruption, and a perceived decline in social stability in the 1990s, such cinematic tours of Okinawa promise fictional recuperation for weary mainland spectators.

In *Free and Easy 11*, tourism is a national practice shifting back and forth between sameness and difference. Okinawa is both the other that reminds one of the benefits of home, and the lost self that, once found, restores Japanese uniqueness. Visiting Okinawa reunifies the nation, first, because it is reinserted through the "Free and Easy" series into a chain of commodified equivalences with other parts of Japan, and second, because it reconfirms common memory and history. Episode 11 does not ignore the war or the U.S. military bases. The driver takes Su-san to visit the peace memorials, and military jets are clearly present in at least one shot. Neither item is stressed or leaves any significant mark on the subsequent narrative, but both occasion a unity between Okinawan and mainlander. Su-san actually tells the driver that he was a military construction officer stationed in Okinawa for a time during the war. The potential conflict raised in such an admission—recalling the oppression of Okinawans by the Japanese military during the war—is elided by the driver's change in attitude: She is instead happy to hear that and now treats Su-san not as a customer but as a friend, inviting him to her house for a home-cooked meal. Both are now Japanese, even if this means ignoring the specific tragedy of Okinawa (note that Su-san declines to visit the memorial to the school girls of *The Tower of Lilies;* narratively this is because he is too depressed by the corporate decision pressed upon him, but it also implies he is tired of hearing wartime stories).

As is perhaps appropriate to a fishing movie, Okinawa is best symbolized by fish. At one point, there is a cut from Usami and Hama-chan deliriously catching an abundance of tropical fish to some fish underwater. While the muffled voices of the two are still audible, as if we are hearing them from underwater, we then see Su-chan and the diver watching these fishes in an aquarium. The spatial connection is, of course, impossible, but associational montage and the sound bridge set the stage for Su-san's comment: "When one sees these fish swimming freely in the aquarium, one gets doubts about fishing." The spatial association implies that these words are directed in part at Hama-chan, critiquing his compulsion to catch fish, and thus underlines the fact that, despite the film's English title "Free and Easy," the text never fully backs his preference for fishing over work obligations. Su-san's concern also relates to Okinawa, for, although he, too, desires to come to Okinawa to fish and consume the idyllic Okinawa just as Hama-chan does, Su-san reins himself in and limits that consumption (the tourist must never "go overboard" or "go native," as Usami and Hama-chan seem to do in their native *sabani*). The tourist must return home and leave the site alone before its authenticity is destroyed. The irony, of course, is that the fish he calls "free" are contained in a tank, just as the touristic Okinawa is free and authentic only to the degree it is confined to the mainland discourse of authenticity.[9]

An independent production, *The Legacy of the Sea, Sky, and Reef* has fewer financial ties to tourism, but it offers more of the touristic pleasure of visual spectacle than does *Free and Easy*. The story focuses on a single mother, Etsuko,[10] who, unhappy about her relationship with a boyfriend, returns from the mainland to her home on a small Okinawan island with her young teenage daughter Kaori in tow. The film shifts back and forth between different characters on the isle, including Etsuko's parents, her former classmate Kenzō, and especially Takashi, a boy Kaori's age whose father has died at sea. While becoming friends with Kaori, Takashi is also learning the fishing trade from his grandfather, and it is his trips to sea with Kaori and the other children that offer the most striking views of beautiful Okinawan nature. The narrative, at its source, feeds off the touristic fantasy of immersion and renewal before return. One of the central plot lines is Kaori's shift from outsider, ignorant of local customs and teased by the island children, to acceptance by the group, and thus participation in a deep experience of another land and culture that any tourist would dream of. At the same time, Etsuko, defined by her clothing as a city woman despite her Okinawan birth, also ultimately finds energy (*genki*) in her visit to Okinawa, and thus the ability to return to the mainland and continue on her own.

The paradox of *The Legacy of the Sea, Sky, and Reef* is that its visual aesthetics and music render Okinawa traditional and natural only through a contemporary set of "artificial" signs. The film values the transmission of traditional knowledge of nature, but in terms of its own film style, there is nothing in its knowledge (articulation) of nature that is analogous to this traditional form; little differentiates it from a skillful Discovery Channel documentary. Note that Shiina has made a small movie career out of pursuing similar themes (the value of traditional knowledge, the importance of harmony with nature, etc.) in spaces such as Mongolia (*White Horse* [*Shiroi uma*, 1995]) as well as other natural locales in Japan. Okinawan dialect and music does repeatedly appear on the soundtrack of *The Legacy of the Sea, Sky, and Reef*, but, interestingly, those aural signs of specificity disappear at many crucial moments when music is called on to participate in the narrative enunciation. A good example is when the children go diving at sea, a pivotal scene emphasizing the bounty of the ocean and the coral reefs that define and defend the island. The musical score, far from emphasizing a special Okinawan relationship with nature, uses a recognizable, globalized, new age style featuring flowing synthesizers that offers spectators a clear emotional reading of this narratively and visually spectacular moment.

The otherness of Okinawa in these two films is restrained and corralled by their styles of representation and rendered familiar and comprehensible within mainland codes. Difference, even when it is promoted in a touristic gaze, is ultimately domesticated within universalized signification systems like music or the narrative formulae of *Free and Easy* that render Okinawa understandable and assimilable to mainland audiences. Otherness itself, one could say, is not wholly other—incomprehensible and unknowable—but is instead readily legible to an implied reading community that, in the end, is homologous to the Japanese nation. I will argue later that the cinema of filmmakers like Kitano, Sai, and Takamine resists this representational containment of otherness, preserving its alterity. Before investigating their work, however, I want to explore a narrative of apparent respect for otherness that ultimately fails to undermine either the nationalistic or the touristic containment of Okinawan otherness.

THE OTHER REVIVING US: OKINAWA AND MAINLAND DISCONTENT

Quite a number of recent Japanese films use Okinawa to criticize some aspect of mainland Japan. One of the subplots of *The Legacy of the Sea, Sky, and Reef*, for instance, revolves around mainland businessmen inconspicuously buying up land on this quiet, pristine island in order to construct a large-scale resort. Some of the residents sell their land; others get enraged and chase the necktied salarymen down the street. The film never makes this a central issue, however, and thus refuses to become a work of environmental protest; its concern is with the transmission of traditional knowledge and communing with nature. Yet the resort development hovers in the background as a potential threat to end this legacy of nature and knowledge and ruin this island paradise. Audiences, by identifying with Etsuko, Kaori, and their friends and family, but also through a privileged opportunity to overhear two of the businessmen insult the Okinawans for their backwardness, are positioned on the side of the islanders in this possible conflict. *The Legacy of the Sea, Sky, and Reef* is by no means a political film, but it nonetheless constructs a spectatorship that ostensibly identifies with the margins against mainstream corporate Japanese.

This brings us back to a question originally posed of *Goodbye Japan!*: Why would a Japanese film take the side of "non-Japanese"—that is,

Okinawans—against Japan? And why would it assume that Japanese spectators desire this identification? In the genre of political cinema, articulation of an unfavorable image is designed to spur spectator action, but clearly neither *The Legacy of the Sea, Sky, and Reef* nor *Goodbye Japan!* depicts haughty mainland Japanese in order to call for political change.[11] Indeed, the representational processes within *Goodbye Japan!*, far from undermining conventional articulations of self and other, utilize sympathy for the other as a means of rejuvenating a deteriorating national imaginary.

Goodbye Japan! sets up a series of binary oppositions that, in one form or another, are often present in Japanese films on Okinawa, but which appear here in more exaggerated form. The island is embedded in spacious, picturesque nature, while the Tokyo visible in the film is a mass of traffic jams. The islanders are a deeply religious people, who observe the taboos and follow the advice of their priestess (*miko*), while mainland construction companies violate sacred land and even the Okinawan bureaucrats who visit the new "nation" in the film ridicule its "backward" spirituality. Akaoneko's culture celebrates its natural abundance, but the Okinawan governor is portrayed as a fat glutton who merely consumes and wastes. The extremity of these oppositions contributes to the comedy (though to my mind, it conforms too much to stereotypes of Okinawa to be truly funny). Yet what is more important to this study is the absence of "regular" mainlanders from these oppositions. While everyday Tokyo is included in some of the contrasts, in general, the counterpoint to the Akaoneko residents is the bureaucratic and governmental elite of Japan. The opposition in *Goodbye Japan!* is less "Akaoneko versus Japan," than "Akaoneko versus the Japanese bureaucracy."

There is a long tradition in postwar mainstream cinema of criticizing the elite, especially in war films, in which officers and politicians are condemned for their misuse of power and authority. Responsibility for the war is often projected onto such figures, thus clearing nonelite Japanese (and the emperor) of guilt. *Goodbye Japan!* mirrors these texts, as well as other contemporary discourses criticizing the bureaucracy, but the opposition it relies on is slightly different: Instead of the conflict "Japanese versus the bureaucrats," it is reformatted as an antagonism between an ethnic or cultural other and the bureaucrats. Structurally, spectators are encouraged to identity neither with Okinawans as essentially the same as Japanese nor with Japanese mainlanders in opposition to Okinawans who are "different," but rather with Okinawa against representatives of the Japanese bureaucratic elite.[12] There is a touch of the touristic attraction to the exotic other, but the other in this case is actively rebelling against what is supposedly the national self (to Japanese viewers). Precisely because ordinary Japanese are missing in the opposition "Akaoneko versus the Japanese bureaucracy," we must ask what the film offers to them.

A clue can be found in another contemporary genre that similarly encourages Japanese spectators to identify with the other: the *kaijū* or monster in monster films. Kaneko Shūsuke, in his remakes of the "Gamera" films (e.g., *Gamera the Guardian of the Universe* [*Gamera daikaijū kūchū kessen*, 1995]) and in horror movies like *Crossfire* (*Kurosufaiya*, 2000), in particular has pursued a certain tradition in the monster genre of siding with the monster. In Kaneko's hands, Gamera is a hard-to-understand creature, battling even worse monsters, but often at the cost of slaughtering thousands of innocent people. Gamera's otherness is thus foregrounded, something evinced by the fact that Gamera is hated by most people in the narrative. Nonetheless, the film's spectators are given the "minority" position of sympathy for his predicament. A similar structure can be found in *Crossfire*, a horror film about a race of oppressed peoples with the power of pyrokinesis (the ability to start fires mentally). The heroine Junko, a descendant of these fire users, is, like Gamera, an essentially good person in possession of horrible powers that are not always in her control. We spectators identify with her and her desire for normalcy and equality, but when she tries to halt a series of brutal thrill killings, she becomes the monster to all the authorities represented in the film. This is a melodramatic turn, but it is clearly aligned in the film with a history of systematic oppression of the minority by the majority. *Crossfire*, like *Goodbye Japan!*, asks its spectators to side with the "other" against the representatives of "good" society.

One can sense in these films dissatisfaction with a post-Aum, post-bubble Japan of corruption, widespread unemployment, crime, and insecurity. Yet *Crossfire*'s sympathy for the other in no way undermines the basic binary opposition between self and other. In fact, since the evil mastermind behind the thrill killings turns out to be Hasegawa, a top police official, the articulations of self and other are merely reversed. The conventional modes of representing the other (as inhuman, irrational, etc.) are all transferred onto Hasegawa and his ilk, and socially valorized qualities are confirmed in the "monster." Spectator identification with the other is then less a first step in breaking down the structures of identity that created the monstrous other (using the different to define the self) than a convenient means of distancing the viewer from corrupt authorities and the forces that oppressed Junko's ancestors in the first place. Although contemporary criticism of corrupt established authority probably lay in the background of *Crossfire*, the film in effect seeks a renewal of the corroded self by appropriating the purity of victimization of the other.

Goodbye Japan! operates essentially along the same lines. The Okinawan governor and officials are not monsters, but they are definitely opposed to the "we" constructed for the spectator through conventional structures of identification. Perhaps this framing of Okinawan bureaucrats alleviates the guilt of ordinary Japanese in the oppression of Akaoneko (Okinawa) and enables them to identify with the purity of the rebellious islanders. What is renewed through this identification with the other is precisely the nation, the one ruined by these wasteful and destructive forces. The film is, after all, the story of the birth of a nation, of "love for the land" (which, to Oshire, defines a person), and of fighting and dying for that nation. These values, as popular nationalists like the influential manga artist Kobayashi Yoshinori currently complain, are precisely what is lacking in a contemporary Japan rendered weak, by affluence, Americanism, and the pernicious influence of the left. *Goodbye Japan!* promises fulfillment of the nationalist desire for these values without the historical baggage of war and oppression. (The memory of wartime Japan's military offenses against Okinawan "imperial subjects" is interestingly elided when Self-Defense Force jets prepare to bomb these Akaoneko others who are supposedly part of the nation.) Just as *Crossfire* simply transferred the self onto the other, *Goodbye Japan!*, by creating a new nation apart from Japan, projects a reborn Japan away from its history and onto this Akaonekoan/ Okinawan space.

It is significant that the central symbol of not only the Akaoneko state but also the cinematic representation of that space, is the sun, which appropriately sits in the middle of its national flag, just like Japan's. Akaoneko is a model of what Japan should be (or should have been): full of people, defined through identification with the soil, who love the nation, respect the environment, are self-sufficient, and behave as pacifist world leaders, capable of manipulating the Americans. Conveniently, they are also in possession of oil. As such, the "independence" depicted here is really the manifestation of Japanese fantasies. While nationhood causes a loss of innocence (symbolized by the loss of Sachiko, the child-like oracle, at the end), it reaffirms a culturally essentialist conception of identity, as well as other markers of the state, such as masculinity (Oshire, with his many lovers, is praised as the most "proficient" of world leaders), patriarchy (Oshire evinces knowledge of the sacred texts superior to that of the female *miko*), and capitalism (since the discovery of oil ensures the island's future riches). The title speaks of a farewell to Japan, but note that graphically, a Japanese expression, "sayonara," is followed by a hybrid mix, in which *katakana* syllables, often used for foreign loan words, spell *nippon* (an old-fashioned reading of the national name). Perhaps, then, the projection of nation onto Okinawa is precisely a farewell to this corrupted mixture and a return to the culturally pure.

DETACHING FROM THE APPROPRIATED OTHER

Goodbye Japan! paradoxically supports an independent Okinawa in order to confirm a unified Japan. This stance, however, is not simply a result of its narrative decisions. While the film could have been more critical of this point by inserting everyday Japanese into an opposition "Akaoneko" versus "Japan," the cinematic structures of the film themselves fail to implicate spectators in the governmental neglect depicted by the movie. Instead, through point-of-view shots and other filmic devices, audiences are inserted into an unproblematic identification with the islanders that, by placing them on the side of the Akaonekoans, not only excuses them from being the target of the movie's (minimally) critical gaze but also allows them to temporarily forget their own difference from these other people (in experience and memory) and vicariously enjoy the birth of a "true" nation.

The film's offering of a vicarious experience of otherness, soon to be reinserted into the national fold, is due significantly to its usage of two visual styles dominant in contemporary Japanese cinema and television, one a contemporary version of the classical Hollywood style,[13] the other a valorization of spectacle. Both ultimately reduce alterity to the understandable codes of the nation. In the first case, a version of the classical Hollywood style remains prominent in films like *Free and Easy 11* and in present-day Japanese television drama. As with the classical style, the central ideological imperative is narrative clarity, in which cinematic devices are mobilized to analyze, emphasize, and then reemphasize narrative points for the viewer. Cinematic devices such as editing, framing, and variable camera distance thus analyze the scene for maximum narrative lucidity and ease of understanding. Ambiguity is strictly forbidden in a unified narrative with definite closure. Everything is ultimately explained for the audience (it is, in many ways, a cinema of the obvious), which can merely follow along passively. Within this style, what characters think and feel is rendered readily accessible, through point-of-view shots, music, and other codes of characterization. As a mode of knowledge, this style refuses all forms of alterity—except, of course, when it has been accommodated within character codes of, for instance, "evil" or "monstrosity" (as is the case with Hasegawa in *Crossfire*).

The other style, that of spectacle, does not necessarily obey the commands of narrative clarity but may reinforce national ideologies in different ways. Purely visual, as opposed to narrative, pleasure is predominant here, as the mise-en-scène, camera aesthetics, and editing are manipulated to visually offer viewers the new, the beautiful, the stimulating, and the stunning. Understanding what is seen or said is less important than aesthetics and spectacle. This style has become prominent in recent American film largely due to the influence of television (especially commercials and music videos) and the changing economics of film making and viewing, but Japanese cinema of the 1970s through the 1990s has largely maintained the classical style. However, young directors such as *Goodbye Japan!*'s Tsutsumi Yukihiko utilize spectacle to reify and visually commodify the object of their glances, reducing the films to the (often national) codes of what the viewer can consume and find visually pleasing.[14]

These two styles work in different directions—one toward narrative, the other toward spectacle—even though in today's cinema they are often combined. What is important here, however, is the fact that each effectively delineates others within cinematic codes of knowledge and visuality that appropriate the other by implied spectators whose boundaries are seen to overlap those of the nation. Audiences, by going along with these codes, can end up confirming them and the national boundaries they imagine. And, alternative representations of Okinawa—for instance, those hoping to narrate the truth of Okinawa's suffering under American or Japanese domination—cannot easily avoid the implications that style poses on their own political project. Films such as *Gama: The Getto Flower* (*Gama: Getto no hana*) or the documentary *The Untaught War: Okinawa—The Fight of Ahagon Shōkō and Iejima Island* (*Oshierarenakatta sensō: Okinawa-hen—Ahagon Shōkō, Iejima no tatakai*), for instance, do tell much about the history of the Battle of Okinawa and postwar Okinawan struggles over the memory of that event and its lingering effects (the American bases, etc.). As an exercise in remembering, for instance, *Gama* effectively depicts the tragic contradictions wartime Okinawans faced, such as discrimination by Japanese and "suicides" more forced than voluntary. However, by being filmed in the same classical style as *Free and Easy*, even *Gama*'s more "truthful" narrative may, within the political dynamics of style in contemporary Japanese cinema, leave Okinawa appropriable within codes of national knowledge.

A number of contemporary filmmakers have consciously chosen alternative styles precisely because they see stylistic decisions as politically important. Their focus has been on how to depict the other in its otherness. While not all have taken up the question of Okinawa in their films, a brief introduction to their stylistic choices provides a crucial context to understanding not only why Okinawa has become an issue in recent cinema, but also how Okinawa has been alternatively represented and the meanings of those different styles. One young director, Aoyama Shinji, for instance, has declared that cinema should revolve around "the sole point of how to treat the other from a political perspective," which, to him, means depicting it as something that "cannot be generalized or universalized"—that is, as something never fully knowable.[15] Directors such as Hashiguchi Ryōsuke and Suwa Nobuhiro have sought out cinematic means to respect the other through what I call the "detached style" to counter universalizing assumptions that the other is just like us and knowable. Whereas a more classical style would use close-ups and point-of-view shots to analyze narratively the scene and give spectators access to character psychology and emotion, thereby formulating an identity between viewer and character, the detached style maintains distance from the characters through long shots and a lack of point-of-view editing. There is also less use of analytic editing. Viewers are thus denied easy access to the individuals on the screen, who remain opaque and indeterminate. Filmmakers instead prefer long takes that maintain the ambiguity of the scene and demand that viewers read the image on their own. Asked to interpret for themselves, viewers remain detached from the individuals in the film, but never completely indifferent. They do concentrate on what is going on, but what matters is that this concentration refrains from invading or appropriating the other. In some films, such as Hashiguchi's *Like Grains of Sand* (*Nagisa no Shindobaddo*, 1995) and Suwa's *M/Other* (1999), this style is actually coupled with narratives that describe the harm created by knowing others, by violating their right to be different and free of prying eyes. The choice not to look, or at least to pull the camera back and let the characters act on their own is in many ways a cinematic style embodying an ethical stance toward the "Other." That project is aligned with other efforts to use Okinawa as a way both to critique the oppression of nationalistic knowledge in Japan and also to celebrate the possibilities inherent in difference and heterogeneity. While dominant representations of Okinawa place it in a shifting position between Japan's other and self, ultimately to confirm the nation, these alternative representations seek to separate Okinawa from the self, precisely in order to respect its otherness and undermine the homogenizing processes of the nation.

A HETEROGENEOUS JAPAN

Okinawa and the Ethnic Mix

Some of the directors who depict Okinawa, such as Sai Yōichi and Kitano Takeshi, utilize elements of the detached style as part of this larger effort to free the different, the individual, the other in all its forms, from nationalistic modes of representation. Neither Sai nor Kitano is exclusively concerned with elucidating the *specific* difference of Okinawa; rather, they use Okinawa to contest the versions of cultural homogeneity and essentialism that are at the heart of Japanese national ideology. Their concern is less with articulating Okinawan identity than dearticulating Japanese identity through forms of cinema that foreground otherness. Their approaches are varied and produce different results, but both share elements of the detached style. Sai celebrates heterogeneity by undermining the tendency of homogeneity to generalize all that are different. Kitano figures Okinawa as an empty space, often associated with death, that can denude Japanese identity itself.

As mentioned before, many films use Okinawa as a locale that essentially could have been filmed somewhere else. This could be said of the films of Sai Yōichi,[16] but in his films, this "somewhere else" is not a Japan of cultural and ethnic homogeneity. His films can be accused of using Okinawa for his own purposes, but unlike Imamura, for instance, he self-consciously undermines the "Japanese" position surrounding his films. Sai, a *zainichi* Korean, has always portrayed a heterogeneous Japan even in such seemingly innocuous teen pics as *The Flowering Asuka Gang* (*Hana no Asuka-gumi!*, 1988), an interest that perhaps stems not only from his heritage but also from his work as an assistant director for Ōshima Nagisa, who has a long history of decentering Japanese national identity through depictions of social marginals like Koreans (*Death by Hanging* (*Koshikei*, 1968) and Okinawans (*Dear Summer Sister* [*Natsu no imoto*], 1972). Sai is known for his award-winning comedic look at *zainichi* society, *All under the Moon* (*Tsuki wa dotchi ni dete iru*, 1993), but he is also the mainland director most consistently drawn to Okinawa. He has shot a total of four films in the region: *Rest in Peace My Friend* (*Tomo yo, shizuka ni nemure*, 1985), *Via Okinawa* (*A-Sain deizu*, 1989), *Attack* (*Shōgeki*, 1991), and *Pig's Revenge* (*Buta no mukui*, 1999).[17] The first three are basically genre films, but all share a concern for the chaotic, material/physical side of Okinawa.

Via Okinawa, for instance, is a narrative of Okinawan rock and rollers around the time of reversion based on the lives of Kyan Yukio and his wife Marie. Most of the story is set in a rock club catering to the American military (the "A-sign" of the original title refers to the permit the American military gave to clubs that GIs were allowed to enter). The band, The Bastards, plays American rock tunes for GIs, many of whom are about to be sent to Vietnam. Yet while there are plenty of fights between patrons and the band, there is no simple binary dividing Okinawan from American, nor any allegory of national conflict. Just as there are fisticuffs, there are also friendships between Okinawans and Americans; while the heroine Eri rejects her mother's invitation to come to the United States, she also is enamored of American rock. Yomota compliments the film's "cultural creolization of the rockers' experience, incapable of being perfect in either Japanese, Okinawan, or English." In the end, Sai neither idealizes this melting pot nor laments its lack of purity.

The nonsymbolic depiction of Okinawans as "minorities who don't belong to any community"[18] concerns Sai most, sharply distinguishing him from Miyamoto Amon, whose debut film *Beat* (1999) was set in about the same time and place. *Beat* neither critiques the Japanese myth of homogeneity nor employs the detached style. With "story help" from Matayoshi Eiki, the narrative of a meddlesome Okinawan bartender and the bar hostess he loves but can't quite measure up to, features interaction with GIs (somewhat sympathetically depicted) fearfully awaiting their call to Vietnam. Yet Miyamoto's mixture of historical reality and fantastic situations (e.g., a car flying through the air), coupled with stylish, often rhythmic editing, a garish color scheme, and artificial set design for the entertainment district, shapes his film as national allegory. One shot featuring a traumatized Takashi (the bartender), alone in a spotlight surrounded by darkness, dissolves to a map of Okinawa, with the island compositionally occupying the same spot on screen as Takashi. This obvious equation between Takashi and Okinawa ostensibly marks his character and experiences as those of Okinawa, and it is within these depictions that an Okinawan identity is performed. Takashi's experience is certainly that of trauma, a lack of power related to his tendency to escape when the going gets tough. The film implies that the solution to his trauma, and thus that of Okinawa, lies in a bold assertion of identity tied to place (the decision to stay put). That assertion is represented by the use of mortar flares, stolen from the American military, at both the beginning and the end of the film. Takashi launches the first, but the second both stops Takashi from leaving and brings Okinawa to the attention of the American astronauts circling in space. Through this phallic discharge, Okinawa has been recognized by the other. Yet as with *Goodbye Japan!*, there is always the danger that this confirmation of identity or nationhood translates less into an assertion of Okinawan independence than a reassertion of Okinawans' Japanese identity. Recognition by America has long been a Japanese cultural fantasy, and thus the astronaut's sighting of Okinawa, by furthering a slippage between Okinawa and Japan that pervades the film, can equally be a confirmation of Japan. In the end, without a clear difference asserted between Okinawa and Japan, Takashi can equally be the sign of the mainland, rendering Okinawa merely the subordinate space for playing out national desires.

Sai avoids Miyamoto's pitfalls by refusing the allegorical impulse through a style, influenced by the detached style, that is thoroughly grounded in the chaotic mundane. Take, for instance, his most recent film shot in Okinawa, *Pig's Revenge*, based on the Akutagawa Prize–winning story by Matayoshi Eiki (figure 10.1). The opening scenes, in which a herd of escaped pigs invades a bar and sends one of the young hostesses, Wakako, into a state of shock, invites a reading of essential Okinawan difference when the bar madam immediately asserts that Wakako has lost her "mabui" (Okinawan for "soul"). If this were *Goodbye Japan!* this would

Figure 10.1. Sai's *Pig's Revenge* resists categorizing Okinawan difference.
Source: Aaron Gerow film still.

be an assertion easily accepted, but in *Pig's Revenge,* Wakako simply gets up a minute later, as if nothing happened, in spite of the others' discussions about calling a *yuta* ("medium") to help her. Sai does not deny these spiritual beliefs, especially when the madam, Wakako, another hostess Shoko, and their customer, Shōkichi, travel to an island to pray at its *utaki* ("shrine"), but he renders them matter-of-factly, without explanation or characterization. Sai's select use of long shot, long take scenes, such as the lengthy scene when Shōkichi and Wakako meet and kiss on the porch, reinforces this sense of the unelucidated everyday. Since the camera is quite far from the two characters, who are partially in shadow, we are not quite sure what to make of their kissing and then their sudden parting. Especially since a romantic relationship doesn't really develop between the two, we are left with incomplete access to the characters' motivations and actions. Simply put, they and the other characters are so concretely mundane, with little abstract explanation or meaning attached to them, it is hard to insert them in allegorical categories like "Okinawa" or "Japanese." Yomota Inuhiko contrasts Ōshima, whose stories are "in the end events in a conceptual world traced along a historical temporal axis, to Sai, whose "world is spatial and physical."[19] We can only look at his characters from without, in space, their physicality preventing abstraction into a conceptual world.

The *utaki* the characters eventually pray to is not even an established one, but one Shōkichi just built for the bones of his father, who, after dying at sea twelve years before, was by custom given only a temporary above-ground burial. Shōkichi hopes that if they pray to his father, his father will become a god and help them. This is a very practical sense of religion. Note the difference between Shōkichi and Takashi in *The Legacy of the Sea, Sky, and Reef,* both of whom lost their fathers at sea: While Takashi resolutely works to carry on his island's heritage, Shōkichi remains ambivalent and confused—not taking over his father's profession, yet feeling he must bury him; reminded by elders about his father's wandering soul, yet ultimately creating a *utaki* on his own in his own way.

As Yomota notes, Sai's depiction of ethnic minorities "is in no way based on a humanistic desire to historically enlighten Japanese spectators, nor does it have a nationalistic motivation." Rather, by taking up "what postwar Japan has tried hard to ignore, such as the bases in Okinawa, left-wing internecine killings, the ennui of a lowly cop"[20]—by showing the differences elided in national and cultural generalizations, Sai focuses on singular realities which resist national metaphors and metanarratives. Sai's approach to difference recalls Naoki Sakai's distinction between specific difference (*sai*) and categorical difference (*shūsa*) when discussing the relationship between language and nationalism. At its most basic, cultural difference is on the level of the incomprehensible, something without limit. It is the process of language, and specifically articulation, that renders difference into categorical difference, and makes it comprehensible, limited, and acceptable by those who use the language. Categorical difference is the basis of the concept of race and ethnicity, so, to Sakai, nationalism, and its attendant ideology of discrimination, fundamentally arises through this process of rendering difference categorical.[21]

Sai Yōichi, I would argue, uses elements of the detached style to counter an analogous process in cinema; precisely by distancing his camera and his narrative stance from his Okinawan characters, he endeavors to resist the processes of categorization and limitation that render the other comprehensible and thus within national categories. It is, in effect, his emphasis on materiality which blocks the process of transforming his characters into signs of ethnicity. In a sense, Sai's conception of ethnicity is less as essence than as practical construction, where identity is an ungeneralizable factor of creation and inheritance, negotiation and acceptance. Whether Sai's perspective on Okinawa is that of an outsider is not the point. His cinema counters Japanese cultural essentialism and homogeneity by focusing on material specifics, the nonconceptualized differences that cannot be reduced to all-encompassing metanarratives such as the nation and its other.

Okinawa, Death, and the Limits of Nothingness

Kitano Takeshi (also known as Beat Takeshi), in his early films before *Fireworks* (*Hana-Bi*, 1998), also uses elements of the detached style to block the processes that appropriate Okinawa into the national imaginary. In fact, his camera aesthetics in *Boiling Point* (*3-4x10-gatsu*, 1990), and *Sonatine* (*Sonachine*, 1993) are so detached from the Okinawan other that it becomes denuded of any substance, with the result that any essential or national identities built in a dialectic of sameness and difference with Okinawa are themselves rendered empty. In Kitano, Okinawa becomes a space approximating death, one signaling the death of Japan itself.

The association between Okinawa and the borderline between life and death is evident in other films. For instance, Shimizu Hiroshi's black comedy *Ikinai* (1998) is all about a tour group who travel to Okinawa precisely in order to die, so that their families can earn the insurance money and pay off mounting debts. Miike Takashi's *The City of Lost Souls* (*Hyōryūgai*, 2000) ends with the main character trying to escape from Japan, only to be shot dead on an Okinawan beach.[22] Death on the border of Japan is not unusual in recent Japanese film; in fact, the inability to escape Japan is a prominent theme. Aoyama Shinji's debut film *Helpless*, for instance, features talk of the British television show *The Prisoner*, especially the episode in which Number 6 escapes The Village only to be tricked into returning to it.[23] The implication is that Aoyama's hero is helpless precisely because Japan is The Village, a closed society with no escape. Contemporary Japanese cinema in fact abounds with images of characters on the margins fleeing to the border areas of Japan, only to die there.[24]

Kitano Takeshi has developed the theme to the fullest that Okinawa is a liminal space in between life and death that reveals the emptiness of Japan itself. Okinawa has appeared in two of his films, *Boiling Point* and *Sonatine*, both times as a free space of play in contrast to the confined world of Tokyo. While the mainland city is a realm of dark lighting and confinement, both spatially and socially, the Okinawan beach is a bright expanse where Kitano's characters, who have in effect escaped from the mainland, can frolic in a virtual return to childhood. This opposition could replicate the touristic discourse of rejuvenation were it not for the fact that Okinawa here is an impossible space, equivalent to death, for characters too empty to be rejuvenated. In *Boiling Point*, two members of a sandlot baseball team, Masaki and Kazuo, venture to Okinawa to buy guns to rescue their manager, an ex-yakuza who has run afoul of the mob.

Yet as Yomota notes, there are no shots of them moving between Tokyo and Okinawa.[25] In fact, the shift to Okinawa is extremely jarring: One of them declares he is not going in one shot, while the next reveals them already there. This technique helps literally cut out a separate space for Okinawa that is both utterly mundane and unreal. An Okinawan gangster, Uehara, helps them acquire guns, but only by shooting an aloha-shirted American soldier willing to sell guns within yards of a U.S. military base. Uehara takes his share, leaving Masaki and Kazuo with large weapons and a dead body in plain view to all in the base. Impossibly, no one notices as they clumsily carry their weapons past the base fence; nor does anyone stop them when they wander around the airport with the barrel of a rifle clearly visible. These function, in part, as typical Kitano gags (some directed at the Americans), but they also render Okinawa a space where the normal rules of social action do not apply, where the abnormal is treated as the mundane. In particular, what is lacking here, as in the aftermath of the killing of the aloha-shirted soldier, is the reaction of others, something most notable in *Sonatine*. A mob lieutenant, Murakami, is sent to Okinawa with some men to help in a gang war, only to find out his boss is scheming to eliminate him. In the ensuing battles, all the killings take place without anyone, Okinawan or mainlander, screaming, crying, or batting an eyelid. This is not Japanese or yakuza stoicism but rather the absence of both other and self: other, in the sense that people don't respond to the doings of others, acting as if the other does not exist; self, in the sense that identity can only be constructed in a dialectic with the other. Without that reactive mirror of the other, the self is void.

Kitano's camera is so detached, then, that it fails to impart an internal life to its subjects. While Kitano does use more close-ups than other directors who employ the detached style, the faces seen are lifeless and deadpan, and the often abrupt editing fails to articulate them smoothly into a unity of space, narrative, and individual identity. He frequently uses long shots and rarely relies on point-of-view editing, so spectators have little access to these characters, who remain distinctly other: opaque, distant, and incomprehensible. They are in effect near death, with Okinawa a playful Valhalla enhanced by Kitano's close association of play and death. In Kitano's films, there is a pleasure in being nowhere, at no time—the pleasure of playing on the Okinawan beach—but it is always a short step away from annihilation: Murakami dreams of smiling as he shoots himself on the idyllic beach, and the mob's assassin also strikes there first. This deadly but pleasurable emptiness is, as I have argued elsewhere, not unrelated to issues of national identity.[26] As Uehara and his lieutenant head off for a showdown against a mob boss, they eliminate or abandon their others—those outside their male yakuza world—one by one: first the American GI, then a black woman, then the Tokyoites

Masaki and Kazuo, and then Uehara's moll. Generically, the film resembles 1960s Toei yakuza films, in which the hero must throw off the girl in order to participate in the male camaraderie of the revenge attack. But given Uehara, with his ambiguous but aggressive sexuality (he makes no distinction between raping his male lieutenant and raping a woman), and the lack of cathartic reaction shots, this elimination of the other practically performs the *reductio ad absurdum* of masculine Japaneseness, revealing its inherent emptiness. The films seem to argue that the relentless logic of the same, of appropriating the other within the self, paradoxically results in the denuding of Japanese identity itself. In Kitano's early films, where all identities, including the ethnic and the national, are rendered null, the opposition between Tokyo and Okinawa is ultimately ambivalent: Okinawa's freedom is ultimately death, while Tokyo is just as void of the other as is the pristine white island beach. To Kitano, Okinawa is both a space of escape and the pleasure of death, the confirmation of the meaningless of identity and the impossibility of escape.

This use of Okinawa as a liminal space between life and death speaks little of the people who live there, but it reveals the emptiness of a mainland Japan that has no concern for the everyday existence of others like Okinawans (and Koreans, Burakumin, Ainu, etc.). Kitano's Okinawa is undoubtedly a creation of certain Japanese desires, but instead of a space of redemption or rejuvenation, it simply promises the end of it all for the weary Japanese. Kitano turns the Japanese gaze on Okinawa back on Japan, to reveal nothing there.

Thus, various mobilizations of the detached style in representations of Okinawa operate to free its inhabitants from cinematic processes that assume knowledge of Okinawa and tie it into mainland assumptions about cultural essence, homogeneity, and national identity. The stylistic choices of Sai and Kitano reemphasize the point that politically progressive representations of Okinawa cannot be effected simply by creating more accurate or authentic content but must work against dominant cinematic styles that can appropriate those "more accurate" images within cinematic codes of national understanding. I do not, however, wish to assert a one-to-one correspondence between style and politics or to argue that there is one style that best represents the Okinawan other. Film style is inherently multivalent, and it only assumes a political tendency in interaction with surrounding discursive conditions. The detached style, for instance, can operate to cinematically respect the otherness of the other in part because it is in contrast with dominant styles, like the classical or the spectacular, which appropriate the other. This multivalency, however, suggests potentially problematic articulations of the detached style, some of which are evident in particular films. With Sai's work, for instance, the detached style renders his characters mundanely physical, but by denying access to their psychology, it can potentially render the thoughts and feelings of the characters irrelevant for a viewer or even assert their absence altogether. Indeed, Kitano did that in his early films, albeit in a critique also directed at Japanese. However, in another problem, his association of death with the border can imply that life outside Japan is impossible (an implication played out in his more nationalistic *Brother* [2001][27]). Separating the camera and the viewer from the Okinawan other protects it from the power of interpretation of camera/viewer and so maintains the otherness of Okinawa, but often this is achieved at the expense of communication, conveying a lack of involvement. That distance also can turn into aesthetic detachment, again rendering the other into spectacle. Such detachment is evident in *The Legacy of the Sea, Sky, and Reef,* which sometimes uses a narratively slower, more distanced camera style to evoke the leisurely pace of island life and insert its characters in the landscape, thereby unfortunately equating the islanders with the beautiful waves and island landscape.

The main problem with the detached style is that detachment is a spatial operation that demands a point from which the object is detached. The other is spatially freed from the operations of the interpreting subject, but there is still a site/sight from which it is being viewed. This geography interpolates a viewing subject, defined as that which watches, against an other that is watched. The danger, then, is that the detached style can reproduce, especially in relation to a cultural other such as Okinawa, a version of "us" (the viewers) versus "them" (the Okinawans being viewed). Some of the most interesting filmmakers—such as Aoyama—in contemporary Japanese cinema, however, use elements of the detached style to critically address the problem of reinforcing the binary of the other against the nation. Takamine Go, especially in his most recent work, *Tsuru-Henry,* has used a different approach, the multiple perspectives of collage, to upset the viewer/viewed binary, encourage difference against homogeneity, and propose a wandering form of Okinawan identity that strategically uses articulation of that identity to mold, reshape, and reinterpret place and memory.

COLLAGE AND THE ARTICULATION OF OKINAWA MEMORY

Takamine Go is one of the few directors born in Okinawa to enter the commercial industry. We should not, however, focus on his work simply because of the location of his birth. The only other significant commercial filmmaker born there, Shinjō Taku, has been condemned by some film critics for creating "banal images [of Okinawa] on the level of 'Yamato-uchinā'"[28] and thus a form of "self-orientalism" in which Okinawans adopt the mainland's vision, performing stereotypes in a form of self-abnegation.[29] Takamine's work is important because it successfully challenges the dominant representations of Okinawan identity that Shinjō accepts, using representational strategies to contest and reshape definitions of that identity.

Takamine began making experimental films while studying art in Kyoto. He is best known for the 35mm commercial films *Paradise View* and the award-winning *Untamagiru* (1989), both of which are almost entirely in Okinawan dialect. His early work, like *Sashin-gu* (1972), *Okinawan Dream Show* (*Okinawan dorimu sho*, 1974), and *Okinawan Chirudai* (1978), combined an articulation of Okinawan public history with issues of personal memory, influenced in part by the fact that Takamine's father died around the time that Okinawa reverted to Japan. His own life bridges different geographies; while he is a staunch proponent of Okinawan culture, he has not lived there for over thirty years (he resides in Kyoto). I will, however, concentrate my analysis on his most recent work, *Tsuru-Henry*, which was made on video then released theatrically (figure 10.2). This

Figure 10.2. Takamine's *Tsuru-Henry*: guerrilla performances for a multitextual moving Okinawa.

Source: Aaron Gerow film still.

work not only stresses the heterogeneity of Okinawa, disturbing any simple designation of self and other but also, far more than Sai or Kitano's films, foregrounds the problem of textuality and representation, thus emphasizing Okinawa as an issue of performance. In Takamine's politics of collage, historical realities and Okinawan memories are recombined to produce a rebellious subjectivity that evades both nationalistic and touristic discourses.[30]

Tsuru-Henry has less a story than a set of intermeshing texts that question the nature of textuality itself. Tsuru is a popular Okinawan singer who does live "guerrilla" radio performances across the islands (she is played by the singer Ōshiro Misako), by suddenly showing up in a location, hooking up a transmitter, and beginning to play. One day she finds the script for a movie, "Love's Love," in a tree. Visiting its author, the director Mekaru and learning that he has no interest in filming it, she decides to make it herself, using her karate expert son, Henry, to play the lead character, James. James, according to the script, is the product of the union between an Okinawan woman and a high commissioner of the U.S. Civil Administration of the Ryukyu Islands (USCAR), who goes to study film at UCLA in order to find his father. He finds out too much, however, and has his memory wiped out by the CIA (how, we don't know) before being sent home. *Tsuru-Henry* follows Tsuru's efforts to produce "Love's Love," but it is never just the story of the making of this film, since *Tsuru-Henry* and "Love's Love" overlap in crucial ways. Henry, according to Tsuru's not always reliable account, is also the son of a USCAR high commissioner. James and Henry are thus equated in a cinematic structure that consciously breaks down the borders between the "real" and the "fictional" worlds. In fact, Mekaru's script in the fiction is a version of a story Takamine intended to film in reality but could not because of financial and other considerations, taking the border-crossing between fact and fiction to another level. *Tsuru-Henry*, which includes many scenes of Henry shooting the film and even a sequence with cartoon drawings of the film's staff, is partially a fictional documentary of its own generation.

Just as *Tsuru-Henry* reflects on itself, different texts and media appear in this film mirroring and overlapping one another. These include Okinawan songs, painted posters (by Takamine himself), photographs, 8mm archival footage, drawings, performance art, and finally a theatrical staging. Utilizing the combinatory effects of video, Takamine presents visual images on screen in collage form, either through double and triple exposures or shots of collaged texts (like the script, which contains words, photographs, and drawings). *Tsuru-Henry* is also replete with songs in different styles and languages, and the verbal texts are overlapped as well: The dialog often shifts from standard Japanese to Okinawan to Chinese to English, sometimes in midsentence. Takamine's film is a veritable rainbow of cultures, as the series of rainbows and prisms on screen attest. But it is also a multiplicity of perspectives, of different texts (some of which are not Takamine's) that prismatically refract the vectors of vision and undermine any effort to construct a singular viewing subject. Far more than Sai's and Kitano's films, the unity of the text itself is under question as many visions and voices resound throughout *Tsuru-Henry*.

The basic division of "us" versus "them," implied in the detached style, is problematized through a more nomadic form of identity. Kosa, Mekaru's neighbor, at one point kids Tsuru about depending on another person's script, asking, "Don't you want to free yourself from the 'Base as Salvation Economy and the Dependency Culture'?" The question echoes debates within Okinawa over the problem of the economic dependence of Okinawa, which lacks a strong productive foundation, on the U.S. military bases. While Takamine is certainly critical of the bases, he uses Tsuru's reply to Kosa to critique the "us" versus "them" binary assumed in that statement. Tsuru says, "I am a Ryūkyūan folk movie wanderer once known as 'Movin' Tsuru'; by character, I can't ignore a scenario I've picked up." She thus asserts a freedom to strategically move between positions and identities, a situation that many Okinawans find themselves in as a matter of necessity but that Takamine seems to assert they can strategically use. The nickname "Movin' Tsuru" (*katsudō no Tsuru*[31]), in its polysemy, actually implies multiple identities: moving Tsuru, Tsuru of the movies, and even activist Tsuru. As an artist, she constantly moves in space, performing just about anywhere, willing to use just about anything. At one point, she even appropriates the infamous "Zō no ori"[32] to broadcast her show, to distinctly collage-like effect: Her song gets mixed both with American army radio and a Chinese rendition of "The Internationale" that the listening station is monitoring. This is not presented as an affront to the purity of her Okinawan song, since later in Taiwan she does another show deliberately combining her Okinawan lyrics with other musicians singing in Chinese.

The film's refusal to distinguish identities essentially through a narrative of origins extends to its playful use of DNA. Mekaru studies DNA to confirm his origins, claiming that he descends, on his father's side, from a nationalist leader who escaped to China in 1879 when the Ryūkyūs were forcibly annexed by Japan, and on his mother's, from the adopted child of Commodore Perry. He laments that he is like a "*machibui* rolling stone" (*machibui* being both an Okinawan word for "chaos" and a central motif in the film), and claims this chaotic mixture of different tendencies "is without a doubt determined by the genes of Commodore Perry and the Okinawan nationalist." The assertion is of course symbolic of differences in Okinawa's past that have mixed to form the present, but the association with DNA is absurd: He could not possibly bear the genes of the *adoptive* parent of his ancestor. Critiquing essentialized conceptions of identity, the film asserts that Mekaru is confused not because he combines two essentially different genetic lineages but because of the way his origins have been articulated historically. Mekaru is associated in the film with James, the mixed-race child who is himself linked with other characters like Henry, who plays him in "Love's Love," and Kosa, who plays him in theatrical performance. The confusion James and Mekaru experience is in part allegorical of Okinawa, but given James's lack of identity (the different actors, the different voices), his representation of Okinawa is only of an Okinawa whose identity itself is unrepresentable, preserving its otherness, but without either asserting a subject viewing it from afar or aligning the film's viewers with that subject. James's voice-over admits to this lack of identity when he declares, "I am not an American. I am not a Japanese. I might not even be an Okinawan." Takamine echoes this himself; having lived in Kyoto for the last thirty years, he is sometimes described as a mainlander by Okinawans and as an Okinawan by mainlanders.[33]

Music is central to Takamine's work, but the mixing of sounds and music rarely matches rhythms on the aural register, let alone creates a utopian synthesis between bodies and sound.[34] Music is only one element in the narrative world of the film, and in the collage of *Tsuru-Henry*, it collides and overlaps with other elements. During the final theatrical performance, the opera singer Kaneshima Reiko suddenly stands up from the audience and begins singing. The audience reaction, "Ah, that opera singer's come again," is both bemused and detached, glad to have her there, but not necessarily joining in the chorus. Without a love story to unite all these disparate elements, *Tsuru-Henry* emphasizes the confusion of a colonized culture as well as the thrill of manipulating elements in a collage.

The latter is in effect what Tsuru does, and thus she becomes a model for what *Tsuru-Henry* and Takamine are attempting. As mentioned earlier, she is a guerrilla performer who has no problem in using the material of another; she has little desire for authentic, original expression. Yet at the same time, she is not merely inheriting the texts of others. As is noted in the film, she rewrites Mekaru's script, drawing in new texts such as the theater performance, and even broadcasting on her own without permission from her station. Her activism is less one of original creation than articulation, taking what is already there and shaping it through collage, action, and performance. Her texts (and *Tsuru-Henry* itself) thus do not presume a unified point of knowledge—in the form of an author, a viewer, or a nation—that restricts Okinawa to the homogenizing, essentializing, identifying gaze. Rather, they wander through different points, strategically multiplying and combining different views of Okinawa and expanding them often in productive directions (e.g., potential solidarity with Taiwan and the rest of Asia, suggested by Tsuru's trip to Taipei).

That Takamine's Okinawa is similarly a process of articulation is evident from the film's theme of memory. Memory, particularly the memory of what has been lost, is often an important subject in Takamine's films, but in *Tsuru-Henry*, the loss of memory is central. This loss can be related to American rule and the accompanying *machibui*, both of which can be seen as tragic states. Takamine is keenly aware of the disappearance of not only the memory of the war and the American occupation but also of Okinawan cultural heritage. *Tsuru-Henry* offers reminders of this history, as well as a virtual catalog of famous Okinawan songs. Yet unlike his earlier films, *Paradise View* and *Untamagiru*, which sometimes work toward preserving the purely Okinawan, the film consciously avoids a serious program of historical recollection, in favor of a more jesterlike play with Japanese and American identities, and the possibilities of rearticulating Okinawa. Takamine remains conscious of the historical background of Okinawa's chaotic *machibui*, but his solution here is not the assertion of an ideally unchaotic state but rather positive use of memory within life as a "rolling stone." In Tsuru's rewritten story, James learns from his mother that his American father was in fact a supporter of Okinawan independence, knowledge that the CIA wanted to suppress. He learns this, however, only after he has caught fire and just before he walks into the sea to die with his mother. This tragic end, which several commentators have felt invokes the memory of Buddhist monks who immolated themselves in protest of the Vietnam War, is partially rendered as an absurdly everyday event: a man actually comes up to the burning James and asks him for a light—and James obliges. James's effort to remember his father is also contrasted to Henry, who has no interest in learning about his father. Memory in *Tsuru-Henry* is less an absolute necessity than a matter of practical choice and action within a struggle over the past.

This past is constantly reinterpreted and revived in the film. Toward the conclusion, *Tsuru-Henry* shows 8mm footage of the aftermath of an anti-American riot in Kōza in 1970, mixed with James's voice-over and a musical imitation of Jimi Hendrix by Tsuru. Nakahara Shogo describes how the continuation of the music into the riot footage gives it "the color of a carnival." This device not only reinterprets the riot, it detaches its images from the existing definitions of the riot "in a political context as a necessary protest against the power structure of ruler and ruled." Nakahara does not reject those definitions but praises Takamine's effort to "defamiliarize" present versions of memory and reconsider the original event.[35] The effect of Takamine's collage of memories, then, is to render the past strange, to take it out of both the realm of forgetfulness and the confines of existing discourses, in order that it may be seen anew, realigned with other factors, and even reinvented.

The best example of this in *Tsuru-Henry* is the *rensageki* performance at the end. *Rensageki* was a popular form of performance mixing scenes on stage with scenes filmed; in a performance, these staged scenes and scenes on film using the same actors would be presented alternately in a kind of "chain" (the "rensa" of *rensageki*, which is sometimes translated "chain drama") to compose a single story. This performance form was quite popular on the mainland in the 1910s until theater fire safety regulations, which banned the showing of films (which were made of flammable stock in those days) in stage theaters unequipped for motion pictures, made them more difficult to perform. Yet while *rensageki* largely died out in the mainland, except for some avant-garde appropriations, the form continued well into the 1960s in Okinawa, and it was one of the few kinds of film produced locally. *Tsuru-Henry* revives this form, but, in Takamine's words, "That is not just a reproduction of old-time rensageki, but an attempt to bring it back to life as a new mode of expression."[36] Thus, while the stage scenes are shown in *Tsuru-Henry* in what is practically a documentary of a theater performance, the film scenes not only use different "actors" (Kosa for the stage James, Henry for the film James), they are not shown to the audience in the world of the film, but directly to us. This new kind of *rensageki*, mixing stage and video, in some ways epitomizes the style of *Tsuru-Henry* itself. Takamine's text then, in its very form, is both the embodied memory of the Okinawan past and a restructuring of that past to intersect with a variety of present-day forces. In this process, Okinawa, like Tsuru, wanders between the past and the present, bearing the burden of the past yet taking multiple views to rework it into new forms of expression.

CONCLUSION

I have shown how dominant representations of Okinawa in contemporary Japanese film enact for spectators the power relations that render Okinawa both different and the same within Japanese national identity, ultimately confining it to regimes of knowledge that rob Okinawa of its alterity. The films of Sai, Kitano, and others remind us that cultural resistance against such depictions can never simply be on the level of offering more accurate and authentic images but must contest cinematic structures that reinforce the nationalist tendency to appropriate and absorb the other.

Takamine's work, however, makes the argument that the struggle over representations of Okinawa is not just over how the islands are represented or a matter of delineating "good" and "bad" cinematic strategy. While, as we have seen, mainland representations of Okinawa try to revive a unity in the Japanese national imaginary, Takamine, the jesterlike guerrilla artist, deftly advocates an Okinawa that celebrates its own shifting collage of political positions. In his own way, Takamine is adding a voice to debates over political action in Okinawa itself. He seems to argue for the mobilization of multiple "hows," of a kaleidoscope of perspectives that not only frees Okinawa from mainland definitions, but also prevents the self-defeating problem of creating essentialized and permanent self-definitions of Okinawa. Against an Okinawa confined by mainland representations, he and Movin' Tsuru sing overlapping songs of a movin' Okinawa.

NOTES

1. When available, I have used official English titles. Otherwise, translations are my own.

2. I concentrate here on analysis of textual strategies and their intertextual and discursive contexts, to emphasize these often conscious tactics. I plan a subsequent study of the reception of these films.

3. Takamine's real name is Takamine Tsuyoshi, but he often uses the reading "Go" as his directing name.

4. Two lists of films related to Okinawa can be found in Nakae Yūji and Nakae Motoko, "Okinawa eigashi," in *Okinawa poppu karucha*, ed. Tenku Kikaku (Tokyo: Tokyo Shōseki, 2000), 154–75; and Iki Ichirō, *Eizo bunkaron: Okinawa hatsu* (Naha-shi: Henshu Kobo Toyo Kikaku, 2000), 55–57.

5. Matsuda Masao, "Ryūkyū eiga no tame no memorandamu: Okinawa wa ika ni egakarete wa naranai ka," *Gendaishi techō* 34, no. 10 (October 1991): 110. The film scholar Yomota Inuhiko relates this mode of representation to conceptions of the nation:

> In [*The Tower of Lilies*], there is absolutely no idea that Okinawans during the war were subject to linguistic and ideological identity formation under the discriminatory gaze of mainlanders. The young women, up to the instant of their deaths, use the same standard Japanese as mainlanders. . . . Undoubtedly Imai Tadashi believed that the mentality of these Okinawan girls was completely identical to that of mainland girls.

In this representation, the purity and lack of difference of the Okinawan Lilies molded them as the "representatives of Japanese defined as war victims." Yomota Inuhiko, "Okinawa to eiga," *Geijutsugaku kenkyū* 11 (2001): 52.

6. See Alan Christy, "The Making of Imperial Subjects in Okinawa," in *Formations of Colonial Modernity in East Asia*, ed. Tani E. Barlow (Durham, N.C.: Duke University Press, 1997).

7. Yomota Inuhiko, *Nihon eiga no rajikaru na ishi* (Tokyo: Iwanami Shoten, 1999), 151.

8. *Free and Easy 11* is actually the thirteenth film of the series because of two special unnumbered episodes.

9. For more on tourism as the experience of signs of authenticity—as a simulacrum of signs—see John Frow, *Time and Commodity Culture* (Oxford: Oxford University Press, 1997).

10. It is interesting that both Etsuko and the driver in *Free and Easy 11* are played by Yo Kimiko, a *zainichi* Chinese actress born in Yokohama who has repeatedly been cast as Okinawan or in Okinawan-related productions (her other Okinawan works include Sai Yōichi's *Via Okinawa* and the NHK *asaren* morning drama set in Okinawa, *Churasan*), suggesting an equation of *zainichi* and Okinawan that emphasizes their difference from the Japanese and also erases differences among such "non-Japanese" as *zainichi* and Okinawan.

11. Shiina screens his films in public halls coupled with discussions, which could politicize reception. Note that the rental videotape of *The Legacy of the Sea, Sky, and Reef* actually begins with an advertisement for *The Deep Sea World* (*Shinkai sekai*), a video documentary on the natural mysteries of the ocean. In its video context, the film is located in the nature documentary genre.

12. A similar identification with Japan's other is evident in Yukisada Isao's *Go* (2001). While *zainichi* Koreans have historically been victims of virulent racism in Japan, in this commercially successful film, the teenage *zainichi* Korean hero essentially becomes the cool rebel in the vein of James Dean, suffering from Japanese racism but eventually winning the Japanese girl. The film's success may indicate dissatisfaction with existing forms of Japanese identity among young Japanese, but it also negates the *zainichi* challenge to Japanese identity by reducing it to the conventional formulae of youth cinema.

13. See David Bordwell, Janet Staiger, and Kristin Thompson's *The Classical Hollywood Cinema* (New York: Columbia University Press, 1985).

14. For the relation of this aesthetics (in the case of Iwai Shunji) with a form of "consumer nationalism," see my "Consuming Asia, Consuming Japan," in *Censoring History*, ed. Laura Hein and Mark Selden (Armonk, N.Y.: Sharpe, 2000).

15. Aoyama Shinji, "Yo wa ika ni shite Gareru shito ni nari shika," *Cahiers du Cinema Japon* 21 (1997): 166–75. For a longer analysis of Aoyama's stance, see my "Aoyama Shinji," in *Fifty Contemporary Film Directors*, ed. Yvonne Tasker (London: Routledge, 2002).

16. The director Takamine Go has made this argument about Sai. See the interview "*Sashin-gu* kara *Untamagiru* made," *Eiga jidai* 2 (1992): 104–5.

17. Sai's 1985 *Someday. Someone will be killed (Itsuka dareka ga korosareru,* 1984), while not filmed in Okinawa, features a male lead character who is Okinawan.

18. Yomota, *Nihon eiga*, 180.

19. Yomota, *Nihon eiga*, 178.

20. Yomota, *Nihon eiga*, 172.

21. See Sakai Naoki, "Joron—Nashonariti to bō(koku)go no seiji," in *Nashonariti no datsukochiku*, ed. Sakai Naoki, Brett de Bary, and Iyotani Toshio (Tokyo: Kashiwa Shobō, 1996), 9–53.

22. *The City of Lost Souls* multiplies the signs of identity as a part of a general critique of the image of homogeneous Japan. In a wonderful parody of the signification of national identity, one of the first scenes features a bus full of captured illegal immigrants driving on the right side of the road through the desert. On the

screen appears the explanatory title "Saitama Prefecture," just as the bus passes a billboard for curry featuring a geisha and Mount Fuji. The image is humorously absurd—Saitama is no desert, vehicles drive on the left side of the road in Japan—but it thoroughly mocks the signs of national identity—place names, "geisha," and "Mount Fuji"—in order to reveal their status as mere images and ones that are always mixed (curry plus geisha).

23. *The Prisoner* was the brief running but highly acclaimed "sequel" to *Secret Agent* starring Patrick McGoohan as a secret agent who, when he announces his intention to leave the service, is kidnapped and placed in The Village, a clean but thoroughly bureaucratic prison town where all inhabitants have numbers for names (the hero is "Number 6"), are constantly monitored, and cannot escape. Rarely has television offered such a compelling and disturbing vision of the jail that is the modern nation-state.

24. Iwai Shunji's *All about Lily ChouChou* (*Riri Shushu no subete*, 2001) also depicts Okinawa as an encounter with death, but its meeting with the Okinawan other also becomes the starting point for the bullying and killing that ensues in the narrative, as if it is the other that ruins the idyllic Japanese country and lives of the heroes of the film

25. Yomota, "Okinawa to eiga," 54.

26. For more on Kitano's deconstruction of the nation in his early films, which is abandoned in *Fireworks* (*Hana-Bi*, 1998), see Aaron Gerow, "'Nihonjin' Kitano Takeshi," *Yuriika rinji zōkan* 40, no. 3 (February 1998): 42–51.

27. This definition of Japaneseness through death is never fully articulated in the Okinawan films because of the liminality given to Okinawa itself. If a clear geographic distinction between the inside and outside of Japan is established, as there is in *Brother*, in which racism also serves to reconfirm divisions between Japanese and Caucasians, life apart from Japan is considered death, even if life in Japan entails suffering.

28. Matsuda Masao says this of Shinjō's *Okinawan Boys* (*Okinawa no shonen*, 1983): Matsuda, "Ryūkyū eiga no tame no memorandamu," 113. "Yamato-uchinā" refers to the Japanese (Yamato) version of Okinawa.

29. Yamashiro Masae levels this charge against Shinjō's 1998 feature *Hisai*, a film scripted by Ishihara Shintarō about a Japanese man who, upon visiting an Okinawan island to plan a resort, is murdered by the secretive islanders after he learns of their esoteric rites (*hisai*). To Yamashiro, Ishihara's attempt to see in Okinawa a purer, more premodern identity that could act as "a mirror for Japan," ends up merely imagining a connection with the land predicated on exoticist visions of the sexuality of the other: "Okinawa o sudorisuru 'Okinawa' eiga," *Inpakushon* 108 (June 1998): 141. The film scholar Yomota Inuhiko is also critical of *Hisai*: "Here Okinawa is not presented as the self-made energetic chaos emerging from within, but only as a mysterious, threatening realm spied upon from the outside." Yomota, "Okinawa to eiga," 56.

30. Thanks to Ōgawa Takao and Ōnishi Ikko of the Shimin Producer's System for lending me a tape and materials on this work.

31. Although the original term is in Okinawan, my analysis here is based on the Japanese equivalent provided in the official pamphlet.

32. The U.S. military listening station in Yomitan which, because it looks like a tall, circular cage, is somewhat paradoxically called "The Elephant's Cage" (*zō no ori*).

33. See, for instance, Nakayama Marumi, "People: Takamine Go eiga kantoku, *Asahi gurafu* (27 August 1999).

34. This nonutopian use of music sets *Tsuru-Henry* apart from *Nabbie's Love* (*Nabi no koi*, 1999), even though they share multiple cultures and even actors. Nakae Yuji's film is about love on an Okinawan island, where, on the one hand, the young Nanako is drawn to the wandering mainlander, Fukunosuke, and, on the other, her grandmother Nabbie, forced by island customs to separate from her lover SunRa long ago, finally escapes with SunRa when he returns from exile. The pleasure offered by the film stems in part from the wide variety of music, ranging from Okinawan folk to Irish folk to European opera, played almost continually. In fact, its vision of Okinawa is of a space where everyone sings and plays an instrument, where no one is so repressed they can't suddenly break out dancing. The place of music in Okinawan everyday life is, of course, central, but the world offered here is distinctly utopian. It is, in effect, a musical in the classic sense, presenting not only a utopian synthesis of body, rhythm, and sound, but also a mythical union through song of two opposing paradigms represented in the couples. As Yomota notes, this can have two potential valences, one touristic (a singing and dancing Okinawa served up for the touristic gaze of tired Japanese) and one ideal (a utopia to either be proud of or aim for), thus problematically addressing itself to both mainland and Okinawan spectators. See Yomota, "Okinawa to eiga," 60.

35. Nakahara Shogo, "Kioku no monogatari," in *Mugen Ryūkyū Tsuru Henri* (Okayama: Shimin Purodyuda Shisutemu, 1999), 12. This is the official pamphlet for the film sold at theaters.

36. Ogura Mushitarō and Takamine Go, "Futsu no eiga wa toritakunai," *Yuriika* 31, no. 10 (September 1999): 275.

SELECTED JAPANESE FILMS THAT FEATURE OKINAWA

Ah, The Tower of Lilies (*Aa himeyuri no tō*), dir. Masuda Toshio, 1968
All about Lily ChouChou (*Riri Shushu no subete*), dir. Iwai Shunji, 2001
Attack (*Shūgeki*), dir. Sai Yōichi, 1991
Beat, dir. Miyamoto Amon, 1999
Bodyguard Kiba (*Bodigado Kiba*), dir. Miike Takashi, 1993
Boiling Point (*3-4x10-gatsu*), dir. Kitano Takeshi, 1990
The City of Lost Souls (*Hyōryūgai*), dir. Miike Takashi, 2000
Dear Summer Sister (*Natsu no imoto*), dir. Ōshima Nagisa, 1972
Extreme Private Eros (*Gokushiteki eros, renka* 1974), dir. Hara Kazuo, 1974
Free and Easy 11 (*Tsuri baka nisshi irebun*), dir. Motoki Katsuhide, 1999
Gama: The Getto Flower (*Gama: Getto no hana*), dir. Osawa Yutaka, 1997
Goodbye Japan! (*Sayonara Nippon!*), dir. Tsutsumi Yukihiko, 1995
Hisai, dir. Shinjō Taku, 1998
Ikinai, dir. Shimizu Hiroshi, 1998
The Legacy of the Sea, Sky, and Reef (*Umi sora sango no iitsutae*), dir. Shiina Makoto, 1991

Nabbie's Love (*Nabi no koi*), dir. Nakae Yōji, 1999
Okinawa Gang War (*Okinawa yakuza sensō*), dir. Nakajima Sadao, 1976
Okinawan Boys (*Okinawa no shonen*), dir. Shinjō Taku, 1983
Okinawan Chirudai, dir. Takamine Go, 1978
Okinawan Dream Show (*Okinawan dorimu sho*), dir. Takamine Go, 1974
Okinawan Islands (*Okinawa rettō*), dir. Higashi Yōichi, 1972
Oyake Akahachi (*Oyake Akahachi*), dir. Toyoda Shiro, 1937
Paradise View (*Paradaisu byū*), dir. Takamine Go, 1985
Pineapple Tours (*Painappuru tsuazu*), dirs. Makiya Tsutomu, Nakae Yōji, and Toma Hayashi, 1992
Pig's Revenge (*Buta no mukui*), dir. Sai Yōichi, 1999
The Profound Desire of the Gods (*Kamigami no fukaki yokubo*), dir. Imamura Shōhei, 1968
Rest in Peace My Friend (*Tomo yo, shizuka ni nemure*), dir. Sai Yōichi, 1985
Shakking the Movie: The Okinawa Scam (*Shakkingu the Movie: Okinawa daisakusen*), dir. Izumi Seiji, 1999
Sonatine (*Sonachine*), dir. Kitano Takeshi, 1993
The Stormy Petrel (*Umitsubame Jo no kiseki*), dir. Fujita Toshiya, 1984
Tora-san's Tropical Fever (*Otoko wa tsurai yo: Torajirō haibisukasu no hana*), dir. Yamada Yōji, 1980
The Tower of Lilies (*Himeyuri no tō*), dir. Imai Tadashi, 1953
The Tower of Lilies (*Himeyuri no tō*), dir. Imai Tadashi, 1982
The Tower of Lilies (*Himeyuri no tō*), dir. Koyama Seijirō, 1995
Tsuru-Henry (*Mugen Ryūkyū: Tsuru Henri*), dir. Takamine Go, 1999
Untamagiru, dir. Takamine Go, 1989
The Untaught War: Okinawa—The Fight of Ahagon Shōkō and Iejima Island (*Oshierarenakatta sensō: Okinawa-hen—Ahagon Shōkō, Iejima no tatakai*), dir. Takaiwa Jin, 1998
Via Okinawa (*A-Sain deizu*), dir. Sai Yōichi, 1989
The Vindictive Snake (*Shūnen no dokuhebi*), dir. Yoshino Jirō, 1931

Index

About the Contributors

Laura Hein (history, Northwestern University) has a number of recent publications, including *Living with the Bomb: Japanese and American Cultural Conflicts in the Nuclear Age* (coedited with Mark Selden; Sharpe, 1997) and "Savage Irony: The Imaginative Power of the 'Military Comfort Women' in the 1990s," *Gender & History* (Summer 1999). She is just completing *Reasonable Men: Japanese Economists and the Twentieth Century.*

Mark Selden (Binghamton and Cornell Universities) has recently published the books *Censoring History: Citizenship and Memory in Japan, Germany, and the United States* (coedited with Laura Hein; Sharpe, 2000); *Bitter Flowers, Sweet Flowers: East Timor, Indonesia and the United States* (coedited with Richard Tanter and Stephen R. Shalom; Rowman & Littlefield, 2001); and *The Resurgence of East Asia: 500, 150 and 50 Year Perspectives* (coedited with Giovanni Arrighi, Takeshi Hamashita; Routledge, 2003). He is the editor of The War and Peace Library and the Asia/Pacific/Perspectives series at Rowman & Littlefield.

Matthew Allen (School of Asian Studies, University of Auckland) is the author of *Identity and Resistance in Okinawa* (Rowman & Littlefield, 2002) and *Undermining the Japanese Miracle* (Cambridge University Press, 1994).

Linda Isako Angst's (anthropology, Lewis and Clark College) Yale doctoral dissertation is entitled "In a Dark Time: Community, War Memory, and the Making of Ethnic Selves in Okinawan Women's Narratives."

Asato Eiko, a scholar based in Okinawa, is the author of several books, including *Yureru seiiki, rizōto to kaihatsu to shima no kurashi* (Confused Sanctuary: Resort Development and the Life of the Islands; Okinawa Taimuzusha, 1991).

Gerald Figal (history, University of Delaware) is the author of *Civilization and Monsters: Spirits of Modernity in Meiji Japan* (Duke University Press, 1999) and is at work on a study of tourism in Okinawa.

Aaron Gerow (Yokohama National University) is the author of "Consuming Asia, Consuming Japan: The New Neonationalistic Revisionism in Japan," in *Censoring History,* edited by Laura Hein and Mark Selden, and "Recognizing 'Others' in a New Japanese Cinema," *Japan Foundation Newsletter* 29, no. 2 (2002).

Michael Molasky (Asian literatures, University of Minnesota) is the author of *The American Occupation of Japan and Okinawa: Literature and Memory* (Routledge, 2001) and coeditor, with Steve Rabson, of *Southern Exposure: Modern Japanese Literature from Okinawa* (University of Hawai'i Press, 2001). He is currently working on a study of jazz in Japan.

Steve Rabson (Department of East Asian Studies, Brown University) is the author of *Okinawa: Two Postwar Novellas* (Center for Japanese Studies, 1989) and *Righteous Cause or Tragic Folly: Changing Views of War in Modern Japanese Poetry* (Center for Japanese Studies, University of Michigan, 1998).

James E. Roberson is a senior lecturer in the Department of Anthropology, Oxford Brookes University, Oxford. He is the author of *Japanese Working Class Lives* (Routledge, 1998) and coeditor (with Nobue Suzuki) of *Men and Masculinities in Contemporary Japan* (Routledge, 2002).

Julia Yonetani is a lecturer at the University of New South Wales. She is the author of "Ambiguous Traces and the Politics of Sameness: Placing Okinawa in Meiji Japan," *Japanese Studies* 20, no. 1 (May 2000); "Playing Base Politics in a Global Strategic Theatre: Futenma Relocation, the G-8 Summit, and Okinawa," *Critical Asian Studies* 33, no. 1 (2001); and an essay on Ōta Masahide, in *Japan and Okinawa: Structure and Subjectivity,* edited by Glenn Hook and Richard Siddle (Routledge, forthcoming).